Evidence, History
and the Great War

EVIDENCE, HISTORY AND THE GREAT WAR

Historians and the Impact of 1914–18

Edited by

Gail Braybon

Berghahn Books
New York • Oxford

First published in 2003 by

Berghahn Books
www.berghahnbooks.com

© 2003 Gail Braybon

Library of Congress Cataloging-in-Publication Data

Evidence, history, and the Great War : historians and the impact of
   1914–18 / edited by Gail Braybon.
      p. cm.
   Includes bibliographical references and index.
   ISBN 1-57181-724-7 (alk. paper)
   1. World War, 1939–1945--Historiography. 2. War and society. 3. World
   War, 1939–1945--Women, 4. World War, 1939–1945--Medical aspects.
   5. World War, 1939–1945--Social aspects. I. Braybon, Gail.
   D522.42.E85 2003
   940.3'072--dc22

                                                          2003057826
                                                          CIP

British Library Cataloguing in Publication Data
A catalogue record for this book is available from the British Library.

Printed in the United States on acid-free paper

ISBN 1-57181-724-7 hardback

Contents

List of Illustrations

Note on Terminology

The war of 1914 to 1918 is known by several names, including the Great War, the First World War and World War I, each of which implies something about the conflict. For example, the 'First World War' is inevitably linked in our minds with the 'Second World War', making connections, or suggesting similarities, which may be misleading. I deliberately did not specify its nomenclature, and have left the contributors to use their own preferred titles, as I feel this reflects something of their own view of the war and its place in history.

Introduction

14–18: Retrouver la Guerre is the title Stéphane Audoin-Rouzeau and Annette Becker chose for their recent book on France and the Great War.[1] The word 'retrouver' can be translated as 'recovering', 'regaining', 're-finding', and more. It implies that something has been lost – and Audoin-Rouzeau and Becker do indeed discuss the war's neglect in French national history – but also that this is an event to be looked at again, afresh. This is not a feeling confined to France. The 1914–18 War is seen as ripe for reconsideration and analysis amongst historians of other nations too. The organisers of one recent conference began their email announcement by citing Pierre Nora, who has suggested that 'the Great War has undergone the kind of reappraisal applied to the French Revolution a decade ago …' They went on to draw attention to the influence of L'Historial de la Grand Guerre at Péronne, and the collaborative projects which have ensued once French, British and German historians are gathered together.[2] This work, they wrote, 'epitomises what could be dubbed the second upheaval of the Great War: the academic upheaval, which has meant that the isolated study of the military, cultural or economic facets of the war is no longer possible.'[3] The same year saw other conferences in Britain; these were well attended by graduate students, making it quite clear that there has been a resurgence of research into the war. I would add only that this 'reappraisal' is not yet complete, and that there is much work yet to be done.[4]

The focus of study has shifted. There is a new enthusiasm for tracing the way in which the war has been remembered – or forgotten – over time, which in turn is connected with research into the nature of memory and has been influenced by the rise of 'public history'. There is also a renewal of interest in how different groups of people lived through the war, and what we really 'know' about their various experiences. As a result there has been an increase in research with a comparative European perspective (as exemplified by Jay Winter and Jean Louis Robert's edited collection, *Capital Cities at War*) but, at the same time, a willingness to break down the vast, multi-faceted edifice of war history, and look for *detail*.[5] Both kinds of approach are to be found in recent writings and are necessary if we really are to 'look again' at all aspects of 1914–18. While many solid and well-con-structed social and economic texts on the war have been published since the 1960s, we have also seen far too many books which are weighed down with symbolism, or dominated by over-arching theories. When I read, for example, that a particular new work is about 'one of the most devastating conflicts in modern history. The Great War traumatised a generation, and shaped the whole of the twentieth century', warning bells ring.[6] This kind of statement demands to be deconstructed, and raises questions in my mind about what other 'devastating conflicts' around the world are implic-itly ignored or marginalised, what is meant by 'a traumatised generation' (who, exactly?), and quite how the twentieth century was, or was not 'shaped' by four years of European war.[7] A succession of texts in the 1970s and 1980s fed this kind of approach, including books by Paul Fussell (1975), Eric Leed (1981), Roland Stromberg (1982), and Modris Eksteins (1989), all of which are to be found on every university's bookshelves, and are invari-ably included in reading lists on the social and cultural impact of war.[8] These books concentrate on Western Europe, particularly the supposed effect of the Western Front experience, lean heavily on literary sources, and seek to show how the war separated the old world from the 'modern', innocence from experience, and so on. The influence of the classic British image of the war – as created in part by a select group of war poets, and known and loved by the population at large – can be seen in the work of Fussell in particular, with his quotations from Philip Larkin, who talked of '… the innocents of the remote Great War, those sweet generous people who pressed forward and all but solicited their own destruction.'[9] In this world of patriotic, naive, middleclass young men (volunteers in Britain until 1916, though not, of course, in France or Germany), who threw themselves into war and faced death, or survived bitter and disillusioned, even the weather is co-opted as a symbol of some other, sweeter, era. Fussell writes:

> Although some memories of the benign last summer before the war can be dis-counted as standard retrospection turned even rosier by egregious contrast with what followed, all agree that the prewar summer was the most idyllic for many years. It was warm and sunny, eminently pastoral. One lolled outside in a fold-ing canvas chaise, or swam, or walked in the countryside. One read outdoors, went on picnics, had tea served from a white wicker table under the trees … Siegfried Sassoon was busy fox-hunting and playing serious county cricket.[10]

It is clear that Fussell has fallen under the spell of a romanticised Edwardian England and become fascinated by 'the English' – fascinated above all by the sincerity and patriotism of the upper and middleclass young men who volunteered. He is writing about the making of a 'myth', yet his own prose further promotes the idea of 1914 as the last golden summer and the end of innocence. He subscribes to the idea (as often claimed during the war, and in the years that followed) that '… a whole generation was destroyed that might have furnished the country's jurists, scholars, administrators, and political leaders …'[11] He freely admits that he is trying, with his descriptive prose, to 'illuminate' a different world for the benefit of American readers, which perhaps accounts for the feeling of nostalgia which permeates the book. Although he is a literary, not social, historian, his work has certainly influenced not just his compatriots, but many British and Europeans writing on the wider emotional and cultural impact of war as well.

For all his faults – and Martin Stephen, Brian Bond and John Terraine all, in their different ways, make serious attempts to point out his inaccuracies and misconstructions[12] – it is clear that Paul Fussell has a personal interest in his subject. He is moved partly because of his own memories of the Second World War. He writes about young men who died a generation before, but he is also remembering his contemporaries. Whether one agrees with his approach or not, he did indeed have some new things to say about literature, war poetry and the English 'memory' of war. Other less original writers, who claim that the war symbolised something deep and dark in the twentieth-century psyche, or marked the birth of a cynical modern age, are troubling. They write as though the war has some kind of universal historical significance. They write with hindsight, yet with a strange lack of awareness that this may have coloured their judgement. They also write as though the sequence of events which followed on from 1914 was inevitable: world history was fixed from that moment. As Pierre Sorlin, writing about cinema and the war, has said:

> In pictures, the War has been turned into myth. It is like a Greek tragedy: we can tell the story again and again; we can create new characters and circumstances; but we can change neither the plot nor the symbols which define the period.[13]

Some have placed a major part of the blame for this portentous approach amongst historians fairly and squarely on Fussell's immediate predecessors, the writers of the 1960s who readily adopted the English war poets as the voice of a generation, and influenced countless readers, young and old. However, attempts to use the war as representative of a new kind of evil (with the implicit assumption that 1914–1918 was worse than any other conflict in history), or as a symbolic watershed between old and new societies, or as the inevitable product of a decadent civilisation's malaise – and any of these contradictory claims may feature in books which generalise about its wider impact – began long before. Daniel Pick, in *War Machine: the Rationalisation of Slaughter in the Modern Age*, traces this preoccupation back to nineteenth-century dread about the nature of 'future' warfare, and points out that even in 1914 there were writers who greeted the conflict with a kind of grim satisfaction. The war they prophesied had arrived, and they anticipated that their worse fears would be realised – but this was before a trench was dug or a war poem published. Pick looks at how more recent writers have interpreted these sources, and pleads for a more subtle interpretation:

My point here is not to make the (absurd) claim that wars, least of all perhaps the First World War, should be seen as simply continuous with a 'pre-war' culture and society, but to suggest that a highly idealised juxtaposition of past and present may come to operate, imbuing the war with a range of philosophical, evolutionary and psychological functions which eerily echo the war philosophy of the nineteenth century. These need to be analysed, not taken for granted. The First World War cannot be seen as either the final signified or the new signifier which emerges out of nothing – and yet so often it is.[14]

As he points out, it is possible to lean too heavily on some of the gloomy, or apocalyptic commentaries of the time without understanding the personal views of those writing or the intellectual debates about the nature of warfare which had characterised the preceding decades. His book also shows how writers (of all kinds) have always been willing to utilise the war in support of their fears about the future, or their judgement of the past. This is demonstrated well by Roland Stromberg's 1982 book, *Redemption by War*. Although he begins with the admirable aim of showing that there was no simple division across Europe between warmongering (elderly) politicians and pacifist (young) intellectuals, his anxieties about his own time somehow come to dominate the text and influence his conclusions about the war. Thus he writes that:

The resemblance between today's youth and a much smaller band of intellectuals and artists in 1914 continually strikes us. Violence, often of the most extreme sort (*à la* Charles Manson, *Clockwork Orange*, urban guerrillas), is invoked as an answer to the unendurable clockwork society; a thirst for community, adventure, spirituality, can lead to the neoprimitivism of hippy communes but is within a hair's breadth of street battles with the police, demonstrations turning into riots, or Tupermaro-style terrorism ... the disaffection of Timothy Leary, Paul Goodman, Frantz Fanon, and Herbert Marcuse, for example, seem only vulgarized versions of the 1914 malaise.[15]

Are these comments helpful? Do they tell us anything at all about 1914? Even Bernard Bergonzi, in his thoughtful critical text on war poets, *Heroes' Twilight: a Study of the Literature of the Great War*, nevertheless concludes by writing:

The Great War is not likely to be forgotten: the memory of its waste and dumb heroism is part of twentieth century sensibility. It started as a war to end wars, but instead it pointed forward to the totalitarian state, to an even greater war and a concept of unlimited conflict in which not merely uniformed armies but whole populations, down to the smallest child, are regarded as appropriate victims for destruction on a scale that makes the slaughter on the Somme appear ordinary.[16]

Key aspects to note here are references to 'dumb heroism', 'the war to end wars' (although it could not possibly have 'started' as this), the inevitable connection with totalitarianism, the claim that this war created a new kind of warfare, and the suggestion that civilians first became legitimate targets during 1914–18 – an idea which is clearly untrue, as any cursory look at military campaigns across the centuries will show. And does the slaughter on the Somme now 'appear ordinary'? When such generalisations about the effect of the war on world history dominate the text there is no place for dispassionate analysis or discussion.

While this kind of approach remains common in popular history books, school curricula and internet sites – all of which, perhaps inevitably, seek to tell simplified stories about the war – it has also featured in enough academic writing to be problematic. For example, all the books I have mentioned so far will be found on the average reading list for undergraduates, and they are influential – they are the starting point for many of those who begin research into some aspect of the war. This is why recent trends in the field of the social and cultural history of the war are so important. From the 1990s onwards there has been an increasing interest in the complexity of the war's impact on different societies and social groups, and a growing recognition that there was no one 'war experience'. There is also a new willingness by diplomatic, economic, military, social and cultural historians to share information, and to compare the war's effect across different nations. Conferences and edited collections of papers have become an extremely important part of this process: it is necessary for the different strands of history to mix. If we are to have detail, we need people to look closely at small parts of the jigsaw – but at the same time, these pieces need to fit together.

At this point I could offer lists of 'useful' books or papers which exemplify the encouraging trends evident in the last few years, but lists are, in isolation, not that interesting. Instead, as an example let me consider some of the background reading one might need to do if researching some aspect of the wartime experiences of young men in the British Army in France. What kind of work has already been done, and what debates are going on? The work of a substantial number of historians has already provided a great deal of information, and demonstrates that there were many kinds of war for young white men alone, let alone their wives or sisters, their parents, and their allies or foes. Key texts on the Army would include the work of Tim Travers and Tony Ashworth. In *The Killing Ground: the British Army, the Western Front and the emergence of Modern Warfare 1900–1918*, and *How the War was Won: Command and Technology in the British Army*, Travers gives us practical detail on the nature of warfare, including how the British Army transformed itself and turned near defeat to victory in 1918. He also places the army in a social context and considers how war was viewed by strategists in the years before 1914.[17] Ashworth, in *Trench Warfare, 1914–18: the live and let live system*,[18] is informative on the practicalities of warfare, the diversity of experience in the trenches, and the nature of day-to-day life in the army. He shows how the ordinary soldier spent a considerable amount of time behind the lines, and how both the British and German soldiers often tried to keep life in the trenches as quiet as possible, avoiding direct engagement with each other. Joanna Bourke and Ilana R. Bet-el both offer valuable information on the more mundane aspects of army life – what happened when men joined up, what was training like, what did soldiers write home about?[19] The former, in *Dismembering the Male*, goes much further, including interesting discussion of soldiers' sexual behaviour (including some reluctance to visit prostitutes) and providing useful material on the treatment of disability, sickness and 'malingering'. Several writers have recently published work on wounded soldiers, and what became of them. How were 'the crippled' viewed in early twentieth-century Britain, and how were these views influenced by the arrival home of so many young disabled men? These issues are discussed, for example, by Seth Koven in 'Remembering and Dismemberment: crippled children, wounded soldiers and the Great War in Great Britain', and Jeffrey Reznick in 'Work Therapy and the disabled British Soldier in Great Britain in the First World War: the case of Shepherd's Bush Military Hospital, London.' Deborah Cohen, in *The War Come Home,* compares the British and German treatment of returning disabled soldiers, and the political repercussions in the years that followed.[20]

When considering the culture within which these young men grew up, Graham Dawson's book *Soldier Heroes* is useful, while Fuller's *Troop Morale and Popular Culture* offers a picture of what men did with their leisure time, including concert parties, sports and entertainment. For a critical view of the war poets, who they were, their social and cultural background, how their work was received, Martin Stephen, already mentioned, is enlightening, and so too is Elizabeth Marsland, who compares the poetry of Britain, France and Germany in *The Nation's Cause,* placing it in its literary and social context, and looking beyond famous names.[21] In the field of political/military history, Keith Grieves' book, *The Politics of Manpower, 1914–18*, gives us information about how the army was raised, describing the relations between army and government, the move to conscription and its impact. This was published the same year as Peter Simkins' *Kitchener's Armies: the Raising of the New Armies 1914–16.*[22] It is educative to read these alongside *A Nation in Arms: a Social Study of the British Army in the First World War* (edited by Ian Beckett and Keith Simpson) which includes Jay Winter's essay on workingclass recruits, their economic/social background and their health. One glance at the photograph on page 192 – headed 'Specimens of men in each of the four grades', and showing examples of physical fitness – will emphasise the separation between the world of the workingclass soldier and Fussell's England of wicker chairs and tea in the garden.[23]

Of course, the enthusiastic scholar might also be interested in how the army experiences of British men compared with those of the Empire, whether New Zealander, Australian, Canadian, or West Indian, African, Indian and Chinese? Or, how different was life as a French or German soldier, or American, whether black of white? And what of conscientious objectors or deserters? The list of books and articles grows accordingly, and it is soon apparent that one needs to appreciate work produced by writers from a range of different disciplines, from the military historian to the feminist, from the literary to the economic; all have their own particular skills and knowledge to bring to bear on the material. The few books I have mentioned here all have a different approach to the subject of men in the army, and all are illuminating in one way or another. This range of material reveals both the advantages and disadvantages of working on the war. The literature is vast, especially if one is also interested in the way it has been interpreted and remembered over the years by each separate nation – and I must recommend Keith Wilson's *Forging the Collective Memory: Government and International Historians through two World Wars*,[24] which is invaluable for showing how governments (and official historians) attempted to justify their own nation's part in the war from the outset. (This book is a sobering reminder of the extent to which all of us, as historians, have been influenced by prevailing national wisdom regarding the war's origins and influence.) The amount of research, across all areas, with which one needs to keep pace is therefore daunting. On the other hand, this very richness is what now allows us to review the war so effectively. For the more one finds out about the experiences of individuals, social groups, armies, populations, the more one sees that the classic, simplified picture of the war, as described by Fussell, Leed, Eksteins or others like them, is not only disturbingly Eurocentric, but deeply flawed, even on its own terms. The Western Front, for example, was not the only kind of battlefront in 1914–18; in other areas, environment and strategy were different. Those seeking to use the mud, the blasted landscape of No Man's Land, and the tunnels and trenches as some kind of metaphor for a dark twentieth century have usually ignored this inconvenient fact. In contrast, as Ben Bar-Yosef writes in a recent article, 'The Palestine campaign, with its feasible objectives, linear narrative, relatively few casualties and, most important, its unequivocal victory, simply could not – and cannot – be moulded into an Apocalypse.'[25] The impact of war was more complex, more diverse, more interesting, than some 'classic' texts would have us believe. This is why reading across historical disciplines is useful. Again, a single example will suffice. The development of 'modern warfare' is an issue for debate amongst recent military historians. It is *not* widely accepted that 1914–18 was the 'first modern war', or that it was some kind of template for twentieth-century warfare. It has to be viewed in the context of developments in weaponry and tactics during the American Civil War, the German wars, the Japanese-Russian war and, indeed, the Boer War. 'Modern war' certainly does not just mean using machine guns, digging trenches or killing thousands of soldiers, as far too many social/cultural historians seem blithely to assume.[26]

We may well be past the point of needing 'big', single author, books about the war – it is not possible for any one person to understand, let alone interpret, all aspects of the conflict across continents. (I say this even though Hew Strachan's multi-volume history promises to be an excellent survey and analysis of the war's political, military and social scope.[27]) The future lies in collaboration and comparison. A more modest approach to writing about the war in general would also be useful, together with an acknowledgement of how much there is still to find out. It sometimes seems as though writers about the war feel obliged to make grandiose statements or dwell on wide-ranging themes, as though only such an approach will suit the magnitude of the conflict; this does not necessarily add to our understanding.

The essays in this book all bring something fresh to debates about the war. Some of these debates are long running, and others are new; one interesting facet of war history is the way some arguments fall out of fashion while others continue to inspire research. The first two chapters, by Catherine Moriarty and Deborah Thom, join the growing body of work on the way in which the British have interpreted the war, and continue to remember it. No other country marks Armistice Day with the same fervour, although all have their own ways of viewing the war, as essays in John R. Gillis' *Commemorations: the Politics of National Identity*, show well.[28] Adrian Gregory (another contributor to this book) has written elsewhere about Armistice Day's shifting meaning over the decades, and many historians expected its importance to fade away as the last few old soldiers died.[29] However, it has seen a renaissance in recent years, and the fluctuating public focus between Remembrance Sunday and 11 November has served to make both days part of a formal or personal festival of remembrance. It is often difficult for historians from other nations to understand the extent to which the war has entered the consciousness of the 'ordinary person' in Britain, or to believe that there can still be arguments (as there have been) about whether or not TV newsreaders wear poppies. People will tell you they *know* about this war – even though they are unlikely to claim much knowledge of many other historical events.[30] In England, Wales and Scotland the war occupies the kind of space in our collective imagination filled by the 1789 Revolution in France, or the Civil War in the United States. Furthermore, the historians of Eire too are now eager to recognise the part played by Irishmen in the British Army, and there has been a wave of new work on this subject.[31] The war is widely seen as some kind of defining moment for the nation, while the ambiguities inherent in the way we remember it are glossed over. Even in France, with whom we share the experience of the Western Front, the war has been less prominent in national memory – although recent work suggests that the French people (particularly the young) are rediscovering it.[32] The classic British war story has also been nurtured from the 1960s onwards by television drama, documentary and films, including the BBC's *Great War* series, the dramatisation of Vera Brittain's *Testament of Youth*, the ITV serial *Upstairs, Downstairs*, and the film of *Oh What a Lovely War*, all of which are part of popular culture. The importance of film is discussed in Michael Paris' book, *The First World War and Popular Cinema*, and he may well be right when he suggests that this, rather than literature, has embedded a particular view of war in our national consciousness.[33] Pierre Sorlin, in the same volume, describes how 1918 newsreels, often showing staged scenes, have been shown over and over again ever since, 'so that spectators accept them as authentic'.[34] This story, or series of pictures, is not passing away with time: the war poets are still favourite subjects for school English lessons, while Pat Barker and Sebastian Faulks have written popular novels which revolve around the Western Front, and which build on what we 'know' about the war.[35] Even in 2002, the BBC was prepared to give us a bizarre interpretation of the 'soldier's experience' with its 'reality TV' series, *The Trench*.[36] As Paul Fussell discovered, the British story is one of lost Edwardian summers, enthusiastic young men, poetry, disillusionment and battles waged by doltish army commanders who cared nothing for the soldiers who died. Implicit in this too is the idea that the war was unnecessary and pointless: that it should not have happened; 'never again' is the motto, even after another world war, the Falklands, the battle against Iraq and Afghanistan.[37] (Cynics might say that recent wars are acceptable as long as *our* men do not die in their thousands.) Yet still we see, again and again, how the war exerts its power on those seeking connections between our own time and 'the past'. It is extraordinary that nearly thirty years after Fussell, another American (with British connections) can write an eight page article for the *London Review of Books* in 2002 about her search for a great uncle's war grave in France, and her own obsession with the war and that generation. Again, we see how present preoccupations interact with one person's view of the war; in this case her interest was revived by the events of 11 September 2001.

> He [the uncle] lives in the same world as I do – the familiar valley of sorrows, fuck-ups and relentless, chain-reaction human disasters. (How acutely one feels the 11 September violence to be, like so much in our time, simply one of the hundreds of geopolitical aftershocks of the First World War.[38]

But of course, not only was Terry Castle moved to write this, an editorial team was happy to publish it: the *London Review of Books* knew that its readers would recognise the issues, the connections and the relevance of such a piece, even now.

An increasing number of historians are looking at why the British picture of the war has remained so potent and so resilient. In his introduction to *Forgotten Victory*, Gary Sheffield, a military historian, grapples with the origins of the standard idea that the war was simply futile, and that Britain's military commanders were inept fools, tracing the way it has been interpreted by TV, film and radio.[39] Daniel Todman (a social historian), explores the way so many people still feel connections with the war, long after the death of grandfathers or great uncles, and take pride in their role.[40] Both these writers look at the influence of the 1960s, and the fiftieth anniversary of the war, and both see the importance of family memories. For many of us, family history (middle class and working class alike) began with that war: photographs, letters, medals and other memorabilia, are treasured. They are also our immutable connection with a great event in history – our ancestors were *there*. At the same time, the rise of research into material culture, as exemplified by the work of Nick Saunders, has established valuable connections between art, archaeology and social history, together with an appreciation of the visual impact of war iconography, and an awareness of the psychological effect of war memorabilia, from postcards to war memorials.[41]

Both Catherine Moriarty and Deborah Thom are here concerned with some of the early representations of the war in Britain, and the way in which these have affected us, as 'ordinary people' and as historians. Catherine Moriarty's chapter, '"Though in a Picture Only": Portrait Photography and the Commemoration of the First World War', explores two forms of memorial, and two aspects of the powerful visual record with which we live in Britain.[42] The war memorial is concrete, symbolic and designed to unite a community in mourning. Soldiers' photographs – the product of the rise in portrait photography during these years – in contrast remind us that every man who fought was an individual. These pictures, of the young or middle-aged, the handsome or plain, the smiling or serious, were often the only mementoes of lost husbands, fathers or sons. En masse, as seen in the Imperial War Museum's collection of portrait photos, this can be shocking. Photographs add an extra dimension to the national 'memory' of the war, and even outside the context of the family album their resonance remains. Who has not seen, as Catherine Moriarty describes, a sepia-coloured postcard in a junk shop of a young soldier, and wondered whether he survived, or died during the war? From the photograph alone we cannot tell whether he perished on some muddy battlefield or returned home to a good job and a long and prosperous life, but there is always the fear that he too must have been a victim of the war. As for war memorials, Moriarty reminds us that in both Britain and France these were specifically *designed* to reach out to the viewer and make an emotional impact: they were supposed to act as a focus for those – individuals and communities – who had been bereaved.[43] It is hardly surprising that these were, for many of us, a childhood introduction to 1914–18. Their carved angels, their stone soldiers – departing with one last wave of the hand – their alphabetical lists of 'the Fallen', all affect us still. This is a legacy bequeathed by the survivors of the war. Such powerful imagery, public and private, goes some way to explaining why this long-gone conflict still maintains such a hold on our imagination – and inevitably affects us as writers about the war, for better or worse. I would say we 'remember' the war exactly as sculptors wanted us to, but that the impact of their formal memorials is, ironically, re-inforced by the personal photograph.

Deborah Thom, in 'Making Spectaculars: Museums and how we remember Gender in Wartime', writes about the Imperial War Museum, and in particular the origins of the Women's Work Collection, which has had an enormous impact on both popular and academic views of women's participation in the war. As Thom shows, exhibits were chosen for a particular reason: the collection was to exemplify what women *could* do in time of war, and thus the emphasis was on the unusual, the heroic, the picturesque. The theme of women's splendid war work was dear to the hearts not just of patriots or politicians, who hoped to mobilise volunteers and illustrate support for the war effort, but to feminists as well. Agnes Conway, the organiser of the collection and a feminist herself, was delighted to have the opportunity to show how skilled and resourceful women could be when the nation called. The Women's Collection is a wonderful and unique resource, yet there is a danger that it is seen – partly because of its sheer scale – as 'the truth' about women and the war. As Thom reveals, it is important to be aware of what was left out, or marginalised. Furthermore, the very quality and variety of the photographs, as seen in exhibitions at the time, or reproduced in countless books since, has influenced public perception of women's role. There is a telling contrast between these pictures and those discussed by Moriarty. While the men are frozen in time as soldiers, victims of war, their civilian identities disguised by uniform, the women appear to be workers of all kinds and all classes: clerical, professional, industrial, rural, they all appear vibrant and alive. However, it is notable that there are few pictures of women working in the 'traditional' industries, let alone mopping floors, cleaning stairs or cooking (unless they are in the Army Corps) and no pictures of women campaigning about low pay and long hours. And, while we frequently see pictures of wounded men, photographs of sick or injured women are rare, even though they suffered from the effects of TNT poisoning and a variety of industrial injuries. Nor do pictures or models tell us anything about why women took up their war work. Was it for patriotic reasons or for the money – or a mixture of both? Photographs show much, but require careful examination, and knowledge of what the photographer was trying to achieve.

The next few chapters examine some aspects of the war which are supposedly 'known', but are open to reinterpretation. Adrian Gregory, in 'British "War Enthusiasm" in 1914: a Reassessment', looks critically at the widely accepted belief that the British public greeted the prospect of war, and indeed that their jingoistic response helped urge politicians into declaring war – as suggested by so many historians for decades, including a number of recent writers. He quotes W. J. Reader's confident pronouncement that 'The suddenness of the onset of war fever and the way in which it smothered all other national pre-occupations ... is one of the best documented aspects of the outbreak of the Great War.'[44] Nor is this claim made for Britain alone. Marc Ferro's words represent the standard picture: 'In Paris, London and Berlin they left exuberant, "with flowers in their rifles".'[45]

Niall Ferguson raises the subject afresh in *The Pity of War*, but provides little new evidence for his counterclaim that the amount of enthusiasm was exaggerated.[46] While Becker challenged this idea for France over twenty years ago, and Verhey has recently reassessed the German response, there is still little sign of detailed work on the British response.[47] In his chapter for this book Adrian Gregory uses newspapers, diaries and autobiographies in an attempt to find out more about the views of those who were more cautious in the summer of 1914. His careful reading of these reveals a more measured approach amongst both journalists and other observers, from clergymen to union officials, and shows the way in which opinion seemed to change as the conflict shifted from threatened to real.

It should be noted, however, that Gregory does not claim that enthusiasm did not exist. We have all seen the pictures of cheering crowds, though the date of such pictures is important, and so too is the context. Are these pictures of crowds waiting for news of war's declaration, or of men queuing at recruiting offices in the autumn, or of families gathering to greet returning soldiers? Film of women smilingly waving off their men is real, but we do not know what lies behind any of these pictures. There are many reasons why crowds gathered – there was the desire to give volunteers a good (often civic) send-off, there were genuine feelings of patriotism or pride, but at the same time there were often doubts and fears amongst those who stayed at home. 'Enthusiasm' for war need not have been the sole, or even dominant response.[48] It is important to acknowledge that the response to talk of war was often more ambiguous and varied amongst ordinary people than is usually suggested. The views of those who were more phlegmatic, nervous or fearful at the thought of war are no less valid. If we accept this then we can see that the idea of 1914 'enthusiasm' and later inevitable 'disillusionment' is simplistic. Just as some people remained against the war, others supported it throughout. The neat picture of innocence and experience is immediately undermined. There is also much more, as Gregory points out, for us to discover about the response to war in different geographical areas, even within the United Kingdom. Reactions may have varied between town and country as well as between regions. Furthermore, it is surely time that men's feelings of duty, obligation, or patriotism (as individuals and as groups) were looked at more closely by historians.[49] Gregory's essay shows that a range of opinion existed, but does not seek to replace one dogmatic assumption about what 'the British people' felt with another.

Chapters 4, 5 and 6 all discuss some aspect of the long running debate about 'women and the war'. This is an intriguing subject, as it crops up in different ways in different strands of history writing. The supposed impact of the war on 'women' (and the all encompassing word is singularly unhelpful in this context, given differences in age, class, race, region) is always mentioned in general history books, whether they are about Europe (for which read Britain, France and Germany) or Britain alone, where women's war experiences as VADs (volunteer nurses) and munition workers are a key part of the greater war story. Deborah Thom's chapter on the Imperial War Museum goes some way to explaining why the images of working women are so familiar to us, as the photographs from its collection are widely used by press, magazines and TV. In addition, women's own experiences, the effect of their work on them as individuals, and the longer term impact of war on their role at home and work are often cited in both popular and more academic texts. The amount of space given to this varies from a few paragraphs to several pages in those many books concerned with broader arguments about the war, while of course whole volumes are devoted to the subject by writers within the field of women's history. The latter, however, include practitioners from a range of historical disciplines, and their approach varies accordingly. For convenience, one might divide these into 'social historians' and 'gender historians', though these terms are problematic as the main proponents are by no means as sharply defined as their names imply. Deborah Thom's book, *Nice Girls and Rude Girls*, includes an extremely useful chapter on 'The History of the History of Women and War' which outlines the developments of the last forty years, and lists some of the key texts; I would recommend this to anyone seeking more information about the shifts in methodology within women's history.[50]

British social historians (women and men) have long been interested in the impact of war on different social groups, and the apparent change in what was acceptable work for women, together with the emergence of new kinds of factory work in the postwar period, the extension of suffrage, smaller family size, changes in the nature of marriage, and so on. These have all been subjects for detailed discussion – sometimes linked together, and sometimes as separate topics. Penny Summerfield's valuable essay on 'Women and War in the Twentieth-century' in June Purvis's book, *Women's History: Britain, 1850–1945*, gives an excellent overview of writings about social policy, and the search for dynamic effects on 'society' as a result of war. (It is intriguing that so many of the same issues emerged from discussions about the Second World War as well, given the vastly different economic, social and political background.)[51] 'Progress' is usually accepted as being the expansion in women's employment opportunities, higher wages, work for married women, availability of birth control and childcare, improved diet and health. These areas of women's physical/social/economic lives seemed to be improving during the early twentieth century, and the question is the extent to which such a process was accelerated by what happened during the war. This kind of approach to women and war should ideally be read alongside other research examining just how much of an impact the conflict may or may not have had on a variety of institutions, industries and individuals. Constantine, Kirby and Rose list the main areas of debate in the introduction to their edited collection of essays, *The First World War in British History*.[52]

The rise in the history of gender – often closely linked to cultural history – over the past twenty years has encouraged the fragmentation of 'women's history'. This in turn has promoted a different kind of approach to women and the war. The years between 1914 and 1918 have been defined as a critical time for issues of gender: women appeared to step outside their usual arena, but were still barred from heavy or skilled work, and from the battlefield. Their social world was thus seen as expanding, but certain territory was still 'male' and still forbidden. This fact has nurtured the idea that 1914–18 instituted a 'sex war', encouraging hostility between men and women. Another question then arises: did the war result in longer term changes in gender roles and relations or not? Again, it must be said that English language writing in this area is extensive, although books are usually firmly focused on Britain and France. In many ways the debate has shifted towards issues of psychology and perception, and it is significant that the primary sources used to support this strand of history are often literary.

There is nothing inherently contradictory in these two kinds of approach, but there are sometimes tensions between practitioners, as well as a lack of cross-disciplinary discussion. This may be in part because the 'social' historians are often European, with their own strong links to other areas of French and British writings about war and society, and frequently with politically left wing or liberal ideology too, while many of the 'gender' historians are American, working within a rather different intellectual and political tradition – though this statement is itself a generalisation, and may be seen as provocative! It is notable, however, that continuing interest in women and war has resulted in so much English language writing, while issues of race and racism lag far behind. A few key texts have emerged over the years, but there is little of the wide-ranging and heated debate one finds about women. It is perhaps surprising that historians interested in the war's supposedly liberating effects on wider society have rarely chosen to compare the experiences of a range of socially disadvantaged groups and set them in context.[53] Intriguing similarities can appear. For example, there were expectations amongst a wide variety of groups campaigning for economic and civil rights that the war would bring about change. Thus women's suffrage organisations and unions in Britain and France, black leaders and recruits in the United States, and ordinary black or Asian troops from nations within the British Empire all expressed the hope that they would prove their worth as citizens, and would gain respect, if not reward. Disappointment was thus widespread in the 1920s amongst those who returned home from war service to find that, on the contrary, the world had not really changed. Hostility towards working women in Britain led to critical newspaper articles or insults in the street. In contrast, racism led to murderous attacks against African American soldiers who returned to the United States with a greater sense of self-worth. 'Rights' did not automatically follow war service in any of the combatant nations. There are thus interesting comparisons to be made in this area which seldom appear in general books about the war, and are rarely noticed by those who concentrate only on issues of gender.[54] This is disappointing.

My own contribution to this volume, 'Winners or Losers: Women's symbolic role in the War Story', looks at the superficial approach to women which characterises those many books which refer to the war as a 'watershed' of some kind. A number of writers, writing about the war in general, merely repeat the familiar claim that women's status was raised by their war work, their higher wages, greater independence and so on. Authors of these kinds of book have no particular interest in women's experiences: they simply seek a few sources which will provide a synthesis of what they already 'know' about the war and women, given this is part of the classic war story – in Britain, and to some extent in other nations. (One of the problems is the frequency with which the 'British experience' is then adopted as the norm.) Arthur Marwick's work is often cited, particularly *The Deluge* and *Women at War,* and there is usually no mention of the debates which have featured in feminist history since the 1970s.[55] One or two quotes from books asserting women's changed wartime/postwar role will suffice, and idea that the war instituted major social reform is then reiterated. Yet, curiously, a number of books by the 'new' gender historians share many of the same faults. Authors such as Susan Kingsley Kent (*Making Peace: the Reconstruction of Gender in Interwar Britain)*, and Sandra Gilbert (*No Man's Land: the Place of the Woman Writer in the Twentieth Century*) are now widely read, and they are seen as specialists on women and war, but they too eschew detail, satisfy themselves with a small range of sources, and choose to discuss 'women' as though all ages and classes went through a single, defining, war experience.[56] Evidence which points to other interpretations is simply not used; variety is ignored and discussion of what actually happened to women as individuals or social groups is still dominated by literary texts.

In contrast, Susan Grayzel and James McMillan look closely at particular claims made for women's changing role, both during the war and since, and test these. Grayzel, in 'Liberating Women? Examining Gender, Morality and Sexuality in First World War Britain and France', offers a perfect illustration of the complexity of women's experience. Women were sometimes described as behaving 'like men' in the wake of widening employment opportunities. This claim, although apparently humorous – as in the cartoon analysed by Grayzel – could also be seen as critical, or even hostile. In what ways were women perceived as being 'like men'? Was this because the newly visible young workers were more independent, smoked, drank, or were sexually predatory? Grayzel duly examines three related subjects: anxieties about workingclass women's drinking habits; maternity and abortion; and public debates about women's sexual behaviour, prostitution and venereal disease. She looks at what *seems* to have been taking place, in social/economic terms, and what a number of commentators *believed* – or even feared – was taking place. The distinction is important: as I have written elsewhere, when considering the history of women during the war one always needs to take account of the way in which ingrained prejudice about 'women's proper role' influenced the comments of their critics. It is clear from Grayzel's essay that while cultural norms and anxieties may have varied between Britain and France, for many workingclass women in both these countries the idea of greater sexual freedom was an illusion. Women certainly did not, and could not, behave 'like men'.[57]

In 'The Great War and Gender Relations: the Case of French Women and the First World War Revisited', James McMillan engages with what evidence really exists for the idea that the War instituted a 'crisis in gender relations' as maintained by Mary Louise Roberts, one of the new wave of feminist cultural historians (whose work is also mentioned in Grayzel's chapter). Roberts is best known for her book, *Civilization without Sexes: Reconstructing Gender in Postwar France, 1917–1927*, which, as McMillan points out, suggests that '... debate concerning gender identity became a primary way to embrace, resist, or reconcile oneself to changes associated with the war'.[58] Implicit in this approach is the assumption that attitudes changed, although, as McMillan points out there is often very little comparison with anxieties and debates before 1914. McMillan goes on to test the Roberts hypothesis by considering the war's apparent impact on three aspects of gender relations. Under the category of 'Power Relations' he looks at the range of work available to women, and the way their war work affected the suffrage debate. In 'The Body and Sexuality' he considers how the war impacted on the physical lives of men and women: for the former it meant, as always, the possibility of injury and death; for the latter, it could mean rape, and the risk of abortion, but not the danger of the battlefield. Finally, under the heading of 'Private and Public', McMillan looks for signs of any change in the prevailing belief that women's primary role was maternal. In all these areas he finds, that 'traditional' views of men's and women's place in society remained as strong as ever, and that the experience of war probably reinforced a conservative agenda after 1918. It is true to say, therefore, that James McMillan's view of the war's effect on women's status in general (as also expressed elsewhere in his own books) is fairly negative,[59] but again it needs to be recognised that he, like Grayzel, is not arguing that some changes, whether temporary or permanent, did not occur: of course women entered various new trades, of course there was criticism and debate about their wartime and postwar role, but this can hardly be interpreted as a 'crisis'. Both Grayzel and McMillan illustrate that the only way to engage in argument about the war's impact is to look in detail at what did or did not appear to change, at economic, political and personal levels.

Much used, but little understood, the term 'shellshock' is the subject of Laurinda Stryker's essay, 'Mental cases: British Shellshock and the Politics of Interpretation'. The trauma of war, and its impact on the fighting man, remains an issue for doctors and psychiatrists. Post-traumatic shock syndrome is now discussed by those looking at the health of soldiers who fought in the Falklands and Iraq, and its cause is by no means established. Over the past few years there has also been renewed interest in this subject amongst social and military historians and historians of psychiatry, as evidenced by the work of Paul Lerner and Ben Shephard.[60] A complete issue of the *Journal of Contemporary History* was dedicated to the subject in 2000, and included essays by Jay Winter, Marc Roudebush, Catherine Merridale and Joanna Bourke, as well as Lerner, with themes ranging across Britain, France, Germany, Ireland and Russia in the twentieth century.[61] This more historical, and historicist approach is to be welcomed, but it still remains true that one of the most well-known contemporary writers on shellshock is Elaine Showalter, a cultural historian, whose arguments have received attention and widespread acceptance amongst many historians and literary critics, as well as journalists. Her feminist credentials have made her work well-known to those outside the academic arena, and encouraged the notion that shellshock should be compared to women's 'hysteria' as defined by Victorian physicians – with all this implies for discussion of gender roles, sexuality and power during the war years. Such an approach is beginning to seem rather dated in the context of recent medical debate, but nevertheless Showalter is often seen as a reliable source of solid information on diagnosis and treatment. (It should also be noted that several contributors to a recent collection of essays on medicine and war point out how the kind of approach to shellshock exemplified by Showalter has even distorted arguments within the history of psychiatry and mental illness.[62]) We therefore find that even Joanna Bourke cites Showalter as a reliable source, in *Dismembering the Male*, within in a chapter otherwise well supported by primary material.[63] In this essay, Stryker looks closely at Showalter's hypothesis and her evidence, including the influence of Eric Leed, whose own original source material – concerning a variety of subjects, it has to be said – is scanty. She goes on to show that even within the British medical establishment (and Stryker is adamant that national differences need to be recognised to a far greater degree than Showalter allows), treatment varied from doctor to doctor, and changed over the course of time. Stryker reveals a more practical, even humane, approach amongst many doctors than Showalter claims, and suggests that her wider arguments lack logic and consistency. Given that a brief mention of shellshock and its connection with the Edwardian concept of 'masculinity' is almost obligatory in many recent books about the social history of war, it is important to encourage a more questioning attitude to the Showalter thesis and remind ourselves that an interesting idea, strongly influenced by a limited number of literary sources, is not actually 'proof' of very much. At this point it is worth wondering whether the intensification of the debate about sex roles and sexuality in our own time has allowed anachronistic attitudes about the war, and those who experienced it, to gain a footing. Does a preoccupation with shellshock as an issue of gender, rather than as a medical condition – allowing for the influence of social and cultural nuances, as with many other psychiatric illnesses – reveal more about *our* times than those of our forebears?

Keith Allen, in 'Food and the German Home Front: Evidence from Berlin', takes as his theme rationing and the provision of hot food to Berlin's inhabitants. The allied blockade caused food shortages and increasing hardship from late 1914 onwards, and there are few doubts about the physical and mental anguish endured by Germany's civilian population. However, the wider *significance* of this hardship has exercised political, social and economic historians. It is ironic that while there is often a tendency amongst writers to isolate the years between 1914 and 1918 from the period that followed, in the case of Germany attempts to connect wartime events with the political developments of the 1920s and 1930s are almost obsessional. Why did Weimar fail, is the call, and why did the Nazis come to power? What fault lines may be traced back to the divisions and jealousies of the home front, or the way local bureaucracy and national government seemed to fail the people as food shortages grew desperate? These are perhaps natural questions, particularly in view of the voluble discontent expressed by Germany's ex-servicemen in the 1920s, yet does hindsight adversely influence both focus and judgement? The efficiency of the allied blockade is acknowledged, and it is recognised that civilian hardship was inevitable (particularly during cold winters) yet there is still more than a hint of a suggestion in the work of many writers that the German nation, or its people, were tested and in some way found wanting – that there were clearly moral shortcomings in a country which allowed the blackmarket to flourish, and failed to distribute its limited resources fairly and efficiently. Avner Offer's superbly provocative book, *The First World War: an Agrarian Interpretation*, has perhaps encouraged this judgmental approach, with its claim, for example, that an obsession with meat was part of Germany's downfall.[64] Yet food shortages are bound to engender conflict, and rationing will always raise strong feelings: the latter requires that judgement is made about which groups of workers are most important to the war effort, as well as most needy. It will often set one group against another, and this was not (and is not) a problem unique to Germany. Belinda Davis's recent book, *Home Fires Burning: Food, Politics and Everyday life in World War I Berlin*, has shifted the debate further, considering the role of popular protest and, in particular, the experiences and influence of the so-called 'women of lesser means'.[65] She raises further questions which certainly have a particularly German dimension. What was seen as a 'proper' German meal at the time, under what circumstances would people use soup kitchens, would married women accept state provision of the main family meal, who were defined as 'weak' or 'strong', and how were they treated by the rationing system? What class divisions were reinforced by feelings of injustice? One has also to agree that her account of women's protests, and their role in food riots, does indeed beg the question of 'what constitutes politics, who are the political actors, and where [do] they act politically'.

However, she too sees Berlin's food administration as failing the people. Keith Allen's view is rather different. He looks as how the city tried to deliver nutritious food to its inhabitants through dining rooms or the provision of 'take home' meals, and how it managed bread rationing. His conclusion is that, despite the difficulties caused by a complex government structure and genuine food shortages, Berlin did remarkably well – it was not until after the war that things started to fall apart. The city succeeded to a considerable degree because it forged a unique partnership with both volunteer groups and tradespeople. The former were usually middleclass women, and it is rare to read an account – of any nation – which recognises their crucial wartime role in the maintenance of day-to-day food preparation and provision, although it is true to say that thousands were involved in running factory or troop canteens and soup kitchens across Europe. Allen also suggests that the role of local bureaucrats was far more important than is usually claimed – particularly by those who concentrate on the increase in state control during the war. Allen's chapter, and his recent book, thus offer an alternative interpretation and a different kind of emphasis, but both he and Davis are adding to a debate which will no doubt continue.[66] In one crucial regard they are similar: they both show how necessary it is to look at what was happening 'on the ground' amongst city dwellers, and to examine the nature of ordinary life and urban administration at an extraordinary time. There are no easy generalisations to be made about the German people during these years.

With the last two chapters, we move into a less familiar world. There are many spaces in Western Europe's history of the war, even within the realm of the British Isles. In each nation, regional variations have often been neglected, and so too have the experiences of different age groups (particularly the children who made up such a large portion of the workforce in industry and farming), various other social groups, and a whole range of industrial workers who fell outside the arena of weapons production. Nevertheless, although we should certainly be cautious in our interpretation of autobiographical data, a vast amount of oral testimony, personal opinion and description does exist. The British, or French, or German histories of the war include many voices, for all their omissions. When considering the history of Russia and Italy we enter a different arena. These two major participants in the war have been excluded from the greater picture not merely because of the general preoccupation with the Western Front (and the relative familiarity of English/American academics with the French and German languages), or because their experiences lie outside some of the standard paradigms of Great War history, but because their own records, and their own memories, have been damaged or occluded by succeeding communist or fascist governments.[67] To a large extent the neglect by English-speaking historians has thus reflected the unavailability of written and oral evidence within both Russia and Italy. Furthermore, while many of us in Western Europe and the United States have grown up immersed in a film culture which has shown us, over and over again, what the war 'means' for us, reiterating (for good or ill) its importance to national pride, its tragic waste, its impact on ordinary men and women, Russia and Italy also lack a familiar visual fictional and documentary record.[68]

Russia is an extreme case. As the authors of one recent article have written, it is 'a society, possibly unique in the whole world, where remembering has been dangerous at least since the 1920s'.[69] The history of the years between 1914 and 1917, defined by communists as an imperialist struggle, was completely overshadowed by revolution and civil war: it was deemed irrelevant to Soviet society. This silence lasted not just for years, but for generations. Although oral historians are, painfully, beginning to piece together a record of the experiences of ordinary Russian people in the twentieth century, it is too late to find survivors of the 1914–17 war. Opinions and feelings about wartime life must be gleaned from contemporary writing. Even now, the sheer scale of the political and social conflicts of the 1920s and 1930s, or the military struggles of the 1940s, continue to marginalise the experiences of those who lived through the earlier war, destructive though that was.[70] In his essay for this volume, 'The Epic and the Domestic: Women and War in Russia, 1914–1917', Peter Gatrell is therefore reconstructing part of a history which was almost literally 'lost'. There are other ways in which he is making the obscure 'visible' too. Firstly, little has been written *at all* about Russian women during the war. Here, Gatrell offers us some background on life before 1914, and discusses the kinds of attitudes towards women which were carried forward into the war. Secondly, although millions of people were displaced by the fighting in Eastern Europe, their experiences are virtually unknown: there is even less written about their lives than about the civilians who struggled through four years of occupation in northern France.[71] When Gatrell turns his attention to refugees, many of whom were women, he shows us something of what life was like for people who have been doubly neglected by history, as women, and as the displaced. Historians of women will recognise some familiar themes – including anxiety about what was 'fit work' for women (both refugees and the charitable workers who organised them), and fears about the sexual behaviour of young women released from family supervision. At the same time it is clear that while gender influenced experience, class and ethnic background also influenced the way refugees were perceived in their new communities, and indeed the kind of work they saw as appropriate for themselves. This chapter is, therefore, a revealing example of how one historian sensitive to issues of gender, but not dominated by them, may include these as part of a wide-ranging exploration. It also becomes clear that in Russia, as elsewhere, there could be no all-encompassing general 'women's experience' of war.

Simonetta Ortaggi, in 'Italian Women during the Great War', begins by discussing the impact of Fascism on the historiography of the war in Italy. The Fascist regime literally marginalised and threatened the women who had been activists during the war, and also influenced the way in which the conflict was defined and remembered. Ortaggi's work is rooted in the vibrant tradition of oral history which emerged in Italy in the 1970s, and which has given a voice to many workingclass people. Yet ironically (or perhaps not!) this strand of writing, which sprang from the history of organised labour, has itself sometimes down-played or side-lined the role of women during the war.[72] Anna Bravo and a small group of feminist historians shifted the perspective of oral history to women, and in this essay Ortaggi continues the process, concentrating on the way in which Italian peasant women and workers reacted to a deeply unpopular war. Many were 'politicised' (my term) by their experiences, and played their part in resisting the war effort, even while they maintained food production or laboured in munitions factories. They spoke out: they tried to stop their men from going to war, and protected the deserters who sought refuge in the countryside. There is little doubt about the fact that the war had a drastic effect on many workingclass women. However, Ortaggi makes it clear that any 'gains' in independence were often illusory or temporary. Both this chapter and Gatrell's thus bring extra data to the debate about the war's impact on women, and show how dramatically different lives could be, even while anxieties and suspicions about their changing wartime role were remarkably consistent across national boundaries.

Each chapter in this book can be read alone, as a separate essay which engages with one or more of the critical themes in current war history. Common concerns run through them all – what is the nature of the evidence available, what is its provenance, how has it been used by historians over the years? However, if the essays are read together other connections will fall into place; comparative pictures also emerge, particularly in the areas of women's history, and the development of 'received wisdom' about the impact of war in general. The key words here are *detail* and *context*.

These essays fit into a history of 1914–18 which is not only vast, but multi-dimensional. We need to know about national experiences, and look across boundaries for similarities and differences, but we also need research which concentrates on small groups, individual lives, the events of a few days or weeks. We need to appreciate the scale of the war's disruption, but at the same time we need to put this into perspective and see it as part of the longer term. There was a time before 1914, and attitudes to the war were moulded by this. There was also a time after 1918, and other disasters played their part in people's lives – the general strike and the depression in Britain, the rise of Fascism in Italy, the reign of Stalin in Russia were not minor events, and could easily overshadow 1914–18. I hope that micro and macro research mean that the picture should become more complete in time, and also more complex. This is all part of the writing of history.

However, in one respect the war is unique. No other event in modern history has generated so much writing over the last ninety years. Nor has any war inspired so many novelists, poets and artists, thus attracting the attention of cultural and literary historians too. But much of this writing is

in English; it is dominated by the interpretation of anglo-american historians, and strongly influenced by the British war story – even writings in
French are seldom translated, which is a grave loss to the English-speaking readership. Also, the bulk of available visual material, from portrait
photography to film, is Western European. There are two inherent 'problems' with this emphasis. Firstly, although the arena of research is now
expanding to encompass Russia, Italy, Austria and, one hopes, many
smaller nations, there remains the danger that the main perspective
remains white and concentrated on Britain/France/Germany, with conclusions about the war's impact still tailored accordingly. If issues of gender are still perceived as a minority interest, this is even more so of other
social, racial and ethnic groups. The role of colonial troops, their interaction with standing armies, and the effect of war on their home nations
remains shamefully neglected by all but specialist researchers. We need
more diversity in the 'greater' war story.

The other 'problem' could be viewed as more of an opportunity. We
have an event which has been discussed for so long, and in such a public manner, that we can chart the changes in emphasis over the years.
People of the 1920s and 1930s wrote about it in a different way from those
of the 1960s and 1970s, let alone historians of the 1990s. Layers of story-
telling have built up, many of which need to be examined carefully, some
of which may be misleading – like the idea that Europe was gripped with
war enthusiasm in 1914 – but the emergence of these stories is itself
important. How has the war been *interpreted* by journalists, or historians,
or politicians, or policy makers, in different nations at different times? The
writers of 1914–18 were part of their own time with particular preoccupations and concerns, but so too were the historians of the 1960s or the
1990s. The focus has varied accordingly. For example, it is clearly no coincidence that the 1970s saw an increase in the number of people researching women and the war or the women's peace movement. This makes
the use of 'secondary sources' challenging, and implies, I think, that there
are *always* themes which need to be re-examined, not merely as more
papers come to light, or new collections are utilised, but in a conscious
attempt to refine, and if necessary revise, the standard picture. We should
never depend on what historians have already said. It is also true, of
course, that we can choose to look back at the shifting interpretation of
texts, memoirs, reports, descriptions, as national and international events
impinged, and comment on this process. The history of writing about the
war may be as absorbing as the event itself, and all the essays in this
book are, to some extent, about this aspect of war history as well.

So, to return to the word 'retrouver'. One commentator, to whose
rather jaundiced views I have referred in my own chapter as well, complained that:

Since the World War ended, a thousand writers have set down their impressions of the conflict, and a thousand more have declared the falsity of these

impressions. Already the truth about the War has been told so often by eye-wit-nesses whose accounts are mutually destructive that history in the future must, as plain history has always done in the past, confine itself to the bare bones of event ...[73]

Can we really 'recover' what Ward, with unconscious grimness refers to 'the bare bones' of 1914–18? My conclusion has to be cautious. There is no universal 'truth' about the war, beyond its magnitude and its destruction of countless men. Statements about what impact it had on individuals, groups, or societies must always be tempered. But at the same time I understand what he means, just as I understand all those others who complained so bitterly in the 1920s (and indeed in the decades that followed) about the way 'their' war had been appropriated, defined and *used* by novelists, poets and journalists.[74] If we are to respect the people for whom the years 1914–18 were part of life, or death, we must be careful how we utilise their experiences or their opinions, and delicate in our interpretation. Our view of events cannot possibly resemble theirs, no matter how well we feel we know the war: it is a superimposition of interpretations built up over time. Sometimes it is enough to recognise this and work with it, but sometimes we need to look beneath, and, quite simply, start afresh.

Notes

Simonetta Ortaggi died shortly after finishing the main text of her chapter for this book. I am grateful to Simonetta's husband, Paolo Cammarosano, for his work on completing the references, and making publication of this chapter possible. Simonetta's work has been translated by Guido Franzinetti, a colleague and friend of hers. My thanks to him for undertaking this task, and also for his patient discussion of the subtle issues of interpretation which emerged during the translation of Italian into English.

1. Stéphane Audoin-Rouzeau and Annette Becker, *14–18: Retrouver la Guerre*, Gallimard, France, 2000.
2. This is both a museum and research centre, and the connection between the two is important. Jay Winter describes its establishment in 1989 in 'The Generation of Memory: Reflections of the "Memory Boom" in Contemporary Historical Studies', in the German Historical Institute Bulletin (U.S.), *http://www.ghi-dc.org/* (accessed 2002). My thanks to Pierre Purseigle for this reference.
3. Email announcement by Pierre Purseigle and Jenny Macleod, June 2001, of *La Grande Guerre aujourd'hui: actualité de la recherche*. Lyon, 7–8 September, 2001.
4. *Mars in Ascendant: the Great War and the Twentieth Century*, 31 July–4 August, 2001, University College, Northampton. This five day conference included an enormous number of papers on less familiar aspects of the war, bringing together social, military, cultural and film historians. The 2001 West of England and South Wales Women's History Network 8th Annual Conference theme was *Women and War*, and included many papers on the Great War. See *http://humanities.uwe.ac.uk/swhisnet/2001prog.htm* (accessed 2002). The Imperial War Museum was also the venue for *Materialities of Conflict: Anthropology and the Great War 1914–2001*, 8 September 2001. For new scholarship see the University of Sussex on-line postgraduate *Journal of Contemporary History*,

accessed via the University, *http://www.susx.ac.uk* (2001). Articles in issues 1 and 2 include Peter Edwards, 'Mort pour la France: Conflict and commemoration in France after the First World War'; Martyn Oliver, 'Addressing the Crisis in the Representation of Traumatic Events: Great War historiography and the Lessons of the Holocaust'; Dominic Harman, '"The Truth about men in the Front Line": imagining the Experience of War in Memoirs of the Western Front'. Issue 3 includes Jenny Keating's article on postwar adoption, 'Struggle for Identity', which contains material on illegitimacy during and after the War.

5. Jay Winter and Jean Louis Robert (eds), *Capital Cities at War*, Cambridge University Press, 1997.

6. Longman's History catalogue, 2000.

7. For a useful article on the wider impact of history books written by academics, but aimed at a general readership, and their dangers, see Susan Carruthers' review of three books on the twentieth century, 'Small Corners of a Century's Killing Fields', *Times Higher Education Supplement*, 21/01/00.

8. Paul Fussell, *The Great War and Modern Memory*, Oxford University Press, 1975; Eric Leed, *No Man's Land: Combat and identity in World War I*, Cambridge University Press, 1981; Roland Stromberg, *Redemption by War*, Regent Press, 1982; Modris Eksteins, *The Rites of Spring: the First World War and the Modern Age*, Peter Davidson, 1989.

9. Fussell, *Great War*, 19. As Fussell acknowledges, Larkin was writing many years later, but I am not sure that he fully engages with the relevance of this fact.

10. I fear he is not being ironic. Paul Fussell, *The Great War*, 24. It is not pedantic to point out that as cricket and fox-hunting take place at different times of year, Sassoon would not have been hunting in July, and that although an enthusiastic cricketer he did not play 'county cricket'. See Jean Moorcroft Wilson, *Siegfried Sassoon: the making of a war poet*, Duckworth, 1998, for more on Sassoon's life in summer 1914. Fussell's description is similar to many others in tone, particularly in the field of popular history; for example Lyn Macdonald, who writes 'There was hardly a hint, in that golden summer of 1914, that the world was about to come to an end,' and proceeds to wax lyrical about the weather, garden parties, village fetes, courting couples and so on. *The Roses of No Man's Land*, Michael Joseph, 1980, 2.

11. Fussell, *The Great War*, 337.

12. Martin Stephen, *The Price of Pity: Poetry, History and Myth in the Great War*, Leo Cooper, 1996; John Terraine, *The Smoke and the Fire: Myths and Anti-Myths of War*, Sidgwick & Jackson, 1980; Brian Bond (ed.), *The First World War and British Military History*, Clarendon Press, 1991, Introduction.

13. Pierre Sorlin, 'Cinema and the Memory of the Great War', in Michael Paris (ed.), *The First World War and Popular Cinema; 1914 to the present*, Edinburgh University Press, 1999.

14. Daniel Pick, *War Machine: the Rationalisation of slaughter in the Modern Age*, Yale University Press, 1996, 196. Pick also includes a useful critique of the work of Paul Fussell.

15. Roland Stromberg, *Redemption by War*, 9–10.

16. Bernard Bergonzi, *Heroes' Twilight: a Study of the Literature of the Great War*, Macmillan, 1980, 222.

17. Tim Travers, *The Killing Ground: the British Army, the Western Front and the emergence of Modern Warfare 1900–1918*, Allen and Unwin, 1987, and *How the War was Won: Command and Technology in the British Army*, Routledge, 1992.

18. Tony Ashworth, *Trench Warfare, 1914–18: the live and let live system*, Macmillan, 1980.

19. Joanna Bourke, *Dismembering the Male: Men's Bodies, Britain and the Great War*, Reaktion Books, 1996; Ilana R. Bet-el, *Conscripts: Lost Legions of the Great War*, Suttons Publishing, 1999. For an interesting insight into the way men were treated in hospitals, and wartime medical techniques, see Eileen Crofton, *The Women of Royaumont: A Scottish Women's Hospital on the Western Front*, Tuckwell Press, 1997; these women were working with French soldiers, their offers to the British Army having been rejected.

20. Seth Koven, 'Remembering and Dismemberment: crippled children, wounded soldiers and the Great War in Great Britain' in *American Historical. Review*, 99, October 1994;

Jeffrey Reznick, 'Work Therapy and the disabled British Soldier in Great Britain in the First World War: the case of Shepherd's Bush Military Hospital, London', in David A. Gerber (ed.), *Disabled Veterans in History*, University of Michigan Press, 2000; Deborah Cohen, *The War Come Home*, University of California Press, 2001.
21. Graham Dawson, *Soldier Heroes*, Routledge, 1994; J. G. Fuller, *Troop Morale and Popular Culture in the British and Dominion Armies 1914–1918*, Clarendon Press, 1991; Elizabeth Marsland, *The Nation's Cause: French, English and German Poetry of the First World War*, Routledge, 1991.
22. Keith Grieves, *The Politics of Manpower, 1914–18*, Manchester University Press, 1988; Peter Simkins, *Kitchener's Armies: the Raising of the new Armies 1914–16*, Manchester University Press, 1988.
23. Ian F. W. Beckett and Keith Simpson (eds), *A Nation in Arms; a Social Study of the British Army in the First World War*, Manchester University Press, 1985. Jay Winter's chapter is one of many useful essays: 'Army and society; the demographic context.'
24. Keith Wilson (ed.), *Forging the Collective Memory: Government and International Historians through two World Wars*, Berghahn, 1996. A very useful chronology of the ebb and flow of 'who was to blame' for the war can be found in Annika Mombauer, *The Origins of the First World War: Controversies and Consensus*, Longman, 2002.
25. Ben Bar-Yosef, 'The Last Crusade? British Propaganda and the Palestine Campaign, 1917–18', *Journal of Contemporary History*, 36 (1), January 2001, 108. For a complete history of events see Anthony Bruce, *The Last Crusade: The Palestine Campaign in the First World War*, John Murray, 2002.
26. I am indebted to Alan Scott for many of these references. Brian Bond, *British Military Policy between the Two World Wars*, Oxford, 1980, and Bryan Ranft (ed.), *Technical Change and British Naval Policy 1860–1939*, Hodder and Stoughton, 1977, both demonstrate that there was no 'straight line' between the warfare of 1918 and that of 1939. Lieut.-Colonel G. S. Hutchison DSO MC, *Machine Guns: Their History and Tactical Employment*, MacMillan & Co, 1938, illustrates just how tactically and practically complex the implementation of machine guns actually was. Timothy Lupfer, *The Dynamics of Doctrine: the changes in German tactical doctrine during the First World War*, Leavenworth Papers No 4, Ft Leavenworth Kansas, 1981, demonstrates the sheer complexity of the German system of defence in the West, possibly the largest fixed position ever to be tested by frontal assault in European warfare. Jay Luvaas, *The Military Legacy of the Civil War: The European Inheritance*, Chicago, 1959, is interesting not just because he shows just how soon the new firearms forced field entrenchment, or how difficult it is to extrapolate from one war to the conduct of warfare on another continent, but for illustrating many of the practical problems of the time, like the difficulty of reducing earthworks by artillery fire; W. R. Murray and A. R. Millett (eds), *Military Innovation in the Interwar period*, Cambridge University Press, 1996, includes excellent essays on changing technology and the nature of warfare; Denis E. Showalter, *Railroads and Rifles: Soldiers, Technology and the Unification of Germany*, Hamden, 1975, offers indispensable insight into infrastructures and technical development, and the willingness or otherwise of combatants to sacrifice troops in the face of the new firearms as a battle tactic; Hew Strachan, *European Armies and the Conduct of War*, Routledge, reprinted 1993, is a remarkable synthesis of issues to do with politics, economics, industry, technology, strategy and tactics of war in Europe in the modern period; John Terraine, *Right of the Line*, Wordsworth Editions, 1997, illustrates how circumspect it is necessary to be about the idea that large scale strategic bombing 'began' during the Great War; M. F. Boemeke, R. Chickering and S. Förster (eds), *Anticipating Total War: the German and American Experiences, 1871–1914*, Cambridge University Press, 1999, and S. Förster and J. Nagler (eds), *On the Road to Total War*, Cambridge University Press, 1997, both include essays which show how sophisticated the current debate about technology, strategy and war is.
27. Hew Strachan, *The First World War*, Vol. I, Oxford University Press, 2001.
28. John R. Gillis (ed.), *Commemorations: the Politics of National Identity*, Princeton University Press, 1994. See also the war's impact on Australia, once part of the Empire,

where its memory remains important. For an overview, see Joan Beaumont, *Australia's War 1914–18*, Allen and Unwin, 1995, and for a comparison of memorialisation, see David W. Lloyd, *Battlefield Tourism: Pilgrimage and the Commemoration of the Great War in Britain, Australia and Canada 1919–1939*, Berg, 1998. George Mosse, in *Fallen Soldiers: Re-shaping the Memory of World War I*, Oxford University Press, 1990, offers an interesting interpretation of the immediate postwar-war years in Britain, France and Germany, and compares the way the war story was used by politicians and nations.

29. Adrian Gregory, *The Silence of Memory: Armistice Day 1919–1946*, Oxford, 1994.

30. Of course the 1939–45 war is also 'remembered', but is usually seen as a 'good' war, rather than an event to be mourned. Although more people across the world died during this conflict (including far more civilians), there is no talk of a 'lost generation' in 1939–45. See Williamson Murray, 'Armoured Warfare: the British, French and German Experience', in Murray and Millett, *Military Innovation in the Interwar period*; footnote 11, on page 35, discusses relative casualties, and the mistaken perception that the 1914–18 war was 'worse' in terms of numbers killed and wounded across the warring nations.

31. 'For Evermore: Fading Evidence of the Great War', an exhibition at the Gallery of Photography, Dublin, 2000, raised much interest; its catalogue includes extracts from discussions about Ireland's part in the war. Also, soldiers from Catholic areas of Ulster were often forgotten or ignored in British history until the 1990s. One speaker at a recent conference reported how his own family had no idea that his grandfather's name appeared on the local war memorial, as remembrance ceremonies were effectively run by the Orange Order: Jim Haughey, 'The Great War and an Irish Town', unpublished paper presented at *Mars in Ascendant* Conference. See also Adrian Gregory and Senia Pašeta (eds), *Ireland and the Great War: 'A War to unite us all?'*, Manchester University Press, 2002, and Keith Jeffrey, *Ireland and the Great War*, Cambridge University Press, 2000, (which includes a useful bibliographical essay).

32. Apart from the Revolution of 1789, French historians have to engage with the Napoleonic era, the revolutions of 1830 and 1848, the Franco-Prussian War and the Paris Commune, all of which mean that there can be no suggestion that the 1914–18 war marked the end of a peaceful century – which is a key part of the British war story. However, Stéphane Audoin-Rouzeau and Annette Becker suggest that since 1998 the war is the subject of growing interest; see *14–18, Retrouver la Guerre*.

33. Paris, *The First World War and Popular Cinema: 1914 to the present*, Introduction. See also Jill Liddington, 'What is public history? Publics and their pasts, meanings and practices' in *Oral History*, 30 (1), Spring 2002, for discussion about the rise of 'public history' and its influence. The work of John Lowenthal, cited by Liddington, is also important when considering nostalgia and the lure of the past: *The Past is a Foreign Country*, Cambridge University Press, 1985. Samuel Hynes has much to say about the importance of 'myth' and the way we use this, in 'Personal Narratives and Commemoration', in J. Winter and Emmanuel Sivan (eds), *War and Remembrance in the Twentieth Century*, Cambridge, 1999, 207; see also Samuel Hynes, *A War Imagined*, Pimlico, 1992, and *The Soldiers' Tale*, Allen Lane, 1997

34. Pierre Sorlin, 'Cinema and the Memory of the Great War', in Michael Paris, *The First World War and Popular Cinema*, 13.

35. Pat Barker, *The Regeneration Trilogy*, Penguin, 1992–96; Sebastian Faulks, *Birdsong*, Vintage, 1994. The interpretation of war in these novels remains largely unchallenged in Britain, but see M. Loschnigg, '… the-novelist's-responsibility-to-the-past: History, myth, and the narratives of crisis in Pat Barker's "Regeneration trilogy" (1991–1995)', in *Zeitschrift fur Anglistik und Amerikanistik*, 47 (3), 1999, 214–228, and Esther MacCullum-Stewart's essay at http://www.whatalovelywar.co.uk/Regeneration.htm (accessed 2003.)

36. This was screened in March 2002. Volunteers lived in a reconstructed trench, complete with mud, noise, bugs, etc., and were supposed to understand the physical discomfort of life as a soldier. Of course, sudden death was not included. To be fair, the BBC also co-produced (with PBS) the recent *1914–18* series on the Great War, with its rather more sophisticated approach to the conflict.

37. The British view is very confused: we are at once proud of the men who died, and therefore, by extension, proud of our nation's role, and yet we accept the idea that the war was wrong and unnecessary. What exactly are we commemorating on Remembrance Day?
38. Terry Castle, 'Courage, mon amie', *London Review of Books*, 4/04/02.
39. Gary Sheffield, *Forgotten Victory*, Headline, 2001. Brian Bond engages with the British preoccupation with the war's disasters and the usual jaundiced view of the Army in *The Unquiet Western Front*, Cambridge University Press, 2002.
40. Daniel Todman, '"It's a family affair": the First World War and family history in Britain, 1918–1998' unpublished paper presented to *Mars in Ascendant* Conference.
41. Catherine Moriarty, 'The Material Culture of Great War Remembrance', *Journal of Contemporary History*, 34 (4), 1999; Saunders, *Trench Art: a brief history and guide, 1914–1939*, Leo Cooper, 2002.
42. See also Catherine Moriarty, 'The Absent Dead and Figurative Sculpture', *Transactions of the Ancient Monuments Society*, 39, 1995. For a fascinating discussion of the imagery of soldiers wearing greatcoats used by memorial sculptors, see Moriarty, '"Remnants of patriotism": the sculptural appeal of the greatcoat after the First World War', unpublished paper for the *Drapery and Visual Culture* Conference, National Gallery, London, August 2002.
43. It is hard to avoid the feeling that for some people war memorials may have made both mourning and the process of recovery more difficult, just as many war widows and old soldiers chose to avoid formal Remembrance Day gatherings. For a detailed discussion of war memorials, their building and their symbolic status, see Alex King, *Memorials of the Great War in Britain: the Symbolism and Politics of Remembrance*, Berg, 1998
44. W. J. Reader, *At Duty's Call: A Study in Obsolete Patriotism*, Manchester University Press, Manchester, 1988, 104.
45. Marc Ferro, *The Great War, 1914–18*, Routledge & Kegan Paul, 1973, xi.
46. Much of his argument is based on secondary sources. Niall Ferguson, *The Pity of War*, Penguin, 1999.
47. Jean-Jacques Becker, *1914: Comment les Francais sont entrés dans la guerre*, Presses de la Fondation Nationale des Sciences Politiques, 1977; J. Verhey, *The Spirit of 1914: Mobilization, Militarism and Myth in Germany*, Cambridge University Press, 2000.
48. It might also be instructive to compare the reports of 1914 with press coverage of other twentieth-century wars. The Falklands War, for example, was greeted by a jingoistic tabloid press, and pictures of departing Royal Navy ships showed cheering crowds of friends, wives and children waving their men off to war. However, many of us will recall that there was little celebration or enthusiasm amongst a substantial part of the population, and that this cynicism about the necessity for war was not widely reported at the time.
49. An article by Keith Grieves is an indication of what local history can bring to the debate. In '"Lowther's Lambs": rural paternalism and voluntary recruitment in the First World War', *Rural History*, 4 (1), he discusses men's reasons for volunteering in Sussex. He suggests that there was a strong feeling of local community spirit, and loyalty to the county, in urban areas as well as rural. This was probably more influential than patriotism.
50. Deborah Thom, *Nice Girls and Rude Girls: Women Workers in World War I*, I. B. Tauris, 1998. Thom also cites June Purvis, 'From Women Worthies to Post-structuralism', in Purvis (ed.), *Women's History: Britain 1880–1945*, UCL Press, 1995. This explores developments in women's history.
51. Penny Summerfield, 'Women and War in the Twentieth-century' in Purvis, *Women's History*. The experiences of women in Britain in the two wars are contrasted and compared by Penny Summerfield and myself in *Out of the Cage*, Pandora, 1987.
52. Stephen Constantine, Maurice Kirby and Mary Rose (eds), *The First World War in British History*, Edward Arnold, 1995.
53. George Robb's book, *British Culture and the First World War*, Palgrave, 2002, is an exception. The first chapter of this very useful overview is devoted to aspects of the war's impact on 'Nation, Race and Empire'.
54. For essays on the varied experience of men and women in African nations, see Melvin Page (ed.), *Africa and the First World War*, Macmillan, 1987. Men were sometimes con-

scripted, sometimes forced into the army by tribal obligations, or were even volunteers. While some sought to show themselves as too soft and weak for battle in order to avoid call-up, others took pride in a fighting heritage, and were then frustrated by the fact that they were confined to work as porters and labourers, never trusted to be soldiers in the front line. The scale of recruitment is surprising. For example, according to Geoffrey Hodges, in Kenya the British utilised 50,000 African soldiers, who were accompanied by over a million followers and casual labourers, while 130,000 men were sent to Belgium. See Hodges, 'Military Labour in East Africa and its impact on Kenya' in Page, *Africa and the First World War*, above. See also Albert Grundlingh, *Fighting their own war: South African Blacks and the First World War*, Ravan Press, 1987; and Myron Echenberg, *Colonial Conscripts*, Heinemann, 1991 for the French African experience (about which far more has been written); for the colonial context see David Killingray and David Omissi (eds), *Guardians of Empire: the Armed Forces of the Colonial Powers c. 1700–1964*, Manchester University Press, 1999; David Omissi, *Indian Voices of the Great War*, Macmillan, 1999. For the expectations of black American soldiers see A. Barbeau and F. Henri, *The Unknown Soldiers: Black American troops in World War I*, Temple University Press, 1974. For American Indians, see Thomas Britten, *American Indians in World War I: at home and at war*, University of New Mexico Press, 1997. There is also plenty more to be discussed about the experiences of other minorities within each nation, and postwar life. See, for example, P. Panayi, *The Enemy in our Midst: Germans in Britain during the First World War*, Oxford University Press, 1991, and Mark Connelly, 'Assimilation and integration: East End Jewish Ex-Servicemen, the memory of the Great War and the fight against fascism', unpublished paper presented to *Frontlines: Identity, Gender and War* Conference at Monash University, Melbourne, July 2002. It is a sad fact that more words have been written about the British war poets than about all the non-white troops put together.

55. Arthur Marwick, *The Deluge: British Society and the First World War*, Macmillan, 1965 (reprinted 1991); Arthur Marwick, *Women at War*, Fontana, 1977.
56. Susan Kingsley Kent, *Making Peace: the Reconstruction of Gender in Interwar Britain*, Princeton University Press, 1993; Sandra Gilbert and Susan Gubar, *No Man's Land: the Place of the Woman Writer in the Twentieth Century*, Vol. II, *Sexchanges*, Yale University Press, 1989.
57. In passing it should also be noted that, as Frances Bernstein points out, the figure of 'the dangerous single woman' in wartime was common to many other nations too, whatever their differences. Frances Bernstein, 'Visions of Sexual Health in Revolutionary Russia' in Roger Davidson and Lesley A. Hall (eds), *Sex, Sin and Suffering: Venereal disease and European Society since 1870*, Routledge, 2001. This book includes valuable discussion of attitudes to single women and prostitutes during both wars.
58. M. L. Roberts, *Civilisation without Sexes: Reconstructing Gender in Postwar France, 1917–1927*, University of Chicago Press, 1994, 5.
59. James McMillan, *Housewife or Harlot*, Harvester, 1981.
60. See Ben Shephard, *A War of Nerves: soldiers and psychiatrists*, 1914–1994, Cape, 2001, and Paul Lerner's review of this, 'Hard Cop, Soft Cop: the awkward paradox of military psychology' in the *Times Literary Supplement*, March 9, 2001. See also Lerner's article, 'Hysterical cures: hypnosis, gender and performance in World War I and Weimar Germany', in *History Workshop*, 45, Spring 1998, and 'Rationalising the Therapeutic Arsenal: German Neuropsychiatry in World War I', in Manfred Berg and Geoffrey Cocks (eds), *Medicine and Modernity: Public health and Medical Care in Nineteenth- and Twentieth Century Germany*, Cambridge University Press, 1997. For the Irish dimension, see Joanna Bourke, 'Shell-shock, psychiatry and the Irish soldier during the First World War', in Gregory and Pašeta, *Ireland and the Great War*.
61. *Journal of Contemporary History*, 35 (1), January 2000, entire issue, but especially Jay Winter, 'Shell-shock and the cultural history of the Great War', Paul Lerner, 'Psychiatry and the Casualties of War in Germany, 1914–18', and Joanna Bourke, 'Effeminacy, Ethnicity and the Evil of Trauma: the suffering of "shell-shocked" men in Great Britain and Ireland 1914–39'. For a German perspective on the experiences of discipline in different

armies, see Christoph Jahr, *Gewoehnliche Soldaten. Desertion unde Deserteure im deutschen und britischen Heer 1914–1918,* Göttingen, 1998.

62. See Roger Cooter, Mark Harrison and Steve Sturdy (eds), *War, Medicine and Modernity,* Sutton, Publishing, 1999, in particular Roger Cooter's own essay, 'Malingering in Modernity: psychological scripts and adversarial encounters during the First World War', and Mathew Thomson, 'Status, Manpower and mental fitness: mental deficiency in the First World War'. The volume is also notable for its editors' attempt to define and describe what they mean by 'modernity' in the introduction, an essay which includes a useful critique of the way many historians have employed the words, 'modern', and 'modernism'.

63. Joanna Bourke, *Dismembering the Male*; see also Jason Crouthamel, 'War Neurosis versus Savings Pychosis: Working-class Politics and Psychological Trauma in Weimar Germany', in *The Journal of Contemporary History,* 37 (2), April 2002. This is an interesting article, but he nevertheless directs the reader to Showalter 'for research on male hysteria and British psychiatrists' assumptions about social class' in a footnote on page 163.

64. Avner Offer, *The First World War: an agrarian interpretation,* Clarendon Press, 1989.

65. Belinda Davis, *Home Fires Burning: Food, Politics and Everyday life in World War I Berlin,* University of North Carolina Press, 2000; see also her essay, with Thierry Bonzon, 'Feeding the Cities', in Jay Winter and Jean Louis Robert, *Capital Cities at War.*

66. Keith Allen, *Hungrige Metropole. Essen und Wohlfahrt in Berlin*, Ergebnisse, 2002

67. There is still little written in English about many other smaller nations during and after the war, including Serbia and other parts of the Austro-Hungarian empire.

68. See Giovanni Nobili Vitelleschi, 'The Representation of the Great War in Italian Cinema', and Denise J. Youngblood, 'A War Forgotten: the Great War in Russian and Soviet Cinema', in Paris, *The First World War and Popular Cinema.*

69. Daria Khubova, Andrei Ivankiev and Tonia Sharova, 'After Glasnost: oral history in the Soviet Union', in the *International Yearbook of Oral History and Life Studies,* Vol. I, Oxford University Press, 1992 (Special editor, Luisa Passerini).

70. For example, one otherwise useful volume on the changing face of Russian history includes no essays on the 1914–17 war, although it is mentioned in passing by some of the contributors. See Nurit Schleifman (ed.), *Russia at a Crossroads: History, Memory and Political Practice*, Frank Cass, 1998. For a powerful description of the nature of work as an oral historian in Russia today, see Catherine Merridale, *Night of Stone: Death and Memory in Russia*, Granta, 2000.

71. Life during the invasion is now attracting more attention. See Annette Becker, in *14–18, Retrouver la Guerre*, and Helen McPhail, *The Long Silence; civilian life under the German Occupation of Northern France, 1914–1918*, I. B. Tauris, 1999. A good overview is to be found in Margaret H. Darrow, *French Women and the First World War: War Stories of the Home Front*, Berg, 2000.

72. For more on oral history and Italian fascism see *The International Yearbook of Oral History and Life Stories*, Vol I, Introduction, by Luisa Passerini, and the Review article, by Alfredo Martini, 'Oral History and Italian Fascism.' For the shifting view of the war in Italy, and its later co-option by fascism, see Vitelleschi, 'The Representation of the Great War in Italian Cinema,' in Paris, *The First World War and Popular Cinema.*

73. A. C. Ward, *The Nineteen-twenties,* Methuen, 1930, 1.

74. Martin Stephen, *Price of Pity*, on page 78 quotes from memoirs cited by G. A. Panichas, *Promise of Greatness*, Cassell, 1968: 'I never met an 'old sweat', as we liked to describe ourselves, who accepts or enjoys the figure in which we are now presented ... Is it any use to assert that I was not like that, and my dead friends were not like that, and the old cronies that I meet at reunions are not like that?'

1

'Though in a Picture Only'
Portrait Photography and the Commemoration of the First World War

Catherine Moriarty

The First World War memorial at Houilles, north west of Paris, takes the form of a high platform; upon it at one end a uniformed soldier, who is about to walk away and join his comrades, turns to gesture farewell to his child, who with a mirroring outstretched arm stands with its mother at the other end (Figure 1.1). The most striking feature of this memorial is the way in which the composition emphasises the space in between the soldier and his family. The spectator knows that this space, although barely a few feet, represents separation. In the instance depicted, the time of farewell, it is yet to be determined whether the separation is temporary or not, but by the nature of this sculpted object and the many names inscribed upon it, we know that for many it was permanent.

The First World War separated millions of individuals from their families and home communities. Sometimes this separation lasted the duration of enlistment with periodic returns home on leave, but in many instances death made it permanent. This essay considers two types of material culture which played an important part in assuaging the pain of separation in circumstances both temporary and permanent. It will look at the ways in which photography's part in the processes of remembering compares with the part played by war memorials in stone and bronze that were built at the end of the conflict. While considerable attention has been paid to monumental war memorials in recent years, this essay argues that the material culture of Great War remembrance occupies a wider plane, and that war memorials were but one part of a diverse remembering landscape.

Figure 1.1 First World War Memorial at Houilles, France, sculpted by Jean-Joseph Galle (1859–1923). Photograph by Catherine Moriarty.

Although monuments tend to occupy conspicuous public spaces, they have been a neglected component of the built environment until recently. In Britain, listed building status is conferred only on memorials deemed to be of significant artistic merit or those of group value – for example, a cross on a village green, forming part of the picturesque overall scene. Few are included in architectural surveys, such as the Buildings of England series originated by Nikolaus Pevsner in the 1950s.[1] Certainly, they were overlooked by art and architectural historians and were marginal to studies of twentieth-century sculpture that focused on the development of British modernism, and the sculpture of the avant garde, rather than the public monument. Likewise, war remembrance was once an activity that fell beyond the concerns of historians of the First World War, who concentrated on the events leading to the outbreak of war, the duration and conduct of the conflict. Studies of the postwar years emphasised the economic and political ramifications, as did social histories, which acknowledged innumerable private tragedies but rarely developed this theme.[2] A continuing interest in the literature of the war, and the broadcasting of documentary television programmes such as the BBC's *Great War* series in 1964, promoted greater understanding of the conflict. The body of writing on the circumstances of the First World War evolved, with new emphasis on the experiences of the ordinary soldier and life in the trenches.[3] Yet, as the war receded in time, it came to be experienced by new generations through, or *as*, acts of remembrance. Armistice Day was identified as a public ceremony, which had a key role in the shaping of national identity, and from this platform interest in regional and localised acts of remembrance developed. Never a serious object of study for art historians, memorials were attractive to cultural historians keen to investigate the neglected components of twentieth-century life that fell between the strictures of traditional historical practice. From research that began during the 1980s, an important bibliography of texts on war memorials, commemoration and remembrance has evolved.[4]

This body of work has had a significant impact on the way in which wars, both historical and current, are discussed, taught or reported. The impact of mass death, the impact of individual deaths, and the activity of memory in public and private – these are now key issues.[5] This essay seeks to add to this work by continuing to focus on what was marginalised for so long, the memorial, but to add to it an investigation of that which was considered ephemeral: the personal photograph.

In 1918, a report on the policy of the newly established Imperial War Graves Commission was published. Compiled by Sir Frederick Kenyon, the Director of the British Museum, it was entitled *War Graves: How the Cemeteries Abroad will be Designed*.[6] The Commission's proposals were brought to a wider audience in 1919 with the publication of *The Graves of the Fallen*. Written by Rudyard Kipling, it was intended to soften the impact of Kenyon's report. It included illustrations of the cemeteries by Douglas Macpherson, with mature shrubs and trees in blossom: a glaring contrast to stark, bleak landscapes depicted in photographs of battlefield cemeteries at this time.[7] Public outcry followed these publications, fuelled by campaigns led by the *Spectator* and the *Daily Mail* and culminating in a debate in the House of Commons in May 1920.[8] The major issues centred on the role of the state in the commemoration of the dead, the ban on repatriation and the decision that headstones, rather than crosses, should mark graves. The sculptor Eric Gill was incensed by Kenyon's report. He wrote a letter which was published in the *Burlington Magazine* in April 1919, and it is worth quoting at some length:

> The commission's attitude in the matter [the design and production of headstones] is the more easily understood inasmuch as it is the whole trend of our time to impose the ideas of the few upon the many while being careful to hide the process under a guise of democratic sympathy and social reform. Thus the idea that half a million headstones should be made according to the ideas of a few architects (an idea worthy of the Prussian or the Ptolemy at his best) instead of according to those of several thousand stone-masons and twenty million relatives is not surprising, and under the plea of commemorating 'the sense of comradeship and common service' and 'the spirit of discipline and order',

etc. (vide 'Report'), it is hoped that the very widespread desire of relatives to have some personal control of the monuments to their dead will be overcome.[9]

Following this shrewd assessment of the motives of the Commission, Gill went on to discuss the appropriation of the bodies of the dead, the preference for headstones rather than crosses and the limited space allowed for personal inscriptions. Gill suggested that stone masons across the country should carve headstones for the dead of their locality over several years. In this way uniformity would be replaced by slight variations in style, quality and materials, from grave to grave, which he suggested would reflect the characters of the dead themselves, some good, some bad.[10] It is easy to imagine Gill's scheme causing as much upset as the policy of the Commission, yet he was determined that the latter should not go unchallenged.

Later in 1919, the pages of *The Times* included substantial comment on Commission policy. Whether or not the dead should be repatriated was a major issue, and Gill's questioning of the appropriate role of the state in commemorative activity was reiterated. A letter from Lady Cecil was published on 23 December; she wrote:

> these memorials to the dead do not as a rule appeal to mourners either collectively or as individuals. The bereaved desire consolation from personal tributes to their dead, not from well-drilled patterned uniformity.[11]

Cecil's view, expressed in support of her husband's objections to Commission policy, raises the issue of what sorts of objects were used for different kinds of remembering. Many felt that the bodies of their loved ones had been absorbed in an Imperial plan, many were unable to travel overseas to see a grave, indeed for the relatives of the Missing there would be no grave to see.[12] Consequently, memorials in home communities acquired great significance as substitute graves. Thousands of memorials were built by communities up and down the British Isles and in other countries that had suffered losses in the war.

A great deal of work has taken place in recent years investigating how communities organised the building of their First World War memorials.[13] Extensive examinations of local newspaper reports, and the minutes of commissioning bodies held at county record offices, have provided the details of how local commemorative projects were initiated, organised, funded and discussed. With no funding from central government, most regional projects were financed by public subscription with the local council or other community representatives organising the process. There were often public meetings, where the form, location and inscription were debated at length. It has been argued that it was this process of decision making that enabled individuals to give meaning to memorials, and that this meaning was not necessarily the same for everybody. The forms and wording of memorials were regarded as appropriate for remembering the dead but flexible enough to absorb a great diversity of opinion.[14] Nevertheless, is this where the bereaved actually remembered? The historian Samuel Hynes has argued that the constraining, officially endorsed language, and form of memorials prevented any alternative or opposition view of the war. It is certainly true that representations or inscriptions indicative of individuals' experience of the war are rare. Instead we are faced with a collective statement, a collective solution to individual loss.

Public war memorials are an acknowledgement of a community's loss, expressed in forms and words that are publicly acceptable, but they tell us virtually nothing about how people mourned or remembered away from these structures. Many memorials commemorating one individual or siblings were installed by bereaved families in local churches. Yet these objects required substantial funds and influence, and the vast majority commemorate officers. Bronze plaques, stained glass windows and other conventional ecclesiastical memorial objects were popular. There are a few examples which take the form of portraits sculpted in relief and we must assume that the artist worked from a photograph in order to achieve a likeness of the deceased.[15] Yet the vast majority of commemorative portraits would have remained as a photographic print rather than being remodelled in bronze or carved in stone.[16]

During the war, many villages and city neighbourhoods constructed temporary shrines that listed those who were serving, and which became memorials to the dead as casualty figures increased. Sometimes these incorporated photographs of the dead which were arranged around the list of names.[17] Located in streets or churches, shrines were often heaped with flowers and ribbons. The devotional significance of these objects is made clear in a contemporary photograph of the interior of the village church at Raunds, Northamptonshire (Figure 1.2). Moreover, the inclusion of photographs on shrines illustrates the transference of an object created for remembering one individual into a collective assemblage where he, or much less often she, becomes one among others.

After the war some shrines were dismantled to make way for more enduring constructions made from resilient materials, and usually crafted and designed by professional masons or sculptors. Yet many communities sought to make permanent the accumulated photographs. A framed roll of honour comprising twenty-two head and shoulder portraits commemorates those from the Dent Congregational Sunday School, Cumbria (Figure 1.3), who served in the war.[18] Each portrait, of twenty-one men and one nurse, all in uniform, emerge ghost-like from evenly spaced oval frames within the rectangular whole. The four who were killed are placed centrally with a black border separating them from those that returned. The framed roll was compiled by a photographer in Eccleshill, Bradford, presumably working with images sent from the congregation at Dent. Other memorial objects were created after the war by a similar process, but often in a more controlled format – for example, published rolls of

Figure 1.2 Raunds Parish Church, Northamptonshire. Photograph from the National Inventory of War Memorials, Imperial War Museum.

Figure 1.3 Dent Congregational Sunday School and Church Roll of Honour, Cumbria. Photograph from the National Inventory of War Memorials, Imperial War Museum.

honour, which will be considered below. First, however, it is important to consider the production of portrait photographs during the war years.

Portrait photographs, which could be displayed at shrines, positioned on mantelpieces, or kept safe in wallets and lockets for frequent viewing, were precious.[19] Photographers experienced a boom in the war years; their services were sought when uniforms were issued, before leaving for training or active service, while in camp and while on leave. These images were retained by the families of those who left to serve, and photographs of those at home would accompany those at war, an exchange of images common to all, but exacerbated by the absences and removals brought about by war.[20] Indeed the exchange of photographs, or rather evidence that those who purchased them intended them to travel, is emphasised by the number which were printed as postcards. Those produced by the photographers W. A. Brown and Son (Figure 1.4), who had studios in London and Manchester, included the title *Postcard* and sub titles *Correspondence*, *Address* and an area marked *stamp here* on the back, and these were accompanied by a translation into French.[21] The photographers produced a photographic object with a clear understanding of its intended function, as an item which could literally traverse the gap of separation, so poignantly

Figure 1.4 Family portrait mounted on a postcard produced by the photographers W. A. Brown and Son.

represented by the memorial at Houilles, and which would enable those at home or at war to see again loved ones from whom they were apart.[22]

In 1917 Ivor Gurney wrote a poem entitled *Photographs*.[23] It is a perceptive consideration of the importance of photographs to those at home and to those on active service, and the irony of these captured faces amid the misery of life in the trenches:

> With pity and pride, photographs of all colours,
>   All sizes, subjects: khaki brothers in France;
> Or mother's faces worn with countless dolours;
>   Or girls whose eyes were challenging and must dance,
>
> Though in a picture only, a common cheap
>   Ill-taken card; and children – frozen, some
> (Babies) waiting on Dicky-bird to peep
>   Out of the handkerchief that is his home
>
> (But he's so shy!). And some with bright looks, calling
>   Delight across the miles of land and sea,
> That not the dread of barrage suddenly falling
> Could quite blot out – not mud nor lethargy.

Gurney refers to the distance which the images traversed between home and front, seeing them as a link between places and people, the past and the present, peace and war. Amid the official communications and the censoring of letters the photograph assumed authenticity; incorruptible evidence of dearly loved faces.[24] Thousands of similar photographs would have been destroyed in battle or returned to families with servicemen's 'effects', and in death the portraits of soldiers gained even greater value as the last portrait of an individual, and thus acquired a memorial function.[25] The fear of not seeing a loved one again is evoked by the following postwar reminiscence, 'when, after their short spells of leave from the front we saw our boys off again, with the haunting fear that we should see their faces no more'.[26]

The all-encompassing official commemorative activity of Imperial governments, wrought mainly in stone and bronze, with fixed meanings, makes a stark contrast to the highly personal rituals of remembrance, centred on the photographic image. These are the images that remain in family albums or stored with medals. For every headstone in a Commission cemetery there would be at least one photographic counterpart of an individual. Portraits of the dead were made public in various ways. They were included in rolls of honour which were framed in churches and places of work, as in the aforementioned example at Dent, or published as volumes, particularly by schools and businesses; they were also printed with obituary notices in local newspapers and incorporated into films which were shown after newsreels in cinemas.[27] Photographs brought together in this way become cemented in a framing structure, be it a film, plaque or page in a published roll of honour. Before this final placement, the photograph, or copies of it, would have experienced a more fluid and private life as a totem attached to particular individuals, perhaps secure in a father's wallet or a loved-one's locket.[28]

This practice of amalgamating portrait photographs taken at different times, by different photographers, in different situations and in different formats, which together formed a collective memorial by combining individual memorial items, was adopted by the Imperial War Museum for a project it initiated in 1917. During that year a step was taken to try and bring together this dispersed photographic collection of the war dead, a step which could be regarded as a means of absorbing the private into the national.

When the Imperial War Museum was established in 1917, photography was recognised as an important component of its future collections. The curator of photography, Kenneth Hare, acquired official photographs documenting the conduct of the war from British sources as well as the Dominions. He also collected photographs of war memorials as they were built, and virtually any photograph relating to any aspect of the war was accepted. One project, however, differed from the others. On Saturday 21 July 1917 the Museum placed an announcement in national and local newspapers calling for the submission of portrait photographs of those serving, the aim being to compile a national record. The announcement was headed We Want Your Photograph.[29] As soon as the responses began to arrive, the Museum realised the enormity of the project it had initiated. Hare wrote to one enquirer, 'we are most anxious to receive photographs of every man who served, but as there are some millions of these, you must understand that they will take a great deal of time to collect'. Although the project was to encompass serving individuals, the files relating to this project are filled with black-edged letters and it seems as if most of those submitting photographs were the bereaved. One woman wrote from an address in Liverpool, 'I would feel it an everlasting honour to my son, to send his photograph so that friends and relatives can recognise him when making pilgrimages in the near future.' This then was more than a record; it was to be a memorial, and those sending photographs seemed to have no doubt that these images would be displayed. But this was not to happen. The files tail off towards the end of 1919. Perhaps the impossibility of administering such an enterprise had dawned on the Museum, which certainly did not appear to have renewed its requests in the press, or perhaps after the Armistice public interest waned? Some of the prints were bought directly from commercial photographers, deposited in bulk rather than with personalised commemorative intent. Overall almost 15,000 photographs were collected, a small percentage of the Empire's dead, but a considerable collection nonetheless. Mounted on card, filed alphabetically and stored in boxes, the photographs have been housed off-site at the Museum's stores at Duxford barracks for many years.

These hidden images are disquieting. Looking at these photographs now, they possess an 'ironic reinscription of the present on the past', as Marita Sturken has described the study of photographs of Holocaust victims: 'that is, our capacity to read the weight of this particular historical event upon them.'[30] The young man in a new uniform, standing in the photographer's studio, perhaps contemplated death, but would have been unaware of how and when this might happen, and his family would have faced the same uncertainty, at first. Confronted with the simple statement of place and date of death on the board mount, or through its inclusion on a memorial plaque, roll of honour, or, as is often seen in France, on an enamel plate positioned by a memorial or in a cemetery,[31] we recognise the shift in the context of this image: rather than assuaging a temporary absence, it has become a document of that which has gone forever – the 'posthumous irony' of the photographic image, as Susan Sontag has described it.[32] Indeed amalgamations of portrait photographs, which were taken before the fact of death united them, are characterised by the disparity in scale, pose and quality between the individual images comprising the assemblage, even though the framing structure may be uniform. The Imperial War Museum cards are a standard 27 by 31 cm, yet the portraits mounted upon them range from postcard size and smaller, to much larger formats. In some, the individual looks to the left, sometimes face on, sometimes right. Some are face only, some three-quarter, some full length, some have white backgrounds, others dark. Some look pensive, others resigned, some cheerful. Most are young, a few are older, some are handsome. Some look comfortable in uniform, others seem to be in costume.

While memorials in stone and bronze were built to endure, photographs are characterised by their fragility, their mere paper support. If the former, through the processes which determined their form and meaning, have lost their connection with the individual experience of pain or bereavement, photographs retain the sense of immediacy, or rather the existence of a life that ended during the war; we imagine the process of looking at this image by those who knew the individual depicted. The names on memorials have an indexical relationship to one particular war death, and while we may imagine the physical counterpart of a particular name, this cannot compete with the impact of looking at the face of the one who died. The Imperial War Graves Commission imposed various structures to ensure equality in death. It insisted that each headstone should appear the same, that the inscriptions should adhere to a prescribed system, that the wording by relatives, at the very base of the memorial should be restricted to sixty-six characters. Even then a charge was made per letter and the inscription had to be approved by the Commission.[33] As Eric Gill expostulated, 'under the cloak of culture [the government] denies to mourners even the unfettered choice of words!'[34] Yet the Commission's measures to standardise commemorative activity in order to ensure equality also had the effect of diminishing the understanding of graves and inscribed names as representations of individuals.

Despite official efforts to order the photographic record in a similar way, they belie such control.

Portrait photographs, originally created to relieve the pain of temporary absence, 'Calling/Delight across the miles of land and sea', as Gurney put it, were, as we have seen, later incorporated in devices to commemorate a permanent absence.[35] Yet memorials in stone and bronze to groups of casualties, which attempted to denote the physicality of the dead, had to depend on idealised representative figures. Apart from the practicality of this step, sculpted soldiers could be endowed with qualities that the dead may never have possessed in their lifetime: physical stature, heroism, beauty. The entire monumental vocabulary, in word and image, was constructed to enhance and embellish the dead 'as memory'. Photographs on the contrary have the power to remind us of the humanity of the dead, their ordinariness and their differences, which the language and representative devices of monumental structures are unable to accommodate. Indeed, 'the dead', as a collective pronoun for all those different deaths brought about by bullets, bombs, sickness or accidents, evokes the generalised rather than the particular. The specificity of the photograph is the counterpart to generic monumental sculpture. I have discussed elsewhere the ways in which the work of contemporary artists, in addressing the memory of wars, can inform our understanding of the First World War.[36] One comment by Christian Boltanski on his assemblages of portrait photographs is especially pertinent in this context, and in understanding the Imperial War Museum collection and published rolls of honour: 'they are not a group they are always one person. It's always one and one and one, never two thousand.'[37]

John Berger has commented on the cathartic role that poetry can play, stating how all human pain, apart from physical pain, is caused by 'one form or another of separation'. He writes, 'Poetry can repair no loss, but it defies the space which separates. And it does this by its continual labour of reassembling what has been scattered.'[38] A similar process took place at war memorials in all combatant nations. The inscribing of names and their positioning in a public or sacred place was a symbolic reassembling. At Stalybridge outside Manchester a memorial bridgehead was unveiled in 1921. The souvenir programme reads:

> In number equal to a battalion going into action, they were sprinkled in a hundred regiments. Together in time they did not fall – each year took its steady toll; nor yet in place – they rest now in scattered graves in both hemispheres. But now, in this Memorial is achieved perfect unity: here in one place, at one time, are they united as never before – spirits of a nobler mould, who died for you and yours, for me and mine.[39]

At the unveiling of the Jedburgh Memorial in the Scottish borders, in December 1921, the Secretary of State for Scotland delivered an address which recounted the way in which the local men had left for war:

We remember today with what readiness – nay, with what alacrity – the men and youths of this parish and town went forth to fight the foe.

He went on to describe how,

... some of them have come back to us – warworn and scarred, but victorious and triumphant. And we have welcomed them and congratulated them on their return. Some, alas, will never come back. Today they sleep peacefully in lands far from the homeland, and all that seems to remain is perchance a simple wooden cross in France and an aching heart in Scotland.

The only means of traversing this gap becomes spiritual; the speech ended, 'Their names are engraved on our memories as well as on this memorial: they are enshrined in our hearts.' A similar sentiment had been expressed the year before at the unveiling of a plaque in Jedburgh Parish Church: 'Whilst the men whose memory they were honouring were absent in body ... their spirits were with us still.'[40]

In the same way that the portrait photograph was often the last record of the dead's appearance, the last sight of the dead was an evocative image which some memorials, in addition to Houilles, attempted to represent. The order to mobilise was often sudden, after weeks of expectation and speculation, and the departure of local men usually took the form of a band-led march to the railway station with townsfolk gathered en route to say good-bye. The site of departure became especially poignant, all too frequently the site of the last glimpse or farewell. At Manchester's Victoria station a plaque was raised, 'IN MEMORY OF THE MANY THOUSANDS OF MEN WHO PASSED THROUGH THIS DOOR TO THE GREAT WAR 1914–1919 AND OF THOSE WHO DID NOT RETURN.'[41] When the 1921 Armistice Day service at Brighton railway station was reported in the local newspaper, the location was described as 'whence so many Sussex men went out in defence of their beloved Motherland'.[42] Incorporated in the Scottish National War Memorial is a stained glass window which depicts a scene at a railway station, a couple kiss, an officer holds his daughter high.[43]

The honourable marching off to war was another popular commemorative subject. It applauds the spirit of all those who served, and in Britain there is never any distinction between those who volunteered and those who were conscripted; but it also has significance in depicting the last sight of the dead.[44] At Hastings an elegant column surmounted by Victory was unveiled as the town's memorial in 1922. One of three bronze reliefs, sculpted by Margaret Winser, depicts soldiers marching away, looking over their shoulders and raising their helmets in farewell.[45] At Carnforth, Lancashire, a small bronze relief on the memorial's pedestal, below a surmounting bronze soldier, depicts ranks of marching helmeted soldiers in profile, one figure turned towards the spectator, similarly, raises his hand in farewell. Below, one reads the title OFF TO THE FRONT, and indeed, the memorial is only yards from the railway station.[46] While one figure turns to wave we see only the backs of the other soldiers, a device which only enhances the illusion of a re-creation of the 'last sight' as members of the community might have remembered it.

In 1929 Christopher Hussey, writing on Tait McKenzie's seated soldier figure at the front of the American-Scottish Memorial, 'The Call', in Edinburgh, described how the sculptor had given 'the universal symbol', by which he meant the Cenotaph, 'human shape and temporal reality in such a way that the simple-minded may see in it their own lad who went away.'[47] This seems a harsh comment on such an instinctive reaction to a generic soldier representation. Indeed the depiction of an event that would be especially emotive to the bereaved, such as the last farewell, is bound to have evoked recollections of their own goodbyes. Several memorials in Britain and France depict the last moment of familial 'togetherness'. At Houilles the soldier has already stepped away, but at Workington, Cumbria, Alexander Carrick sculpted a relief where the touching heads of the soldier and his wife, their interlocking hands and the encircling action of their child's outstretched arms creates a binding unified composition, the group are as one (Figure 1.5). The St. Anne's-on-Sea

Figure 1.5 Bronze panel on the Workington War Memorial sculpted by Alexander Carrick (1882–1966) and unveiled in 1928. Photographer, Tom Kay, Cumbria.

Memorial, Lancashire, sculpted by Walter Marsden and unveiled in October 1924, includes a similar image described in the unveiling programme as, 'the parting of the soldier returning to the Front, who gently releases himself from the caresses of his wife, while their child stands by in bewilderment.'[48] While these depictions encourage recollections of a family that was complete, many were devastated by war deaths, indeed the Workington memorial was unveiled by a woman who had lost four sons and her brother.[49] Yet it was precisely the generality of memorial forms, iconography and inscriptions, with their emphasis on sacrifice, rather than mass death, that enabled them to be largely uncontested sites of memory. As Adrian Gregory has described it, 'The multivocality of British commemoration helped it to serve as a healing process, defusing war-time resentments and re-emphasising the essential shared values of society.'[50]

Yet if memorial forms and iconography presented an idealised model from which to construct one's past, photographs were specific in their commemorative reference. As John Taylor has described it, 'During the war, the [photographic] industry made a virtue out of its ability to produce the illusion that time was fixed in photographs. By apparently stopping the passage of time, the photograph could keep a dead relative in the family.'[51] While the Cenotaph commemorated the Empire's dead, and local memorials a community's dead, a photograph was a specific record of one individual, and while an inscribed name might signify a loved-one it would not have brought him directly into view. The public memorial was an encompassing commemorative structure that located loss within the Empire, the Nation and the community, but the photograph was acute in its specificity, a direct trace of one who had died. Yet it is important to remember that the studio portraits of First World War servicemen were fictions themselves, forming part of a mode of representation where the subject dressed-up, posed and was pictured within a staged setting. Many portraits show the subject in front of a painted back drop, sometimes a garden setting or a country landscape, and some photographers even took these props to camps behind the lines where muddy boots belie the fiction of the idealised scene. Nevertheless it is the details of these images that create the complexity of individual lives – the shaving cut, the badly-ironed collar – and it is these interruptions from idealised sculptural representations of the dead which make them so arresting.

At the end of the First World War ambitious monuments in permanent materials were seen as a means of ensuring that the memory of the dead would endure 'forevermore'. Such great loss of life required a significant gesture: clearly the public demanded this from the governments which had sent their men to war. In retrospect, the Imperial War Graves Commission project can be seen as a success: its equanimity in treatment of the dead and lack of overt military reference, ensures that its memorials and cemeteries remain a moving experience for a wide audience of all ages and beliefs. What of the Imperial War Museum's portrait photograph project? Although incomplete, this collection evokes the loss of 'lives' with unparalleled power. It provides a glimpse of the scale of photographic portraiture during the war years and encourages us to imagine the many thousands of photographs that remain in family albums, cherished or forgotten, and those that have been destroyed over the years, or those that have come unstuck from their familial associations and now emerge at postcard dealers and market stalls. Moving from one image to another is disturbing and maybe this is why the Museum's collection has remained in storage for so long. Should a collection such as this be displayed? An assemblage of photographs of individuals is one of the dramatic moments at the United States Holocaust Memorial Museum in Washington. The 'Tower of Faces' has been discussed at length elsewhere, but it is the 'ironic reinscription' of these portraits that creates 'a more profound sense of loss than that provided by the most graphic and painful images of the Holocaust.'[52] If stone and bronze are the main media of memorials, they should be understood to function in conjunction with the media of mourning – the photograph.[53]

Notes

I would like to thank Gail Braybon, David Chandler, Nick Hewitt, Hilary Roberts and George Walter for their help and guidance with this essay.

1. Considerably more war memorials have been added to editions republished in the last ten years.
2. For example, John Stevenson, *British Society 1914–45*, Penguin, 1984, 94.
3. For example, Denis Winter, *Death's Men*, Penguin 1978.
4. The most significant publications include Angela Gaffney, *Aftermath: Remembering the Great War in Wales,* University of Wales Press, 1998; Ken Inglis, *Sacred Places: War Memorials in the Australian Landscape*, Melbourne University Press, 1998; Alex King, *Memorials of the Great War in Britain: The Symbolism and Politics of Remembrance*, Berg, 1998; Sergiusz Michalski, *Public Monuments: Art in Political Bondage 1870–1997*, Reaktion Books, 1998; J. M. Winter, *Sites of Memory, Sites of Mourning: the Great War in European Cultural History*, Cambridge University Press, 1995. For a consideration of these works in the historiography of writings on war and remembrance see Catherine Moriarty, 'The Material Culture of Great War Remembrance', *Journal of Contemporary History*, 34 (4), October 1999: 653–662.
5. An example of the inclusion in contemporary journalism of issues of remembering and monuments would be the account of post Gulf War Iraq by James Buchan. He begins by recounting a meeting with a bereaved mother whose family was killed by US bombing in 1991 and he describes the photographs of the dead which adorn the walls of the shelter where 1186 people were incinerated. Later he considers the victory arch in Baghdad built to commemorate the war with Iran, regarding its form as expressing 'all that the Ba'ath has by way of ideology. It is a monument to pure violence.' *Guardian Review*, 25 September 1999, 1–3. After September 11 2001, issues of photography and memory engaged the world's press.
6. Sir Frederick Kenyon, *War Graves: How the Cemeteries Abroad will be Designed,* HMSO (London), 1918.
7. Imperial War Graves Commission, *The Graves of the Fallen*, HMSO (London), 1919.
8. The heated parliamentary debate took place on 4 May 1920. The intentions of the Commission were argued at length when the House was asked to approve a grant of £991,000.

The anti-Commission lobby in parliament comprised Lord Balfour and Lord Lansdowne in the upper House and Sir Edward Carson and Sir Robert Cecil in the Commons. During the war Cecil had run the Red Cross office in Paris and had played an important role in the recording of war graves before the formation of the Army Graves Registration Commission. See Philip Longworth, *The Unending Vigil*, Leo Cooper, 1985, 48.

9. Letter from Eric Gill, *Burlington Magazine*, Vol. XXXIV, no. 193, April 1919, 159.
10. Eric Gill, 160.
11. *The Times*, 23 December 1919
12. For a detailed investigation of pilgrimages to the battlefield cemeteries see David Lloyd, *Battlefield Tourism: Pilgrimage and the Commemoration of the Great War in Britain, Australia and Canada, 1919–1939*, Berg, 1998.
13. See Catherine Moriarty, 'Public Grief and Private Remembrance' in M. Evans and K. Lunn (eds), *War and Memory*, Berg, 1997; Alex King, *Memorials of the Great War in Britain*, particularly Chapters 3, 4 and 5; and Gaffney, *Aftermath: Remembering the Great War in Wales*.
14. King, *Memorials of the Great War in Britain*.
15. More unusual than a portrait relief are portrait statues commemorating individuals, for example Ellis Humphrey Evans at Trawsfynydd. See Jo Darke, *The Monument Guide to England and Wales. A National Portrait in Bronze and Stone*, Macdonald, 1991, 122–23; also the equestrian sculpture to Edward Horner at the Church of St Andrew, Mells, Somerset.
16. For a discussion on idealised sculpted figures as representations of all who died see Catherine Moriarty 'The Absent Dead and Figurative Sculpture', *Transactions of the Ancient Monuments Society*, 39, 1995.
17. Alex King refers to one example in Hackney in his detailed account of war shrines and rolls of honour, see King, *Memorials of the Great War in Britain*, 44–61. See also Edward Warren, *War Shrines*, Civic Arts Association (London), 1917, a booklet advising the 'seemly form' the Civic Arts Association felt shrines should take.
18. A record of this memorial is included in the National Inventory of War Memorials, Imperial War Museum. Ref: 494.
19. For a discussion of portrait photographs in relation to photographs of war memorials see Catherine Moriarty, catalogue essay to accompany an exhibition of photographs by Chris Harrison, *Sites of Memory: War Memorials at the end of the Twentieth Century*, Imperial War Museum, 1997.
20. See John Taylor, *A Dream of England. Landscape, Photography and the Tourist's Imagination*, Manchester University Press, 1994, 120–21.
21. Portrait postcard in the author's possession.
22. Derek Jarman makes this point in his 1989 film *War Requiem* and brilliantly elucidates the function of the photograph over time. An early scene depicts a First World War veteran (Sir Laurence Olivier) being pushed to a remembrance service by a nurse (Tilda Swinton). As the nurse stoops to rearrange his blankets, the soldier shows her 'an Edwardian miniature hidden in his wallet of a young nurse whom she resembles.' Jarman, in his diary described acquiring the photograph. 'March 1988. Drove to Hythe with Tilda Swinton. We found a beautiful miniature of a First World War nurse in a junk shop.' In this brief scene Jarman juxtaposes official memory, represented by the memorial service and the soldier's medals, alongside hidden forms of remembering represented by the soldier's flashbacks and the old photograph. Derek Jarman, *War Requiem*, Faber and Faber, 1989, 2–3.
23. Ivor Gurney, *War's Embers*, Sidgwick & Jackson, 1919. I am grateful to George Walter for sharing his detailed knowledge of Gurney's work.
24. The Great Western Railway memorial at Paddington Station (1922) by Charles Sargeant Jagger is perhaps the best known instance of the commemoration of the postal link between home and serving men. A soldier, cloaked by his greatcoat reads a letter, the ripped seam of the envelope visible in his right hand, implying the haste with which it was opened.

25. In 1919 *The Times* reported how burial officials were able to name a dead soldier after a photograph depicting a woman, 'was found in the man's right hand, clasped against his heart. At the bottom of the card, which contained a cheerful message from the original, was the name of the hitherto unidentified man.' *The Times,* 9 December 1919, 9.

26. Senator H. B. Armstrong at the unveiling of the Lurgan War Memorial, Northern Ireland, May 1928, National Inventory of War Memorials, Imperial War Museum. Quoted in Moriarty, Imperial War Museum catalogue 1997, 136.

27. See the collection of Rolls of Honour in the Department of Printed Books, Imperial War Museum and for Rolls of Honour on film see examples held in the Department of Film, Imperial War Museum.

28. C. R. W. Nevinson's painting *He Gained a Fortune but Gave a Son* of 1918, in the University of Hull Collection, depicts a head and shoulders portrait of a bereaved father with a framed photograph of his dead son on the mantlepiece behind. The allusion to this individual's profit from the conflict makes the private display of the portrait photograph especially disturbing.

29. Photographs: Memorials for the Fallen: Appeals for Photographs, Central Files, Imperial War Museum.

30. Marita Sturken, 'Imaging Postmemory/Renegotiating History', *Journal of Media Arts and Cultural Criticism*, 26 (6), May/June 1999, 10–12.

31. Photographs incorporated on memorial plaques can be found in the collection of postcards of French war memorials housed at the National Inventory of War Memorials, Imperial War Museum for example, Bouzincourt and Colincamps. See also Daniel Sherman 'Art Commerce and the Production of Memory in France after World War 1' in John R. Gillis (ed.), *Commemorations: The Politics of National Identity*, Princeton University Press, 1994, 186–211, 190, Sherman describes the images on enamel plaques as an 'echo' of the names inscribed on the main memorial.

32. Susan Sontag, *On Photography*, Farrar, Strauss and Giroux, 1977, 70.

33. Thomas W. Laqueur, 'Memory and Naming in the Great War', in Gillis, *Commemorations*, 150–167, 152.

34. Gill, letter in *Burlington Magazine*, Volume XXXIV, no. 193, April 1919.

35. Gurney, *War's Embers*.

36. Catherine Moriarty, 'The Material Culture of Great War Remembrance', *Journal of Contemporary History*, 34 (4), 1999, 653–662.

37. Christian Boltanski, [Video recording] edited and presented by Melvyn Bragg, Phaidon, 1995.

38. John Berger 'The Hour of Poetry', in Lloyd Spencer (ed.), *The White Bird*, Hogarth Press, 1988, 249.

39. *Stalybridge Book of Remembrance*, 1921. Imperial War Museum, Department of Printed Books.

40. *Jedburgh Gazette*, 24 December 1920. The memorial commemorated the 79 members of the congregation and it was unveiled by Lieutenant-General Sir Francis Davies.

41. National Inventory of War Memorials, Imperial War Museum (NIWM) 1419.

42. *Sussex Daily News*, 12 November 1921.

43. Depictions of soldiers embracing their children before departure can be found also on French memorials, for example at Lure and Mesnil.

44. Ken Inglis provides thoughtful discussion on the British practice of commemorating those who served as well as died. French *monuments aux morts* refer exclusively to the dead. K. S. Inglis, 'The Homecoming: The War Memorial Movement in Cambridge, England', *Journal of Contemporary History*, 27 (4), 1992, 583–605, see 586–587.

45. NIWM 2073.

46. NIWM 2229.

47. Christopher Hussey, 'Tait McKenzie, a Sculptor of Youth', *Country Life*, 1929, 71.

48. NIWM 2214. Unveiling programme in IWM Department of Printed Books Ephemera Collection, 26(=427.2):36 [Lytham St Anne's]. In his essay 'Appearances' John Berger provides a provocative analysis of the photograph 'A Red Hussar Leaving, June 1919,

Budapest' by André Kertesz. Berger explains that while the image is identified as a particular historical moment, the parting look between the Hussar and his wife is exclusive to their understanding of their lives: in this look 'their being is opposed to their history'. John Berger and Jean Mohr, *Another way of Telling*, Writers and Readers, 1982, 81–129.

49. Darke, *The Monument Guide to England and Wales. A National Portrait in Bronze and Stone*, 210.

50. Adrian Gregory, *The Silence of Memory: Armistice Day 1919–1946*, Berg, 1994, 226.

51. John Taylor, *A Dream of England: Landscape, Photography and the Tourist's Imagination*, Manchester University Press, 1994, 135

52. Liss, *Trespassing through Shadows: Memory, Photography and the Holocaust*, University of Minnesota Press, 1998, quoted in Sturken, 'Imaging Postmemory/Renegotiating History', 10. Another war and another city show the power of combining photography with concrete memorials. An accumulation of 2059 portrait images of war dead, transferred to ceramic tiles and framed together, comprises the memorial to Second World War Resistance casualties located on the exterior wall of the Palazzo Comunale in the Piazza del Nettuno, Bologna. Such a display of the individual cost of collective endeavour is particularly powerful due to the unexpected sight of intimate portraits placed in a public location. The spectator becomes aware that he or she shares the past gaze of family, friends and lovers.

53. Marianne Hirsch, *Family Frames: Photography, Narrative and Postmemory*, Harvard University Press, 1997, quoted in Sturken. Writing on the Tower of Faces, Hirsch describes how the installation provokes the perception of photography as a 'media of mourning'. See also her discussion of *Camera Lucida*, first published in French in 1980, this text by Roland Barthes remains an indispensible source on photography and memory.

2

Making Spectaculars
Museums and how we remember
Gender in Wartime

Deborah Thom

'Memory makers' is what Suzanne Brandt calls museums and exhibitions of the First World War, and Gaynor Kavanagh suggests that museums make history, as well as shaping memory.[1] These authors have elegantly demonstrated some of the ways in which posterity's sense of the experience of war is shaped by its public presentation, in glass cases, away from the dangers and excitements of the battlefield. They have also pointed out how material objects are an essential part of such presentation, which is never merely didactic or moralistic but includes the real thing in the shape of the kit the soldier wears, the gun he fires, and the tank or aeroplane which was the new technology of its day. Ludmilla Jordanova wrote recently about the concept of 'public history' – the idea of the creation of a public space where the notion of the social, the shared and the official can jostle for attention, incorporating street furniture, statues, drinking fountains, posters, buildings – areas which are never personal but may carry powerful symbolic meanings to the individual.[2] Because most public functions, and public lives, are male, one of the problems with this when thinking about gender in our past is that this form of public history tends to privilege masculinity. Such histories have helped to shape and create a popular and populist history in all the combatant countries of Europe. These histories, as Brandt makes very clear, carry with them different national traditions of remembering the war – or, of course, they encourage the other process of memorial making, which is making it possible to *forget* aspects of the war, which is sometimes as important a point of departure in the making of memorials. There were also other 'new technologies' involved in the First World War which helped to provide potent symbols for the purpose of memory making, and the placing of the war in history – namely cheap printing and photography. Popular illustration and family record keeping expanded the production of photographs many times over, as people kept mementoes of those they loved, or communicated with them through photographs on postcards across the sea, or commemorated them in newspapers when they died. Government too stimulated the production of vast amounts of pictorial material, first as a stimulus to recruitment and production, then as an arbiter in disputes, and finally as a formal record of sacrifice and endeavour. Hence the photographic image as much as the object in the case became an essential part of those museums where the memory of war was being produced.

This memory was one in which gender was an integral structure of thought, an assumption that was built into wartime administration and popular rhetoric, and thence into public and private memory. But it was also a *social* memory, that is, it was reinforced by numerous rituals and ceremonies which included the unexpressed bases of social relationships. Because it was social it was assumed, and taken for granted in general, but not necessarily uncontested. For example, the discussion of whether a task was a man's or a woman's job had profound implications for both the wartime and postwar labour markets, and, although it has often been described as a unilateral process of men keeping women out of the jobs that they themselves wanted, a cursory glance at the organisation of wartime production shows that it reflected deep-seated, very old, assumptions about male and female habits, relative strength and physical advantage that were held by both men and women, and by the organisations that represented them. Similarly, the natural connection between masculinity and soldiering was so intrinsic to the process of enlistment and mobilisation that it was identified as central by the postermakers for one of the first campaigns to create an expeditionary force for the British Army. 'Women of Britain say Go' is the famous message, and in this classic example, the soldier strides down a road whose end is not yet visible as wife and daughter, or mother and sister or childbride, gaze steadfastly after him.

It is the implication of that image that I want to address by suggesting that we should be very careful to avoid the anachronism of ignoring the conscious process of making a spectacle of the war in the museum, the gallery or the exhibition, and how this might have influenced how we remember the participants later, when only the objects, not the living remain. The 'Great War', as it was already being called during the first atrocities of late 1914, was presented to the public using material objects from very early on, and these objects are often preserved in museum displays which have themselves become objects of academic study. War was primarily seen as men's work during 1914–1918, and men's activity. For example, although there is a book entitled *Waac: The Womens' Story of the War* (by Anon), it is only obliquely in the delicately referential title, *A Man Could Stand Up*, of one of Ford Madox Ford's Great War tetralogy, that we find much interrogation of the idea of manhood which even attempts to decouple it from wartime. And the most striking factor in any museum display, as Gaynor Kavanagh and Suzanne Brandt have both argued, is that the original collectors and recorders of the objects that war generated should have emphasised that there should be no blood, no bodies. They cannot allow the physical suffering that war creates to be shown.

In displaying the conflict to civilians during the war, or to soldiers enlisting, images of recent wars were not used at all in exhibitions. Images and artefacts of the South African War, or the Mahdi, for example, were not used to represent war. Instead of statues or photographs, cardboard cut-outs of soldiers, and uniforms on stands or as worn by drummers in ceremonial kit, were used to express or demonstrate the idea of being a soldier in 1914.

For women, on the other hand, the presentation of themselves as spectacle began in the earliest years of the war. Their bodies and physical experience could be used to demonstrate their contribution to the war, and was built into the concept of *formal* memory making from the outset. The members of the Women's Social and Political Union, whose recent political work had been conducted in secret, with its leaders in exile or in prison on hunger strike, reverted to using again the kind of enormous demonstrations of its heyday in the years between 1906 and 1910, making visible in spectacular and expensive form the desire of British women to replace men so that they could fight at the front. The images ranged from the historical, such as two virgin warrior/leaders, Joan of Arc and Queen Elizabeth, to the mythic figure of Britannia, but the emphasis was on women as contributors to the nation state. As Mrs Pankhurst was reported as saying in the *Daily Chronicle:*

> The women of France, of Serbia, of Belgium – to say nothing of the women of Germany – are sharing in the effort and burden of the war to a greater extent than the women of England have yet been enabled to do.[3]

For the suffragettes, arguing that their chance to prove themselves lay in the war was but a short step from arguing that the war was an opportunity for women. Other women's organisations were less ready to move towards a description of what could be in the future, than to exploit an image of women in the past, which could also be seen as summing up women's nature. This creation of an 'exhibit of womanhood' is characteristic of many philanthropic and commercial images of womanliness in wartime. The poster – and postcard – image used by the Professional Classes War Relief Council (PCWRC) for their bazaar of Christmas 1914, which was to fill the Albert Hall, looks like the kind of image later to be exploited on chocolate boxes, and harks back to the illustrations of Dickens or Thackeray. It shows a woman gazing at a picture covered in holly, wearing flowers in her hair and a very full 1860s type flounced skirt, while another woman, partly obscured, possibly a servant, stands behind her. This central image is an interior scene in an oval frame, around which are depicted trees, small birches frosted with snow, and a cavalry-man in Napoleonic hussar uniform, wearing the tall shako hat, with his head and his horse's bowed against the storm. Here women are again inactive, the ones who watch but are safe, comfortable, and certainly decorative, while men endure the cold of cavalry warfare in the snow. The image is 'historical', it dates back to some past great conflict, using a style of warfare in which Britain had been victorious. Although it was miles away from the mass killing which had already begun on the Western Front it also carried visual echoes of Goya and other presenters of nineteenth century warfare, like Tolstoy. Of course it would be a mistake to read too much into the work of one professional artist, who had been given some support, and a small commission to compensate for the loss of luxury trade work at the outbreak of war, but this poster was the one chosen by the PCWRC to send to the newly formed National War Museum as representative evidence of what they had done in the war. It thus becomes an example of what people *hoped* would be remembered, and which they wished to preserve and to present in a public display. It was after all solicited as a deposit in a museum, which, it had been explicitly argued, was not a war memorial, but a war record. The same PCWRC programme advertises cigarettes on the back in different sizes: tenor, basso and soprano, this last for 'ladies'. Genders are sizes too, in this gendered world where men are soldiers, and women, while they might as young girls wear sailor suits, by 1914 had not yet been seen in military uniform.[4]

As an impatient and republican historian I started looking at the Women at War Collection of the Museum nigh on twenty-five years ago, and did not at that time do anything more than impatiently turn over the pages of programmes of memorial concerts, the accounts of royal patronage and the descriptions of jubilees and fundraising. I have learnt better now that what is important enough for people to preserve as a sample of what the war means, must also have helped to play a part in people's understanding of what the war was – and so indeed such preservations, deposits and images prove to be. Recent cultural historians of the war have looked at verbal and pictorial images of the working girl, the mother, the whore, the flapper and the mother-worker, but they have not used the objects that are kept in museums or attics, or the collections of photographs that illuminate them, to talk about the contemporary constructs of a gendered history of wartime.[5] Where this has been done at all, historians have tended to accept the positivistic bias of these collections, by ignoring the process through which the collections were made, or permanent exhibits were laid down and the history of the war given its preliminary and formative mapping.

In 1914 the problem of women was deemed to be the problem of unemployment, poverty and potential prostitution or promiscuity. Exhibitions had been used to demonstrate this plight previously in years of low employment before the war, with the Sweated Industries Exhibition of 1906 at Bishopsgate, for example, or in demonstrations by striking chain-makers in 1911, and in the great fairs and exhibitions in modernising cities all over Europe, such as Paris or Lyons, where workers did their work in public view – and sometimes these workers were female. In Britain there was also a long tradition of the public presentation of women's work as an interesting exhibit, as revealed by the photographs of Sutcliffe at Whitby, or Munby's fascinated delight in female muscularity during his campaign for the rights of working women to be recognised.[6]

The First World War was to add government to the list of those who turned working women into public exhibitions. Dilution officers, employed to encourage employers to replace their skilled male workers (or to spread their skills more widely), appeared with 'dilutees', who could do most of their new jobs with the aid of adapted machinery. These officers toured the provinces accompanied by women working on machines, and photographs in loose-leaf booklets to show sceptical employers, worried about female insubordination and the cost of separate lavatories, that women could indeed do tasks previously only done by skilled men.[7] Government photographers were sent by the new Ministry of Munitions to photograph women doing all sorts of activities, and the pictures were then used in two booklets which were sent all over the country to large employers: *Women's War Work on Munitions* and *Women in Non-munition Industries*.[8] This activity was at its peak between 1915 and 1917, years of labour shortage, expanding armaments production and war on two fronts. When one front later closed, and munitions production began to be scaled down, the continuing need for wood, forage and food led to the expansion of the Women's Land Army, which in turn sent caravans of young women in uniform with pitchforks, hay, horses and sheep to show, in practical terms, what could be done by women on the land, rather as the socialist weekly *Clarion* had done before the war, and birth controllers were to do later.

These practical demonstrations meant that even people who did not read much, or did not often go to the cinema (where working women were seen on newsreels very frequently indeed), would still have a strong sense of the tasks women had done, the novelty of those tasks, and the high value being placed on them, because they were applauded and lauded as they were produced for public view. This sense of the visibility of innovation, of the public acceptability of work and women doing it, was thus a direct by-product of using exhibitions as a way of making visible a complex phenomenon like the labour market. It is one of the ways in which the Imperial War Museum's collection enshrines a profound statement, even a national truth, about what the war was for women, and therefore itself helped to shape a gendered history of the war, a history which overvalued the temporary achievements and innovations of wartime at the expense of noticing the diversity of reactions to gender, and the continuity of some ideas of gender, changes in others. The Museum collections contain the assumption that gender above all is the dominant division between people in wartime – and this is therefore the guiding principle of organisation within the Museum. Women have their own special section, and are never included in other categories alongside their male counterparts. This was true at the time of the Museum's foundation, and in commemoration of the First World War thereafter.[9]

These early exhibitions of work had been meant to mobilise, not to record, but they very quickly changed in 1918 and 1919 into exhibitions of what *had* been done rather what *could* be done. The Queen, who often visited war factories, tended to go and see the women workers when she did so. In 1918, before the war ended, it was decided that women workers should return the compliment. The 'women war workers' were to appear in a procession of homage to their majesties '… on the occasion of their silver wedding'. On Saturday 29 June the Ministry of Labour was to present this procession, and they specifically required that all marchers were to wear uniform. However, it would be truer to describe it as a march of 'women in organisations', as most of them were not workers in the sense of *manual* workers – the term 'war worker' was being used in its older meaning of 'women doing voluntary work', and many of them did not usually wear a uniform at all. Not surprisingly, those that predominated were those who could identity themselves in some way as the people who had created new war institutions, like the women police, the military services, the Voluntary Aid Detachment, and the Women's Legion (which organised troop refreshment). The Ministry of Munitions was represented, of course, but as a Ministry rather than as a body of workers. The procession thus

Figure 2.1 A very staged photograph of women police 'warning boys'. Imperial War Museum, Q31089.

showed how far the war had lead to the creation of new women's organisations, but it was exemplary in that the number of marchers from each group was roughly the same, despite the difference in the number of women workers in each organisation. Of 2,540 women who marched there were very few who represented munitions workers, and these were in no way proportionate to their numbers in the workplace, while there were virtually no women representing the large number of women in shops and offices, whose work had expanded during the war. They were not in uniform, not visible as war workers, and not remembered in a war procession marking a war that was not yet over.[10]

Their absence from the procession is also echoed to some extent in the array of documents in the Women's Work Collection of the Imperial War Museum, and therefore in the process of the construction of the war's history. So those who had some organisation which spoke up for them, like the women aircraft welders (who had the Women Welders' Society) appear prominently, despite only having forty members. Their trade was seen as a classic example of the male exclusion of women from the wartime workforce, while those women whose organisations had a more ambivalent view towards the war feature less.

The Museum itself included women from the outset in one story, but as an afterthought in another. Its original brief in 1917 was to create a national war museum, and the first version of a national display was shown in the Crystal Palace, amidst massive potted palms. The first exhibits were mixed, consisting mostly of soldiers' outfits and weapons, and the very first national showing of them was in touring exhibitions in 1916, which took what were then called 'war relics' around the major cities of Britain.

The inclusion of women in the collection came through the imaginative vision of Sir Alfred Mond, original chairman of the appeal, in appointing Martin Conway as the Museum's first Director, and then his daughter Agnes as the official responsible to Lady Norman for the Women's Work section.[11] Agnes Conway kept a diary, as well as her letters and other papers, and the biographer of three generations of Conways, Joan Evans, fortunately deposited these papers in the Cambridge University library.[12] Agnes was, as her diary shows, both not very interested in conventional politics, and an enthusiastic supporter of the National Union of Women's Suffrage Societies, representing Maidstone at the NUWSS general meeting in February 1917, for example.[13] She had been educated at Newnham and was a valued and valuable collaborator in her father's archaeological expeditions, generating photographs of archaeological sites and artefacts. She had been involved in war voluntary work, and spent 1916 to 1917 helping run a depot supplying bandages to the front and looking after Belgian refugees. Like many women of the middle and upperclass she was busily engaged in working for the war effort, but not in paid employment. She recorded her enthusiasm when the possibility of her father being the Director was raised in March, 'Which I should like extremely', and even was more enthusiastic when Sir Alfred Mond asked her to join the Women's Sub-committee, which she hailed with the exclamation 'What fun!'[14] She solicited material and deposits with initiative and determination. People were very responsive to her requests for information, objects and photographs, and she marvelled at how easy it was to obtain whatever she wanted 'in an official capacity', although her biographer records how little people were prepared to proffer unsolicited.[15] She acquired the records of the War Cabinet Committee on Women in Industry, including the typed transcripts of evidence, not just the published and sanitised version of this most revealing document.[16] She asked factory managers and members of organisations representing women to send documents, photographs and objects, and she used ephemera from the state's encouragement of women's work, particularly the posters and photographs, to provide an extensive archive of the war as it had been for women.

Conway was particularly interested in the 'real' object, as well as the photograph, as a modern means of recording and demonstrating. She commissioned models from sculptors of actual women working. The women's shrine in the Museum's first permanent display at Crystal Palace was flanked by two life-sized figures, which, as Sue Malvern has pointed out, were of Edith Cavell (nurse and midwife), fast assuming the status of martyr, and Dr. Elsie Inglis, of the Scottish Women's Hospitals. Thus

Figure 2.2 War shrine. The exhibit which most clearly demonstrates the sense of commemoration in a display of women's activity framed and dominated by national flags. IWM Q 31113.

Figure 2.3 Models of pitbrow women demonstrating the effect of three dimensions as being somehow less dramatic and monumental than many of the photographs. IWM Q 31105.

women were represented by those who sacrificed themselves and served, doing caring, but not transgressive, wartime tasks. Other heroines of the Museum display included the two 'Women of Pervyse', who were famously the only women actually at the Western Front, tending and rescuing the wounded. Conway and Lady Norman met them on their trip to France in 1919, while gathering artefacts for the Museum's collection and viewing the battlefield, and persuaded them to donate the actual corrugated iron sheets which formed their shelter to the Museum. Lady Scott, the widow of the polar explorer, was one of the sculptors asked to think about making models, in part because as the widow of a famous hero she was thought to be a particularly appropriate choice to contribute to a national process of recollection. Model making was part of the conventional presentation of history in the Museum, but it was the Women's Section which particularly used life-size models to demonstrate information, as well as graphs to convey statistical data, the other innovation of the period and a new way of making abstract concepts visible, as Sybilla Nikolow has shown in her work on exhibitions of public health.[17]

The depiction of real women doing the new activities of wartime was already something of a convention in the presentation of the war, as the women had been commemorated in an exhibition organised in Manchester in 1917, and then later in a bigger one in Whitechapel, which had recorded women's contribution to the war. In the London exhibition the people who provided, managed and even sat with the exhibits, were the main figures in the systematic extension of women's work in wartime. The people working on exhibition stands, mounting photographs, writing captions and organising models, and workers showing the tasks they could do, included Adelaide Anderson (the chief woman Factory Inspector and author of *Women in Industry*) and Miss Monkhouse, the chief woman Dilution Officer (in other words the woman singly most responsible for advocating, organising and encouraging the replacement of skilled male labour by semi- or unskilled labour – which was nearly all female in this period). When the first exhibition of the Imperial War Museum's new collection was set up in Crystal Palace, the main occasion in its honour was a visit by the Queen, continuing her wartime interest in the working woman's contribution. Men did not have to go through the crude process of asking themselves or others whether they had made a contribution to the war, had been good soldiers or engineers or tram drivers, but the women's contribution was systematically appraised and assessed, and constantly compared with work as done by experienced male workers in the past. This was often not a very scientific measure of their activity at all, and certainly gave little indication of what women as a whole did or did not achieve.[18]

The continuing emphasis on making war visible without any need for verbal explanation tended to encourage the use of dramatic tableaux as photographic evidence, as shown both in the pictures donated to the collection, and those specially set up and taken for it, especially those by Horace Nicholls. Nicholls had already participated in one war as a recorder of the Boer War, eager to gain credibility as a war correspondent with a 'series of large photographs which would appeal to the artistic sense of the most fastidious, knowing that they must as photographs have the enhanced value of being truthful.' He also had a sense of their public interest, travelling Britain with a lantern show of his images 'Fresh from the Front' in a speaking tour which went from the West Country to London, then Hawick to Hastings. He made a living after his return to England in 1902 from photographing English life, with a strong line in photomontage to make a more accurate but less directly representational view. By 1917 his persistent efforts to obtain war employment where he could use his skills had paid off, and for £350 a year he was employed by the Ministry of Information as their official photographer, released by the National Service department where he was a Substitution Officer on 7 August 1917. He came to this work with a clear understanding of the processes of dilution and substitution, with a brief to take 'photographs in Great Britain for publication in neutral and allied countries for propagandist purposes'.

Conway had asked Nicholls to get pictures in the first instance for the Whitechapel exhibition, but she specifically requested that he also keep in mind the question of their contribution to the war effort and the change in women's labour and people's perception of it. The pictures were carefully lit in some examples to give a sense of the future – they were young, given radiance by the use of filters; groups are posed like stage groups. Some are haunting images of women substituting for dead or absent husbands or fathers, unsmiling, looking slightly away from the camera. In all 2,300 negatives of the Home Front went with him when he transferred to being in charge of the archive at the Imperial War Museum in December 1918, which was when that part of the Ministry became a section of the Museum. His photographs were thus at the heart of the Collection, and fully reflected the consistently feminist stance of Agnes Conway and her assumptions about how the war was putting women into the national history in an new and unforgettable way. But they also influenced the perceptions of historians, leading to the tendency to overemphasise munitions work, and encouraging a history of innovation which understates the persistence of some aspects of industrial life. Also encouraged was the idea that war was a distinctive period in which women did factory work, as though they had not done it in the past. Rarely had working women been portrayed with such skill and to such artistic effect before, and they were rarely seen in this way later. However he also dramatises the war. The remarkable series of pictures taken at Chilwell have frequently been reproduced, and they show extraordinary, magical, images of people sprouting amongst the ranks of shells, or floating in the cranes which lifted and moved them, since, when filled, these shells were too big for people to carry without help. The theatre of war and the surrealism of its constructions are thus given a large part in the historical record of the war, just as happened with the soldiers and battlefields when portrayed in pencil and paint by Paul Nash or Edward Wadsworth. It is not clear how far the

Figure 2.4 Crowds looking at the photographic bureau the day before the official opening of the exhibition, showing how popular these were at the time. IWM Q 31117.

Museum organisers, or the people thus portrayed, appreciated these images, which add so considerably to our perceptions of the shocking aesthetic of war. During my own research, I never found a munition worker who had any of Nicholls' photographs, either from the time or in later books written about them. The exhibits in the early Whitechapel show were more exemplary than dramatic, more of individual heroines than of anonymous workers. Subsequent exhibitions, as in 1976, did however echo Nicholls' photographs in that they made heroines out of all women, not just those who came nearest to the fighting men at the front. Perhaps it is only with the long hindsight of social history that Nicholls' work can be assessed as itself a major element in the process of history making.[19]

The task of presenting innovation in distinctive images sometimes proved hard for the photographers. Gravedigging was one timely wartime activity that women were thought to be doing. Nicholls had written to a Greenock cemetery and decided on 20 July not to trouble them further when he was told that 'Women are only employed trimming edges of grass, weeding and hoeing walks and that no women are doing any gravedigging'.[20] In a sequence of letters sent to firms arranging tours in 1918 by both Gilbert Lewis and Horace Nicholls, they sought to obtain clear evidence of the rigours of the work. A typical request was the one made to Austin Motor Company at Longbridge.

> We should like as far as possible to secure photographs showing machinery as it is in this way that the public will be impressed by the arduous nature of women's labour.[21]

Again and again the stories of women's work turned out to be only partially true, or to demonstrate a difficult or ambiguous situation. Work with Borax and cyanide were too frightening in abstract, and yet uninteresting as images. Even glass blowing, which had been thought to be ideal, turned out to be less dramatic than anticipated. The manager of the works wrote: 'Of course women do not do the actual blowing of glass but they do what is known as wetting off and taking in and do it very well too.'[22]

Nicholls ended up taking some striking images of women doing other tasks, but the limits of the process are evident in the surviving correspondence, indicating that the factory manager's confident 'of course' was not an unusual response. The photographs were to go a long way towards rewriting people's image of the working woman and they were very popular with the workers themselves, or so the correspondence records at the time.[23] The problem was recorded by the official responsible for collecting photographs for the exhibition in 1919 in a memorandum:

> What was excellent from a TOPICAL point of view is now deplorable from the HISTORICAL point of view – *the only point of view which will matter tomorrow*. The problem is the absence of proper documentation.[24]

It is debatable how far Nicholls and Lewis themselves ever thought in terms other than the historic in the ways they presented the images and selected their subjects. They clearly did move rapidly to record things that were changing fast themselves, but they were consistently moved more by concern for good propaganda than for an accurate record or a representative sample.

One of the models that Conway wanted to commission from a sculptor was of shell filling. She planned to show a shell being filled with Lilian Barker standing by.[25] When she was gathering evidence about munitions work she went to the Woolwich Arsenal for a night shift, and watched Lilian Barker carrying out her job as Lady Welfare Superintendent. She was very impressed by the charismatic Barker, of whom several photographs were taken. She described her thus,

> She has all those girls eating out of the palm of her hand owing to her extraordinarily ready wit and to her being such an absolutely so thorough good sort.[26]

The Women's Work Collection bears traces of this visit and the impression it made, as the Woolwich Arsenal generated many photographs in the collection, ranging from these interior shots of Barker to pictures of women on the danger platform walkways, and images of the royal visits to this, the most visited of war factories.

Agnes Conway had other good ideas for material that would last as a representation of the war. She went out and found participants in the war and interviewed them, starting a tradition of participant observation that informs the Museum's collection to this day. This is the first use of oral testimony in a public collection that includes the voices of women. She went to meetings, where the conduct of the war and women's contribution were being assessed, to gather data. She found the speakers at one such meeting of the National Union of Women Workers (the organisation of social workers rather than a trade union) 'frumps' who depressed her, except for one speaker, the economist Kirkaldy, who had written a report on women's war work in 1916 (which many historians have subsequently found of use).[27] Conway did not always find her task easy. Some people were hostile to the whole enterprise, especially those campaigning for a negotiated peace. Trade unionists, however, were rather eager to join in. Conway prepared for her meeting with Mary Macarthur, leader of the National Federation of Women Workers and the Women's Trade Union League, by reading the 1917 Fabian Women's group report, written by Barbara Drake, *Women in the Engineering Trades*.[28] (Drake was to be the author of the historical section of the Report of the War Cabinet Committee on Women in Industry, which summed up the problem of historic assumptions about female labour, and the way these assumptions were still built into the negotiation of women's introduction into the workplace.) She found Macarthur and Susan Lawrence, who came with her, generous with their offers of help and material: it was a 'most satisfactory interview'.[29] Here we can see the slow accumulation in the Museum's written collections of the official Labour/suffragist view of the war experience.

Dissenting voices tended to come from one particular point of view. Two people in particular objected to what was being done for the Women's Collection because it was done by charitable ladies (amateurs) rather than by professional participants like themselves. Dr Flora Murray, for example (who had organised the Scottish Women's Hospitals which had been especially active on the Eastern Front as the Army did not welcome them in the West) initially refused to give them an interview or to share her records with the Museum because, 'She did not want amateurs to investigate her work, that Lady Norman was an amateur of amateurs and knew nothing about hospitals and it's "Hands off our work" for her.'[30]

The other critic was someone who became a far more serious problem for the Museum in the early days because she was a disgruntled employee, who called into question, as Flora Murray had done, the ethos of the lady volunteer. A Miss Wolfe Murray had been employed by the founders of the collection on a wage (as neither Conway nor Lady Norman were) to provide administrative support. She was clearly a rather neurotic woman, who herself suffered some sustained bouts of ill health. Martin Conway tried to limit her activities, first by banning the use of official secretaries in people's own homes. She refused to acquiesce and argued, when asked to resign her post because she had taken so much leave, that not she but Agnes Conway should resign because, 'Volunteers and relations were not wanted in government offices'. A month later, when she finally went, she said it would be because of 'nepotism and corruption' and two days later threatened a slander suit because Conway and others had been saying 'her nerves were not normal'.[31] After some rather dramatic encounters involving stolen keys and illegal entry into offices, she finally departed, leaving Agnes Conway relieved but sickened. However the incident revealed rather starkly, in ways the records do not otherwise show, that Miss Wolfe Murray was in many ways right. The collectors were amateurs, as everyone seeking to create new institutions which reflected the novelty and drama of the war was bound to be. But they were also *amateur* in that this work did not reflect their need to earn a living and they therefore had only to act according to their own attitudes, and their own understanding of the civic task the Museum was designed to fulfil. As a result the Museum's purpose is explicit: those who worked on the collection did not have to think commercially, or even particularly politically. When they decided in December 1917 to allow no 'propaganda' in the Museum's first display, it was because they wished to rise above the quotidian, and to demonstrate the existence of a universal national mission, rather than show the immediate needs of the war labour market, or the shortage of soldiers, or problems of conscription. When Martin Conway made a speech to a packed meeting, demanding the urgent prosecution of the war, he said that we must do so because we are 'trustees of the dead'.[32] The view of the war that all these individuals represented may have been the dominant one, but it was not the only one, and it means that the Museum did not stand against the official and public record: it helped in its creation and reproduction at the time, and remains a memorial to that view.

For example, there is one particular group of women created by the war whose contribution to the peace was to be significant, and whose legacy has been important in twentieth century culture and politics, but who were not contacted by Conway, nor represented in the Museum at the time. These were the campaigners for a negotiated peace, who organised the Women's International League for Peace and Freedom, or who resisted taxation through the Women's Freedom League, or who opposed the war, like Lenin's correspondent, the author of *The Home Front*, Sylvia Pankhurst. There is also very little about the group that grew slowly after conscription was introduced, The No Conscription Fellowship, organised to resist this aspect of militarism, or about the people who hid conscripts on the run from the battlefield. We should not be surprised that Agnes Conway did not seek these out; her instincts were fairly inclusive, but although she had some impulse towards writing a comprehensive history of the war, her entry for the *Encyclopaedia Britannica* (written between 1921 and 1922) shows that she was entirely devoted to the idea of the war as benefit, rather than loss, for the image of women and their capacities. She took no particular view on militarism but certainly did not deplore it.[33]

The Women's Collection is organised roughly alphabetically, starting with Albania and Army, and ending with Welfare and Volunteers. Chronologically, Conway started with her own work with the Belgian relief operations, and it is an indication of her systematic way of proceeding that when one reads the diaries alongside the Index to the collection, one finds it is actually organised rather along the lines of the timing of her own visits and solicitation of sources. Different sectors of the people surveyed responded with varying degrees of vigour, but in general the best represented women are those who belonged to institutions which used uniforms, or those which had some sense of being part of corporate innovation – in other words, those who could claim to be part of change, rather than those who still carried on doing what they had done before the war. There are very interesting sections on the military uniformed services, the Red Cross, the Voluntary Aid Detachment (VAD) and the two bodies organising police patrols, but Employment and Munitions are the largest single sections. The photographic record is extremely rich and continues to expand. Not least of Agnes Conway's achievements was her use of her own skill in making photographs of archaeological finds to encourage other photographers to make a record of the war for the Museum. This is a large part of the Museum's original photographic collection and one of the most aesthetically successful.

The idea of the Museum as a public record of private experience and achievements was given greater validity when people were encouraged to deposit diaries and letters in the 1970s, and by adding a Department of

Sound to the Museum's collections at the same time, when recollections were recorded from all over the country. The Museum had become sensitive to the absence of the voice of the people from their collections. Here again the Women's Collection had already included far more material about everyday life than other sections of the Museum had initially been able to do, but it is also the case that the collectors of the original material, whether men's or women's, did not consciously go for the voice of the ordinary worker, or the ordinary nurse or soldier. There is also an odd asymmetry about the original displays, in that models of women were life-sized but because of the problem of portraying death or wounds or blood, the models of soldiers are small-scale, and uniforms are shown without bodies inside them. When the soldier was shown in the original displays he was usually behind a gun. Active combat shows him in battle, as if he fights alone. That asymmetry was to be overcome in the late twentieth century to some extent with the Museum's oral history recording programme, and the rise of the word rather than the image. In the 1990s the Museum's own review recorded these innovations, and the enormous expansion of public use of the Museum for education, television and even comedy. Thanks to the National Curriculum, the First World War appears in the syllabus for most GCSE courses in History and in English. It is a defining element of our national culture. But this representation, whether through objects or text, does simplify and it does reduce. As a result men are always soldiers, while women make munitions or are nurses.

The pivotal moment for this in terms of gender issues was probably the Museum's exhibition of 1976, which drew upon the collection to display the uniforms, the cap badges, the posters, the propaganda encouraging enlistment and dilution, and the films of the period. What these reproduced was the sense of national unity, of a positive contribution warmly received, and which was rewarded by 'the vote' – a view in which Conway believed when she set the collection up. Those who were still under-represented were the embittered, who felt that their achievements before the war had been overwritten by those of the war, and those whose records of facing hostility, misogyny and difficulty could not be dramatised or publicised in the simple material narratives of image and model that the Museum encouraged.

It is a simple and obvious point to make that gender was prioritised as an organising principle in the British Imperial War Museum from the very first, in the way that men's experience was the war, and women were an 'additional other' of significance. While other similar museums in France and Germany collected material too, they did not have so effective a section specifically allocated to women in their collection policy, nor in their exhibits when they finally opened in Stuttgart (1921) and Paris (1924).[34] For them, the history of remembering war was initially difficult because defeat had been experienced by both France and Germany, and was further complicated by the later rise of National Socialism in Germany, and occupation and collaboration in France in the Second World War, where the idea of achievement is undermined to some extent by the contested notion of the popular, the public, and whether indeed there can be either ceremonies or institutions which reflect any collective experience at all.[35] There has been much recent debate on the question of 'collective memory', and, as Jay Winter argues in his *Sites of Memory, Sites of Mourning*, the history of commemoration itself is often a return to previous ways of thinking, rather than an innovation in cultural form.[36] However, we see distinct national differences in the way in which women are incorporated or forgotten in the processes, both official and cultural, of commemoration. In France and Germany the divide of gender is itself fractured by other divides of loyalty and politics, of race and subordination, so that there was not at the time, nor in the later construction of the museum collections, any single unitary gender experience which could be addressed. Also feminist movements in these other nations did not go through a unifying process during the last stages of the struggle for the vote, as happened in Britain. Here, the existence of organised feminism, with its conscious articulation of a feminist history expressed in suffrage parades, and ephemera which focus on heroines of the national past, helps to explain the inclusion of women in that national past. Yet their inclusion in the imaging of statue and photograph was in the end to emphasise the singular, the volunteers, and those who had developed new institutions, rather than the mass, and those who had worked at old tasks in new places. In the end the most significant contemporary women included in this depiction of national experience were probably the 'lady volunteers' in voluntary associations, and, echoing the concept of national service, the specific form that these took within feminism in Britain. Just as most British feminism before the war emphasised, not undermined, sexual difference, so the Museum which one feminist helped create was to underpin assumptions about gender roles in the subsequent history and historiography of women and war.

Notes

1. Suzanne Brandt, 'The Memory Makers: Museums and Exhibitions of the First World War', *History and Memory*, 6 (1), Indiana University Press 1994, 95–122; Gaynor Kavanagh (ed.), *Making Histories in Museums*, Leicester University Press, Cassell, London 1996.
2. Ludmilla Jordanova, *Defining features: scientific and medical portraits, 1660–2000*, Reaktion in association with the National Portrait Gallery, 2000.
3. It is part of the process of history making that I am describing that the Imperial War Museum Women at War Collection has now been copied onto microfilm and can be consulted in that form all over the world. Records from it therefore retain the IWM's own cataloguing, using their classification system Emp. 13.4, but are reproduced in Harvester microform microfilm reel 39. (Hereafter the microfilm reel number comes first, the IWM category second – hence 39/Emp. 13.4.)
4. 39/Emp.4.1: poster for Professional Classes War Relief Council (PCWRC) for Christmas in War-Time, programme 4.1/36
5. Mary Louise Roberts, *Civilization without Sexes*, University of Chicago Press, 1994; Susan Kingsley Kent, *Making Peace: the Reconstruction of Gender in Interwar Britain*, Princeton University Press, 1993.
6. Michael Hiley, *Victorian working women: portraits from life,* Gordon Fraser Gallery, 1979; Angela V. John, *By the Sweat of their Brow: Women workers at Victorian Coal Mines*, Routledge & Kegan Paul, 1984.

7. Gail Braybon, *Women Workers in the First World War*, Croom Helm, 1981; Gail Braybon and Penny Summerfield, *Out of the Cage*, Pandora, 1987; Deborah Thom, *Nice Girls and Rude Girls*, I. B. Tauris, 1998; Marion Kozak, 'Women Workers during the First World War, with special reference to Engineering', unpublished Ph.D. Thesis, University of Hull, 1977; Arthur Marwick, *Women at War*, Fontana, 1977.
8. Deborah Thom, *Nice Girls and Rude Girls*, chapter 3.
9. Brandt argues that the divides are Near/Far; Dead/Living; Present/Future and demonstrates this extremely well. I would want to argue that gender creates the fourth great binary as significant but totally asymmetrical. Kavanagh talks about stereotypes when she points out that exhibitions about hygiene and housewifery operated for women, and that children too were divided by sex, but does not, interestingly, think about stereotypes of masculinity in thinking about the absence of the body of the soldier in the war museums she describes.
10. 39/Emp.15/2.
11. Lady Norman (Florence Pricilla, d. 1964) was also active in the suffrage movement and remained involved in the Imperial War Museum until she died. She was also busy in many welfare organisations. Two collections of papers describe some of her activities c1873–1918: Correspondence and papers related to work for suffragette movement at London Metropolitan University, The Women's Library (formerly the Fawcett Library) Reference: 7/NOR; 1920–62: Correspondence and papers related to work as Trustee of Imperial War Museum at the Imperial War Museum, Department of Documents, NRA 43205 Norman.
12. Cambridge University Library manuscript collection, the Conway papers, Additional documents (Add.doc.) 7676, henceforth cited as Conway. The diaries are in small volumes each containing one year's record, in Z; letters are R, denoting letters to her parents from Agnes Conway; U for letters to Agnes Conway. See also Joan Evans, *The Conways: a history of three generations*, Museum Press, London 1966.
13. Conway, Z, 1917, 21 February.
14. Conway, Z, 1917, 21 March, 17 April.
15. Conway, Z, 1917, 1 May; Evans, *The Conways*, 233–4.
16. These transcripts take up four reels of microfilm.
17. Nikolow, 'Measuring Public Health', unpublished paper at the Social History Conference, *Rethinking the Millennium*, Gonville and Cauis College, Cambridge, 6 January 2000.
18. Laura Lee Downs, *Manufacturing Inequality: gender division in the French and British Metalworking industries, 1914–1939*, Cornell University Press, 1995; Braybon, *Out of the Cage*; Health of Munition Workers Committee, Final Report, 1918, Cd.9065; Reconstruction Committee, Final Report, 1918, Cd. 9239.
19. Gail Buckland, *The Golden Summer: the Edwardian Photographs of Horace Nicholls. A Life in photography*, Pavilion Press, 1989, 122–3 and 133.
20. IWM, Wellington House papers, Box 2/10.
21. IWM, Wellington House papers, Box 2/10, letter 10 May. Similar letters were sent to a mining company, a quarry, cyanide works, salt company, paint varnish, consolidated Borax, two sugar companies and two glass jar and bottle factories.
22. Letter dated 10 June, from a Mr. Stairfoot (? – writing unclear).
23. IWM, Wellington House papers, letter of 19 June from Miss N. Spry to H. Nicholls which says that 'the girls are simply delighted with their photos.'
24. IWM, Wellington House papers, 1/7, filed next to a letter of 22 January 1919 which records that the exhibition must make a profit.
25. Conway, Z, 1918, 19 April.
26. Conway, Z, 1917, 29 June.
27. A.W. Kirkaldy, *Industry and Finance*, Vols. I and II, Isaac Pitman, 1917 and 1920.
28. Barbara Drake, *Women in the Engineering Trades*, Labour Research Department (London), 1918.
29. Conway, Z, 1918, 6 May.
30. Conway, Z, 1917, 7 December.
31. Conway, Z, 1917, 5 October; 8 November and 10 November.

32. Conway, Z, 1917, 4 August.
33. The first curator, Charles ffoulkes, had come from the Royal Armouries, of which he remained the curator, and his interest in guns is evident in the collection to this day. See Sue Malvern, 'War, Memory and Museums: art and artefact in the Imperial War Museum', *History Workshop Journal*, 49, Spring 2000.
34. Brandt, 'The Memory Makers', 95–96.
35. There has been extensive debate about history and memory, often read backwards through the traumatic and difficult history of remembering the Holocaust. See, for example, the discussion between Omer Bartov and others, in the *American Historical Review*, December 1997, forum on 'History and Memory', 1371–1412.
36. Jay Winter, *Sites of Memory, Sites of Mourning*, Cambridge University Press, 1995.

3

British 'War Enthusiasm' in 1914
a Reassessment

Adrian Gregory

For over eighty years there has been a largely unexamined assumption about British popular attitudes at the outbreak of the First World War. Arthur Marwick summarises it succinctly, 'British society in 1914 was strongly jingoistic and showed marked enthusiasm for the outbreak of war.'[1] Images of cheering crowds outside Buckingham Palace, of long lines outside recruiting offices and of soldiers marching away singing 'Tipperary' dominate folk memory. Peter Parker states the Government's decision to enter the war was 'a popular one and there is a feeling for some that it seemed that the holiday was to be extended indefinitely.'[2] Noel Annan, after listing competing explanations for the outbreak of war states, 'They do not explain why the war was greeted with such enthusiasm. For one of the waves of emotion that overwhelmed the sea wall was the willingness of so many to accept war as a solution to the problems of the times.'[3] W. J. Reader has gone as far as to state that 'The suddenness of the onset of war fever and the way in which it smothered all other national pre-occupations ... is one of the best documented aspects of the outbreak of the Great War.'[4] Countless other writers have repeated these assertions, but have cited few sources in support of their claims. Recent historians may have shown a willingness to engage and criticise a variety of myths about the war, but the idea that Britain was seized with a desire to wage war has remained surprisingly resilient. It is true that in *The Pity of War*, Niall Ferguson counters claims of 'war enthusiasm' amongst both the common people and politicians across Europe with alternative reports of those who confronted the idea of war with gloom, cynicism or dread. Likewise, in a nuanced account Hew Strachan has pointed to mixed emotions and ambiguity in the European responses to the outbreak of war, and has characterised the typical response as one of acceptance rather than enthusiasm. Despite this, a more measured response to claims that all Europeans marched joyfully to war has yet to filter through to the wider historical community.[5]

The continuing popularity of this image of mass bellicosity is interesting. It reinforces our sense of superiority to our forbears. *We* know that war is horrible and futile, but *they* were naive. The image of war enthusiasm offers something to all parts of the political spectrum. For conservatives it is the tragic coda to the lost golden age of Edwardian Britain, for socialists it is the extreme case of false consciousness, as working men were led by the pied piper of patriotism into an Imperialist war instead of overthrowing the social order, and for liberals a striking demonstration of the irrationality of the mob. Never mind the fact that a society as complex, subtle and nuanced as Edwardian Britain would seem unlikely to have had a single, uniform reaction to such a major event as the outbreak of a European war, it has proved an immensely satisfying image ever since its creation.[6]

Some of the major proponents for the idea of mass enthusiasm had obvious reasons for promulgating the myth. For wartime pacifists the war was irrational, therefore support for the war was irrational. It flattered the self-proclaimed heroic image of the pacifists to perceive themselves as isolated and far-sighted individuals who were 'above the melee'. The classic text in this regard is Bertrand Russell's *Autobiography*. Russell describes how he 'spent the evening walking the streets, especially in the neighbourhood of Trafalgar Square, noticing cheering crowds, and making myself sensitive to the emotions of passers-by. During this and the following days I discovered to my amazement that average men and women were delighted at the prospect of war.'[7]

This short passage is worth interrogating on a series of grounds. For one thing, it was written half a century after the fact, by which time the image of cheering crowds was well established in popular mythology. How exactly did Russell make himself sensitive to the 'emotions of passers-by'? How could Russell have been 'amazed' in 1914 at 'average' people's delight in war when the idea of 'jingoism' had been firmly established in Liberal circles at the time of the Boer War?[8] Russell was undoubtedly brave in his stance in 1914, but it is quite clear, from his other writing, that what really disturbed him was not so much 'mass enthusiasm' as his own isolation in Liberal political circles after the invasion of Belgium.

This image of 'war fever' also received significant support from the memoirs of politicians. The decision to go to war in 1914 was taken by a very small number of men, but the idea that it was resoundingly endorsed by the population as a whole later became a useful fiction in spreading the blame and avoiding awkward questions of personal culpability. Lloyd George gave a classic *post facto* description of 'war enthusiasm':

> The theory which is propagated today by pacifist orators ... that the Great War was engineered by elder and middle aged statesmen who sent young men to

face its horrors, is an invention ... I shall never forget the warlike crowds that thronged Whitehall and poured into Downing Street, whilst the Cabinet was deliberating on the alternative of peace or war. On Sunday there was a great crowd. Monday was a Bank Holiday and multitudes of young people concentrated in Westminster demonstrating for war against Germany.[9]

This passage, sometimes cited uncritically, must be regarded with enormous caution. When Lloyd George implies that the people impelled the declaration of war he is justifying his own decision to come out in favour of war after the German invasion of Belgium. The description of 'war enthusiasm' is clearly a defence against the accusation that 'old men' sacrificed the young. But the fact remains that the 'crowds' did not declare war on Germany, the Cabinet did, and Lloyd George, by default, played an important role in persuading Liberal Britain to accept war.

Any reassessment of the events of 1914 should start by acknowledging that the very idea of a uniform enthusiastic reaction from the 'masses' owes more to contemporary beliefs of the excitability of mass society, widespread amongst liberals and conservatives alike, than it does to empirical evidence. The evidence for mass enthusiasm *at the time* is surprisingly weak. Part of the problem is methodological: the domestic surveillance capacities of the British state were small compared with continental counterparts and there was relatively little attempt to gauge popular morale at the outbreak of war. Thus the kind of evidence that has been brought to bear on this question by revisionist historians on the continent – the most important being Becker and Verhey for France and Germany respectively – is largely unavailable in the British case.[10] One point that such European studies make strongly, and which ought to be emphasised in the British case too, is that chronology matters. Responses before the outbreak of war differed from responses after its outbreak, and public opinion continued to evolve. It will not do to take rowdy manifestations at midnight on 4 August, resigned editorials accepting war in the Liberal press over the next few days, or the rush to the colours at the end of the month as evidence of attitudes *before* the outbreak of war. In this chapter I will look closely at the evidence we do have, in the form of articles in the national and local press, to show the kind of issues which were being discussed publicly, and the shifting views of a variety of individuals and groups over those critical few days. Detailed analysis reveals an altogether more complex picture.

Finally, discussion of responses to the war in Britain have been remarkably blind to major divisions in Edwardian society, particularly region (or nation), class and gender. Any reconsideration must break down generalisations about 'the British' and examine more closely particular groups.

A reassessment might therefore usefully begin with analysis of a notably unenthusiastic case, namely that of Wales.

Wales in early August 1914

Wales might well have been expected to act as a focus for anti-war senti-ment. Dominated in the south by trade unions with a well developed sense of workingclass consciousness, and in the rural centre, and north, by non-conformist liberalism, Wales had been a major area of 'pro-Boer' opposition to the war in South Africa and had provided anti-war senti-ment at the turn of the century with its most charismatic leader in David Lloyd George. Nevertheless, it is blithely assumed that in 1914, anti-war sentiment whether of the socialist or Christian variety was swept aside by patriotic fervour. Kenneth Morgan, the standard authority, states, 'the overwhelming mass of the Welsh people cast aside their political and industrial divisions and threw themselves into the war with gusto.'[11] This is far from true.

In fact the first major response to the war in the principality came from the South Wales Miners Federation (SWMF) which ostentatiously refused to accede to a government request on 3 August 1914 to cut short the annual holiday. This decision was reaffirmed on 5 August 1914, the day *after* Britain entered the war. The pro-war *Merthyr Express* stated on 22 August 1914 that despite appeals to return to work, only 100 of the 11,000 South Wales Miners on holiday had actually done so. This was not an explicit anti-war stance, but it does indicate that generalisations about war fever over-riding civilian concerns need to be reconsidered.

Nor was rural Wales swept fervently into the Imperial cause. The Welsh language press was full of foreboding; *Seren Cymru*, the Baptist weekly paper predicted on 7 August, 'the Napoleonic wars will seem as nothing but playing compared to coming conflict'. The same day, the Methodist paper, *Y Goleuad*, saw, 'civilization breaking down'. *Y Dinesydd Cymreig* predicted on 12 August, 'the remains of this war will be left behind for generations, in hate, jealousy, misery and poverty'.[12]

Wales as a whole did come round quite quickly to accepting the idea of war. But people did so for local and specific reasons. Welsh Liberals were motivated principally by loyalty to what they very much saw as *their* gov-ernment. The story in the coal fields was more complex. On 9 August, the government and owners requested that the miners should work an extra hour per day. This was widely resisted until the end of the month and as late as 30 August a mass meeting of miners at Merthyr overturned a union recommendation on this score. It was only on 1 September when a spe-cial conference of the SWMF itself resolved to back the extra hour that the dispute was settled. But the context is significant: the conference in return demanded higher pay for soldiers and better separation allowances. It could well be suggested that the Federation was widening its remit to pro-tect those of its members who had enlisted. It is also the case that by the end of August the military context had changed dramatically. Britain as a whole appeared to be facing defeat and the decision of the SWMF to 'rally' corresponded with a general upsurge in defensive patriotism.

It might be possible to dismiss lukewarm Welsh reactions to the out-break of war as the response of an atypical periphery of the United Kingdom. But the response to war at the undoubted centre of both nation and empire was also less overwhelmingly enthusiastic than is generally assumed.

London in early August 1914

It is instructive to compare the description of the crowds in central London written retrospectively by Lloyd George (cited above), with a con-temporary account:

> ... thousands of holiday makers who in other circumstances would have been only too happy to get out of town made their way to Whitehall in the hope of catching a glimpse of Ministers as they arrived. Quiet and orderly, this typical English crowd, obviously comprising all classes of people bore itself well. There was no feverish excitement. Downing Street itself was kept clear by Police – a duty easily managed by a handful of men, so correct was the behaviour of the crowd ... As usual on a fine August Bank Holiday, St James Park and Green Park were invaded by good humoured crowds, bent on enjoying themselves to the utmost. Hundreds of people from the squalid districts of London, many of whom had brought their families and their day's provisions were either playing games, boating or watching their children fishing for tiddlers, when suddenly the sound of military music was heard from the direction of Wellington Bar-racks. Immediately there was a stampede. Fathers packed up their children, mothers gathered the bottles of milk, bags of cake and fruit and there was a general rush in the direction of the Palace. Here some thousands of people had already gathered with the object of seeing the visitors to the palace and the cer-emony of the changing of the guard. Round the Queen Victoria memorial and in front of the Quadrangle all available space had been taken up with the excep-tion of the carriage way on either side of the memorial.[13]

This description appears in an evening paper of Tory persuasion, there-fore unlikely to downplay pro-war enthusiasm, and it was written imme-diately after the events described. Not only does it contradict Lloyd George in detail, it places the crowd in a very different context, as essen-tially a *normal* August Bank Holiday crowd. These people seem to be interested spectators rather than a jingoistic mob baying for war.

Close examination of the 'pro-war' crowds in the metropolis during the war crisis causes them to dwindle almost to the point of disap-pearance. Estimates of numbers are very imprecise. I have been unable to find a police estimate of numbers in the Metropolitan Police files (in itself a point of some significance, suggesting a real lack of concern). Reliable estimates of numbers are hard to find, even in the press. The *Evening Standard* estimated the crowd outside Buckingham Palace on 3 August as 6,000, the *Star* at 10,000. Given the fluid nature of crowd assembly on that day, this order of magnitude is about as useful a guide as we can get. An interesting quantitative measure might be the receipts of the London County Council's tramways for the August Bank Holiday. The record receipts for that Monday, 3 August, as reported in the *South London Observer*, were £ 9,622 as opposed to £ 8,451 for the Bank Holiday in 1913. The newspaper attributed this to the 'many thousands of people who journeyed by tramcar to Westminster and Victoria to witness the exciting scenes in the neighbourhood of the Houses of Parliament'.[14]

These numbers should be seen in the perspective of a city of almost seven *million* inhabitants. To grasp what this implies, a crowd of 8,000 (halfway between the estimates quoted above) would imply the presence of little over one in a thousand of the metropolitan population! A useful 'control' on these numbers is the estimated 100,000 Londoners who flocked to central London upon the news of the Armistice in 1918 and continued to do so for several subsequent days.

Moving away from the centre of London, to the areas in which the vast majority of Londoners spent their Bank Holiday the mood was noticeably different. Hampstead Heath, the pre-eminent gathering spot, saw a holiday which according to the local paper was:

> a dismal affair ... the true holiday spirit as only was to be expected was absent. Many attempts were made to infuse gaiety into the proceedings, but even when these attempts were partially successful, incongruity was afforded by the harsh and discordant voices of news vendors shouting out the latest war news ... Nowhere was their the slightest sign of 'Mafficking' and it was obvious to the observer that the idea of war was distasteful to all.[15]

The *South London Observer* concurred: 'It has been a black Bank Holiday, people have tried to enjoy themselves but have been conscious of the presence of a skeleton at the feast.'[16] The *Kentish Mercury* commented that, 'Greenwich Park and Blackheath were quieter than usual' and suggested that the reason for this was the absence of the military personnel who usually gathered there on a Bank Holiday.[17]

Other newspapers however noted a determination to get on with the holiday. 'On the Bank Holiday the general population of Woolwich seemed bent on enjoyment. Here and there knots of men anxiously discussed the situation, but the tramcars and omnibuses bound for Borstal Woods, Bexley and Eltham were packed all day long.'[18] The *Islington Daily Gazette* even suggested that the crisis had added to enjoyment:

> The North Londoner didn't forget all about what people call the European situation ... but remembrance of it did not weigh heavily upon him ... If anything the war lent a zest to the holiday making ... The burning topic of the war brought members of every company, whether on tram, 'bus or tube, in the park or restaurants into an immediate and friendly touch ... Here is a scrap heard on top of a bus going from Finsbury Park to Finchley. 'Pretty go this here war.' 'Bust up all round seemingly.'

'What do you reckon England will do?'... 'Why stick up for her friends as soon as they're set upon – France in particular.' Quite a little burst of applause greeted the speaker's conclusion.[19]

Whilst this might suggest that there was a rather pro-interventionist popular attitude, it is worth noting that the major *organised* manifestations of public opinion were pro-neutrality and anti-war. The biggest socialist manifestation, the famous Trafalgar Square demonstration on Sunday 2 August, polarised press reporting. There was clearly heckling from middleclass youths present, but what followed seems to have generated quite different accounts depending on the political bias of the reporting.

According to the Conservative press, the meeting was disrupted, red flags were torn down, blows were exchanged between socialists and their opponents, H. M. Hyndman was heckled into inaudibility and Ben Tillet was challenged to a fistfight.[20] Naturally the *Daily Herald* differed on this point considered the meeting generally a success and dismissed the hecklers as 'a few rowdy clerks'. With no great commitment on either side, the *Daily Chronicle* also dismissed the hecklers as 'a negligible contingent of youths in front of the Southern plinth'. These hecklers, 'clerks by appearance', shouted patriotic songs until a heavy shower of rain dampened their enthusiasm and the mounted and foot police who had arrived to avert trouble found themselves with nothing to do. The *Daily Chronicle* stated that with the exception of these youths, the crowd gathered in the square was completely unanimous in passing a resolution which 'deplored the impotency to which the democracy of Germany had been reduced and in calling on the British government in the first place to prevent the spread of the war and in the second place to see that the country is not dragged in to the conflict'. Not all was unanimity. The paper also noted that the 'Red Flag' was carried around the square to the annoyance of the many present who were neither socialist nor jingoes.[21]

Class and gender helped shape responses. As a generalisation the most jingoistic element of crowds appear to have been middleclass youths. Photographic evidence shows more 'boaters' than 'cloth caps' amongst the more pro-intervention gatherings. Such groups are also predominantly male.

The Public Mood up to the Outbreak of War

The Trafalgar Square resolutions were far from untypical of a great deal of comment in the press throughout the country immediately prior to the outbreak of war. This was far from being confined to the most vehement Liberal newspapers, the *Daily News*, edited by A. G. Gardiner, and the *Manchester Guardian*, edited by C. P. Scott, both of which ran strong anti-war campaigns up until 4 August.[22] But much of the provincial press, both Liberal and Unionist had initially expressed a firm preference for neutrality.

On 28 July the *Cambridge Daily News* stated that, 'British interests in the current dispute are quite negligble', and on 29 July it suggested that, 'The ordinary man has heard too much of European conflagrations to believe it until he sees the flames as well as the smoke.' On 27 July, the *Yorkshire Post* editorialised, 'Is it conceivable that Europe can be on the eve of a conflict between the tremendous forces represented by all those great military nations? Happily we see no reason why Great Britain should be drawn in.' The *Northern Daily Mail* put it more strongly on 28 July, that Britain 'could and ought to remain neutral'.[23] The *Oxford Chronicle* on 31 July editorialised that Britain's first duty was to localise the conflict and that 'our second duty is to preserve our own neutrality'.[24] Although it came to be widely believed in Liberal circles that the Unionist press was trying to engineer a war, the Unionist press in the country at large was not universally belligerent. Certainly Lord Northcliffe's papers, *The Times* and the *Daily Mail*, took a strong anti-German line from early in the crisis, but in some respects their belligerence was as unrepresentative as the pacifistic tendencies of the *Daily News* and the *Manchester Guardian.* To some extent the 'jingo' and the 'cocoa'[25] press cancelled each other out (or more likely simply confirmed what their well-defined readerships already believed). Away from the extremes the press could be quite flexible and even surprising; a full page advertisement placed by the Neutrality League, appealing to 'Britons' to 'keep your country out of this wicked and stupid war' appeared in the Unionist *Yorkshire Post* on 4 August.[26]

The fact that the appeal of the Neutrality League appeared in the press on the day that the war broke out indicates sharply the main barrier to the organisation of widespread anti-war feeling – the sheer speed of the crisis and its ultimate resolution in British intervention. A letter to the press from Eleanor Rathbone illustrates the sense of helplessness which the fairly widespread anti-war opinion felt in the face of unfolding events:

> Sir, Before this letter can appear in print the die may have been finally cast for war. But if it is not so … ought not those Liverpool citizens who feel strongly on the question of Britain's neutrality to take some steps such as are being taken in other towns to make their convictions known? This might be done by a public meeting, or better because it could be done more quickly a collectively signed letter in your columns … many people I think shrink from taking this step from a feeling that it is a dangerous presumption of private citizens to express an opinion on an issue of such supreme importance and difficulty. No one imagines that manifestos of the kind in question are likely to exercise a preponderating influence on the deliberations of the Cabinet. All they are and all they are intended to do, is to reflect the feelings of different sections of the public, and so assist the Government to gauge how far they have the country behind them.[27]

In the event, a large amount of anti-war sentiment was expressed through various means. Letters to the newspapers expressed a great deal of pro-neutrality opinion, much of it strongly anti-Russian and often with an extremely powerful vision of war as a catastrophe for civilisation.

Norman Angell's views on the likely consequences of a European war were well known in Britain in 1914.[28] The immediate effects of the war crisis appeared to justify Angell's vision of the disastrous collapse of credit and trade that war would entail. On 30 July, the *Liverpool Daily Post* outlined the grim prospects for trade:

> The fears and apprehensions of the citizens were reflected in melancholy vigour in the business done on various marts and exchanges. There was a sensational drop in the cotton market, whilst the corn market was excited and nervous, the price of flour is going up 1s 6d per sack, making 2s 6d advance in a couple of days. The Liverpool stock exchange is practically paralysed ... The effect of a great European war on Liverpool would be disastrous.[29]

On the eve of the war a trade union official in Norwich 'outlined a terrible picture of the consequences of war with food at famine prices and ordered government at an end'.[30] Sombre realism was widespread, Radnor Hodgson wrote to the *Yorkshire Post*:

> War is death and destruction. All who participate in war, of course, intend to put the death and destruction on his enemies; but history shows that the crushing punishment has often fallen on those who thought they could impose it on others. War is not a game to be trifled with.[31]

Reading the newspapers either side of the outbreak of war suggests very strongly that the public were not as naive about the consequences of war as is often imagined. Even those who were pro-intervention were quite clear-headed about the perils of war. Contrary to popular belief, the idea that 'the war would be over by Christmas' is entirely absent, except in the apocalyptic sense that civilisation was on the verge of complete and imminent collapse.[32]

A very real sense of concern about the risks of war did not in itself create widespread opposition. Such opposition needed a focal point. In the event, although quite a lot of opposition was publicly expressed, the speed of events prevented it coalescing into a clear anti-war movement. Church of England sermons, for example, generally followed a predictable line of concern, tempered by national loyalty, on Sunday 2 August, but individual clerics did speak out. The most prominent of these was the Bishop of Lincoln, in a sermon at Cleethorpes. He predicted, 'a continental war could be nothing short of disastrous when one thought of the militarism of Europe, of the hell of battlefields, of the miseries of the wounded, of ruined peasants'. He was reported as saying, 'we had no quarrel with Germany and to go to war without a reason was tempting providence. Moreover it would inflict upon our industrial community one of the most terrible curses possible to inflict. He asked them all to pray to God to keep our people from war.'[33] At a less exalted level, the Rector of St. Mary's, Newmarket, painted an apocalyptic picture of what a war would entail:

All the horrors of war in ancient times would be nothing to the horrors of war today ... All the resources of science had been called upon to perfect weapons of destruction for mankind ... no town in England was now safe. At night it might be turned into a smouldering ruin and its inhabitants into blackened corpses.

In the parish of Bowerchalke in Wiltshire, the Reverend Collet wrote in his parish magazine:

THE CONTINENTAL WAR – which has unfortunately broken out and may possibly affect our country is very greatly to be deplored. Whatever the cause of it may be, the inevitable consequence cannot fail to be bloodshed and misery for many. It is true that a nation's honour must be upheld but surely that might be accomplished without loss of life.[34]

Anti-war opinion was expressed much more vigorously in sermons and in resolutions within the nonconformist chapels. The Muswell Hill Brotherhood unanimously passed a resolution calling for the Government to maintain 'the honourable position of pacificators'.[35] In Leicester, two Primitive Methodist Chapels, the United Free Church and the Baptists sent petitions to Edward Grey calling for neutrality. The *Banbury Advertiser* reported that special prayers for the limitation of conflict were offered at most places of worship, and that the Grimsbury Brotherhood had passed a revolution that viewed 'with horror the terrible outrage to humanity and the menacing challenge to Christianity involved in a European war'.[36] The nonconformist response to the actual outbreak of war was perhaps more sorrow than anger. The sermon at the Unitarian Chapel in Banbury the next weekend regretted that, 'the moral development of the people of Europe had not kept pace with their intellectual growth'.[37]

Organised non-conformist opposition to the war was actually on the point of becoming quite significant over the weekend before war broke out. On Saturday 1 August Robertson Nicoll presented Lloyd George with a letter stating that the free churches would strongly oppose any war. On Monday 3 August George Riddell visited Nicoll and persuaded him that the government had to stand by its responsibilities towards France. This information was passed on to Lloyd George by Charles Masterman in order to stiffen his resolve.[38]

Socialist and trade union opposition was also widespread. On the morning of Sunday 2 August a trade union official in Norwich 'outlined a terrible picture of the consequences of war with food at famine prices and ordered government at an end'. On the same day an Independent Labour Party (ILP) meeting was held in Leicester, where Councillor Hallam stated that: 'War would not make the capitalists or workers any better off. Was England to range herself on the side of Russian diplomatists?'[39] In a less conciliatory tone that evening, at the Birmingham Bull Ring, George Cook expressed his opposition to being drawn into a quarrel between Austria and Servia (sic) because, 'the workers already had on hand an industrial battle for better economic conditions which was far more important than entering into a war with their brothers on the continent'.[40] Charles Hobson of the Sheffield Branch of the International Metal Trades Federation wrote to his local paper expressing his trade union's opposition to the war, and the British Socialist Party in the same town passed a resolution against it.[41] On 2 August, a young Ernest Bevin addressed a trade union meeting on Bristol Downs which called for a general strike against war.[42] In Islington, under the auspices of the local British Socialist Party and the ILP, two anti-war meetings were held at Highbury Corner where it was decided to form a procession to march to Trafalgar Square and join the Peace Demonstration. This was followed by a further meeting in the evening where resolutions against the war were passed.[43]

But once again there was some movement towards a reluctant acceptance of war, should it come. At a Labour fête held on Bank Holiday Monday at Abbey Wood, Will Crooks pledged loyalty to the government in the following terms:

> I cannot help myself, we have fought for peace to the last moment, but if war has got to come, you and I must shoulder the burden … our next order is to look after the food for the people, not at famine prices, but at reasonable prices that the poor can afford. Then we have to look after the women and children. Do not forget that our obligations are beginning now. We have got to see the job through and present a united front to the enemy.[44]

It was reported that Crooks was 'loudly cheered'. The question inevitably arises as to which sentiment provoked the cheers, standing by the government or the condemnation of 'famine prices'. It is quite possible that both sentiments did.

Generalisations about public attitudes are very difficult. There *was* a widespread sentiment of sympathy with France and a sense of a moral obligation; on the other hand, there was a widespread dislike of Russia, and a downright contempt for Serbia, best exemplified in the *John Bull* headline, 'To Hell with Servia'. Anti-German prejudice was expressed during the crisis, but so was pro-German sentiment. The possible effects of war were not romanticised, but duty and sacrifice were accepted. On balance it is completely untenable to suggest that the politicians were forced into war by the public.

In this context, the German invasion of Belgium becomes significant. The invasion of Belgium does not appear to have changed many minds in the country at large. Attitudes had tended to polarise around responses to a German attack on *France*: pro-intervention sentiment was largely fixed before 2 August, and anti-intervention sentiment did not change. But within the Cabinet the invasion of Belgium did have an important effect. It provided both an excuse, and a cover, for the Liberals who had already decided that Germany should be resisted. By far the most important of these was Lloyd George. It was the decision of Liberal politicians, and to a lesser extent certain influential newspaper editors, to back the war effort that guaranteed that anti-war sentiment remained marginalised once hostilities finally broke out.[45]

Mobilisation and the Outbreak of War

The actual declaration of war, when it finally came, was greeted with more clear-cut enthusiasm in the strict sense of the word. The *Daily Chronicle* reported that up to this point there had been no 'Mafficking', but that the declaration of war had produced enthusiastic demonstrations akin to 1899:

> Earlier in the evening a procession starting with 30 people outside Buckingham Palace marched through the City to Mansion House, increasing in numbers until 3,000 were taking part in it. Many carried Union Jacks, others displayed the French Tricolour and the Green Flag of Ireland waved triumphantly over several sections of the demonstration. On the return from the Mansion House a company of the 1st Division (London) of the Royal Fusiliers was held upon a brake by Police. Instantly cheers were raised and hats and caps were lifted in salute to the Territorials ... All the way from West to East and East to West, soldiers in Scarlet or Khaki, and sailors with their kitbags slung over their shoulders were greeted warmly. Outside the Palace an immense crowd had been assembled all evening. As the hours advanced it grew in numbers until it reached about 12,000. All sorts and conditions of men and women were there. Lord Lonsdale in evening dress was seen rubbing shoulders with one of the costers to whom he is a good friend and patron. Mothers brought their babies in arms with them and many quiet young children were held up by their parents that they might see the King and Queen. The enthusiasm was long sustained ... In contrast with the exuberance of the demonstrations outside the Mansion House was the quiet demeanour of the people who had gathered in the neighbourhood of Parliament Square.[46]

Because the *Daily Chronicle* was a morning newspaper, the reporting more or less breaks off at midnight, but the *Globe*, an evening paper, picked up the story as the crowds became more exuberant still:

> The receipt of the news was the climax to the evening's demonstration and for the next two hours stirring scenes were witnessed. Gaily decorated motor-cars crowded inside and out, passed round and round the Victoria memorial in processional order, men and women standing on the tops of taxi-cabs and waving flags continuously ... when the police began to clear the vicinity of the palace people proceeded up The Mall and demonstrated in other parts of the city until well into the morning ... There were scenes of great enthusiasm in Trafalgar Square and Piccadilly Circus when the news of the declaration of war spread. A great roar of defiance was the answer of a vast crowd in the Square at the news.[47]

All of this corresponds much more closely to the stereotype of war enthusiasm. (Indeed, this was the scene into which a depressed Bertrand Russell walked and which made such an impact upon him.) But such a view must be heavily qualified. One aspect of 'enthusiasm' was the desire to give mobilising troops a good send-off. This could be found either side of the actual declaration of war. The *Eastern Daily Press* reported on the scenes surrounding the departure of Territorial soldiers from Norwich:

> The men as they were making the final preparations for leaving were in the highest of spirits. They sang their favourite melodies with vigour and shook hands cordially with friends who came to have a last word with them … Girls rushed forward with merry laughter just to tap their military friends on the back and receive a warm glance of recognition as a reward. Umbrellas were waved in the air, handkerchiefs were flourished and all was done to make the Territorials feel that they were carrying away with them the best hopes of the ancient city.[48]

It is in the nature of the case that public manifestations of solidarity and enthusiasm attract notice. What is less easy to estimate is how many people privately reacted with shock and resignation. Actual opposition, whilst not unknown, was thin on the ground once war was under way. On 6 August the *Labour Leader* carried the slogan 'Down with War!' on its front page and on 11 August the National Council of the ILP reiterated the solidarity of the Second International. The majority of ILP branches endorsed this stance. On 9 August, the ILP, the British Socialist Party and the Peace Society held a joint demonstration in Glasgow demanding an armistice. But at this stage the first instinct of most of the war's opponents was to keep a low profile. Even within the ILP, the London Divisional Council admitted that, 'We cannot at this moment take steps to stop the war'.[49] It took a month or so for Liberal and Socialist opponents of the war to coalesce and organise what would become the Union of Democratic Control. The truth was that those who had opposed the war before 4 August were now deeply divided. There were various reasons for supporting the war or choosing to stay silent. Some had changed their minds and had accepted the British moral case for war. Some retained doubts about the moral case, but hoped that the war could nevertheless be invested with moral purpose. Some accepted the war as a pragmatic reality and looked to ameliorate its effects. These three groups probably made up a very substantial section of the population. Even amongst the little band of outright opponents there were differences. There were even some, like Ramsay MacDonald, who basically accepted the 'moral' validity of Britain entering war, whilst continuing to oppose it.[50]

Recruiting

The standard 'evidence' for a generally enthusiastic response to the outbreak of war is the 'rush to the colours' that created Kitchener's Army. This is taken to stand both for the 'group psychology' of war enthusiasm, and the transformative effect on individuals seeking the romantic excitement of war. But when the chronology of recruitment is examined this phenomenon appears in a different light.

Large numbers did join up in the first few weeks of August. Between 4 August and 8 August, 93 men enlisted, and by 22 August over 100,000 men had enlisted. Of those who joined up, a substantial number probably *were* motivated by enthusiasm and a desire to fight. But this should not lead us to overlook that there were other and perhaps more powerful reasons for enlistment at the outbreak of the war. Most traditional accounts of enlistment in 1914 have tended to overlook that the *first* impact of the war (and indeed the war crisis) was mass unemployment. Economic distress had always been the British Army's best recruiting agent and the slump at the start of the war was, in the *short term*, probably the most severe bout of economic distress in Britain in the twentieth century. Trade Union reports to the Board of Trade indicated that unemployment amongst union members rose from 2.8 percent at the end of July to 7.1 percent at the end of August. Between July and September male employment fell 10 percent. This does not begin to express the whole impact of the war on the economy. Much of the rest of the workforce was working on short time by mid August 1914.

The burden of economic hardship fell on all classes, but perhaps most severely on sections of the workforce which were already the principle recruiting ground for the army – the urban unskilled. It was reported from Birmingham that 78 percent of the volunteers in August came from the same classes which had joined the peacetime army. The disproportionate numbers of the early volunteers who enlisted in London is further evidence that the bulk of this enlistment was an intensified version of pre-war recruitment, driven by economic distress.

The beginnings of a real mass recruitment movement came later in the month. The key moment was the publication of the Mons Despatch in *The Times* on 25 August. Presenting the battle as a heroic defeat, it ended with an appeal for more men to join up. The response was instantaneous. On the next four days more than 10,000 men enlisted (daily enlistment therefore exceeded the total enlistment for the first *week* of the war.) By 31 August, daily enlistment topped 20,000 and on 3 September 33,304 men joined the army, the highest enlistment for any day of the war. In the week between 30 August and 5 September 174,901 men joined the colours.

This is not merely a technical detail of chronology. If, as these figures suggest, the main rush to the colours occurred not immediately after the outbreak of war, but nearly a month later, it has important implications for understanding the major motivations for enlistment. Far from signing up in a burst of enthusiasm at the outbreak of war, the largest single component of volunteers enlisted at *exactly* the moment when the war turned serious. Men did not join the British Army expecting a picnic stroll to Berlin but in the expectation of a desperate fight for national defence.[51]

Ambiguity

Simplistic generalisations about war enthusiasm not only iron out the complexities of society, they also gloss over the complexities of individual response. The diaries of two middleclass women are indicative of the very mixed feelings, including apparently contradictory responses, that could occur in a single person across the course of a dramatic week. Mrs Eustace Miles, a restaurateur, kept a diary at this time, which she later published. On 1 August she wrote, 'We are having a quiet weekend at W on Sea ... There seems nothing wrong (outwardly) with the world, yet the air is full of whispers of coming trouble: and rumours of war are becoming more and more alarming and more and more persistent.' On 4 August, she noted, 'Since writing these words we already seem to be in a new world. The awful declaration of war has been made and everything plunged into chaos. We are back in London. In the short time that we have been away everything seems to have changed ... awful as it is – it is very thrilling.' The same mixture of foreboding and excitement appears the next day:

> Of course at first we are all feeling terribly shaken and hardly anyone sleeps. The streets are full of people all night long, and the steady tramp of Territorials as they march to Headquarters seems never to cease. There are small and subtle changes too. I notice people in the streets are now singing the 'Marseillaise' and 'God Save the King' and 'Rule Britannia'; the very children are marching instead of walking and carrying bits of stick as bayonets and using old pieces of pails as drums ... We are having to part with some of our most valued employees, who have been with us for years. It seems to bring the tragedy of war into our midst. It is like parting with members of our own family.[52]

In an unpublished diary, Mrs Ada Reece, the wife of an army doctor, shows another mixture of reactions. On 2 August she wrote:

> we are on the eve of a Great European War in which we must engage against our will and the ultimate consequences of which none can foresee. But all are agreed that it will be more terrible than any previous war with all the horrible engines of destruction that science has been perfecting through a hundred years of peace.

Despite this she was firmly convinced that war was necessary; the next day she wrote: 'We must fight, I wrote yesterday, it had never occurred to me that it was possible to do otherwise ... Of course we were not in a part which would be crowded on a Bank holiday, but the people seemed unusually quiet.'

Historians may separate out anxiety and enthusiasm, but for individuals the two could be closely linked:

> I spent all the morning marketing. The CSSA was crowded, the rush to buy food by well to do people last Saturday has been very unfortunate, stocks are

82 | *Adrian Gregory*

exhausted ... those of us who are calmer are forced to buy now before the greedy seize all. I gave an order for a large quantity of sugar which has already risen by 1/2d per lb, some chocolate etc.

On Wednesday 5th we awoke to the glorious news that Great Britain declared war on Germany last night ... Glorious, I say although we undertake hostilities very gravely and reluctantly, but the suspense of the last few days has been great and some papers have been urging that Britain should remain neutral.

War might be glorious, but Reece was not unaware that it also brought misery:

Helene and I started out with Peggy, and walked from Queen's Road to Marble Arch and then by omnibus to Holborn. The buses are crowded, they say 400 chassis have been requisitioned by Government. There were many Khaki uniforms about and horses being lead away by soldiers ... Mother came up in a very sad mood, had seen the London Scottish marching out and wept over them – full of fear for Dick and Harold.[53]

These literate testimonies might be treated as untypical in their complexity, but there is every likelihood that the same mixture of emotions and motivations was widespread.

It is more difficult to trace this ambiguity in actions than in diaries, but there are some intriguing cases where public enthusiasm can be seen in relation to private anxiety. A press account of police court proceedings from Norwich shows how apparent 'jingoism' was a mask for deeper concern:

Clara Mason, married woman, yesterday was charged with being drunk and disorderly ... Defendant said she was insulted by some person on St Andrews Plain. She was singing 'God Save the King' when he told her to shut up. Defendant said 'I shall not, my husband is fighting for such as you.' She then became very excited and did not know what happened afterwards ...

Police-constable Taylor said defendant picked up several pieces of brick and threw them at witness. One piece struck him in the head, Defendant bursting into tears said – My Husband is at the front and all I wanted was to fight Germans. I have been worrying this past month about my Husband and lost my head a bit ... He is at the front and I have not been right since. I cannot eat anything. A friend of mine gave me a drink and it got hold of me.[54]

In an impassioned pacifist attempt to capture the mood of 1914, Caroline Playne wrote *The Pre-War Mind* in 1928. Playne had hated the war and still found it inexplicable. Yet extensive reading of contemporary reporting had convinced her that *prior* to the outbreak of the war there 'was no sudden fit of passionate insanity which annihilated all reasonable action'. Instead, 'Soul possessing, permeating neurosis' had paralysed the public response and had caused a flight into irrational fantasy of anti-German liberal crusading *subsequent* to the outbreak of war.[55] The attempt to psychoanalyse the national mood, and the underlying assumption that support for the war in *any* form was clear evidence of irrationality, undermine some of the specifics of Playne's argument. But it is not without merit. The declaration of war did release some of the growing anxiety and tension, the speed of the crisis did paralyse opposition, and the urge to do *something,* whether it be search for alleged German spies, contribute to relief funds or personally volunteer, was clearly widespread in the first week of the war.

Perhaps an impressionistic view of the mood immediately after the outbreak of the war, which was published in a local North London newspaper, comes closest to capturing the anxiety, excitement and fear of the moment, and the multitude of reactions:

THEY SAY:
That the war greets you everywhere in Islington.
That you turn a corner and blunder into a man obsessed with his newspaper.
That you meet a friend and his first words are, 'What do you think of it?'
That from right, left and in front, news-vendors throw out nothing but war.
That you enter a tramcar and still find the subject being waged with fervour.
That finally, at the end of the day you go home to bed and dream about it.
That the closing of the banks was a move most businessmen were unprepared for.
That a local tradesman remarked, 'It has fairly put the lid on.'
That a number of military reserve men in the local police have been called to the colours.
That the response of the North London 'Braves' to the country's call has surprised the authorities.
That great crowds invaded the picture palaces of Islington last night to see the war movements on the screen.
That when the great clap of thunder burst over North London at 11.30 yesterday many people thought that a German bomb had been dropped from an aeroplane.
That there has been a stampede of Germans from Finsbury Park.
That the appearance of uniformed Territorials in the streets caused considerable excitement in Stoke Newington.
That the rise in the price of commodities is giving grave anxiety in the poorer parts of Finsbury.[56]

This, rather than tired clichés about popular jingoism, captures the way that British people entered the war.

Notes

1. A. Marwick, *The Deluge: British Society and the First World War* Macmillan, 1965 and 1989, 309.
2. P. Parker, *The Old Lie: The Great War and the Public School Ethos*, Constable, 1987, 151.
3. Lord Annan, *Our Age: The Generation that made Post-War Britain*, Fontana, 1990, 93.
4. W. J. Reader, *At Duty's Call: A Study in Obsolete Patriotism*, Manchester University Press, 1988, 104. It is interesting to reflect on a straw poll conducted by the US Senator for Indi-

ana, Albert Beveridge, in the early spring of 1915, which suggested to him, 'the middle classes are unaroused, the so-called lower classes divided between those who are sullenly indifferent and patriotically interested … Only the aristocracy was eager, united and resolved.' A. Beveridge, 'War Opinion in England – Some Contrasts', *The American Review of Reviews*, July 1915, reproduced in H. E. Straubing, *The Last Magnificent War*, Paragon House, 1989, 44–53. This is not to argue that Beveridge was correct, only that a contemporary observer could draw a very different conclusion.

5. Niall Ferguson also explores the scepticism about war, particularly on economic grounds, amongst various members of the governing elite: *The Pity of War*, Penguin, 1998, Chapter 7. Hew Strachan, *The First World War, Volume I: To Arms*, Oxford University Press, 2001.

6. The full story of the creation of the idea of 'war enthusiasm' would require an essay in itself. One interesting aspect is that whilst in Germany the myth of the *Augustgemeinschaft* was largely a product of the political right, in Britain the idea of war enthusiasm was mostly promulgated by the left. One largely unexplored avenue of investigation is how the very real mass enthusiasm at the end of the war in 1918 in Britain was projected back to August 1914.

7. B. Russell, *The Autobiography of Bertrand Russell: 1914–44*, Volume 2, Allen and Unwin, London, 1968, 16.

8. The classic text remains J. A. Hobson, *The Psychology of Jingoism*, Grant Richards, 1901. See also C. F. G. Masterman (ed.), *The Heart of Empire*, Unwin, 1901, a compendium of liberal views. In point of fact most liberal dissidents in 1914 were reacting to a well established 'script' which assumed that the 'mob' would react enthusiastically to war.

9. D. Lloyd George, *War Memoirs*, Ivor Nicholson & Watson, 1938, Volume 1, 39

10. In particular, Jean-Jacques Becker, *1914: Comment les Francais sont entrés dans la guerre*, Presses de la Fondation Nationale des Sciences Politiques, 1977. For the first systematic overview and refutation of the myth of the *Augustgemeinschaft* in Germany, see J. Verhey, *The Spirit of 1914: Mobilization, Militarism and Myth in Germany*, Cambridge University Press, 2000.

11. K.O. Morgan, *Rebirth of a Nation: A History of Modern Wales*, Clarendon Press, 1981, 159.

12. I am very grateful to my student Rhodri Jones for exploring the Welsh dimension, particularly those parts inaccessible to an ignorant Anglo-Saxon. This section is entirely based upon his very original research. R. Jones, 'Wales and the Outbreak of the First World War', unpublished BA Dissertation, Oxford, 1999.

13. *The Globe*, 3 August 1914, 5.

14. *South London Observer*, 8 August 1914, 6.

15. *Hampstead Record*, 7 August 1914, 2.

16. *South London Observer*, 5 August 1914, 3.

17. *The Kentish Mercury*, 7 August 1914, 6.

18. *Woolwich Herald*, 7 August 1914, 2.

19. *Islington Daily Gazette*, 4 August 1914, 2.

20. *Evening Standard*, 3 August 1914, 4.

21. *Daily Chronicle*, 3 August 1914, 6.

22. See *Daily News*, Editorial by A. G. Gardiner, 'Why we must not fight', 1 August 1914. For background see S. Koss, *Fleet Street Radical: A. G. Gardiner and the Daily News*, Allen Lane, 1973, and T. Wilson, *The Political Diaries of C. P. Scott, 1911–28*, Collins, 1970.

23. Cited in P. Esposito, 'Public Opinion and the Outbreak of the First World War: The Newspapers of Northern England', unpublished M.St. Dissertation, Oxford, 1996, 17.

24. *Oxford Chronicle*, 31 July 1914.

25. The derogatory term used for liberal newspapers such as the *Daily News*, which were seen as promoting an unpatriotic agenda derived from their proprietor's Quakerism.

26. For a full discussion of the complexities of the local press in Northern England in early August, see Esposito, 'Public Opinion', 23–33.

27. *Liverpool Post*, 4 August 1914, 7.

28. See H. Weinroth, 'Norman Angell and the Great Illusion: An episode in pre-1914 Pacifism', *Historical Journal*, 17, 1974.

29. *Liverpool Daily Post*, 30 July 1914, 5.
30. *Eastern Daily Press*, 3 August 1914, 6.
31. *Yorkshire Post*, 4 August 1914.
32. The frequently asserted opinion that the British people expected the war to be over by Christmas has very little foundation in contemporary sources. Prognostications on the war's length are actually quite rare in July and August 1914 , either in public or in private. The few that do exist suggest that the war was generally anticipated to last at least a year. For example Harold Cousins' diary entry for 9 August, 'England now being involved in what will probably be known as the First World War of 1914 – probably 1915.' H. Cousins, diary, Microfilm, Imperial War Museum.
33. *Hull Daily Mail*, 3 August 1914, 3.
34. R. L. Sawyer, *The Bowerchalke Parish Papers: Collett's Village Newspaper 1878–1924*, Allan Sutton, 1989.
35. *Islington Daily Gazette*, 6 August 1914, 5.
36. *Banbury Advertiser*, 6 August 1914, 6.
37. *Banbury Guardian*, 13 August 1914, 5.
38. J. M. McEwen (ed.), *The Riddell Diaries*, Athlone, 1986, 87–88. Entry for 3 August 1914.
39. *Leicester Daily Post*, 3 August 1914 , 6.
40. *Birmingham Daily Post*, 3 August 1914, 3.
41. *Sheffield Daily Telegraph*, 4 August 1914, 5.
42. A.Bullock, *The Life and Times of Ernest Bevin*, Vol. 1, Heinemann, 1960, 45.
43. *Islington Daily Gazette*, 5 August 1914 , 4.
44. *Kentish Mercury*, 7 August 1914, 7.
45. The most influential of these were Lord Northcliffe – as a hands on proprietor rather than an editor – and Garvin, of the *Observer*, who was the most important editor as such.
46. *Daily Chronicle*, 5 August 1914, 3.
47. *The Globe*, 5 August 1914, 5.
48. *Eastern Daily Press*, 6 August, 1914.
49. F. L. Carsten, *War against War: British and German Radical Movements in the First World War*, Batsford Academic and Educational, 1982, 26–28.
50. Macdonald wrote to the American socialist Laidler in November, 'there is nothing chauvinist or sordid about our intentions. It is a war for liberty and democracy as far as the man in the street is concerned.' Cited in Carsten, *War against War*, 29.
51. Both the facts and the interpretation presented here are drawn from Peter Simkins' magisterial and definitive account of voluntary recruitment. P. Simkins, *Kitchener's Army*, Manchester University Press, 1988.
52. E. Miles, *Untold tales of Wartime London; A Personal Diary*, Cecil Palmer, 1930, 13–15
53. Ada Reece Diary for 1914, Ada Reece papers, Liddle Personal Experience Archive, Leeds University.
54. *Eastern Daily Press*, 2 September 1914.
55. C. Playne, *The Pre-War Mind*, Allen & Unwin, 1928, 381.
56. *Islington Daily Gazette*, 6 August 1914, 3.

4

Winners or Losers
Women's Symbolic Role in the War Story

―――――――――――

Gail Braybon

Robert Wohl, in his book on the so-called 'lost generation' of 1914, begins by inviting his readers to consider the myth:

> Generation of 1914 – close your eyes and a host of images leaps to mind: of students packing off to war with flowers in their rifles and patriotic songs on their lips, too young, too innocent to suspect what bloody rites of passage awaited them; of trench fighters whose twisted smiles and evasive glances revealed a close companionship with death …[1]

These images are important, for:

> [They] have a privileged place in our conception of the early twentieth century. They colour our memories and creep into the best of our books. They are the prisms through which we view the years between the two world wars.[2]

Yet, he reminds us, this is the stuff of literature and legend, and the task of establishing who the men of 1914 really were, and what they felt about the war, is fraught with difficulty.

> Indeed one could be tempted to argue that if the war generation is 'lost', it is lost because it has no history; lost because its history is overlaid with myth.[3]

There are several key elements to the lost generation story. The first is that in this tableau – and it is peculiarly visual, thanks to film and photography – 'the generation of 1914' is implicitly and explicitly male. However, not just any male will do. To the British, the major players are still soldiers, preferably those who fought on the Western Front – not sailors, miners, munition workers, doctors, or any others involved in the war effort. They are also young, straight from school or university, and idealistic. They are primarily middle or upper class, 'a great generation, marvellous in its promise'[4] and highly literate – although the plucky working class soldier may receive honourable mention.[5] They are also white – not African, Asian, Arab or Indian, though these men too fought for the British Empire, as volunteers or conscripts. And they are the victims of politicians and generals, who exploited their idealism. Furthermore, the 'lost generation' is made up not merely of men who died, but men who were injured, physically or mentally, by their war experiences. There is no place here for the men who tolerated, or even enjoyed, their army life, or those who saw war as an escape from poverty, from crushing manual labour, or even boredom. Graham Greenwell, who wrote in 1935 that 'The horrors of the Great War and the miseries of those who were called to take part in it have been described by innumerable writers. For my own part I have to confess that I look back on the years 1914–1918 as among the happiest I have ever spent ...' was clearly not part of the lost generation.[6] Embittered men, volunteer and conscript, are the subject of more books than any other wartime social group; these include Paul Fussell's *The Great War and Modern Memory* and Eric Leed's *No Man's Land*,[7] both frequently regarded as key texts in any discussion of the impact of war on the twentieth century – at least amongst a coterie of European and American historians. This image is fed by contemporary novelists and filmmakers, and by the continued popularity of the war poets, who remain amongst the more romantic figures of English literature.[8] As Elizabeth Marsland writes, in her book on the war poetry of Britain, France and Germany, for literary historians 'a typical English First World War poet was a combatant, usually a junior officer, apolitical, who, if he lived long enough, was converted by his war exposure from a patriotic idealist to a disillusioned realist, and who then used his poetry as a tool of protest.'[9]

The story of doomed and betrayed youth is very powerful; it chimes with a thoroughly pessimistic view of the century, and it reinforces the idea that the war signified a new chapter in man's inhumanity to man. Yet it is also both one-dimensional and weighed down with symbolism. Douglas Jerrold, writing in 1930, despaired of the growing tendency to see the war in uniformly bleak terms, and the fact that so many writers of the 1920s seemed to dwell on the horror of 1914–18 while ignoring the suffering and injustice around them in their own time. Casting his eye over the numerous newly published books which now claimed to tell the public about the 'actualities of war', he wrote:

> How could I avoid, even at the outset, approaching the conclusion that it was a peculiar, unhistoric and absurdly romantic vision of war which was popular, and that under the clever pretence of telling the truth about the war, a farrago of highly sentimentalised and romantic story-telling was being foisted on to a new, simple and too eagerly humanitarian public.[10]

Yet this preoccupation with the concept of a lost generation is still found in both popular and academic history. As Wohl says, it 'creeps into the best of our books', even though it neglects the experiences and opinions of millions of other men, young and old, before, during and after the war. In many standard British history books, 'men's story' is deemed to be the soldier's story, and the soldier's role is to be betrayed by politicians and generals. Although a number of recent historians have looked critically at descriptions of life at the front and soldiers' experiences, attempting to replace the classic picture with a more realistic and rounded view of army life, it remains to be seen whether these books will have any significant impact on the war story so beloved by Britain.[11]

How do women, the other half of the population, fit into the picture? As non-combatants, they are clearly not part of the lost generation, and there has been relatively little interest in portraying them as the damaged or bereaved partners of soldiers – their mirror image – although Vera Brittain's autobiographical *Testament of Youth* (1930) and Helen Zenna Smith's novel, *Not so Quiet ...* (1933) both sought to show how women too could be devastated by war.[12] Yet women are far from invisible in popular British iconography. On the contrary, it often seems as though women emerged from the dimness of ordinary life into the brilliant illumination of wartime, only to drop back into the shadows once more in 1918 (until the next war). But Wohl's words are worth repeating in this context: women's wartime history was, and often still is, overlaid with myth. They have their own stereotypical roles to fill. There is scope for them to be seen as victims, villains or heroines, depending upon the viewpoint of the writer. The most popular stereotypes are VAD (volunteer nurse) and munition worker. The former – middle or upperclass – has been largely displaced by the latter in recent years, with the implicit assumption that she took up men's work for the duration of the war, earned high wages, and then went home quietly when no longer needed. The increasing interest over time in 'the woman worker' reflects a general shift towards those who did something *different* as a result of war, and in someway challenged the existing social order. The VAD, of course, was performing 'standard women's work': her dedication is seen as admirable, but unsurprising – while her sisters who were professional nurses arouse very little attention at all. The search for 'difference' began during the war itself, as Deborah Thom's essay on the Women's Collection at the Imperial War Museum in this volume shows.

However, there are two similarities between the archetypal female figure of the woman worker and the symbolic male soldier. Firstly, *young* women – preferably photogenic women – were (and are) most likely to receive attention, as revealed by the photographic record of women doing 'men's work' in direct support of war, often dressed in uniforms, and even trousers. Secondly, just as the betrayed or disillusioned young soldier is very familiar in a wide range of books on war, so too is the 'new' woman worker. The interaction between their stereotypical descriptions in academic and popular texts is critical: each source feeds off the other. 'Women' are part of the war story, and their particular role is frequently to exemplify the concept of the war as a 'watershed' in social history. Ironically, their war experiences are therefore seen as the polar opposite of men's: they are said to have prospered while men suffered. To the majority of ordinary people, the war is still seen as handing British women new freedoms. Yvonne Klein, in her recent collection of women's wartime autobiographical writings, remarks on the fact that:

> ... seventy odd years after the Great War, my students tell me confidently every year that the war was a good thing for women: it gave them the vote and jobs.[13]

The public image of women is thus dominated by two strands: their war work (in 'men's jobs'), and their acquisition of 'the vote.' Intriguingly, specialist research seems to have convinced many academics – within the field of women's history and beyond – that the extension of suffrage to women over thirty was *not* the direct result of war in Britain. It is recognised that debates about suffrage during the early years of the twentieth century were complex, and that while many people called for a 'reward' for women workers in 1918, this was not necessarily what motivated either the government or MPs.[14] However, the idea that the war was 'good for women', and that 1914–18 was some sort of 'watershed' for them, continues to crop up with surprising regularity in many academic texts, with or without reference to suffrage legislation.

Joan Scott, in her important essay 'Re-writing History', rightly identifies the major claims in watershed history (women gained new jobs, women won the vote, and their position in society changed permanently) and points out how these themes have so dominated discussions about the war that those of us who disagree with such statements have nevertheless found ourselves arguing on the same territory. Scott's criticism of the limiting agenda imposed by these preoccupations is all too valid.[15] Inevitably such an approach encourages many readers and writers alike to work through a mental list when considering women and the war, ticking off events as 'good' or 'bad' for women, and of 'short' or 'long' duration. Interpretations based on the supposed experiences (and behaviour) of a relatively small group of young women, and the alleged response of what is often referred to as 'society' are bound to lack subtlety and variety, yet they feature in a large number of books about the war in Britain, and indeed Western Europe. Nevertheless, we cannot simply ignore claims that the war was a 'watershed' for women: we need to understand how this idea has been used by historians over the years and, ironically, how this has also influenced a number of those writing about war and gender.

Watershed 1: War and Social Change

It is tempting to identify the 1960s as the key decade for establishing the idea of some sort of inherent connection between the war and 'social change.' Clare Tylee is amongst those who have pointed out how the fiftieth anniversary of the war was marked by a rush of publications and performances, stimulating new public interest in the experience of life on the battlefield and the home front.[16] These included Theatre Workshop's *Oh What a Lovely War* (1963), which was followed by the film in 1969, A.J.P. Taylor's *The First World War: an illustrated History* (1963), new editions of war poetry, and Arthur Marwick's book, *The Deluge,* which appeared in 1967. With regard to women's experiences it is Marwick's work that is critical, and there is no doubt about his continuing conviction that they benefited from the war. This was reiterated in the introduction to *War, Peace and Social Change in the Twentieth Century* (1996):

> Can it be possible that wars (which, after all, are in their very nature increasingly destructive and negative) touch off processes which really do bring about social change?[17]

This appears to be a rhetorical question, given the Open University courses and books Professor Marwick's initial thesis has spawned.[18] Although some recent social and feminist historians have dismissed the Marwick *oeuvre,* and Joan Scott is by no means the only one to find the whole idea of seeking to prove or disprove 'watersheds' counter-productive, it is nevertheless the case that the arguments popularised by Marwick have been enormously influential. There are multiple copies of his books in every university in the United Kingdom, as well as many public libraries. Inspite of Scott's warnings, he is still frequently cited by feminist or cultural historians, often as the sole source for claims regarding women's changed lives. For example, Margaret Higgonnet, in 'Not so quiet in no-woman's land,' simply says, 'See Arthur Marwick, *Women at War, 1914–18,* for the British situation', and Susan Kingsley Kent, *Making Peace: the Reconstruction of Gender in Interwar Britain,* also refers to his work – in a way which is discussed at greater length later in this chapter.[19] He is widely cited on First World War web sites and is one of the few social historians referenced by many military historians. Thus Brian Bond's recently updated book, *War and Society 1870–1970,* refers the reader only to Marwick for information on women and the homefront, even though there are now many other texts he could have mentioned.[20]

However, the idea of attempting to measure the impact of the war on social, economic and cultural life began long before the 1960s, and was not invented by Arthur Marwick. Although there is no real reason why discussion of 'social change' should focus on women in particular, their situation has often been used as a kind of marker of 'progress' (or lack of it) by writers past and present.[21]

For any one considering arguments about women's role during the war, it is important to bear in mind the fact that wide-ranging discussions about women's work and its impact on society had emerged in England by the mid-nineteenth century, and were mature and detailed by the outbreak of war. It was accepted that women's work influenced their social status, affected their relations with men at home as well as the workplace, and influenced their fitness (moral and physical) for motherhood. The nature of the work open to them, their wages, their living conditions, their behaviour – all were seen as a major social and economic *issue*. Evidence was gathered and discussed by trade unionists, Factory Inspectors, feminists, select committees and social commentators like Charles Booth and Seebohm Rowntree. As women moved into 'new' trades soon after the beginning of the war they became the subject of a fresh wave of government reports, investigations and newspaper articles – but many of these were written with a full awareness of the long-running debates on pay, protective legislation, mothers' pensions, and so on. Women – particularly those involved in 'men's work' – were photographed, interviewed, analysed, praised or criticised at length, but this interest was by no means new. Together, these successive phases of intensive investigation have given us a detailed record of women's work in particular industries over many decades, and reflect a wide range of political agendas and social attitudes.[22]

When Marwick sought descriptions of women's new work, or opinions about its impact, these were therefore easy to find. The source material, both visual and textual, is rich; it comes in many forms, and from all political persuasions. However, inevitably the most striking comments about women's wartime role are from highly biased individuals or organisations. They tend to reflect the views of people who either sought change or dreaded it, and who were voluble in their expression of hope or anxiety. These included feminists, journalists, trade unionists and social investigators. The opinions of those who were uncertain, doubtful, uninterested, or merely neutral, are often far less visible in reports whose authors were often *looking* for differences or problems. Furthermore, it was hardly surprising that there was considerable speculation about women's future role and the possibility of drastic change during 1916 to 1918, while the nation was experiencing exceptional wartime conditions, but such speculation needs to be compared with postwar commentaries. What did similar writers have to say about the impact of war a few years later, in 1925 or 1935? Professor Marwick does not tell us. Nor do the others who claim the war was the beginning of a new social order.

What is certain, however, is that when Arthur Marwick talked about the war's positive impact on women, he revived a debate which began during the war itself, and one which will continue to be of interest to many: discussion of social/economic indicators and the effects of war on pay or opportunity cannot simply be dismissed as irrelevant, as Joan Scott may be seen as suggesting. For those tracing the historiography of women and war it is also significant that Marwick did do much to revive interest in women's wartime role, at a time when the work of many labour historians of the 1960s and 1970s was almost completely lacking in any analysis of women's part in wartime production. In books by many of his contemporaries women are usually invisible, or described as a problem – which of course reflected the fact that their labour had been viewed as problematic by many trade unions during the war. Far more research has yet to be done on women in industry and men's wartime anxieties about their labour. There are interesting connections and comparisons to be made with attitudes to women workers in other European nations during the war, where they were often seen as unreliable, emotional creatures, difficult to organise into the standard labour organisations. Concern about whether they would join unions (even though many such organisations were not open to women) were ironically accompanied by the suspicion that they were liable to strike at the drop of a hat – that they had no respect for any tacit understanding between capital and labour which had built up over the years. This reputation was enhanced by their leading role in rent strikes, food protests and riots, from 1917 onwards, in Britain, Germany, Italy, France and Russia.[23] A revealing comment comes from Marc Ferro, in his 1973 book, *The Great War,* which has a general European perspective:

> The working class, at first helped by the campaign for full employment, was in fact handicapped by the influx of new types of worker, prisoners of war, foreigners, and particularly women and adolescents.[24]

It does appear from this that 'the working class' was made up of white males over the age of 21.[25] Lest one become too attached to the idea that Marwick was an early radical in his approach to women's history, however, it is worth quoting from one paragraph which reveals something of his general attitude to women and the nature of 'progress'. He writes that higher wages led to increased spending on clothes and make-up:

> The new pride in personal appearance, especially among a class of women who had formerly become ill-kempt sluts by their mid-twenties, if indeed they had ever been anything else, was one of the pleasantest by-products of the new female self-confidence remarked upon by the Chief Factory Inspector.[26]

The style of this paragraph is a clue to the fact that Marwick's willingness to accept the importance of women as war workers nevertheless disguises an inherently conservative agenda. For, he writes,

> If it really was the war that brought votes for women, was suffragette violence then irrelevant, or perhaps even harmful to women's cause? Does not the way in which many of the most militant suffragette leaders took up an extremely militaristic, and even bloodthirsty stance during the war suggest that it was possibly something odd in their psychology which led them into the militant suffragette campaign in the first place?[27]

He goes on to tell us that 'the absolutely central phenomenon in the changing position of women was their movement into new jobs'.[28] And thus we return to one of the critical tenets of the war-as-watershed approach: the idea that war produced (good) social change (in whatever form, to whatever extent) tends to undermine any discussion of the effectiveness of personal and collective efforts to achieve political rights or economic equality for women, both before and after 1914. As Joan Scott warns us in her outline description of watersheds: good behaviour 'was often the politicians' explanation of why they extended the right to vote to women (a far better justification in their eyes than appearing to give in to the militant tactics of the suffragists).'[29] Here we see the early origins of another part of the watershed story: many of us may now be convinced by research that shows us that the extension of suffrage has little to do with war, but claims were made at the time to the contrary – the war was a convenient excuse for MPs who changed their minds.

I have no wish to engage here with the question of whether the war instituted long-term, permanent gains for women in general in Britain. This is a complex area which requires careful analysis based on detailed evidence, and an understanding of what may or may not be meant by 'progress'. My views of workingclass women's reception into industry, and of the war's more general effects on the way they were perceived by unions and employers, have been aired elsewhere.[30] The problem, as I see it, is that the whole neatly packaged idea of the war as 'a watershed' for women, as reiterated by Professor Marwick, has become embedded in public consciousness. It has left us with a succession of writers who have failed to define 'progress', let alone set women's lives in the context of debates to do with class, age, region, developments in industry, health, insurance and so on.[31] This has duly separated the experience of women in 1914–1918 from the rest of twentieth century history, leading to neglect of all other influences, good and bad, on women's lives during the first few decades of the century. The concept of the war as a watershed has become a cliché, and one which has been accepted unthinkingly by many historians who should know better. The fact that women's history is not their area of expertise does not excuse the sloppy repetition of generalisations, and the re-cycling of material which is merely anecdotal – particularly when vague assumptions about women's changing role are then used to bolster larger arguments about the war in general, and its apparent impact on 'the twentieth century'. No one expects all writers on the war to have a detailed knowledge of women's work, industrial status and social environment during the years 1914 to 1918 – though arguably a rather broader knowledge of gender issues per se might be helpful – but one might hope for a more careful use of secondary sources, and a higher level of debate. Consider the work of Bernadotte Schmitt and Harold Vedeler, and their view of the war's impact as described in *The World in the Crucible*. This includes a couple of pages on 'women' in Europe, near the end of the book. The fact that their 'changing' lives can be summed up in these few paragraphs gives the reader the impression that they are of little importance, and that they are only included to offer a little light relief in the midst of a serious text on war. Readers are told that women were 'emancipated' by the war, that middle and upperclass women were liberated 'from economic dependence on their families' and workingclass women from 'the servitude of domestic work'. Schmitt and Vedeler go on to write that:

> The social behaviour and dress of women altered concomitantly with these changes of status. Women and girls frequented the night clubs that had sprung up during the war, and single women dined in restaurants without escorts. Women began to smoke in public, and their drinking increased. They took up the free use of cosmetics, the bobbing of hair, and the wearing of short skirts or slacks and uniforms at work. Their new social freedom encouraged freer sexual relations, the consequences of increasing promiscuity and illegitimacy.[32]

This picture of Europe's women frittering away their time in nightclubs might be laughable were it not found in an apparently serious book, and it is certainly drawn in part from Marwick's descriptions in *The Deluge*. There were few expensive restaurants or nightclubs outside London, Paris and Berlin (and one can be fairly certain that they were not filled with working class women) while the matter of women's 'promiscuity' is open to considerable debate, as Susan Grayzel discusses elsewhere in this book. But why allow these facts to spoil the picture of modern women wearing short skirts and smoking?

Here is a similar description from *The Rites of Spring*, by Modris Eksteins:

> On the home front, morality loosened it corsets and belts too. Prostitution increased strikingly. In Paris, of 3,907 girls arrested in 1914–15, over half were found to have venereal disease ... The growing independence of women, as they were brought into the labour force by the absence of men, meant that the moral constraints of the home and paternal authority slackened. More women now had their own lodgings in which to entertain their men friends. If the assault on the fixed moral code was well under way before 1914, the war acted like a battering ram.[33]

This book is frequently cited – although its use of primary sources is limited – and will continue to be referred to by the next generation of writers, unless they can be persuaded to look more critically at its claims.[34] Apparent 'facts' about women and war acquire status, and an increasing respectability, as they are told and retold.[35]

Why does the watershed approach to women and the war remain so popular? It is certainly a 'good story' in the tabloid newspaper sense, involving as it does both sex and death, and a charitable view might be that it is also a story which seems to satisfy a certain need to find a more uplifting side to the conflict. This acts as a balance to the misery, and the idea that 'progress' of some kind occurred makes the war itself seem more tolerable. It is also neat and tidy: the war was a great event, and it must therefore have had an enormous impact on everything. Perhaps the war was even 'necessary' to bring about improvements for women? However, the concept of emerging sexual freedom is particularly important in these texts, and is closely connected with the popular assumption that the war helped create 'modern' society – whatever this means. (To quote Bernard Bergonzi, 'the Great War swept away the remnants of Victorian order, and brought into existence what is, more or less, the world we have had to inhabit ever since.')[36] But such a simplistic view of 'social change', or 'progress', ill-defined as these phrases are, means that wartime anxieties about promiscuity and sexuality are doubly neglected by many of these authors. Anxiety about sexual 'freedom' is often dismissed as an amusing foible of the past, and the preserve of the elderly or repressed – the subtext being that we, the liberated people of 'the present' are entitled to snigger a little about our ancestors' concern over 'loosened corsets and belts', to use Ekstein's flippant phrase. But casual dismissal of such anxiety means a failure to analyse its roots. We need to know whether adultery, sex outside marriage, and illegitimacy really increased during the war, and if it did not, we need to look at why people felt that it did. We need to acknowledge the importance of any rise in sexually transmitted diseases to a world before antibiotics, and see how this influenced views of women. We need to look at attitudes to sexual relations before and after the war as well. In too many books we also see the highly dubious juxtaposition of women's new work, their alleged 'sexual freedom', and prostitution. Is growth in prostitution really a marker of progress or freedom? Many would argue the opposite, given its usual connection with low wages and poor job opportunities for women. Did prostitution really increase at all? This too is a complex area, and one through which the historian should tread carefully.[37] Wartime, or postwar, claims that women's 'new' jobs were the cause of profound changes in sexual behaviour need to be treated with extreme caution, as various feminist historians have pointed out.[38] Once again it is clear that the occasional quote from an outraged commentator, or a snippet from a newspaper, should only be viewed as evidence of *opinion*, not used as proof of either continuity or change.

It is unfortunate that many writers about the war in general fail to appreciate the existence of debates about women's role at home and work throughout the nineteenth century, and across all industrialised nations. The particular, detailed, studies of women's labour, wages and poverty, which emerged in Britain in the decades preceding the war, and which I have already mentioned, may be the preserve of the specialist, but general anxieties about women working in factories, or mines, or in heavy industry were expressed over and over again, particularly at times of economic upheaval. Ironically, women were often viewed as the moral guardians of the family (and their husband's behaviour) and yet it was also feared that they could be corrupted by working conditions outside the home. Comparisons across time are therefore useful, and might lead to a less isolationist approach to the years between 1914 and 1918. Similar questions have been discussed constructively by many historians of the eighteenth and nineteenth centuries, whose work could usefully be consulted by those who talk of exceptional wartime attitudes or behaviour.

For a fine *pessimistic* view of 1914–18 as a watershed, at once a contrast to the optimistic picture, yet clearly related in its preoccupations, one might turn to Fischer and Dubois's paranoid classic, *Sexual Life During the World War* (published in 1937). They write that their book will show how:

> ... the primitive, bestial instincts that lie dormant in civilized man exploded in an almost universal orgy of sexual license and debauchery; how the war enthusiasm of the first weeks suddenly broke down the established concepts of sexual morality; how, as the war proceeded, millions of men, deprived of their normal sexual partners, resorted to the most degrading kind of prostitution with official sanction and under official supervision, while women on the 'home front' were driven by sexual hunger to adultery and worse; how sexual perversions, from homosexuality and Lesbian love to the most horrible manifestations of sadism developed and spread through the length and breadth of Europe; how, while the guns thundered and the screams of mutilated and dying men filled the air at the various war fronts, men and women in the big cities of Europe, maddened by the strain of war and sex starvation, indulged in degrading sexual orgies under the influence of drink and drugs; and how, finally, venereal disease increased a hundredfold in all the belligerent countries ...[39]

One's first thought is that this is merely ludicrous exaggeration, but the work merits closer attention. Once again, we see the troubling and thoughtless use of the word 'women' to encompass the entire female sex (in this case, throughout Europe!). About whom did Fischer and Dubois believe they were writing? What did these hysterical claims have to do with the lives of peasant farmers in Italy, transport workers in Britain, or refugees in northern France? Misogyny and sarcasm underlie much of the book. For example, they write of suddenly 'enthusiastic' bright eyed women, who urged their men to fight, adding snidely:

> ... it is undoubtedly true that in the case of poor wives and mothers, the allowances they received from the respective governments sometimes constituted an element in the fortitude with which they allowed or encouraged their men to go to war, while the pensions they received after their men-folk had fallen on the 'field of honour' were undoubtedly a more or less conscious factor in the resignation with which they bore their bereavement. [40]

The implications of this book are clear: all women were aroused by war, ruthless in their pursuit of sex, and cared more for money than for the men they dispatched to the trenches, although the sources for any of these claims are scant. However, the book also illustrates how many of those who talk of 'watersheds' for women hover between praise/amusement and criticism/contempt. While the same stories of shorter skirts, bobbed hair, drinking in pubs and higher wages might appear again and again, interpretation of this as 'good' or 'bad' will depend on the agenda of the writer.

Generalisations about women's sexuality and propriety are also rife in those books which relegate them, en masse, to the fringes of some grand theory. Paul Fussell, whose book, *The Great War and Modern Memory*, contains the barest mention of women as participants, nevertheless finds space to comment on the gender balance of postwar England, and inform us that:

> After the war, women dramatically outnumbered men, and a common sight in the thirties – to be seen, for some reason, especially on railway trains – was the standard middle-aged Lesbian couple in tweeds, who had come together as girls after each had lost a fiancé, lover or husband.[41]

The heterosexist assumption that lesbians were merely women who could not find men is simultaneously amusing and disturbing. One feels that this paragraph is supposed to be an aside, in contrast to the serious main text (about men), but also that Fussell is unwittingly recycling some of the wartime prejudices about single women, and particularly those who wore uniform, or 'mannish' clothes. These anxieties too are a rich area for research, but Fussell's comments are worryingly superficial.[42] (However, as it is also the case that he thinks there is something amusingly innocent about an England whose inhabitants used the word 'intercourse' without sexual connotation, we may assume that his own preoccupations strongly colour his view of the early twentieth century.)[43]

Although nearly all the books I have discussed so far vary slightly in their conclusions about the 'good/bad' nature of social change, there are intriguing similarities. Women – usually referred to as a coherent single group – may be seen as light relief, as decorative, as problems, as symbols, but they are hardly ever part of the main narrative of war. After thirty years of women's history, one might expect that younger writers would have a more sophisticated view of women and war – but all too often in 'serious' books they are still confined to a handful of paragraphs. For example, Niall Ferguson claims, in *The Pity of War*, to offer a new picture of the conflict, its causes, and course. This is not a general social history, but it does include a great deal of material about life in the combatant nations, the state of industry, political aspirations, and the attitudes of soldiers and civilians. In 462 pages, there are just three references to 'women', which amount to about one page in total. How are they perceived by Ferguson? Women in the labour force (of France, Germany and Britain together) merit a few paragraphs, and also an intriguing footnote, which states that:

> In many ways, the whole issue of dilution was overdone. Not many women ended up in the engineering industry; mostly they went into the service sector, taking the places of clerks.[44]

The idea that dilution (the substitution of unskilled labour for fully-skilled craftsmen on particular parts of complex industrial work) was unproblematic would certainly have surprised governments and trade unions of the day, and intrigued the many historians – of various nations – who have since tried to unravel the complexity of wartime employer/labour relations! So, it is clear that Niall Ferguson is not a proponent of the theory that war was a 'watershed for women': he has no interest at all in their economic role or its possible social consequences. His other references to women are equally brief, but provocative. When considering the possible reasons for men volunteering Ferguson suggests an important factor may have been 'Female Pressure', and to support this claim he reports that women handed out white feathers to men not in uniform. He neither discusses this in depth, nor cites the work of other writers on the subject.[45] Finally, in his section on 'The Death Instinct: why men fought', Ferguson informs us that 'those women who got close to the action enjoyed it too', citing the opinions of May Sinclair, Vera Brittain, Violetta Thurston and Radclyffe Hall. This is a painfully simplified and misleading claim.[46] Few people would venture to suggest, for example, that Vera Brittain's final verdict was that she 'enjoyed' the war.

In these few scattered sentences, however, Ferguson has summed up his own view of women's wartime role: they moved into some new jobs, but they made little impact on industry; many were pro-war and encouraged men to join up; and some enjoyed their war experiences. But Ferguson's sources for these claims are intriguing: he cites not Arthur Marwick, and his social change data, but Sandra Gilbert, a recent feminist literary historian. This single, but significant, feminist reference has, alas, done nothing to make Ferguson incorporate women into his mainstream arguments.[47] They are still in a ghetto. However, his citation does indicate the growing importance of a whole new area of writing into which the non-specialist might dip a toe, and cull a few striking ideas about women – an area which at first sight seems very different from the world of Marwick. Which leads me to the work of Sandra Gilbert herself, and current writings about 'war and gender'.

Watershed 2: War and Gender

The rise of feminist, women's and 'gender' history over the past twenty years should have led to a more subtle and detailed approach to women, their place in society, and their relations with men in books about the war. Although there are differences between these three strands of history, as implied by their nomenclature, their practitioners all share a willingness to move women to centre stage. Furthermore, their approach to history includes an implicit acceptance of the fact that experiences and attitudes are influenced not simply by gender, but by age, race, class and geography. In this field too, wars have often been seen as key periods for debate about women and their role in society. A key text of gender history is *Behind the Lines*, a collection of essays on both world wars, which is now widely known. In the Introduction, the editors write:

> As a first step, war must be understood as a *gendering* activity, one that ritually marks the gender of all members of a society, whether or not they are combatants. The implications of war for women and men are, then, linked in symbolic as well as social and economic systems. During total war, the discourse of militarism, with its stress on 'masculine' qualities, permeates the whole fabric of society, touching both women and men. In doing so, it draws upon pre-existing definitions of gender at the same time as it restructures gender relations. When peace comes, messages of reintegration are expressed within a rhetoric of gender that establishes the postwar social assignments of men and women. [48]

This sums up the approach of a number of recent feminist writers to women and the Great War.

Unfortunately, when one looks closely at the arguments articulated in particular books an immediate problem emerges – namely the lack of rigour with which the vocabulary of 'gender' is used. Words such as 'feminising', 'masculinising', 'maternalist', 'emasculating' and 'masculinities' are bandied about in a cavalier manner, although these terms are loaded with existing meaning, and have been used and misused by psychiatrists, sociologists, psychologists and lay people alike for a considerable time. They are not neutral. Yet in many of these texts they appear without definition or analysis. Furthermore, for every writer who talks of the 'feminising' or 'emasculating' impact of the war on men – and the two are not the same – there is another who refers to its 're-masculinising' or sexually polarising effect.[49] Even Billie Melman, in her otherwise excellent introduction to the collected essays of *Borderlines*, succumbs to the following, when writing about Pat Barker's novel, *Regeneration:*

> In Rivers' and Prior's neurotic world the trench is the domesticated habitat of feminized soldiers, and the streets and factories of Britain's cities a masculinized women's territory.[50]

Leaving aside any discussion of the wisdom of using recent fiction as a source, I have to query the implicit generalisations, and suggest that the idea that soldiers were 'feminized' (in what way?) is unexplored, while the claim that the streets of Britain were suddenly 'women's territory' – a concept culled from various literary historians – is both disturbing and unsubstantiated. Similarly, Margaret Higonnet and Patrice L.-R. Higonnet, in their essay 'The Double Helix', rightly draw our attention to the shortcomings of traditional 'social change' texts, and yet simultaneously contribute to the confusion about the war's possible impact on gender roles. They write:

> As sexual acts become political, war itself is eroticized. To some extent it is homoerotic. World War I addressed a 'crisis of masculinity' in France, Ger-

many, Britain; and in the latter case it clearly enhanced the male bonding fostered by the public school system.[51]

What exactly does this *mean*? What 'crisis in masculinity'? How did the war 'address' it? Was it 'solved' by war? Perhaps so, as they go on to write that: 'Anthropologists note that demobilization threatens to feminize the male population' which suggests to me that men must have been 'masculinised' by their front line experience.[52] Is this not in direct contradiction to Melman's remark about 'feminised' soldiers in the trenches? But one seeks further elucidation in vain, for the Higonnets' sources for these claims are the ubiquitous Eric Leed and Paul Fussell, neither of whom define their terminology, nor use a wide range of sources as evidence.

One of the key texts which seems to have influenced Melman (and many others) is Sandra Gilbert's essay, 'Soldier's Heart: Literary Men, Literary Women, and the Great War', which has been published in a variety of different forms.[53] It is to this essay that Niall Ferguson refers in *The Pity of War*. Gilbert is unremittingly cheerful about the impact of war on women in Britain. She maintains that while men were being destroyed by the war (becoming 'no-men', 'nobodies', '*not* men' or '*un*men'), women's star was rising:

> ... as young men became increasingly alienated from their prewar selves, increasingly immured in the muck and blood of no man's land, increasingly abandoned by the civilization of which they had ostensibly been heirs, women seemed to become, as if by some uncanny swing of history's pendulum, ever more powerful. As nurses, as mistresses, as munitions workers, bus drivers, or soldiers in the 'land army', even as wives and mothers, these formerly subservient creatures began to loom malevolently larger ...[54]

Women thus gained access to economic and sexual power, to professions and to politics (in the form of 'the vote') while they literally replaced men in jobs across the nation – though Gilbert does not go on to analyse what 'power' a nurse, or a mistress or a mother might actually have had. Her essay is accompanied by numerous photos of women workers – healthy, happy, attractive – from the Imperial War Museum collection, which are reproduced without commentary or title, and with no apparent awareness of the fact that these can (or should) be viewed as wartime propaganda. Furthermore, although many of them show working class women, the quotations about wartime life used in the text are uniformly from literary women: ordinary workers' opinions of war or work do not appear.[55] Also, I am particularly dubious about Gilbert's use of one photo of injured men, whose legs have been amputated. What point does this illustrate? Again there is no caption. Is Gilbert, like some other cultural historians, accepting the idea that such injury represented 'emasculation'?[56] We are not told. Certainly Gilbert's view of men's wartime experience is dominated by the 'lost generation' model with which I began this chapter.

Gilbert goes on to write about the 'erotic release' for women caused by war, and quotes Eric Leed, who writes that:

Women in particular 'reacted to the war experience with a powerful increase in libido,' even though this libido attached itself to the very symbols signifying the uniformization of roles: stripes on officer's [sic] trousers ... the sound of marching boots, batons, pistols, and so on.'[57]

The astute reader may notice that within this paragraph from Leed there lies another, unattributed, quotation on the subject of erotic symbols. This is, in fact, from Hirschfeld's *Sexual Life of the World War*,[58] although Leed admits he is an unreliable source – a detail not relayed to us by Gilbert. Her sources begin to seem depressingly familiar, and it comes as no surprise that the next quotation is from Arthur Marwick, who tells us in his inimitable style that the war helped 'spread promiscuity upwards and birth-control downwards'.[59] We are back in the land of the same old secondary sources – even though one might expect a feminist literary historian to look more critically at the attitudes of Hirschfeld, Marwick and David Mitchell, whose work she also cites frequently.[60] Unfortunately, her selective quotations, in tandem with the numerous picturesque images of cheerful women workers, must leave many readers unsurprised by her claim that men came to hate women, the true beneficiaries of war. A number of other literary historians, familiar with the deeply painful work of bereaved women writers (who are ignored by Gilbert), have distanced themselves from her approach. She is roundly criticised by Claire Tylee, for example, in 'Maleness Run Riot: the Great War and Women's Resistance to Militarism'[61], and by several of the contributors to Raitt and Tate's *Women's Fiction and the Great War*. Jane Marcus, too, in her contribution to *Arms and The Woman*, is scathing about Gilbert 'searching texts for evidence to support the argument, rather than letting the history emerge with as much force as the literature.'[62] As it is, Gilbert repeats the familiar story of women's war work leading to sexual liberation, basing her theories on secondary sources and the opinions of a narrow range of well-known literary figures. Most social historians would balk at the poor range of sources used.[63]

Gilbert is, however, by no means the only woman writer to adopt the watershed/sex-war approach. Other books are becoming part of a new orthodoxy about the war and gender, and need critical consideration. Amongst these is Susan Kingsley Kent's *Making Peace: the Reconstruction of Gender in Interwar Britain*, which is now widely referred to as a reliable description of the war's impact on British feminism. Kent's basic thesis appears to be that prewar feminists had believed that the sexes could work together in a complementary fashion, but after the war 'new feminists' decided instead to support the 'separate spheres' approach.[64] The change in attitude was due, according to Kent, to the contrasting wartime experiences of key representatives from each camp. Those like

Vera Brittain, who nursed frontline troops, maintained their faith in the idea of the sexes working together. Others were gripped by the fear of monstrous uncontrollable male violence, and retreated from an egalitarian approach, concentrating on a separate agenda for women, including campaigns for the endowment of motherhood.

There are two problems with this conclusion. The first is that Kent seems to imply that feminism before the war was a single coherent movement, with one dominant view of sexual and social relationships, and that this was replaced by a similarly organised group of women after 1918. There is no room in this picture for analysis of all the different strands of feminism which existed before and after the war. The second problem is that she appears to apportion *blame* for this shift in attitude, and accuses the 'new feminists' of holding opinions which were thus 'virtually indistinguishable from those of the anti-feminists'.[65] She writes sternly that '"New" feminism failed to challenge, and in fact contributed to, a reconstruction of gender that circumscribed the roles, activities and possibilities of women'.[66] Susan Pedersen, another historian of the war and its aftermath, comments wryly on this approach:

> The tone of much of this work is often harshly critical of new feminists, who are often seen as betraying the cause of equality to accept a restricted and biologically defined 'place'. Yet the implication of this work – that feminists would have accomplished more had they adhered to a strictly 'egalitarian' program in the post-war period – is certainly open to question. If we examine feminist campaigns not for their adherence to some pre-defined orthodoxy, but rather within the political context of the time, the overwhelming constraints on all feminist activity become more apparent.[67]

Yet Kent's criticism of 1920s feminists is all the more confusing given her claim, in an essay entitled 'Love and Death', that 'women' (*all* women in Britain?) had been permanently damaged by the war, and were thus left incapable of stepping outside gender boundaries:

> ... because many of the legal barriers barring women from public life were being dismantled [in the 1920s], the institutional practices enforcing separate spheres came to be replaced by psychological ones. The power of pychologized separate spheres, the extent of the psychic and linguistic internalization of military occupation by the women of Britain, insured that all the parliamentary reforms in the world would be of little avail to those seeking equality with men.[68]

It could be asked, therefore, whether it is fair to blame feminist leaders for their own internalised oppression as she does in her own book?

However, inspite of this dichotomy it is clear that Kent views the war as a watershed – a bad one – in social/sexual relations, and that her verdict is now widely accepted as a valid interpretation of events. The problem is that just as many generalist historians have quoted little pieces of Marwick or Mitchell – out of context – to bolster their theories of dramatic social change, so some writers of women's history now quote little bits of Kent to support their claim that the war had a seriously negative effect on gender relations. For example, Bonnie Smith, in *Changing Lives* (a history of women in Western Europe) seeks to extrapolate arguments from Kent, Elaine Showalter and various postmodernist writers, and combine them in a single chapter on European women and the Great War. She begins:

> The idea of the traditional home may have faded a bit before 1914, but war made it vivid again. Men were doing their duty, being manly ... War made the feelings of men and women toward one another clear again. Across the great divide that split home from battlefield – an extreme version of separate spheres – societies resurrected gender harmony.[69]

Thirty pages later, in a section headed 'Restoring Gender Order', Smith sums up the effects of war on men and women:

> Although the war had started out in a female return to the home and initial acts of republican motherhood, and although in contrast men had chivalrously taken up arms to protect them, gender definitions had weakened as the war progressed. Women filled men's jobs, while men had spectacular trouble winning battles. Men returned home from war maimed, shell-shocked and hysterical – like women.[70]

Finally, she ends the chapter:

> World War I marked the start of an era in which machines and technology undermined that most sacrosanct of Western values – the human individual. Thus, all the assumptions on which women's social analysis rested fell by the wayside as war and revolution fundamentally weakened eighteenth century principles. Feminists had to regroup over the next half century, adjusting their efforts and their understanding of women's experience in the modern world.[71]

In this fashion some recent striking theories on war and gender percolate into the general (feminist) history book: the result is a new set of generalisations and overarching conclusions.

Kent's work on Britain is often referred to in tandem with Mary Louise Robert's book on France, *Civilization without Sexes*. One of the intriguing features of this style of cultural/gender history is an apparent reluctance to engage with the work of social historians. Roberts, like Kent, criticises their mundane concerns. She writes:

> Despite their opposing views concerning war's impact, these historians all evaluate change in women's lives in similar terms as the degree of advancement in a particular era towards the 'liberated' woman of today. Change is understood in contemporary feminist terms, that is, in employment opportunities, wage scale, legal status, and sexual freedom.[72]

This, she claims, 'short circuits' any attempt to discuss the way 'contemporaries' – writers of the time – tried to look at women's lives. Yet these social/economic indicators were precisely those used by commentators before, during and after the war, when they sought evidence of change in women's lives, or wondered about the war's impact on the family or on women's role in labour market. James McMillan discusses Roberts' work elsewhere in this volume, but here I would merely like to point out certain similarities with Kent's approach. While dismissing social historians, both nevertheless lean heavily on some outdated or misleading secondary works of social history which themselves use few primary sources. For example, Roberts frequently refers to John Williams' 1972 book, *The Home Fronts*, which has long since been superseded by more scholarly work on wartime life in Britain, France and Germany.[73] And like Kent she fails to look back at prewar writings on women, or the wide-ranging discussions about their work and its impact on the family, although this is necessary if one is trying to trace changes in attitude. The fact that she is interested in 'cultural construction' (her words) rather than 'reality' does not mean that the former can be discussed without regard to the latter. There is a world of difference between a society in which soldiers' wives really *are* sleeping with enemy aliens or African soldiers, and one in which paranoid husbands worry that they might. Even Roberts herself, while discussing sexual morality, allows herself to wonder what had 'really' happened to sexual behaviour during the war, in contrast to what people *thought* had happened.[74] Other recent writers – cultural and social historians alike – have been considerably more cautious in their conclusions when writing about what the war did to the lives of women in France, and significantly have used a far wider range of source material.[75]

There is ostensibly little in common between the writer who places women at the heart of the narrative and one who grudgingly allows them a few pages. However, I am struck by the similarities between many of the works I have mentioned, inspite of their various pedigrees. They are characterised by an overdependence on a very narrow range of sources (often secondary), and their failure to view the war as part of a longer timespan. There is an apparent desire to find *change*, or *difference*, rather than seek signs of continuity. Their authors display a distinct reluctance to utilise economic or social statistics,[76] or to consider other forces of social and industrial change. And there is often an enthusiasm for peppering the text with fragmentary quotations to lend veracity to the opinion of the author that the war was either good or bad for women, regardless of the context of these quotations, or the agenda of the original speaker.[77] However, one of the most serious problems is the way in which women are usually described as a generic group, regardless of age, class or nationality, leaving one with the feeling that many feminist writers too have failed to react to the call for a new approach to women, as mooted by Higonnet et al. in their introduction to *Behind the Lines*, where they rightly urge us to recognise the diversity of wartime life, and the 'need to hear the polyphony of historical experience, especially that of women'.[78] They also note that an obsession with 'the impact' of war on women makes them appear to be passive victims, rather than active agents – and, I would add, as mere symbols rather than individuals, whether they are seen as representative of the modern era, or participants in a new 'sex war'. Those marginalised by the current focus would include older women, wives of servicemen, workers in the traditional female industries, professional nurses and doctors, rural women, economic migrants to England from Scotland, Wales and Ireland, women injured by their war work, and even, ironically, the wives, mothers and daughters left bereaved, or caring for wounded men. It is disturbing how little has yet been written about many of these groups.[79]

Other Ways

It may seem from my criticisms so far that all writing on women and the war is in a sad state. Nothing could be further from the truth. The last ten years have seen the publication of monographs, and collections of essays which take a more comparative approach to the war and its place in the lives of early twentieth century women. National differences, class, and the contrast between urban and rural wartime life, are all seen as having an effect on their experiences.[80]

But detail as well as breadth are required, and an essay by Nicoletta Gullace, 'White Feathers and Wounded men: Female Patriotism and the memory of the Great War', is an excellent example of what analysis of some classic 'war stories' can reveal.[81] Reports that women handed out white feathers (symbolising cowardice) to men not in uniform, appear in countless descriptions of the war.[82] Gullace investigates the campaign and its origins, but also considers the way it has been treated by historians since. While many writers have been content to repeat the same old stories (based a limited number of literary sources) recent feminist historians too have neglected the campaign. Gullace suggests that 'patriotic' or 'pro-war' women have been seen as less attractive characters by feminists, who have often sympathised with more radical groups, including the abortive women's peace movement. The fact that the campaign is deemed unpleasant even influenced the researchers for the BBC's 1964 *Great War* series. The wording of their advertisement calling for potential interviewees implied that there were probably few who would admit to handing out white feathers, and in view of this it was perhaps surprising that *any* women were prepared to appear on camera to talk about their actions.[83] Gullace proceeds to look at what women themselves felt about their activities, how men reacted, how this was reported in the press and, critically, how this campaign interacted with official propaganda, which urged women to recruit their menfolk to war. Condemned by many commentators as selfish and militaristic, and mocked by the press when they seemed to hand feathers primarily to wounded soldiers in civilian clothes, or war heroes on leave, many of the women who took part felt –

at the time – that they were doing their duty.[84] It is clear that there is far more to this story than many recent writers appreciate.

When Niall Ferguson refers, in *The Pity of War*, to 'female pressure' and the white feather campaign as reasons why men may have enlisted in 1914–15 he offers no supporting evidence for this claim. The rest of this section of his book is about government propaganda, not about women themselves, and his only reference in support of the claim that 'women' in general were pro-war is the Sandra Gilbert essay I have already discussed. Although Ferguson may not have read Gullace's 1998 essay before this own book went to press, the very absence of good supporting material for this tale should have given him pause for thought. Men's reasons for volunteering, and women's attitudes to their enlistment surely deserve a more subtle analysis.[85] Similarly, when Gilbert, in her own article, reports that 'erotic release' was a key part of women's wartime experience, she needs rather more evidence for this claim than Eric Leed's second hand quotations. Gullace's comments are a reminder: historians are writing stories, and they have the power to pick and choose in order to make their case. The truth is that with millions of words written by those who experienced the war, any writer can find suitable quotations to support any theory he or she cares to adopt. It is up to all us to step away from the well-trodden paths and reconsider familiar legends. It may be difficult for historians to undermine the popular legend of women and the war, given the strange momentum such widely held 'truths' about national events tend to acquire, but it is not impossible. Writers like Ferguson, who produce work which is widely reviewed and read, have a critical role to play as the intermediaries between academic and popular history. We depend on them to take account of work done by colleagues who specialise in women's history, and write this into their own, more 'accessible' volumes. In the Introduction to this book, I have suggested that a more modest and less pretentious approach to 1914–18 in general would be to the benefit of all aspects of the war's history. This is true, above all, of writing about women, the complexity and variety of whose lives is ignored by so many of the authors I have quoted.

We might take heed of the damning indictment of one 1920s commentator, who decided that books about the war were already 'a series of illusions of the past dressed up in the shape of the historians' own predilections.'[86] Eighty years later, can we do better than this?

Notes

1. Robert Wohl, *The Generation of 1914*, Weidenfield and Nicholson, 1980, 1.
2. Wohl, *The Generation of 1914*, 1.
3. Wohl, *The Generation of 1914*, 2.
4. J. B. Priestley, quoted by Claire Tylee, *The Great War and Women's Consciousness*, Macmillan, 1990, 217.
5. Ilana R. Bet-el, in her Introduction to *Conscripts: lost legions of the Great War*, Sutton Publishing, 1999, has suggested that early volunteers are viewed as more heroic figures

than the later conscripts, but I would disagree. The contemporary popular view is that all Great War soldiers were equally idealistic and betrayed.

6. Graham H. Greenwell, *An Infant in Arms: War letters of a Company Officer, 1914–1918*, Lovat Dickson & Thompson Ltd., 1935, ix.

7. Paul Fussell writes, for example, 'Out of the world of summer, 1914, marched a unique generation. It believed in Progress and Art and in no way doubted the benignity even of technology. The word *machine* was not yet invariably coupled with *gun*.' *The Great War and Modern Memory*, Oxford University Press, 1975, 24. Eric Leed, *No Man's Land*, Cambridge University Press, 1981. See also R. Stromberg, *Redemption by War*, Regents Press, 1982, and the introductory texts to many collections of British war poetry.

8. Sebastian Faulks, *Birdsong*, Vintage, 1994 and Pat Barker, *The Regeneration Trilogy*, Penguin, 1992–96, maintain the tradition.

9. Elizabeth Marsland, *The Nation's Cause: French, German and English Poetry of the First World War*, Routledge, 1991, 14–15. See also Martin Stephen, *The Price of Pity: Poetry, History and Myth in the Great War*, Leo Cooper, 1996, for a critique of the literary myth, including the cliché of 'the summer of 1914'. For an interesting outline of American historians' approach, see Henry May, 'The Rebellion of the Intellectuals, 1912–1917', in John M. Cooper jnr. (ed.), *The Causes and Consequences of World War I*, Quadrangle Books, 1972.

10. Douglas Jerrold, *The Lie about the War*, Faber and Faber, 1930, 12.

11. For example, see the following for army life: Tim Travers, *The Killing Ground: the British Army, the Western Front and the Emergence of Modern Warfare 1914–18*, Allen and Unwin, 1987; Tim Travers, *How the War was Won: Command and Technology in the British Army on the Western Front, 1917–1918*, Routledge, 1992; Tony Ashworth, *Trench Warfare 1914–18: the Live and Let Live System*, Macmillan, 1980. There are now an increasing number of books and articles on wounded soldiers, their medical treatment, and some of the emotional and social issues raised by the sudden influx of thousands of disabled young men. See Jeffrey S Reznick, 'Work Therapy and the disabled British Soldier in Great Britain in the First World War: the case of Shepherd's Bush Military Hospital, London' in David A Gerber (ed.), *Disabled Veterans in History*, University of Michigan Press, 2000; also Seth Koven, 'Remembering and Dismemberment: crippled children, wounded soldiers and the Great War in Great Britain' in *American Historical Review*, 99, October 1994. Joanna Bourke's *Dismembering the Male*, Reaktion Books, 1996 is interesting for both discussions on disability, and for its view of the lives of ordinary soldiers. Deborah Cohen, *The War Come Home*, University of California Press, 2001, offers a comparison of the experiences of disabled soldiers in Britain and Germany, and the political repercussions. (Her article, 'Will to Work: disabled veterans in Britain and Germany after the First World War' appears in Gerber, *Disabled Veterans in History*.) These can usefully be read alongside Robert Weldon Whalen's *Bitter Wounds: German Victims of the Great War, 1914–1939*, Cornell University Press, 1984.

12. Vera Brittain, *Testament of Youth*, Virago, 1978. Helen Zenna Smith (Evadne Price), *Not so Quiet …*, Virago, 1988, attempts to show women ambulance drivers as victims of war, with her novel echoing the form of Erich Maria Remarque's *All Quiet of the Western Front*. In a direct assault on the literary myth of the war experience, and any attempt to fit women into a similar pattern, Nosheen Khan explicitly rejects the idea that women's poetry changed from naive and optimistic in the early years to bitter and disillusioned as the war progressed. Khan, *Women's Poetry of the First World War*, Harvester, Wheatsheaf, 1988.

13. Yvonne M. Klein, *Beyond the Home Front: Women's Autobiographical Writing of two World Wars*, Macmillan, 1997, 1.

14. The key text is probably Martin Pugh, 'Politicians and the Woman's Vote 1914–1918', *History*, 59, 1974; see also Martin Pugh, *Women and the Women's Movement in Britain, 1914–1959*, Macmillan, 1992.

15. Joan Scott, 'Re-writing History', in M. R. Higonnet, J. Jenson, S. Michel and M. C. Weitz (eds), *Behind the Lines: Gender and the Two World Wars*, Yale University Press, 1987, 23–25.

16. Claire Tylee, *The Great War and Women's Consciousness*. See also Simon Featherstone, *War Poetry: an Introductory Reader*, Routledge, 1995, who suggests that radical young English teachers in schools influenced many in the 1960s; and see the Introduction to Brian Bond (ed.), *The First World War and British Military History*, Clarendon, 1991, and the chapter by Alex Danchev, 'Bunking and Debunking: the controversies of the 1960s' in the same volume.
17. Clive Emsley, Arthur Marwick and Wendy Simpson (eds), *War, Peace and Social Change in the Twentieth Century*, Open University Press, 1996, 2.
18. Arthur Marwick, *The Deluge: British Society and the First World War,* revised edition, Macmillan, 1991; Arthur Marwick, *War and Social Change in the Twentieth Century*, Macmillan, 1974; Arthur Marwick, *Women at War 1914–18*, Croom Helm, 1977; Arthur Marwick, *Total War and Social Change*, Macmillan, 1988.
19. M. Higgonnet, 'Not so quiet in no-woman's land', in Miriam Cooke and Angela Woollacott (eds), *Gendering Wartalk*, Princeton University Press, 1993, 223; Susan Kingsley Kent, *Making Peace: the Reconstruction of Gender in Interwar Britain*, Princeton University Press, 1993.
20. Brian Bond, *War and Society 1870–1970*, Sutton, 1998; see also E. R. Kantowicz, *The Rage of Nations*, Eerdmans, 1999.
21. For an excellent overview of writings on war, women and social change see Penny Summerfield, 'Women and War in the Twentieth-century' in June Purvis (ed.), *Women's History: Britain, 1850–1945*, UCL Press, 1995. See also Rex Pope's pamphlet, *War and Society in Britain 1899–1948*, Longman Seminar Studies in History, 1991, which contains an outline of many of the arguments.
22. For example, see S. Rowntree, *Poverty*, Macmillan, 1901; C. Black, *Married Women's Work*, Bell, 1915; C. Black, *Sweated Industry and the Minimum Wage*, Duckworth, 1907; F. Bell, *At the Works*, Arnold, 1907; C. Booth, *The Life and Labour of the People of London*, Vol. IV, Macmillan, 1893; J. Boucherette and H. Blackburn, *The Condition of Working Women and the Factory Acts*, Elliot Stock, 1896; E. Cadbury and G. Shann, *Sweating*, Headley Bros, 1907; B. L. Hutchins, *Women in Modern Industry*, Bell, 1915.
23. Peter Gatrell's piece in this book for more about women's role in disturbances in Russia. In Italy, they were often radical activists in war factories. As well as Simonetta Ortaggi's chapter in this volume, see Giovanna Procacci, 'A "latecomer" in War: the Case of Italy', in Frans Coetzee and Marilyn Shevin-Coetzee (eds), *Authority, Identity and the Social History of the Great War*, Berghahn, 1995. For France, see, for example, Laura Lee Downs, 'Women's Strikes and Egalitarianism', in Lenard R. Berlanstein (ed.), *Rethinking Labor History*, University of Illinois Press, 1993. For the United States, see Dana Frank, 'Housewives, socialists and the politics of food: the 1917 New York cost-of-living protests', in Kathryn Kish Sklar and Thomas Dublin (eds), *Women and Power in American History*, Volume II, Prentice Hall, 1991.
24. Marc Ferro, *The Great War*, Routledge and Kegan Paul, 1973, 170.
25. See, for example, B. Pribicevik, *The Shop Stewards' Movement and Workers' Control*, Blackwell, 1959; James Hinton, *The First Shop Stewards' Movement*, Allen and Unwin, 1973. More recent labour historians have not really redressed the balance. Bernard Waites, in *A Class Society at War: England 1914–18*, Berg, 1987, admits that he decided to leave out women, and that this is an omission. Gerry Rubin's *War, Law and Labour: the Munition Acts, State Regulation and the Unions, 1915–1921*, Clarendon Press, 1987, leaves women invisible in Glasgow's labour movement.
26. Marwick, *The Deluge*, 113. See also Marwick's claim that the 'women of Britain became a gigantic mutual admiration circle ...', 96. He also writes that young soldiers soon discovered that the ordinary prostitute was a 'pox-ridden, money grabbing harridan', 110.
27. Marwick, *Women at War*, 12.
28. Marwick, *Women at War*, 12.
29. Joan Scott, 'Re-writing History', 24.
30. Gail Braybon, *Women Workers in the First World War*, Croom Helm, 1981; Gail Braybon and Penny Summerfield, *Out of the Cage*, Pandora, 1987; 'Women and the War', in S.

Constantine, M. Kirby and M. Rose (eds), *The First World War in British History*, Edward Arnold, 1995.

31. 'Progress' is an amorphous concept; it fluctuates according to the politics of the commentator, and while it really requires careful discussion and comparison it often remains ill-defined. As we see in the examples I use here it is usually assumed that the modern reader knows what is meant by the idea. When talking about women's status it is clear that job opportunities and pay are important, but assumptions about the general impact of these, together with their effect on behaviour and expectations, often remain unsubstantiated.

32. B. E. Schmitt and H. Vedeler, *The World in the Crucible: 1914–1919*, Harper and Row, 1984, 461: note the similarity with Marwick, *The Deluge*, 151–153. See also H. Fischer and E. X. Dubois, *Sexual Life During the World War*, Francis Aldor, 1937, Chapter 5, for similar stories.

33. Modris Eksteins, *The Rites of Spring*, Peter Davidson, 1989, 225.

34. Susan Grayzel in this volume discusses the concern with drunkenness, prostitution and women's morality during the war, at greater length.

35. It is hard not to think of Tom Stoppard's character, Henry Carr, in his brilliant play on history and memory, *Travesties*, who, on hearing that a 'social revolution' has occurred in Russia in 1917 inquires innocently – 'A social revolution? Unaccompanied women smoking at the Opera, that sort of thing?' Faber and Faber, 1993, 12.

36. Bernard Bergonzi, *Heroes' Twilight: a Study of the Literature of the Great War*, Macmillan, 1980, 219. For a useful discussion of the way the terms 'modern' and 'modernism' have been used and confused, see Roger Cooter, Mark Harrison and Steve Sturdy (eds), *War, Medicine and Modernity*, Sutton, 1998, Introduction.

37. For discussion of venereal disease, and attitudes to prostitution, see Roger Davidson and Lesley A. Hall (eds), *Sex, Sin and Suffering: Venereal Disease and European society*, Routledge, 2001, which has a valuable comparative perspective.

38. For a more subtle and detailed approach to sexual anxieties, prostitution and rape, see Susan Grayzel, *Women's Identities at War*, Chapel Hill, 1999, and also Grayzel, 'The Enemy Within: the problem of British Women's Sexuality during the First World War', in Nicole E. Dombrowski (ed.), *Women and War in the Twentieth Century*, Garland, 1999.

39. H. Fischer and E. X. Dubois, *Sexual Life During the World War*, Francis Aldor, 1937 (see Introduction, by 'the publisher', 7–8); Grayzel also quotes this paragraph in her chapter of this volume, but each of us chose this quotation quite independently, as a superb example of paranoia, years after the end of the war. For a more down to earth description of soldiers' responses to their separation from home, see Joanna Bourke, *Dismembering the Male*. She claims that most British men did not resort to prostitution in France as they were afraid of upsetting their wives or catching diseases.

40. Fischer and Dubois, *Sexual Life During the World War*, 71.

41. Fussell, *The Great War and Modern Memory*, 316. There is no source for this, and the mention of railways is puzzling.

42. 'Mannish women', to quote Radclyffe Hall, were a source of both anxiety and scorn – ironically, given the opprobrium also heaped upon the supposedly newly voracious heterosexual women. But of course not all 'unfeminine' women were lesbian; not all lesbian women were 'mannish'; not all women in uniform either looked like men, or were lesbian! For discussion about lesbian hopes for a new world for women, see Claire Buck, '"Still some obstinate emotion remains": Radclyffe Hall and the meanings of service', in S. Raitt and T. Tait (eds), *Women's Fiction and the Great War*, Clarendon Press, 1997. See also, Jenny Gould, 'Women's Military Service in First World War Britain', in Higonnet et al., *Behind the Lines,* who discusses the way in which the sight of women in uniform raised anti-suffrage and anti-lesbian feelings. Margaret Jackson, *The Real Facts of Life*, Taylor and Francis, 1994, and Sheila Jeffreys, *The Spinster and her Enemies*, Pandora, 1984, both offer alternative views of sexologists' and feminists' attitudes to sexuality in the aftermath of the war.

43. Fussell, *The Great War and Modern Memory*, 23.

44. Niall Ferguson, *The Pity of War*, Penguin, 1998, 519, footnote.

45. Ferguson, *The Pity of War,* 205.
46. Ferguson, *The Pity of War,* 362
47. Ferguson is by no means the only recent historian one could criticise on these grounds. Orlando Figes' book on Russia, *The People's Tragedy: the Russian Revolution 1891–1923*, Pimlico, 1997, is sadly lacking in material on Russian women. His photographs of the Petrograd Women's Battalion, which attempted to defend the Winter Palace for the Provisional Government, is captioned: 'Members of the Women's Battalion of Death await the final assault on the Winter Palace, 25 October 1917. When the Aurora fired its first salvo the women became hysterical and had to be confined in a basement room' (Photo 61). He seems to confuse the Petrograd Women's Battalion with Maria Bochkaraeva's Women's Battalion of Death, and makes women soldiers appear ridiculous. For more detailed discussion of the women's battalions see Julie Wheelwright, *Amazons and Military Maids*, Pandora, 1989; Alfred G. Meyer, 'The Impact of World War I on Russian Women's Lives', in B. A.Clements, B. A.Engel and C. D. Worobec (eds), *Russia's Women: Accommodation, Resistance, Transformation*, University of California Press, 1991; R. Abraham, 'Maria Bochkareva and the Russian Amazons of 1917', in Linda Edmondson (ed.), *Women and Society in Russia and the Soviet Union*, Cambridge University Press, 1992; Richard Stites, *The Women's Liberation Movement in Russia*, Princeton University Press, 1978; Laurie Stoff, 'They fought for Russia: female soldiers of the First World War', in G. de Groot and C. Penniston-Bird (eds), *A Soldier and a Woman*, Longman, 2000.
48. Higonnet et al., *Behind the Lines*, 4.
49. For an enlightening critique of writings on gender and men, see R. W. Connell, *Masculinities*, Polity, 1995. Talk of the 'feminising' effect of the trenches is almost certainly related to the preoccupation with 'homo-eroticism' in English war poetry, as discussed by certain literary historians.
50. Billie Melman (ed.), *Borderlines: Genders and Identities in War and Peace, 1870–1930*, Routledge, 1998, Prologue, ix.
51. Higonnet and Higonnet, 'The Double Helix', in Higonnet et al., *Behind the Lines*, 37.
52. Higonnet and Higonnet, 'The Double Helix', 38.
53. One version appears in *Behind the Lines*; another, longer version is Gilbert, 'Soldier's Heart: Literary Men, Literary Women, and the Great War' in Sandra Gilbert and Susan Gubar, *No Man's Land: the Place of the Woman Writer in the Twentieth Century*, Volume II, *Sexchanges*, Yale University Press, 1989.
54. Gilbert, 'Soldier's Heart', in Gilbert and Gubar, *No Man's Land,* 262–3.
55. Deborah Thom's comment about present day women historians increasingly choosing to write about 'people like themselves' is perhaps relevant here. Thom, *Nice Girls and Rude Girls*, I. B. Tauris, 1998.
56. See for example Leonard Smith, 'Masculinity, Memory and the French World War I Novel', in Coetzee and Shevin-Coetzee, *Authority, Identity and the Social History of the Great War*. This essay is a marked contrast to those concerned with the reality of disability, and the way soldiers were treated as mentioned in note 11 above.
57. Gilbert, 'Soldier's Heart', in *No Man's Land,* 290. There is a missing quotation mark in Gilbert's version, so it is difficult to work out where Leed's own words begin and end.
58. Magnus Hirschfeld, *The Sexual History of the World War,* Panurge Press, 1934.
59. Gilbert, 'Soldier's Heart', in *No Man's Land,* 290.
60. David Mitchell, *Women on the Warpath* , Cape, 1965. This is a dated book and has been superseded by more subtle and detailed interpretations of the interaction between the war and the suffrage movement.
61. Claire Tylee, 'Maleness Run Riot', *Women's Studies International Forum*, 11 (3), 1988.
62. Raitt and Tate, *Women's Fiction*; Jane Marcus, 'Corpus/Corps/Corpse: writing the body in/at War', in Helen Cooper, Adrienne Auslander Munich, Susan Merrill Squier (eds), *Arms and the Woman*, University of North Carolina Press, 1989, 124–167.
63. A number of her critics have pointed out that you need to know the emotional/social background of those who wrote about a 'sex-war'. See in particular, James Longenbach, 'The Women and men of 1914', in Cooper et al., *Arms and the Woman*, 97–123.

64. Clearly enfranchisement was bound to alter the character of the women's movement; the juxtaposition of this with the end of the war is a complicating factor.
65. Kent, *Making Peace*, 4.
66. Kent, *Making Peace*, 141.
67. Susan Pedersen, *Family, Dependence and the Origins of the Welfare State: Britain and France, 1914–1945*, Cambridge University Press, 1993, 138–9. Also, 'Gender, Welfare and Citizenship in Britain during the Great War', in *American Historical Review*, 95, October 1990.
68. Susan Kingsley Kent, 'Love and Death: war and gender in Britain, 1914–18', in Coetzee and Shevin-Coetzee, *Authority, Identity and the Social History of the Great War*, 172.
69. Bonnie Smith, *Changing Lives*, D. C. Heath, 1989, 368. The last sentence is quoted by Kent, in support of her own arguments, though it is completely unsubstantiated by any sources in Smith.
70. Smith, *Changing Lives*, 399.
71. Smith, *Changing Lives*, 402.
72. M. L. Roberts, *Civilization without Sexes: Reconstructing Gender in Postwar France, 1917–1927*, University of Chicago Press, 1995, 6. However, I am not sure why Roberts assumes social historians would term today's women 'liberated', given the general feminist cynicism about this word.
73. John Williams, *The Home Fronts: Britain, France and Germany, 1914–1918*, Constable, 1972.
74. The words of Francois Dosse, *New History in France*, University of Illinois Press, English translation, 1994, seem apt here: 'Too often, the new historians are happy to record the evolution of representations, the way people perceive their times, without worrying about connecting these representations to what inspired them in the real world', 170.
75. See, for example, Stephen Hause with Anne R. Kenney, *Women's Suffrage and Social Politics in the French Third Republic*, Princeton University Press, 1984, 102; Pedersen, *Family, Dependence and the Origins of the Welfare State*; Mary Lynn Stewart, *Women, Work and the French State: Labor Protection and Social Patriarchy, 1879–1919*, MacGill-Queens University Press, 1989; James McMillan, *Housewife or Harlot*, Harvester Press, 1984.
76. See Gilbert's use of my own figures on numbers of women workers; different versions appear in two versions of 'A Soldier's Heart' – both are misquotations and misinterpretations of these statistics.
77. The way in which autobiographical material – oral and written – is used by twentieth century historians in general, and writers about the war in particular, merits an essay in itself, and is a growing field of research. All I will say here is that its usage is difficult. People writing about war at the time soon realised that this was an important event, and this modified the way they described their own experiences. Furthermore, for those in their teens and twenties the war period often coincided with other life changing events, like falling in love, leaving home, or challenging authority. Later memoirs have inevitably been influenced by shifting public attitudes to the war, and indeed by the reading of other memoirs and war books. As for oral history, almost certainly attempts to uncover women's experiences by interviewing them in the seventies and eighties encouraged an overoptimistic view of women's wartime lives and added weight to the idea that women's work changed radically – only those who wanted to talk about their warwork volunteered to be interviewed, for example. Those whose lives changed little would not have come forward. For interesting discussions on some of these issues see Samuel Hynes, who points out in his essay on 'Personal Narratives and Commemoration' in J. Winter and E. Sivan (eds), *War and Remembrance in the Twentieth Century*, Cambridge University Press, 1999, that the people who left us no spoken or written life stories may not have agreed with the views of those who did record their feelings about the war. We must be wary of assuming that because a voluble minority spoke of particular kinds of change, tragedy or opportunity they spoke for everyone. See also Alistair Thompson, *Anzac Memories*, Melbourne University Press, 1994, who discusses how old soldiers have unwittingly modified their memories after repeating their stories of the war for

decades, and also seeing war films, particularly *Gallipoli*. The water is further muddied by the willingness of many contemporary writers about the war to lift quotations from other books, without regard to the context of the comments in the original autobiographies, or the way they were used in the secondary works from which they have been lifted. For a thought provoking view of the past, and the way we use it, see David Lowenthal, *The Past is a Foreign Country*, Cambridge University Press, 1985.

78. Higonnet et al., *Behind the Lines*, 45.
79. Work which encourages thought about the nature of the war's impact on some of these groups include: Ingrid James, '"I told you as I will tell anyone": war widows and the State 1914–25', unpublished paper at the Anglo-American Conference, Institute of Historical Research, London, 2000; Eileen Crofton, *The Women of Royaumont*, Tuckwell Press, 1997, which gives a detailed picture of one of the Scottish Women's Hospitals; Baroness de T'Serclaes, *Flanders and Other Fields*, Harrap, 1964, gives a fascinating insight into life as a 'war heroine', and shows how hard it was for her to adjust to 'normal' life after the war.
80. A list of books which add to knowledge about a variety of groups might include the following: Richard Wall and Jay Winter (eds), *The Upheaval of War*, Cambridge University Press, 1988, for essays on the impact of wars in history; Jay Winter and Jean Louis Robert (eds), *Capital Cities at War*, Cambridge University Press, 1997, for comparative essays on wartime in Britain, France and Germany, though sometimes the generalisations that inevitably ensue suggest there are dangers in this approach; Melman, *Borderlines*; Ava Baron (ed.), *Work Engendered*, Cornell University Press, 1991, for essays which are sensitive to issues of class, race and gender, in the United States; Cooke and Woollacott, *Gendering Wartalk*, for discussions of these issues in different times and places; Lenard R. Berlanstein, *Rethinking Labor History*, for what labour history has failed to do in the past, and positive developments within the genre. For the Austrian Empire, see David F. Good, Margarete Grandner and Mary Jo Maynes (eds), *Austrian Women in the Nineteenth and Twentieth Centuries*, Berghahn, 1996. Coetzee and Shevin-Coetzee, *Authority, Identity and the Social History of the Great War*, includes some good essays, though some are considerably more useful than others. For recent books on women workers see Thom, *Nice Girls and Rude Girls*; Grayzel, *Women's identities at War*. For rare reminiscences of African American women, see Yvonne Klein (ed.), *Beyond the Home Front*, and the words of Addie Hunton and Kathryn M. Johnson, 'Two Coloured Women with the AEF'.
81. N. Gullace, 'White Feathers and Wounded men: Female Patriotism and the memory of the Great War', in *The Journal of British Studies*, 1997, Vol. 36.
82. See, for example, Jane Gledhill's chapter on 'The War and Women', in Dorothy Goldman with Jane Gledhill and Judith Hattaway (eds), *Women Writers and the Great War*, Twayne Publications, 1995. She writes that 'the women of England joined forces to send their men to war, and in the winter of 1915 white feathers were handed out ...', 13. The same story is repeated by Higonnet et al., *Behind the Lines*, Introduction.
83. For further discussion of women's patriotism, and those who supported the war effort, see also Paul Ward, '"Women of Britain say Go": women's patriotism in the First World War', *Twentieth Century History*, 12 (1), 2001. This article is useful for pointing out the 'ungendered' response of many women who threw themselves into voluntary work, and who saw themselves as part of a larger community fighting together to defeat a common enemy. Many of these women had no regrets about the war after it was over: there was no sense of disillusionment.
84. Even further analysis of newspaper reports would be interesting. The similarities between them almost make one suspect that 'urban myth' took over at some point. Just how many one-legged or one-armed officers were really mistaken for 'shirkers' by roving young women handing out feathers?
85. Gilbert herself quotes Virginia Woolf on white feathers, who is quoting George Bernard Shaw – but even Gilbert points out that Woolf thought Shaw was exaggerating! 'Soldier's Heart' in *Behind the Lines*, footnote, 209.
86. A. C. Ward, *The Nineteen-twenties*, Methuen, 1930, 1.

5

Liberating Women?
Examining Gender, Morality and Sexuality in First World War Britain and France

Susan Grayzel

In an image (Figure 5.1) appearing in the British periodical the *Bystander* in April 1918, two young women in the foreground are pictured smoking.[1] One of them, a window cleaner carrying a ladder and pail but wearing high-heeled shoes, helps the other woman, a bus conductress in a uniform consisting of a short skirt and puttees, to light her cigarette. In the background, a faint outline of an elderly woman in bonnet, shawl and nineteenth-century dress is seen collapsing in a younger woman's arms. The caption below reads '"Oh! My Grandmother!" In her time girls *would* be girls: but now girls *will* be men.'

Such an image would appear to encapsulate one of the dominant ideas – expressed in still influential essays like Sandra Gilbert's 'Soldier's Heart: Literary Men, Literary Women, and the Great War' – that the First World War had radically altered women's experience of themselves and their world through stunning gender role reversals.[2] Succinctly put, in this view the war, by opening up new spheres and spaces to women, had 'masculinised' and therefore liberated them, and that there was thus a sharp disjuncture between prewar and postwar constructions of gender identity. Other historians seeking to explain the fleeting nature of such women's liberation and the need for the *reconstruction* of gender in the interwar era have then stressed the masculine backlash against feminism and the gains that women had made.[3] Nowhere would this model of liberation and backlash seem more evident than in the question of women's morality and sexuality.

" OH ! MY GRANDMOTHER ! "

In her time girls *would* be girls : but now girls *will* be men

Figure 5.1 The *Bystander*, April 1918.

The image in the *Bystander* is worth examining a bit more closely because it suggests the complexity of wartime evidence about gender, sexuality and morality. The women are clearly meant to be acting more 'manly' given the variety of public violations of gender identity evident in this image. We can see emblems that these women are performing 'male' work by the ladder alongside the bucket and also that they are taking on other forms of 'masculine' privilege by smoking in public. The caption makes the symbolic significance of the scene quite explicit by telling us that now 'girls will be men' but it may be a case of protesting too much. The fainting grandmother in the background presumably could never imagine a world in which her granddaughters could take such liberties. Yet the visual effect achieved by rendering the old-fashioned women as a faint background sketch suggests the triumph of the newer, bolder images of women.

Still, while there is some discomfort produced by the idea that 'girls' are no longer just that, these are all obviously women, and the whole image is quite sexually charged. Despite their masculine attire, both women's figures and legs are clearly outlined and both appear to be wearing make-up, with darkened lips and eyes. The uniforms of the modern women do nothing to hide their curves and the way in which the two women lean towards each other and their cigarettes meet presents flirtatious and even lesbian overtones. Thus, like much of the wartime evidence about women in many parts of Europe, particularly in the Allied nations of Britain and France, this image can be read in multiple ways.

Rather than seeing a stark disjunction between pre- and postwar notions of femininity, in this essay I want to stress the complexity of wartime reworkings of gender roles, and seek to refine the view that the First World War was liberating for women, who then suffered a 'backlash' in the interwar period. In doing so, I do not suggest that the war must then have been uniquely constraining for women or that the cultural cues that women received about their roles were easily ignored. Instead, I look at the shaping of public debates about women's behaviour in both Britain and France by examining three related subjects: women and alcohol; maternity and abortion; and debates about 'sex in public', especially prostitution and venereal disease. Of course, a brief essay cannot do justice to the full range of these issues, but all three topics reveal how wartime commentators linked women's behaviour more generally to wider concerns with their morality, sexuality and motherhood, and show the limits of the liberation/backlash model. Despite the images of the 'flapper' and the 'garçonne' of the 1920s, the new sexual freedom allegedly experienced by these young women during and after the war appears short-lived at best.[4]

Most recent English and French histories of the First World War have barely discussed sexual behaviour, and if they do so at all, sex frequently appears as a reward for soldiers and an inducement to good morale amongst the troops. It surely served both these purposes as far as men were concerned. Yet the possible consequences of heterosexual activity, namely pregnancy, also appeared to be of great concern in contemporary public discourse, while it remained a private anxiety amongst women. Of course, getting at the 'private' experience of sexuality is itself a tremendously difficult thing to achieve for the historian. However, it is certain that *unwed* motherhood was seen as one of the main problems by those who concerned themselves with sexuality – particularly women's sexuality – before, during and after the War. The sexual and moral double standard certainly did not come to an end. All of which suggests – despite the images of freer young women acting like 'men' – that while experiences of life during wartime varied greatly, many found it far from 'liberating', in the popular usage of the term.

Women and Alcohol

What is striking in British and French wartime media is the linkage between women's adoption of 'male' vices like cigarette smoking, 'foul' language, and, in particular, the abuse of alcohol, with the collapse of gendered moral codes of behaviour. Thus, among other efforts to restore social order came greater state control over licensing hours and the consumption of alcohol. This explicitly included attempts to 'control' women's behaviour – although it is important to keep in mind that debates in England and France can be read more accurately as expressing fears of what might occur rather than as a reflection of 'reality'.

In Britain, the concern about women's potential abuse of alcohol became evident early in the war as a result of the implementation of separation allowances, which were paid directly to women whose husbands were serving in the armed forces. Since it possessed a volunteer army, the government used such allowances to help recruit men who might not otherwise join up for fear of leaving their dependants facing poverty without a male breadwinner.[5] Consequently, debates occurred in Britain over the extent to which the government then had a duty to regulate the behaviour of women receiving these public funds. Particular attention was paid to women's alcohol consumption and their potential sexual misconduct. The two issues were clearly linked in the public mind. According to the *Daily Call*, one of the extreme problems facing London in late 1914 was 'the evil of dipsomaniac wives of soldiers'.[6] A drunken soldier's wife was especially worthy of condemnation because her home and family suffered while she was 'soddening herself with alcohol in a public house on the money given to her by a solicitous government for the deprivation of her helpmate, while that same helpmate is enduring in his country's service the pains and privations of the war ...'[7]

This prompted an emotive defence of soldiers' wives not only among national politicians such as Labour's Arthur Henderson, but also among local and regional political leaders. In Leicester, for example, Councillor W. E. Hincks 'indignantly' proclaimed the government's actions 'ill-advised and unwarranted'.[8] Hincks, in part, blamed the War Office pronouncements on 'the correspondence of various London newspapers ... [where] during the middle of September, very strong statements were made ... concerning the indulgence in excessive drinking of wives of soldiers and sailors.'[9] He further noted that no evidence had been offered then or since regarding drunkenness among soldiers' and sailors' wives, and that among other investigations in Leicester, in a 'confidential inquiry', eighty out of eighty-three elementary-school head teachers 'repudiate[d] the suggestion of excessive drinking among women'.[10] Thus, while claiming that the honour of the wives of 'gallant' men in arms had been besmirched and that the orders must be withdrawn by Parliament, Hincks simultaneously laid blame not on the government itself, but on the influence of London papers and their unsubstantiated attacks.

By pointing to the importance of the press in disseminating misinformation about servicemen's wives, Hincks acknowledged the influence of public, media-driven debates on public policy, particularly where it concerned women. Other press accounts defended these women, quoting with approval the statement of Mrs Harley, Sir John French's sister, who declared that 'as the wife of a soldier, she deeply resented the insults to her class which were implied by the ... instructions issued to the police to keep the wives and dependants of soldiers on active duty under police surveillance.'[11]

Concern with drinking was not, of course, restricted to those receiving separation allowances or to women. In March of 1915, David Lloyd George denounced alcohol as an enemy akin to the Germans and sought to have the government take charge of the liquor trade.[12] Eventually new licensing laws were put into effect; in London as late November 1915 liquor could only be served from 12.00 till 2.00 p.m. and 6.30 till 9.30 p.m. These changes met with opposition from trade unions generally and those concerned with women workers specifically.[13] However, the consumption of alcohol by women, regardless of whether they were married to soldiers, continued to be widely discussed and, by November 1915, the Central Control Board with jurisdiction over the Liquor Traffic joined with the Ministry of Munitions to create a Committee of Inquiry to investigate and report to the Board on the allegations that women drank excessively.[14]

In what seems at least in part a response to these debates, Anna Martin, a South London settlement worker and suffragist, wrote a detailed analysis of working women and alcohol.[15] Appearing in December 1915, Martin's article sought to balance accusatory reports by demonstrating that women's behaviour compared favourably to men's, insisting in particular that the dysgenic effects of parental alcoholism would not be ameliorated by focusing solely on mothers.[16] Claiming that 'the whole business' of placing women under surveillance to insure sobriety 'showed once more that the home life of the masses remains a sealed book to most of those who so light-heartedly undertake to regulate it', Martin used her years of experience among London's working poor to counter the idea of a pronounced wartime increase in women abusing alcohol.[17]

After demonstrating that overconsumption of alcohol by workingclass women tended to be financially prohibitive, Martin directly addressed the issue of women drinking away their separation allowances. She noted that while there were probably more women in pubs since the outbreak of war, they did not represent formerly sober wives of soldiers newly corrupted by money and drink. Martin quoted reservists' wives on this issue: 'It isn't us proper soldiers' wives at all as is crowding to the pubs … it's them as has always gone when they had the halfpence … [Besides the] sort that hasn't the nerve to face things …' Having further established that women's drunkenness was far less of a problem than that of men by surveying Licensing Statistics from 1905 to 1913, Martin then analysed the excessive attention paid to working women who drank.[18]

She offered a variety of possible explanations for this, and noted that charges of drunkenness against women had not declined as much as those against men, attributing this trend to the increased number of men under military discipline. She also made the specific point that 'public spirited citizens are genuinely anxious for the welfare of the rising generation', and were aware of alcoholism's debilitating effect on motherhood. Martin argued that it was thus easy for the 'Drink Trade' to stand by, and allow measures to be taken against the small number of women who drank, as long as their dealings with men, their primary customers, remained untouched – hence the London brewers' agreement, after Britain's entry into war, to exclude women from pubs until 11.30 a.m.[19] Although Martin persuasively demonstrated that fathers' drinking was more detrimental to their offspring's health, it remained the prevention of maternal drinking that received public attention. She claimed that the public wanted 'to make of women a wall to stand between the nation and the natural results of its drink policy'. In fact, alcohol consumption per se was the problem.[20] She argued that fears about 'the horror of drunken motherhood' were not only exaggerated, but also that 'so strong in fact are the maternal instincts of the race that the drink habit can exist to a surprising extent without destroying them'.[21] Thus, in Martin's opinion, despite wartime exigencies, women's allegedly unchanging and natural maternal goodness prevailed.

The media, prompted by politicians, focused on workingclass women's drinking not only because they were easier targets than men, but also because the war increased national interest in the next generation, for whom *mothers* alone, typically, were held to be responsible. The preoccupation with women as mothers meant that concern with women's abuse of alcohol had much to do with the continuing belief in women's moral influence within the family.[22] Alcohol-abusing mothers threatened the health of Britain's future subjects and, most importantly, its future soldiers.[23]

Concern with women's drinking was not unique to Britain. There is ample evidence of French women's wartime 'war against alcohol' in the pages of the feminist journals *L'Action Féminine* and *La Française* throughout 1915 to 1918. In a 1915 article in *La Française* entitled 'Alcoholism and Immorality in Rouen during the War', G. C. Levillain recounted how strict measures had to be undertaken to prevent not only the consumption of alcohol by allied soldiers, but also the employment of women and girls in cafés and restaurants, as well as the presence of wives of *mobilisés* in such establishments. As in Britain, authorities concerned with where such behaviour might lead, instituted measures that led to the arrest and imprisonment of women:

> the most part of whom were picked up in police raids in the camps, among them mothers of families charged with children, also alas, too many little girls … And some fathers return, convalescent … hastening to their hearths for several days before returning to the front, but the hearth is empty, the mother is in prison and the little ones in a place of refuge! [24]

While speaking of France's heroism, Levillain writes that it must also acknowledge 'our shame', urging the 'Women of France' that beyond the war, 'another beast … alcohol … is at the doors of your hearths.' Similar articles warning of alcohol's direct and indirect dangers to women would follow in *La Française* throughout 1916, culminating in an issue almost entirely devoted to the need for women to fight against alcohol (April) and an appeal to all French women to rid France of this poison (May).[25] Meanwhile, organisations like L'Union des Femmes de France urged women to act as the moral guardians of the home, and to save it from the effects of male alcoholism, while saying little about women's own consumption of alcohol.[26] The government took notice of the dangers of women drinking, however, and responded in October 1917 with laws aimed at what it saw as the most dangerous class of women, by barring prostitutes from all establishments where the consumption of alcohol might occur, throughout France.[27]

Thus, the publicly-voiced concern about women abusing alcohol was directly linked to their morality and sexuality, and to preserving deeply gendered assumptions about appropriate behaviour. The language used by wartime commentators continued to utilise two traditional ideas of womenhood; either women were the social glue that kept the family and society together, or they were potential sexual miscreants, prostitutes, who posed the greatest danger to social order. As they were urged to fight alcohol in defence of their homes and families or else viewed as dangerous sexual predators, women had clearly not become 'like men' in their ability to act freely in public.

Morality, Motherhood and Sex

Public debates about women's consumption of alcohol, like debates on women's morality and sexuality, thus generally bolstered traditional views of womanhood, rather than encouraging a liberating destruction of such norms. In Britain, the focus on women spending their separation allowances on drink suggests a particular conjunction of government interest not just in regulating the spending of state money on questionable behaviour per se, but in safeguarding the mothers of soldier's children and thus the children themselves. This can also be seen in fears about the potential rise in numbers of illegitimate children, which caused a public outcry in Britain during the first year of the war.[28] Here, the disapproval of sex outside marriage was mediated by a number of factors, most especially by the possibility that the fathers might be soldiers. In a measure surpassing Britain's financial support of children conceived out of wedlock by military men and unwed mothers, the French government enacted legislation that permitted soldiers to marry by 'proxy', provided they could prove a previous engagement, cohabitation or support of the mother. Eventually, French legislators approved the legitimising of the children of soldiers who had been killed in battle.[29] That both states were so concerned with supporting women as mothers, even though unmarried, shows how pivotal this role remained and how much historians need to consider the preoccupation with motherhood when looking at wartime sexuality.

Measures of illegitimacy in Great Britain and France suggest that some fears of increased wartime numbers of children born out of wedlock had a basis in reality. However, the rise in numbers did not necessarily correspond with the moments of greatest cultural attention. For instance, the illegitimacy rate in England and Wales barely altered in 1915 (the year of the most vocal anxiety about 'war babies') and did not experience a significant upsurge until 1917. The percentage of illegitimate births in Ireland and Scotland remained relatively stable throughout the war years at around 3 percent and 7–8 percent respectively, but the number of illegitimate births in England and Wales rose from 37,000 in 1914 to 57,000 in 1917 before declining to 42,000 in 1918 and back down to 39,000 in 1919. The actual number of births declined markedly during the war, from 879,000 in 1914 to 688,000 in 1917 and 663,000 in 1918. Figured as a percentage of all births, even at the peak of 1917, the English and Welsh illegitimate birth rate still remained at only 8.3 percent.[30]

In France, statistics regarding illegitimacy and the birth rate only exist for seventy-seven departments, excluding the ten departments occupied by Germany. Here too the percentage of illegitimate infants born alive rose during the war from 8.5 percent in 1914 to a height of 14.2 percent in 1917. This corresponded unsurprisingly with a decline in the number of such infants recognised by the father at birth from 15.9 percent in 1914 to 9.9 percent in 1915 and 1917. Both sets of statistics must be placed in the context of an overall sharp decline in the birth rate from 59.3 percent in 1914 to 31.3 percent in 1916, the wartime low.[31]

What all of this reveals is that illegitimacy rates rose, but not by much, and certainly not in the proportions feared by social commentators and politicians. Explanations for this rise are not difficult to imagine. Presumably many of the men who impregnated these women were in the military and this made it impossible for them to return to marry once the pregnancies became known. Furthermore, statistical evidence about illegitimacy tells us relatively little about behaviour or attitudes; it does not prove that sex before or outside of marriage increased, that this sex was consensual, initiated by the man or woman, or was treated casually. It also gives no indication as to whether the stigma associated with illegitimacy altered in any way. It is worth noting, for example, that in France (where such statistics were kept) the number of illegitimate infants stillborn increased far more rapidly than did the those born alive.[32] All of this rein-forces the impression that women's wartime lives were complex, their heterosexual and maternal experiences being no exception.

Indeed the most obvious, gender-specific consequence of women's sexual behaviour – unwanted pregnancy – has not yet been the main focus of writing about wartime sexuality. Instead, many historians have been drawn to the work of sexologists, which contain some of the most vivid depictions of what the war had allegedly done to behaviour. For instance, postwar sexologists H. C. Fischer and Dr E. X. Dubois, in their *Sexual Life During the World War*, describe the war's effects as follows:

> the primitive, bestial instincts that lie dormant in civilised man exploded in an almost universal orgy of sexual license and debauchery ... the war enthusiasm of the first weeks suddenly broke down the established concepts of sexual morality ... as the war proceeded ... women on the 'home front' were driven by sex hunger to adultery and worse ... sexual perversions, from homosexuality and Lesbian love to the most horrible manifestations of sadism developed and spread through the length and breadth of Europe ... while the guns thundered and the screams of mutilated and dying men filled the air at the various warfronts, men and women in the big cities of Europe, maddened by the strain of war and sex starvation, indulged in degrading sexual orgies under the influence of drink and drugs; and ... finally, venereal disease increased a hundredfold in all the belliger-ent countries, to avenge the sins of a mad world on a generation yet unborn.[33]

Even if we take such statements at face value, and focus on 'sexual license' without looking at its results, this is an astonishing generalisation about the war and its impact. It both ignores the measures put in place to control women's sexuality and also how much women themselves suf-fered in an era when there was no easy access to birth control and abor-tion was illegal.[34] As a result, for many women, heterosexuality and maternity were indelibly linked, meaning an investigation into their deci-sion making about pregnancies can provide an insight into women's wartime sexuality.

Gauging women's experiences of, and attitudes towards, maternity remains difficult in a time where there were strong social stigmas against those who rejected or questioned this most 'natural' of womanly activi-ties. Numerous wartime social commentators in both Britain and France expressed great concern at the falling birth rate, seeing in this a poten-tially diminished postwar population.[35] Enormous public pressure to reproduce for the sake of the nation came into conflict with women's own sense of war's costs, and a continued reluctance, by the public gen-erally, and the courts in particular, to punish severely women accused of procuring or enabling abortions.

However, the war did open up new discussions about the acceptability of abortion, particularly in France. When the French government first reported sexual assaults against women by the invading German army in January of 1915, this produced vocal debates about the possibility of changing legislation to permit women who had been raped by German soldiers to abort any pregnancies which then resulted. Feminists, legislators and intellectuals across the political spectrum took sides as to the effects of allowing even this victimised group of women to obtain abortions. Many felt that the future of the nation was at stake, concerned either that French bloodlines would be corrupted by the Germans, or that abortion permitted the destruction of potential French citizens, future soldiers.[36] Only within the context of this wartime debate over the control that women might exercise over their reproductive capacity does the subsequent legislative change of 1920 – which toughened laws on contraception and abortion – make sense.[37]

Some recent historiography has considered the postwar emphasis on natality and heterosexuality to be a direct response to the war's death toll and the dislocation of society.[38] And, as the quote from Fischer and Dubois above further suggests, this anxiety about women refusing to become mothers went hand in hand with fears of what the war had unleashed: namely, an orgy of debauched women. Yet many of those studying sexuality, then and now, based their interpretations on anecdotes, and on cultural artefacts like Helen Zenna Smith's evocative and provocative novel, *Not So Quiet ...*, treating it as a primary text of the war, rather than the interwar period.[39] 'Smith' was the pseudonym selected by popular author Evadne Price, who based her novel on the diaries kept by a female ambulance driver. *Not So Quiet ...* is itself a devastating anti-war novel, vicious in its portrayal of the generation of women who sent their offspring away to engage in the bloody, senseless waste of the war, and cynical about patriotism, romance and life, as it describes the total disillusionment of one young woman 'doing her bit'. However, by the time that Smith wrote this book in 1930, the outcome of the war, and some of its more dire consequences for women, were well known – for instance, the fact that many women were expelled from their wartime jobs, and lost income and financial security.

Fischer and Dubois use *Not So Quiet ...* in order to claim an explosion of promiscuity, but a subplot dealing with abortion in Smith's novel offers a rather more complex portrayal of such issues. In one particularly striking section, Trixie, the protagonist's younger sister, who has been working as a VAD (Voluntary Aid Detachment worker) in France, becomes pregnant from a casual sexual encounter and seeks an abortion. Fischer and Dubois utilise this incident to suggest that 'there is ample evidence to prove that a great many of the WAACs [members of the Women's Auxiliary Army Corps] entertained erotic relations with combatants and others.'[40] In particular, they cite the moment when Trixie begs her sister, the narrator of *Not So Quiet ...*, for £100 for an abortion. As she explains:

I've got to the stage of wondering what's wrong with my appearance if a sub doesn't ask me to sleep with him – that's what the war's done for me ... Here to-day and gone to-morrow, that's what they tell you, and it's true, it's true, people dying all round you. Makes you determined to get a bit of enjoyment out of life while you're alive to take it – you're not alive very long nowadays if you're young, are you?[41]

This *carpe diem* attitude towards life during wartime is not seen as surprising by the author. However, such freedom from codes of bourgeois moral behaviour has the serious result in the novel of leading to a pregnancy that is terminated in a costly, risky and illegal operation, one that leaves Trixie looking 'miserably thin and white ... [with] lines about her mouth that are not good to see in a girl of nineteen.'[42] She is eventually killed in an air raid in France, by which point, her sister, the protagonist, claims to feel nothing for anyone anymore.

Abortion as presented in *Not So Quiet* ... becomes one of a series of grim experiences for wartime women. Yet a genre of novels written and published during the war also dealt explicitly with the question of abortion, and are often neglected by the sexologists and modern historians. These novels, as in the public debates in France, present abortion as an option for pregnancies resulting from rape.[43] Novels like Annie Vivanti Chartres's *Vae Victis* (1917) sympathetically portray the decision of one raped Belgian refugee to abort her German-fathered foetus once she escapes to Britain.[44] And one wartime French novel, Odette Dulac's *La Houille Rouge* (1916), ultimately attacks both the women who seek, and perform, abortions while underscoring the complexity of their situations. Although Dulac's protagonists ultimately regret their abortions, the novel begins with a scene that offers plausible explanations for why women would seek them – pressure from a husband for whom a child would be an inconvenient expense, the conception of a child in an adulterous union, or merely being a single woman seeking a professional career. While these women and their choices are sympathetically portrayed at the novel's onset, readers soon learn that the midwife (who also serves as an abortionist) has herself become involved with a nefarious German spy ring determined to render all Frenchwomen sterile 'by order of the [German] emperor'.[45] When the war arrives, some of these women find themselves under direct threat from the invading German army, and are then raped and impregnated. It is under these horrific wartime circumstances that they come to regret their earlier decisions to terminate their previous pregnancies, and that a full condemnation of abortion ensues. The novel's conclusion is that having children is the most important responsibility of all true French women.

Another quasi-public source of information about the motivations for, and experience of, abortion can be found in wartime criminal court records. It was through examining the records of women accused of murder in wartime London that I was able to discover a more detailed picture of why women sought abortions.[46] Many of the women accused of murder had assisted with abortions that went badly wrong, leading to the death of the prospective mother. While such records demonstrate that pregnancy outside marriage remained an important factor, these cases also record some different, perhaps war-specific reasons, that vaguely echo the fictional experience recorded by Evadne Price in 1930, of women impregnated by men in uniform. Nor does it seem surprising that – of the many couples separated by wartime exigencies – some women became pregnant through adulterous relationships.

In November 1916, Florence Sturley died from septic poisoning of her womb, the result of an attempted abortion. From the depositions given by her mother-in-law, her lover and her own statements given to a doctor in the hospital when she knew she was mortally ill, the circumstances leading to her death are fairly easy to reconstruct. After her husband went off to France, Mrs Sturley moved in with her mother-in-law, Hannah Sturley. Around Christmas of 1915, Florrie Sturley met a Canadian soldier named Archie Hewitt, who was recently back from France, at a pub near Waterloo. According to Hewitt, she claimed to be single and soon afterwards persuaded him to become a lodger in Hannah Sturley's home; only then did Hewitt apparently learn that she was married. Hewitt lodged with the Sturleys, including Florence Sturley's three children, until Charles Sturley came home on leave at the end of April and 'found Hewitt in the house and there was a bother'. Mr Sturley threw his wife and Hewitt out, and made over his separation allowance to his mother so that she could keep his children. Thus, Florrie Sturley was living with Hewitt when she found herself pregnant by him. As her mother-in-law testified, while she 'did not know there was any improper conduct going on between Hewitt and my daughter in law in my house', she was also certain that when her son came home 'he did not go to bed with his wife that night'. Although Hewitt stated that when he learned that Florence Sturley was pregnant he offered to 'accept full responsibility', Florence wanted 'to get rid of it someway'. Her efforts to do so ended by leading to her death on 14 November.[47]

Lizzie Daisy Armstrong's decision to abort her pregnancy also led to her death. And while her court records provide a less full portrait than that of Florence Sturley, it becomes clear that Mrs Armstrong's unwanted pregnancy also resulted from adultery. As her landlady testified: 'She was nervous about her husband coming back. She did not want him to come back because of her condition.' With the help of her sister, Grace Jenkins, Daisy Armstrong secured the aid of Louisa Davies to try to terminate her pregnancy. This attempt had lethal results. In these records, the circumstances behind Mrs Armstrong's pregnancy are never revealed, but it is clear that the liaison that produced the child was not a lasting one.[48]

The situations of Florence Sturley and Daisy Armstrong point to one major way in which the war might have affected married women's sexual behaviour. It would be difficult to prove that the war led to an increase in adultery or even to these particular cases of adultery; these women might have committed them regardless of the war. However, by simultaneously removing husbands and introducing to many towns a population of soldiers, separated from their families, the war certainly opened up opportunities for extramarital encounters – but to read this as 'liberating', given the end results, is difficult.

In yet another case, two women were accused of assisting in procuring an abortion for Marjory Mary Killpatrick, allegedly raped and impregnated by a Commonwealth soldier, William Richard Willing. According to her mother's testimony, after falling very ill Marjory Killpatrick informed her:

> that Willing one afternoon asked me to accompany him to his Australian Pay Office saying he was going to France … Afterwards she said he made an attack upon her after getting her into a room and shutting the door … She said 'did you notice my clothes going to the laundry, how torn to shreds they were.' … She then said 'I went to a woman at New Cross last Wednesday and she did something to me for this …'[49]

Her mother's account was echoed by her younger sister, Isabel Killpatrick, who testified that her sister 'told me that she was going to have a baby … She said she had been taken advantage of by a Mr Willing in the Pay Office of the Australian Forces'. Isabel Killpatrick then recounted how she and her sister had visited a doctor, who confirmed Marjory's pregnancy and urged her to tell her mother. Instead, the two women sought the aid of their acquaintance, Sonia Craigie, a chorus girl, who introduced them to a Mrs Charlotte Myerscough, through whom they met a 'Mrs Brown' (the alias of Jane Crowe) who agreed to perform an operation. In his testimony, William Willing, while admitting that he knew the deceased, denied that he 'had intimate relations with her' or ever even knew that she was pregnant.[50] Mrs Myerscough denied that she knew that Miss Killpatrick was seeking an abortion, and Jane Crowe denied that she had offered to help Marjory Killpatrick for the price of five guineas. It seems clear that if the operation had not led to Marjory Killpatrick's death, none of the information surrounding this pregnancy would be known. From a distance of eighty years, it is difficult to access the validity of the claim of rape. Yet there is also no compelling reason to doubt it; what could Marjory Killpatrick have gained by confessing that she was pregnant as a result of rape rather than consensual sex as she lay dying? Certainly, this case neatly reverses the popular media images of 'Khaki Fever' and of sexually voracious women posing a threat to men.[51] It might also be read as pointing to the 'old' dangers – of sexual assault – awaiting women who ventured into public spaces.

All three of these cases illustrate why abortion, despite its dangers and criminality, continued. They reveal the diverse ways in which heterosexuality and abortion were experienced during the war, not necessarily because of women's sexual freedom but rather men's. If some commentators suggest that the war unleashed frenzied and sexually voracious women, other wartime sources clearly indicate how serious the consequences of such actions could be. Unplanned pregnancies could still destroy lives, depending on circumstances, both within and outside marriage. It is a truism of historical research that it may often be easier to find 'deviance' than so-called normal behaviour. Yet, these court records provide glimpses of 'ordinary' women, who were directly affected by the war, in two cases because of absent husbands and in another because of the presence of soldiers in wartime London. It would be difficult to see in any of their experiences of wartime sexuality a sense that they had been 'liberated'.

Prostitution, Disease and Regulation

Those participating in public debates about female sexuality and morality during the war tended to look at the most visible emblems of 'sex in public': prostitution and venereal disease. Indeed, contemporary concern with prostitution almost inevitably went hand in hand with apprehension about the spread of venereal diseases. Historians have followed this tendency because these two 'problems' have left easy-to-find traces in the written record. Prostitution was among the more 'visible' signs, and sources such as wartime police reports on the 'esprit' of the Parisian population, which discussed anything seen as disruptive to civilian morale, paid particular attention to interactions between soldiers and women.[52]

The incidence of venereal disease also attracted new wartime attention. Still, reliable statistics for venereal disease rates during the war are difficult to obtain, with the exception of military men and even here, the records exist of those being treated for them (not necessarily all of the infected).[53] The Royal Commission on Venereal Diseases had estimated in its 1916 report that 'in a typical working class population of London, at least 8–12% of adult males, and at least 3–7% of adult females have acquired syphilis.' Some historians, taking this as the national figure for all venereal disease argue that it is a conservative one.[54] The *Bulletin de l'Academie de Médecine* regularly updated French physicians on the spread of syphilis during the war, and whatever the veracity of records, the number of diagnosed cases rose. That this was true in every belligerent nation helped usher in a new era of openness in speaking of venereal diseases, their effects, and treatment.[55]

More recently, historians and cultural critics have shown us how much issues of race and class, as well as gender, were also part of these wartime discussions of sexuality. In specific ways, for instance, sexual encounters between French women and Germans ('Huns') were redefined as 'race' contamination.[56] New attention to the colonial aspects of the war further highlights arenas where power discrepancies and national anxieties were even more pronounced. Two recent studies, by Annabelle Melzer on the representation of Senegalese soldiers in France, and by Philippa Levine on British colonial soldiers, reveal, as the latter puts it, 'an increasingly alarmist link between racial mistrust and a vision of sexual disorder in which "unruly" women and potentially disloyal colonials were subject to far more rigorous controls than other groups.'[57] While not disputing this, Joe Lunn's recent history of Senegalese troops during the First World War reveals that some individual Senegalese men could form ties with French women ranging from friendships to those where marriage was considered. These new studies allow us to see that the wider public fears about racial contamination inherent in attempts to police the sexual activity of white women were as important as the desire to prevent the spread of venereal diseases themselves. Efforts to curtail such diseases during the war led to concrete measures and even 'new' laws.

Changing legislation responded to allegedly changing mores, most notably in Britain, with the enactment under the Defence of the Realm Act of regulations 35C and 40D. The latter became especially controversial since it directly stated that: 'no woman who is suffering from venereal disease in a communicable form shall have sexual intercourse with any member of His Majesty's Forces' nor 'solicit or invite' intercourse. This was later amended to include members of 'allied' nations as well. A woman found guilty of violating regulation 40D could be imprisoned for up to six months.[58]

Wartime interest in preventing the spread of disease thus directly resulted in the return of penal legislation regarding sexual promiscuity, which was in turn met with protests from various feminist and religious organisations.[59] This also led to questions about the impact of the war on sexual behaviour in Britain that might seem to reinforce the idea of war-induced 'immorality'. It was in this climate, under the auspices of the Association for Moral and Social Hygiene, that a Committee to inquire into Sexual Morality was convened in October 1918.[60] Initial financial support to set up a Committee to investigate sexual behaviour came from organisations such as the National Union of Societies for Equal Citizenship, the United Free Church of Scotland, the Women's International League, the Women's Freedom League, and the Young Women's Christian Association (YWCA). Although the committee in its ultimate published report, *The State and Sexual Morality*, noted that 'in the years immediately preceding the outbreak of war ... the British people had been increasingly concerned about the question of sexual morality, its effects upon the status of women, on the birth-rate and general health',[61] it limited its scope from the beginning. At one of its first meetings on 14 October 1918, members decided that they would not investigate such matters as marriage and divorce or illegitimacy but would instead focus on 'the laws and their administration and other methods preventive and remedial dealing with sexual promiscuity'.[62] In early November, the Committee of Enquiry into Sexual Morality decided to begin calling witnesses to deal with, in particular, wartime regulations concerning women's public behaviour, prostitution and the spread of venereal disease.

Those testifying before the committee as experts on the prevention of venereal disease, like Dr Mary Scharlieb, reported how much the war had increased the number of cases, as was evident from army statistics.[63] Others would testify as to the fact that 'girls are becoming more difficult to control, and are showing much greater independence of spirit than they used to do'.[64] As Mr E. B. Turner, who served as Chairman of the National Council for Combating Venereal Diseases, would state in July 1919 when asked his views on the promiscuity of girls:

> I am sorry to say that to my knowledge it is very much increased especially latterly during the war ... I believe a great deal of the going wrong among girls lately is due to what I describe as a wave of patriotic immorality going over the country. They think the soldiers have been prepared to give so much for them, that they would give anything, even their best treasure. I have seen more cases of promiscuity among girls in the last five years than in all the rest of my practice, which now extends over 43 years.[65]

Yet the testimony of Turner, among others, also reflected that the consequences of this promiscuity remained severe, especially for women. In its published report, the Committee attacked the influence of alcohol on prostitution and immorality and also stated that 'it is impossible to ignore the influence of standing armies ... War and preparations for war are a fertile source of the moral and physical diseases associated with sexual promiscuity.'[66] Once again, even at the war's end, such voices upheld traditional notions of gender, and assumed this was for the benefit of women. At the same time, such testimony could suggest that the problem of male violence epitomised by militarism had direct consequences for societal health and morality.

If a sense of wartime crisis prompted these reflections, so too did wartime cultural developments – for instance, the wartime performance of France's Eugène Brieux's *Damaged Goods (Les Avariés)* in Britain for the first time. The plot of the play, reduced to its essentials, is this. In the first act, George Dupont, who has contracted syphilis from a brief sexual encounter, seeks an immediate cure from a noted doctor, as he is to marry in a month. However, the doctor warns him that a true cure takes years and he must not marry. Act II shows the consequences of George ignoring this advice. He has passed on the disease to his family, including his sickly baby daughter. The final act finds his wife's father going to the same doctor for evidence against George in order to obtain a divorce; instead he (and the audience) receive a lengthy lecture – illustrated by the case histories of characters who tell their stories – on the need to alter attitudes towards venereal diseases so that they could be more openly acknowledged and treated.

One of the witnesses called before the Committee of Enquiry was J. B. Fagan, the producer who brought Brieux's play for the first time to the London stage in 1917. The performance of the play suggests the significance of culture, as well legislation, in shaping wartime debates over venereal disease.[67] As Fagan explained to the committee, the Lord Chamberlain (who decided to allow performances of Brieux's work sixteen years after it first appeared in France) was influenced by 'a great number of distinguished and official persons'. Fagan continued that the problem with censorship was that a grave subject 'handled with innuendo and any amount of improper suggestions' would often receive a license, while a serious treatment would not. He then reported on the benefits that he had seen when this play was performed throughout the country: 'I think it has done more good in the way of educating women on a subject on which they ought to know everything than anything that has been written about [it] or preached in my time ... I have travelled all round and been in the audiences and heard the expressions from women.' Even if some attended the play 'from curiosity and even prurient curiosity ... anyone who went with these motives came away with an entirely different frame of mind ... There is no doubt it had a very great effect on young minds, school boys, and even grown-up school girls.'[68]

Wartime commentators supported Fagan's views. Responding to the controversy surrounding the play in April 1917, the critic Norman Croom-Johnson vigorously took issue with the idea that 'its matter is unhealthy or obscene, or in any way unfit for public presentation ... M. Brieux's play deals with a terrible subject, the most appalling scourge of civilisation, but it deals with it simply, seriously, and with the most absolute sincerity.'[69] Instead of allowing the young, in particular, to suffer from their lack of knowledge about sexual relations, Brieux insists that 'they ought to be made to understand that the future of the race is in their hands.'[70] Croom-Johnson claimed that *Damaged Goods* 'is received with a still, tense attention that I have rarely seen in a theatre. Its production in aid of the campaign against venereal disease is a most significant event in the history of our stage.'[71] Another wartime commentator, writing in *The Vote*, the paper of the Women's Freedom League, also noted, 'people are turned away from every performance ... [and t]here are usually large numbers of men in khaki in the audience', while encouraging 'Freedom Leaguers' to attend the play, and even suggesting that free tickets be made available to soldiers for the duration of the war, because its lessons must be learned 'if our race is to continue an Imperial race, the production of damaged goods must cease.'[72]

The public reception of *Damaged Goods,* and the fact that it was licensed for the first time in wartime Britain, suggests the extent to which cultural as well as political interest in venereal disease had elicited seemingly new responses. The regulatory apparatus already in operation in France and set up in Britain under the Defence of the Realm Act attempted to prevent women from infecting men and thereby undermining the war effort. The performance of *Damaged Goods* publicised a decades-old argument against the double standard, seeing it as a threat to the imperial nation. There is little indication of 'liberation' in the subjecting of all women, but not men, to state control or in repeatedly emphasising their fundamental, national duty as mothers.[73]

'Now girls *will* be men.' If we return to the image in the *Bystander* after examining wartime and immediate postwar discussions of women's morality and sexuality, this phrase seems worth further analysis. What exactly did it mean that 'girls would be men' if assumptions about their morality and sexuality had remained unchanged? If the consequences of breaches of the prewar and indeed wartime double standard were likewise unaltered? This cartoon suggests that women could do 'men's jobs' and take on 'men's vices', but this does not mean they had the freedom to be 'men'. As is the case with many wartime cultural texts, this image is fascinating and open-ended. Hence the ability of wartime commentators and postwar interpreters to use such examples to claim, on one hand, the maintenance of gender roles and, on the other, stark disruption to them. However, as this essay has tried to demonstrate, given the ambivalence of much wartime cultural evidence, there are limits to what we can claim. Yet by using both printed texts and archives (like the records from criminal courts or private organisations like the Association for Moral and Social Hygiene, as I have done here), we can begin to delineate the complexity of wartime understandings of morality and sexuality for women.

For we are often left with examples of the continuing power of the 'anecdote'. Some have seen moments of wartime 'liberation' for women in portrayals of gender role reversals like the image in the *Bystander,* or in the sexual promiscuity recorded in postwar fiction like *Not So Quiet*. Others would maintain that so long as control over reproduction remained elusive at best, the repercussions for women choosing to pursue allegedly new sexual freedoms remained severe. On balance, given the tone of wartime public debates over women's behaviour, be it their alcohol consumption or heterosexual encounters, gendered assumptions regarding morality and sexuality would appear to have changed much less abruptly and irrevocably than some have argued. The models of 'liberation and backlash' and of gender 'reconstruction' do not prove adequate to explain the diversity of women's wartime experiences.

Notes

I would like to thank Gail Braybon, Kirsten Dellinger and Joe Ward for their comments on earlier drafts of this essay.

1. 'Oh! My Grandmother!' The *Bystander*, 3 April 1918, Women's Work Collection Press Cuttings, Imperial War Museum [WWC]. That the two women's occupations were window cleaning and bus conductor respectively suggests how visibly they had encroached upon men's jobs.
2. Sandra Gilbert, 'Soldier's Heart: Literary Men, Literary Women and the Great War', *Signs*, 8 (3), 1983. Also reprinted in M. R. Higonnet, J. Jenson, S. Michel and M. C. Weitz (eds), *Behind the Lines: Gender and the Two World Wars*, Yale University Press, 1987. As Gilbert puts it: '... the war functioned in so many different ways to liberate women – offering a revolution in economic expectations, a release of passionate energies, a

(re)union of previously fragmented sisters, and a (re)vision of social and aesthetic dreams …', *Behind the Lines*, 223
3. This is most clearly articulated in Susan Kingsley Kent, *Making Peace: The Reconstruction of Gender in Interwar Britain*, Princeton University Press, 1993. But it is also implied by the subtitle of both her book and that of Mary Louise Roberts, *Civilization Without Sexes: Reconstructing Gender in Postwar France, 1917–1927*, Chicago University Press, 1994.
4. For more on the images of women in the 1920s in Britain and France, see Billie Melman, *Women and the Popular Imagination in the Twenties*, Macmillan, 1988 and Roberts, *Civilization Without Sexes*.
5. Their usefulness for recruiting is illustrated by the posters and leaflets created for this purpose, promising aid to the wives and children of married soldiers and dependants – including children – regardless of the legal relationships of unmarried soldiers. See Item K 33304, Misc. Recruiting, Imperial War Museum (IWM).
6. 'Women and the War,' *Daily Call*, 19 November 1914.
7. 'Women and the War,' *Daily Call*, 19 November 1914.
8. Susan Pedersen, 'Gender, Welfare, and Citizenship in Britain during the Great War', *American Historical Review*, 95 (4), 1990, 997. 'Soldiers' Wives', *Leicester Mail*, 14 December 1914. Others, such as George Cassady, the mayor of Bootle, continued to be extremely critical of soldiers' wives who neglected their homes and families, see for instance, 'Complaint Against Soldiers' Wives', *Liverpool Courier*, 30 June 1915.
9. 'Soldiers' Wives', *Leicester Mail*, 14 December 1914.
10. 'Soldiers' Wives', *Leicester Mail*, 14 December 1914.
11. 'Drinking Among Women', *Evening Times*, 26 November 1914.
12. Trevor Wilson, *The Myriad Faces of War,* Polity Press, 1986, 163.
13. 'Unjust Drink Rules Protest of 3,000 London Women Workers,' *Daily Express*, 25 November 1915. A brief overview of the 1914–1915 changes in licensing can be found in Wilson, *Myriad Faces*, 152–153. A discussion of the reaction to the closing of public houses to women during some hours in which men were allowed is discussed in Sylvia Pankhurst, *The Home Front*, 1932, reprinted Cresset Library, 1987, 98.
14. 'Women and Excessive Drinking', *Eastern Press*, 10 November 1915.
15. Biographical information about Anna Martin can be found in Ellen Ross, *Love and Toil: Motherhood in Outcast London, 1870–1918*, Oxford University Press, 1993, 196–197.
16. Anna Martin, 'Working-Women and Drink', *The Nineteenth Century & After*, LXXVIII, no. 4, 1915, 1391.
17. Martin, 'Working-Women and Drink', 1378.
18. Martin, 'Working-Women and Drink', 1378–1383. Quote is from 1383.
19. Martin, 'Working-Women and Drink', 1389–90. Martin also noted an arrangement dating from July 1914 in Liverpool that forbade publicans to serve women more than two drinks per sitting.
20. Martin, 'Working-Women and Drink', 1389.
21. Martin, 'Working-Women and Drink', 1395. See Ross, *Love and Toil*, on the meaning of motherhood among the working poor as being rooted in mothers' abilities to provide materially for their families.
22. This can be linked with what Susan Pedersen has shown to be an explicit government policy to prevent separation allowances going for drink or for the support of those in adulterous unions. See Pedersen, 'Gender', 996–1003. Later in the war, as women increasingly entered the industrial workforce in Britain and their wages rose accordingly, the effect of 'drink' on their performance as workers also became an issue of concern, and the government congratulated itself on having stemmed the potential problem by limiting the availability of alcohol, see Lord D'Abernon, 'Public Health and Alcoholism among Women', 1917, London, 1–3. Lord D'Abernon's comments are cited in 'Women's Sobriety', *Morning Advertiser*, 20 December 1917 as having been read as a paper at the Institute of Public Health on 19 December and in 'Women and the War', *Birmingham Daily Express*, 22 December 1917, which approvingly noted that despite the

2222 | *Susan Grayzel*

increase in women's wages, excessive drinking and drunkenness had decreased. The *Express* also suggested the Central Control Board was not entirely responsible for this happy outcome: 'we are inclined to set something down to the heightened sense of responsibility and public spirit that have come with the war' and 'the absence of some millions of men, which has had a great effect on the drinking habits of innumerable women, married and single'.

3. This was especially true of those suspected of imbibing an increased amount, due to the wartime strain, the wartime largesse of separation allowances or higher pay. In this last case, public concern was not restricted to mothers and applied to all sorts of women workers, especially in the munitions industry. For more on this see Angela Woollacott, *On Her Their Lives Depend: Munitions Workers in the Great War*, University of California Press, 1994, Chapter 6, and Susan R. Grayzel, *Women's Identities At War: Gender, Motherhood, and Politics in Britain and France during the First World War*, University of North Carolina Press, 1999, Chapters 3 and 4.
24. G. C. Levillain, 'L'Alcoolisme et L'Immoralité à Rouen pendant la Guerre', *La Française*, 1 May 1915.
25. See *La Française*, 29 January 1916, 12 February 1916, 1 April 1916 and 18 May 1916. Also *L'Action Féminine*, especially September 1915.
26. See Mme. Louis Tinayre, *Françaises Il Faut Agir*, L'Union des Femmes de France, 1916.
27. For more on the law of 1 October 1917, see Alain Corbin, *Women for Hire: Prostitution and Sexuality in France after 1850*, translated by Alan Sheridan, Harvard University Press, 1990, 335.
28. For a further discussion of this see Susan R. Grayzel, '"The Mothers of Our Soldiers' Children": Motherhood, Immorality, and the War Baby Scandal, 1914–1918', in Claudia Nelson and Ann Sumner Holmes (eds), *Maternal Instincts: Motherhood and Sexuality in Britain, 1875–1925*, Macmillan, 1997.
29. See the following articles that publicised this law: 'Les Soldats sur le Front pourront se marier par procuration', *La Française*, 10 April 1915 and 'Le Mariage par procuration', *L'Echo de Paris*, 10 April 1915. For the subsequent legislation, see 'La Légitimation Posthume des Orphelins votée au Sénat', *La Française*, 1 July 1916 and 'Légitimation Posthume des Orphelins de la Guerre', *La Française*, 2 December 1916 and 'Au Parlement', *La Française*, 10 March 1917.
30. B. R. Mitchell, *Abstract of British Historical Statistics*, Cambridge University Press, 1962, 30–33.
31. Michel Huber, *La population de la France pendant la Guerre*, Presses Universitaires de France, 1931, 250–51
32. Huber, *La population*, 250
33. H. C. Fischer and Dr E. X. Dubois, *Sexual Life during the World War*, Francis Aldor, 1937, 7–8.
34. This is something that Lesley Hall usefully reminds us of in 'Feminist Reconfigurations of Heterosexuality in the 1920s', in Lucy Bland and Laura Doan (eds), *Sexology in Culture: Labelling Bodies and Desires*, Polity Press, 1998, 145.
35. These were both economic and social, even racial, fears. For more on this, see Grayzel, *Women's Identities At War*.
36. See the discussions of this in Stéphane Audoin-Rouzeau, *L'enfant de l'ennemi 1914–1918*, Aubier, 1995; Ruth Harris, 'The "Child of the Barbarian": Rape, Race and Nationalism in France During the First World War', *Past and Present*, 141, 1993; Judith Wishnia, 'Natalisme et Nationalisme Pendant la Première Guerre Mondiale', *Vingtième Siècle*, no. 45, 1995; and Grayzel, *Women's Identities At War*, Chapter 2.
37. It is this context which has been ignored in recent studies. See Roberts, *Civilization Without Sexes*, Chapter 4.
38. See for instance Francoise Thébaud, 'Work, Gender and Identity in Peace and War, 1890–1930', in Billie Melman (ed.), *Borderlines: Genders and Identities in War and Peace, 1870–1930*, Routledge, 1998, and Kent, *Making Peace*.
39. See Jane Marcus, 'Corpus/Corps/Corpse: Writing the Body in/at War', Afterword to Helen Zenna Smith [pseud.], *Not So Quiet ...*, 1930, reprinted Feminist Press, 1989.

40. Fischer and Dubois, *Sexual Life*, 305.
41. Smith, *Not So Quiet ...*, 200.
42. Smith, *Not So Quiet ...*, 212.
43. See the fuller discussion of rape in wartime fiction in Grayzel, *Women's Identities At War*, Chapter 2.
44. Annie Vivanti Chartres, *Vae Victis*, Edward Arnold, 1917.
45. Odette Dulac, *La Houille Rouge*, Editions Figuière, 1916, 45.
46. These records also provide evidence of infanticides. Here the French evidence is harder to come by because the British records, released after seventy-five years, are now available.
47. Deposition of Hannah Sturley, 18 November 1916, Walter Folliott Blanford reporting the words of Florence Sturley, 18 November 1916, and Archibald Harold Hewitt, 25 November 1916 in CRIM 1 164/2, P[ublic] R[ecord] O[ffice].
48. Deposition of Ethel Martin, 26 June 1917, CRIM 1 168/3, PRO.
49. Deposition of Agnes Maud Killpatrick, 22 May 1917, CRIM 1 167/6, PRO.
50. Deposition of Isabel Myra Killpatrick, 22 May 1917; Sonia Craigie, 22 May 1917; Charlotte Beatrice Myerscough, 22 May 1917; and William Richard Willing, 22 May 1917, CRIM 1 167/6, PRO.
51. See the discussions of this in Angela Woollacott, '"Khaki Fever" and its Control: Gender, Class, Age and Sexual Morality on the British Homefront in the First World War', *Journal of Contemporary History*, 29, 1994; Philippa Levine, '"Walking the Streets in a Way No Decent Woman Should": Women Police in World War I', *Journal of Modern History*, 66, 1994; and Grayzel, *Women's Identities At War*, Chapter 4.
52. See Dossier Ba 1614, Archives de la Préfecture de Police.
53. Report of the Royal Commission on Venereal Diseases, London, 1916, 15.
54. Cate Haste, *Rules of Desire: Sex in Britain World War 1 to the Present*, Chatto, 1992, 50.
55. In a book that focuses mainly on France, Claude Quétel indicates that the war years saw increasing numbers of cases after a previous decline since the turn of the century. See Claude Quetel, *History of Syphilis*, 1986, reprinted by Johns Hopkins University Press, 1990, Chapter 8.
56. See references in note 34 above, especially Grayzel, *Women's Identities At War*, Chapter 2.
57. Annabelle Melzer, 'Spectacles and Sexualities: The "Mise-en-Scène" of the "Tirailleur Sénégalais" on the Western Front, 1914–1920', in Melman, and Philippa Levine, 'Battle Colors: Race, Sex, and Colonial Soldiery in World War I', *Journal of Women's History*, 9 (4), 1998. See also Joe Lunn, *Memoirs of the Maelstrom: A Senegalese Oral History of the First World War*, Heinemann, 1999, Chapter 6. Quote is from Levine, 'Battle Colors', 106.
58. Regulation 40D, Defence of the Realm Act, 22 March 1918. See *Defence of the Realm Regulations*, London, 1918. For a fuller discussion of legislation in wartime Britain, see Susan R. Grayzel, 'The Enemy Within: The Problem of British Women's Sexuality During the First World War', in Nicole Ann Dombrowski (ed.), *Women and War in the Twentieth Century: Enlisted with or without Consent*, Garland, 1999, 72–89.
59. In this sense, those responding in 1918 reflected reactions to the original nineteenth-century Contagious Diseases Acts. For more on this see Grayzel, 'The Enemy Within' and Judith Walkowitz, *Prostitution and Victorian Society: Women, Class, and the State*, Cambridge University Press, 1980.
60. The Association for Moral and Social Hygiene (ASMH) was renamed in 1915. Previously known as the Ladies' National Association for the Repeal of the Contagious Acts, it was created by Josephine Butler in 1869. See Edward Bristow, *Vice and Vigilance: Purity Movements in Britain since 1700*, Rowman and Littlefield, 1977 and Walkowitz, *Prostitution and Victorian Society*.
61. Committee of Inquiry, *The State and Sexual Morality*, London, 1920, 7.
62. Minutes, Meeting of Commission of Enquiry, Association for Social and Moral Hygiene (ASMH) Box 49, Fawcett Library [FL].
63. Testimony of Mary Scharlieb, 5 May 1919, AMSH Box 49, FL.

64. Testimony of E. Basil Wedmore, 27 January 1919, AMSH Box 49, FL.
65. Testimony of E.B. Turner, F.R.C.S., 14 July 1919, AMSH Box 49, FL.
66. Committee of Inquiry, *The State and Sexual Morality*, 70.
67. By April of 1917, the play had not only been presented to London audiences, but had also been reprinted, according to a notice by Mrs Bernard Shaw in *The Times Literary Supplement*, because the performance of the play in London had created renewed demand, *The Times Literary Supplement*, 19 April 1917.
68. Testimony of J. B. Fagan, 3 November 1919, AMSH Box 49, FL.
69. Norman Croom-Johnson, 'Brieux Triumphant', *Review of Reviews*, LV, no. 328, 1917. These censorship battles had revolved around all of Brieux's plays. The lifting of the ban on *Damaged Goods* was hailed as part of a liberalising trend by W. L. George in *Royal Magazine* in 1918.
70. Eugène Brieux, *Damaged Goods (Les Avariés)*, translated by John Pollock, in *Three Plays by Brieux*, 1911, reprinted Brentano's, 1914, 241, 249.
71. Croom-Johnson, 'Brieux Triumphant'. The popularity of the play on the West End may account for its being turned into a British silent film in 1919; see Annette Kuhn, *Cinema, Censorship and Sexuality 1909–1925*, Routledge, 1988, 55–63.
72. C. S. Bremmer, 'Damaged Goods', *Vote*, 11 May 1917.
73. For a more thorough discussion of these issues, see Grayzel, 'The Enemy Within' and *Women's Identities At War*, Chapter 4.

6

The Great War and Gender Relations
the Case of French Women and the First World War Revisited

James McMillan

Introduction

In the 1970s and much of the 1980s, scholarly debate on the impact of the First World War on women centred largely on women's 'emancipation', however that was defined. Most of the protagonists in the debate were historians who were influenced by either the rise of the 'new social history', or the emergence after 1968 of 'second-wave' feminism, or, more usually, by both. The research agenda of the relationship between war and social change, turning on the dynamics of the interaction between 'total war' and 'mobilisation', proved to be a productive one and, enlarged by the perspective of comparative urban history, continued to produce fresh insights well into the 1990s. What all these studies shared was a primary focus on material conditions and wartime experience, though the issue of attitudes to change and representations of change was by no means neglected.[1]

In the wake of the 'linguistic turn' and the rise of 'new cultural' history, however, the question of perceptions of change has moved to centre-stage, especially for historians of gender relations whose main interest is in the ideological work performed by representations of gender and sexual difference. Thus in her study of French women and the First World War, Mary Louise Roberts states that 'change ... has been defined as a cultural construction rather than a social, political or economic reality'.

Appropriating the phrase 'a civilisation without sexes' from a comment by the French writer Pierre Drieu la Rochelle (only one of many European intellectuals to articulate a profound cultural pessimism in the face of the characteristics of the modern world), Roberts seizes on Drieu's anxiety about the blurring of the boundaries between the sexes and argues that 'gender was central to how change was understood in the postwar decade'. She adds: 'The discursive obsession with female identity during these years reveals that a wide variety of French men and women made it a privileged site for a larger ideological project: how to come to terms with rapid social and cultural change, and how to articulate a new, more appropriate order of social relationships. Debate concerning gender identity became a primary way to embrace, resist, or reconcile oneself to changes associated with the war'.[2]

The cultural approach has much to recommend it. As Joan Scott has suggested, 'watershed' history – attempting to assess the Great War as a turning point because of its impact on a particular sector of society – has its limitations, whereas gender history allows new questions to be formulated, such as whether the war challenged or reinforced existing ideas about gender identity.[3] Roberts's starting point is the apparent blurring of gender roles during the war, which generated extensive debate both at the time and in the war's immediate aftermath. Social historians of the 1970s – the present author included – had not been blind to that fact, but it is true that in our concern to investigate social realities we had perhaps been less attentive to the social imaginary than we might have been. What Roberts calls 'cultural realities in themselves' – emotions, preoccupations, anxieties, misgivings, expectations – form part of 'reality' in its widest sense and accordingly are as deserving of study and analysis as material conditions.

The question remains, however, as to whether the Great War produced a crisis in gender relations. It is Roberts's contention that the exigencies of wartime shattered the prewar gender order, which then had to be rebuilt as an integral part of the process of postwar reconstruction. This is a thesis which has already been challenged by another cultural historian, Susan Grayzel, who argues that the Great War consolidated rather than transformed the existing gender system, above all by highlighting the centrality of motherhood in patriotic discourse.[4] The present chapter is an exercise in cultural history designed to support the conclusions of Grayzel rather than of Roberts, but it will conclude on a note of caution. All kinds of history have their limitations, and cultural history is no exception.

To begin with, it might be noted that in discussing the impact of the First World War on gender relations, neither Roberts nor Grayzel devotes any serious attention to the prewar period. Yet change can only be measured against some kind of background or benchmark. Roberts, it is true, rightly observes that gender had long played a crucial ordering role in French society. From the time of the Enlightenment through to the First

World War and beyond, a huge amount of thought and discussion went into attempts to redefine the roles of men and women. The French Revolution, though it enunciated the doctrine of the 'rights of man', refused to extend those rights to women. Rather, in their efforts to set boundaries between public and private life, the revolutionaries insisted that women's contribution to society should be made through their role as wife and mother. Republicanism, the dynamic which drove the development of French democracy in the nineteenth century, was from its inception wedded to a vision of citizenship from which women had been excluded.[5]

In the gender order which emerged in the aftermath of the Revolutionary and Napoleonic periods, domesticity was held up as the highest ideal to which women could aspire. Of course, only a minority conformed to the domestic ideal. In both countryside and town, the women of the people participated fully in the world of work and contributed to the financial resources of the household. Nevertheless, in the nineteenth century not only bourgeois commentators and social reformers but also militant male trade unionists came to regard the *ouvrière*, or working woman, as an affront and a challenge to the social order itself.

What Roberts does not discuss, however, is the question of whether gender relations were already seen as being in crisis on the eve of the First World War. In focusing on the 'new woman' of the 1920s, she overlooks her predecessor, the 'new woman' of the *belle époque* (and indeed the even earlier *femme nouvelle* of the 1830s). The period 1880 to 1914 was one which saw considerable advances in the social status of women. Legal changes (especially the reintroduction of divorce in 1884), along with the expansion of female education at all levels and the rise of an organised women's movement, the main demand of which by 1914 was the introduction of the female suffrage, all combined to convince a number of prominent male commentators that a new Eve had arisen to threaten the gender order presided over by old Adam. One particularly disturbing threat to the male sense of sexual identity was the image of the masculinised woman – one who smoked, wore men's clothes, cut her hair short, rode a bicycle and possibly even expressed a sexual preference for other women. Proust's masochistic and neurotic narrator in *À la recherche du temps perdu*, obsessed with the possible sexual transgressions of his lover, Albertine, with her girlfriends from the little band which had played together as children on the beach at Balbec, was perhaps an extreme example, but he was by no means alone.[6] A lesser novelist, Marcel Prévost, was horrified by the appearance of a female type which he labelled the *demi-vierges*, upperclass young women who took delight in violating the genteel conventions to which they were supposed to adhere.[7] For some historians, therefore, the 'crisis in gender relations' began not with the Great War but was well under way by 1900.

As I have argued elsewhere, however, this vision of a gender order turned upside down in the *belle époque* was neither a widespread nor a representative point of view. The exaggerations of a coterie of frightened male intellectuals hardly characterise society as a whole.[8] Secondly – and this is an even more important point because of its implications for the cultural approach to history – hysterical male fantasies about the masculinisation of women, however 'real' they might be in the realm of discourse and in the social imaginary of an epoch, need to be carefully distinguished from the social realities experienced by women themselves in their everyday lives. Despite the not inconsiderable changes which took place in women's situation in the pre-1914 period, the fact remains that for the most part the traditional gender order had survived relatively unscathed by the eve of the war.

The war unquestionably lent a new immediacy and urgency to the ongoing debate on women's role in French society, but whether it precipitated 'a crisis in gender relations' is another matter. In this essay, it is proposed to test the Roberts thesis by examining three aspects of gender relations which have been acknowledged to be of critical significance in any study of the subject, namely: power relations; the body and sexuality; and the idea of 'separate spheres', based on a division between public and private.[9]

Power Relations

As the First World War developed into a protracted war of attrition which necessitated the mobilisation of entire populations, women in France were called upon to rally to the cause of national unity and to contribute to the war effort – but in their own special feminine ways. Service to the nation could take many forms. Unlike British women, French women could not enlist in the armed forces or wear military uniforms, but, in addition to acting as *remplaçantes* (replacements for absent male workers in industry), they became nurses and did voluntary work in countless charitable initiatives designed to boost the war effort. The *marraine* scheme, popularised by the novelist and nationalist deputy Maurice Barrès, encouraged women and young girls to act as 'godmothers' to 'godsons' in the trenches, by writing them letters and sending them presents.[10] Feminist organisations took the lead in organising charities intended to benefit soldiers and their families. Ostentatiously patriotic, the leaders of the two principal mainstream feminist bodies, the CNFF and the UFSF, refused to have anything to do with attempts by international feminist organisations to promote a negotiated peace. In a manifesto, *To the Women of Neutral Countries and Allied Countries*, they explained that French feminists could not possibly meet with their counterparts from enemy countries while the latter declined to disavow the belligerent actions of their governments or to protest at the violation of Belgian neutrality and the occupation of French soil.[11]

Patriotic propaganda heaped praise on the dedication and sacrifices of the women of France. Mothers who gave their sons and husbands only to lose them on the field of battle were singled out as incomparable patriots. In the invaded regions, the village schoolteacher who remained at her post, sometimes even assuming the role of mayor, became a popular heroine, as did the post-office clerical worker who kept services going often at considerable risk to her personal safety.[12] The nurse – devoted, discreet, calm, orderly – became almost a figure of legend, famed for her ability not only to tend her patients' wounds but to give them back their courage to return to the fight.[13] Propagandists went out of their way to present an image of French womanhood working as one with the civil and military authorities, motivated by a righteous patriotism and ready to make any sacrifice in the struggle to defeat the enemy. Playwright Maurice Donnay, for instance, marvelled at the transformation of the frivolous pleasure-seeking *Parisienne* of the *belle époque* into a devoted and dutiful servant of the community: 'Disorder, independence, blindness, all that becomes order, discipline, altruism and lucidity'.[14] Another well-known writer, Lucien Descaves, identified women as particularly suited to the task of rooting out *embusqués*, men who shirked their patriotic duty. In the charitable activities of women during the First World War – knitting, sending off packets of socks, scarves, gloves and other items of clothing to the soldiers at the front – he detected 'a little of the aggressive ardour of 1793'.[15]

It is clear, therefore, that the women of France gave ample evidence of their patriotism in the course of the war – albeit that its expression almost invariably involved particular, gender-specific, feminine forms of action. And, as in Britain, the idea grew that in return for their massive contribution to the war effort, women should receive a tangible reward in the shape of full rights of citizenship. Henri Robert, a distinguished lawyer, was convinced that the war would be 'the women's 1789'.[16] Bracke, a socialist deputy with a long track record of support for women's rights, declared that all the arguments against women's suffrage were refuted by their wartime achievements.[17] Even some anti-feminists recognised that change seemed to be on the way. Maurice Barrès proposed 'le suffrage des morts', which would give the vote to war widows.[18] Feminist leaders, who had suspended their suffrage campaign for the duration of the war out of respect for national unity, acquired the conviction that their hour had come at last. One of the best known, Marguerite Durand, writing in the newspaper *L'Oeuvre*, anticipated a new deal for women in the post-war period.[19] Suzanne Grinberg, a prominent woman barrister and feminist, conducted a survey of parliamentary opinion in 1917 and pronounced herself confident about the passage of a suffrage bill.[20]

These forecasts of an imminent victory for feminism appeared to be vindicated in May 1919 when the Chamber of Deputies debated the question of women's suffrage. A bill to give women the vote in municipal and other local elections had been tabled as far back as 1906 by the Catholic deputy Paul Dussaussoy but, though the object of a favourable report by its Radical-Socialist *rapporteur* Ferdinand Buisson, it had never been

debated by the Chamber.[21] At the beginning of 1918 the Independent
Emile Magniez, acting on suggestions that women should be rewarded
with citizenship by way of thanks for their contribution to the war effort,
tabled another bill to enfranchise women in municipal elections. Backed
by its *rapporteur*, Pierre-Etienne Flandin, the bill received support at the
committee stage and finally came before the Chamber on 8 May 1919,
where in the course of the debate the socialist Jean Bon tabled an
amendment to the effect that the female franchise should be extended to
include the right to vote in legislative as well as municipal elections.
Numerous interventions reiterated the view that women merited the vote
as a reward for their wartime endeavours – a 'gesture of justice and
recognition', in the words of Jules Siegfried. The most persuasive speech
was made by the former socialist and ex-prime minister René Viviani,
who eloquently rehearsed all the arguments in favour of women's emancipation, including their war record, alongside claims that women had a
special talent for tackling the moral and social problems of society and
drawing on international comparisons which cast France in an unflatter-
ing light on the issue of women's rights. To his plea for the immediate
introduction of suffrage equality for women, the Chamber of Deputies
responded by voting in favour of the bill by a majority of 344 to 97.[22]
Feminists were jubilant. Lucie Colliard, a militant schoolteacher, exulted:
'At last we are going to have it, this ballot paper desired for such a long
time. For the old gentlemen of the Senate, led by the sound arguments
and eloquence of Louis Marin, will not dare to do less than their colleagues in the Chamber.'[23]

Sadly for French feminists, their celebrations proved premature, as at
least some of their number had feared might turn out to be the case. In *La
Française*, Jane Misme and Juliette-Francoise Raspail had warned that
the Senate continued to represent a 'formidable obstacle', and so it
proved.[24] The parliamentary commission of the Senate set up to examine
the Bon bill reflected the dominance of the Radical-Socialists in the house
and their leader, Emile Combes, the veteran anticlerical who had waged
war on the religious orders at the beginning of the century and prepared
the way for the separation of Church and State, was a longstanding oppo-
nent of women's suffrage on the grounds that to enfranchise women was
to encourage clericalism and imperil republican institutions. Not all Radicals in the Senate subscribed to Combes's position – the most notable
dissenter being the Radical senator for the Var, Louis Martin, a consistent
advocate of women's rights – but the great majority did. In particular, the
rapporteur of the Senate commission, Alexandre Bérard, was a fervent
disciple of Combes and his report, published in September 1919, reiterated the stock anticlerical argument that female suffrage posed a mortal
threat to the survival of the republican regime. The threat, indeed, was
deemed to be all the greater since the loss of life occasioned by the war
had increased the imbalance in the population in favour of women. With
two million more voters than men, a female electorate was well placed

to vote the Republic out of existence. Thus, when the second chamber finally got round to debating the issue of women's suffrage in November 1922, it proceeded to reject it by the narrow but decisive margin of 156 votes to 134. The key argument against the measure was the anticlerical one, but the debate provided an opportunity for the parading of outright misogyny from the likes of Senator François Labrousse, for whom women were 'impressionable and suggestible' and their role in public life invariably disastrous.[25]

Thus, far from advancing the cause of women's suffrage in France, the First World War could be seen as a serious setback for it. The defeat of 1922 in the Senate was replicated at various times during the interwar years. In 1925, the Chamber voted in favour of a bill to give women the vote in local elections but in 1927 and 1928 the Senate again proved intractable, contenting itself with the sentiments expressed by the bill's *rapporteur* in the Senate, Pierre Marraud, who wrote that:

> The woman of the Latin race does not feel, has not developed, in the same way as the woman of the Anglo-Saxon or Germanic races. Her position in the foyer is not the same. As a person she is generally more absorbed in her Church, whose dogmatism she does not dispute. It is perfectly reasonable, then, that her legal status should be different.[26]

In 1932, another woman's suffrage bill which received a massive majority in the Chamber was greeted with indifference and a refusal to debate the issue. A subsequent attempt to reopen discussion in the Senate was blocked in December 1933, while a proposal for equal suffrage tabled in the Chamber by Bracke in March 1935 and another by Louis Marin in June 1936 failed to win the backing of either the Senate or government. French 'singularity' – the anomalous position of French women by comparison with women in other democratic polities – remained a feature of the interwar years. Whatever its causes and significance – a matter of some historiographical controversy – it certainly makes it hard to sustain the idea that the First World War had altered the balance of power in relations between the sexes.[27]

The Body and Sexuality

Not the least of the advantages of the historiographical shift from a purely women's history to a wider gender history is the welcome attention that has been paid to the question of male identity and constructions of masculinity. In the study of the First World War and gender relations, it is particularly appropriate to recall that the most immediate effect of war was the destruction and mutilation of male bodies. To date, there has been no French equivalent of Joanna Bourke's *Dismembering the Male*, though a recent issue of *Annales* carries a number of stimulating articles on the theme of 'The First World War and the Body', including Stéphane Audoin-Rouzeau's moving account of the mourning experiences of families who had lost a beloved son or husband and father.[28] Sometimes female relatives were prepared to go to extraordinary lengths in order to recover the bodies of their loved ones for private burial. In Audoin-Rouzeau's article, it is evident that the gender history of the body and the First World War is far from being exclusively a narrative about conflict of the sexes and the subordination of women. Any history of the subject needs to begin by recalling what united bodies as well as what divided them.

Nevertheless, sexual difference remains the key theme in gender history and it has certainly been the case that, in Western society and culture, war has often been conceived as a supremely masculine experience, defining manhood for men in the way that childbirth has defined womanhood for women.[29] On the eve of the First World War, in both Europe and America, nationalist rhetoric had succeeded in making war into a social myth, extolling it as a noble and chivalrous enterprise which would redeem nation states by rescuing their young men from weakness and degeneracy and turning them into vigorous and virile patriots. According to George L. Mosse, the exclusively masculine dimension of war was invariably reinforced by the experience of military defeat, such as the French had sustained at the hands of Prussia in 1870 to 1871. The shame of the defeat was an indictment of French manhood and calls for *revanche* emanating from nationalists such as Maurice Barrès and Paul Déroulède were reaffirmations of French virility and male notions of honour. The 'remaculinisation of culture' was as much a feature of the French *belle époque* as of American society after the Vietnam War.[30] In gender terms, war was a business from which women were to be rigorously excluded. The theatre of battle was a space for men only and at the beginning of the First World War the French government showed its commitment to this ideal by banning all women, including nurses, from the war zone until 1915.[31]

As the Great War dragged on, for some combatants at least the conviction hardened that this war in particular was the ultimate test of French manhood. In a work entitled *Courage*, written by two doctors serving in the French army and published in 1917, the authors claimed to offer a scientific treatment of their subject, albeit one written also in a patriotic spirit and dedicated to Marshal Joffre. Drs Huot and Voivenel defined courage as 'physical and moral firmness in the face of death' and distinguished it from fear, a primitive biological emotion emanating from the instinct for self preservation. Courage, by contrast, represented 'the triumph of the instinct of social preservation over the instinct of individual preservation'. It was an essentially masculine quality. Women were naturally fearful, though the authors admitted that during the current conflict women had begun to learn to show courage. But the supreme test – the response under fire – was not open to women. This was 'the safeguard of the race, of the species'.[32]

Of course, not all men proved to be heroes. Some, like the forty-one year old schoolmaster, Théophile Maupas and three of his comrades were shot as cowards for refusing to obey an order to 'go over the top'.[33] Only when the war was over would it be possible to campaign for the rehabilitation of such men shot 'for the sake of example'.[34] Also, from 1915 onwards, military doctors began to comment on the problems of mental health exhibited by soldiers serving on the Western Front. Interestingly, however, unlike the British, French doctors refused to speak of 'shell shock', preferring the term war 'neurosis' or 'hysteria'. According to the French medical profession, the disorders in question were not so much the product of the war as manifestations of a 'hereditary' tendency to degeneracy.[35] In the words of Huot and Voivenel – for whom such men were in any case a mere handful – it was important not to conflate the very few genuine cases of 'war anxiety' with 'the delirious conceptions of a melancholy, persecuted, or confused soldier, who was a madman, real or potential, before the war'.[36]

Rather than dwell on male neuroses, the likes of Huot and Voivenel preferred to imagine soldiers as conquering heroes, entitled to enjoy the traditional *repos du guerrier*. It was their contention that in all probability – though the authors had to admit that they had no hard evidence for their hypothesis – courage was linked to sexual prowess and it was appropriate that women should assume that the link was there. As they wrote: 'Women need to be persuaded that the heroic soldier is a superb lover – and, to judge by the success of aviators with women, it would appear that they are.'[37] What is astonishing about this text is not just its sexism but also its racism. Animals, the authors suggested, were incapable of courage, because even the fiercest of them like the lion acted first and foremost out of the need to stay alive. Similarly, so-called primitive peoples were deemed to be incapable of courage. In the eyes of the two 'scientific' observers – one of whom, Huot, had lived in Africa and was a strong supporter of French colonialism and its *mission civilisatrice* – black people were lacking in the elements of civilisation and were close to the animals in the way they lived, though the doctors conceded that under the benign influence of the white man Africans could acquire civilisation and therefore a capacity for courage.[38]

In rhetoric as in reality, therefore, the battle zone of the French soldier in the First World War was a uniquely masculine space, a proving ground for the display of manly valour from which women were inevitably excluded. The female bodies most at risk were those of women who were subjected to the atrocity of rape at the hands of the invader. The precise number of rapes committed by German troops in the course of the invasion of France and Belgium at the beginning of the war cannot be determined with certainty. It was a crime never sanctioned by the German High Command, committed for the most part in opportunist fashion by soldiers who may have been motivated at least in part by fear of, and loathing for, a civilian population that offered partisan-type resistance, not least from women who could turn out to be murderesses and poison-ers.[39] Stories of rape, however, rapidly became the stuff of French atroc-ity propaganda, aimed at demonising a brutal and heartless enemy. At the same time, however, these narratives can be read as expressions of mas-culine anguish at a failure to protect home and nation, both of which were symbolised by the feminine body.[40] In this way, from a gender per-spective, narratives of rape served to reinforce rather than to undermine existing ideas about gender identity. It was for French men to be real men, rallying to the defence of women, home and hearth, and for women to turn to their menfolk for protection and revenge.

The debate on the 'child of the barbarian', though multilayered in its meanings and ramifications, likewise pivoted on women's role as wife and mother. From the beginning of 1915, the question of whether or not to abort the foetuses developing in the wombs of victims of '*Boche* rape' gave rise to an extraordinary public debate. On the one side were those who were prepared to countenance abortion on account of the affront to French feminine honour and the impurity introduced into French blood, astrous consequences for the future of the 'race'. On the other re those who, motivated either by humanitarianism or by prona-talist considerations, urged women to keep their children and bring them up as true French nationals. Opinion did not divide easily along either ide-ological or occupational lines: neither feminists nor doctors spoke with one voice. Although no figure was ever put on the number of cases involved, the government took the matter seriously enough to issue a decree on 24 March 1915 which encouraged mothers to go ahead with the birth and then give the child over to the civil authorities, who would issue a false birth certificate and place it in care.[41] First, however, the mothers had to produce a statement signed by a local official, a *juge de paix* or a mayor, testifying to their good moral character previous to the assault. The priority of government, in other words, was not only to pre-vent women from committing a criminal act, which abortion was, in the name of a misguided patriotism, but also to encourage maternity in a society threatened with depopulation. Once again, motherhood took precedence over all other considerations. In war as in peace the existing gender order remained intact.[42]

In terms of a 'war experience', the women who came into closest con-tact with the combatants were the nurses who tended the wounded both close to the front line and in the rear. (Such few women doctors as there were replaced male colleagues at home.) The role of the nurse, however, merely served to underline the massively contrasting histories of male and female bodies in the course of the war and the continuing impor-tance of sexual difference. Nurses, indeed, are worth considering at some length to demonstrate that, during the First World War, there was no real crisis of gender relations in France but rather the continuing operation of a gender system which distinguished sharply between male and female, masculine and feminine.

In the nineteenth century nursing did not enjoy much prestige – rather the reverse. The problem was that France had lacked a Florence Nightingale to make nursing into a respectable profession for middleclass women, with the result that its image remained that of a trade not unlike domestic service, involving the discharge of demanding and disagreeable, even servile, duties. Nurses were traditionally recruited from the ranks of men and women of the popular classes, who were paid low wages for what was regarded as very menial work. The only women likely to serve in hospitals were nuns, since they were prepared to undertake the work as a form of self-mortification as well as of serving society.[43] By the turn of the century, however, the predominance of nuns in the nursing profession had come to seem offensive in the eyes of the anticlerical Republican state and a campaign was therefore launched both to secularise its personnel and to raise standards through the establishment of nursing training schools, culminating in the founding of the Ecole de la Salpêtrière in 1908, which managed to recruit from the ranks of the petty and middling bourgeoisie.[44]

Furthermore, as part of a wider campaign to try to raise the status and profile of the nursing profession in France in the prewar period, a number of parties – feminists, social Catholic activists, propagandists on behalf of the Red Cross – began to portray nursing as the one profession which could give women a role in national life that would equate with men's obligation to perform military service. The Red Cross spokesman, Dr Berthier, who was unusually percipient in anticipating a conflict which would require the mobilisation of entire populations, was particularly insistent on women's fitness for nursing duties.[45] Doctors like Berthier were convinced that, in the era of the so-called 'national revival', there was a well of feminine patriotism to be tapped into for the greater benefit of the *patrie*. Indeed, a staple of Red Cross discourse was the reminder that the French defeat of 1870 had been brought about not just by the superiority of Prussian male military might but by the contribution of women volunteer nurses who had outnumbered their French equivalents by ten to one.[46]

From the outset of the 1914 to 1918 conflict, women were eager to join the ranks of the nursing profession as auxiliaries. By 1918 the Service de santé militaire employed 100,000 women, only 30,000 of whom were paid professionals, the rest being made up of volunteers. The nurse thus became an iconic image of the War, celebrated and commented upon in innumerable works of patriotic propaganda. As one commentator put it: 'Whoever thinks of the French woman of 1914 has an image of a young nurse draped in a white or blue veil, sprightly despite the monastic headdress marked with a blood-red cross.'[47] Most of these nurses worked in auxiliary hospitals in the rear. Very few were sent to the front, though those who went were cited as examples of uncommon female heroism. One such was Mme Charlotte Maître, described in the female roll of honour as:

[a] nurse of the elite, courageous and devoted beyond praise: since the beginning of hostilities has given the most valuable services to surgery and medicine. Posted as a volunteer at the front line, has borne the dangers and the fatigue of the life of the Front in the underground shelters, has shown in the face of repeated bombardment an exemplary courage and decisiveness. Wounded by shell bursts while carrying out her duty, refused to allow herself to be evacuated. Has contracted two serious infections in the course of her service while caring for men with contagious diseases. Has already been cited twice by the order of the day.[48]

But not all nurses won such favourable plaudits. Some commentators, struck by the overwhelmingly upperclass origins of the great majority of volunteer nurses, claimed that these women had flocked to join the profession solely in order to be seen doing the smart thing for women in wartime. One critic deplored how the fashionable woman could do her patriotic duty 'without renouncing anything of her feminine mentality and her high society point of view. She has therefore brought to the task her qualities and defects as a woman along with her class prejudices.' The society woman nurse went out of her way to ensure that her appearance was different to that of ordinary nurses. If she had obtained a diploma, she wore the recognised uniform, but styled by a high-class couturier. If she had no qualifications she wore the decorated Red Cross arm band and the *Médaille sociale*. According to this critic, such young society women often saw their role as being to flirt and chat with the wounded rather than to employ themselves in more laborious chores.[49] Lucien Descaves likewise complained bitterly about how, especially at the beginning of the war, 'ladies played at being nurses beside men who, for their part, had not being playing at soldiers. Some, indeed, en route to the hospital, stopped half-way, at the stations of the route, in order to distribute cakes, cards, flowers and smiles the length of the trains … for them it was just another way to hold a tea reception.'[50]

Nevertheless, it is fair to say that the bulk of the comment on voluntary nurses was in fact favourable rather than hostile. Most observers lauded their patriotism and selfless devotion to duty.[51] Novelists and propagandists marvelled at the way brilliant society women and renowned stars of the stage and women of letters, sometimes to their own amazement, were able to take on all sorts of menial tasks, showing no repugnance for the bandaging of horrible gaping wounds, or washing dirty feet, changing sheets, or emptying hygienic buckets.[52] What needs to be underlined here, however, is the identification of a specifically *feminine* contribution to the war effort, the product of women's nature as women. In wartime propaganda, it was argued that it was precisely women's nature which made them specially suited to the task of ministering to the war-wounded. Propagandists on behalf of the Red Cross argued that even the most ignorant woman indisputably made a better nurse than a man, since women naturally possessed the moral qualities necessary in a nurse – devotion, obedience, discretion, calm, order, and above all, delicacy. Woman, it was claimed, was the nurse of the hearth. Why should she not become the nurse of the *patrie*?[53]

As for the alleged coquetry and feminine mannerisms of some upper-class volunteers, *grands-blessés* themselves testified to the fact that they did not mind a degree of coquettishness on the wards.[54] Nurses, too, sometimes contended that their patients appreciated even more the devoted attention they received than the restoration of health itself, since what they needed to boost their morale and prepare them for a return to the fight was someone who could console their grief and sustain their courage.[55] Léon Abensour claimed that nurses gave men the delicious sensation of rediscovering feminine company after months of deprivation, creating in them a sense of being reunited with their families, their mothers, their sisters, their fiancées. It was these dear images which often symbolised for them the *patrie* itself, the homeland for which they were fighting and dying.[56] In this way, as the prominent politician Louis Barthou argued, the smile of the nurse made an invaluable contribution both to national defence and national unity, and even prepared the way for class reconciliation: 'These society women and bourgeois women, who bent over the beds of wounded or sick peasants, by their delicate hands, expert in the most repugnant of duties, have laid the foundations for a more united and fraternal France where envy and hate will have no rights.'[57] Barthou's sentiments were echoed by the Countess de Courson, who also anticipated in the future a reciprocal and deeper comprehension between the upper classes and the men of the people, thanks to the work of the Red Cross.[58] The nurse, in short, served not as the harbinger of a new social order but as the acceptable face of the existing order, a guarantee that the postwar world would not be radically different from the world of the *fin de siècle*. Women would continue to be womanly, and the gender order, as well as the system of class relations, of the *belle époque* would survive intact.

One aspect of nursing that did give cause for concern in some quarters, however, was its implications for sexual morality. One doctor deemed war 'necessarily a school of sexual liberty'. In the military hospitals, young women had discovered 'the mystery of the other sex' and were thus more sexually aware.[59] Other commentators observed that the war had shattered some of the conventions of the double standard of morality by giving young middleclass girls the right to go out unchaperoned in order to tend the wounded in the hospitals. The novelist Marcel Prévost was struck by the number of romantic attachments which blossomed in 'this place of physical misery, among the groans in the odour of blood and iodine'.[60] Indeed, in one of his own novels Prévost has an aristocratic heroine who converts the family château into a hospital and eventually falls in love with a likeable English aviator entrusted to her care.[61] The result of these wartime romances, according to Prévost, was a new, freer, and more intimate association of the sexes in the immediate postwar period. Yet, even he, a champion of traditional morality, accepted that this development was not necessarily a bad thing. Again, one is hard put to discern a crisis in gender relations. In any case, whatever the fears of the most unreconstructed apologists for the double standard in the face of changes in female fashion and of fictional representations of a new, liberated woman such as the heroine of Victor Margueritte's novel, *La Garçonne*, there is plenty of evidence to suggest that, as in the *belle époque*, the 'new woman' of the 1920s and her adepts were vastly out-numbered by the champions of traditional bourgeois morality.[62]

Private and Public

The idea of a division between private and public spheres had been a staple of liberal political thought since at least the time of the Enlightenment. For feminist theorists and historians, it is a much criticised cultural construct which rests on gender-specific assumptions about the 'natural' attributes of men and women, namely that by nature men are specially fitted for the 'public' world of work and politics while women are best suited to the 'private' world of home and family. If the First World War is to be seen as having given rise to a crisis in gender relations, the best evidence would come from discourses and practices which identified the war as the solvent of the public-private divide, opening the floodgates to confusion in the gender order. These were not entirely absent, but they pale into insignificance by comparison with the continuing – and indeed increasing – emphasis placed on motherhood in the discourse of patriotic propaganda concerning women. As an original and revealing study of patriotic postcards by Marie-Monique Huss has found, the child loomed large in this discourse precisely to remind the *poilus*, the *enfants de la patrie*, what they were fighting for, namely the future of the nation as represented by images of home and hearth, family and children. Some cards even targeted women, the *chères mobilisées* of the home front, with exhortations to bear more children for the future of France.[63]

True, for some contemporaries the massive entry of women into the workforce as *remplaçantes* amounted to a challenge to the existing gender order.[64] Few historians, however, now subscribe to the view that women found freedom and a new and better world for themselves through work in the war factories. Recent research has only served to confirm what pioneers in the field discovered in the 1970s, namely that neither government nor employers regarded women's war work as laying the foundation for any permanent transformation in the sexual division of labour. In the metal industry, for example, employers refused to invest in the training of a skilled female workforce, preferring to use women for unskilled and semi-skilled tasks which could be accomplished using improved machinery under male direction. Much to the satisfaction of male trade unionists, employers were keen to preserve skill as an attribute of masculine work, and always recognised their women workers as women first and workers second.[65] There was no crisis of gender relations in the war factories because few people, apart from the paranoid or those with their own political agenda, believed that the war was responsible for any drastic change in women's role in the workplace.

In conservative and pronatalist circles, of course, there were fears that women's war work would have a detrimental effect on the future of the 'race'. Dr Adolphe Pinard, a militant pronatalist, was commissioned by the Académie de Medecine to conduct a survey into maternity in the war factories. His report produced statistics to show a fall in the birth rate and a rise in the rate of infant mortality, which he attributed directly to war work; consequently he recommended to government that all pregnant women, nursing mothers and women with children under the age of one should be banned from war factories. The factory, in his view, was a *tueuse d'enfants*, a 'killer of children'. But Pinard's findings were disputed by other doctors, including Paul Strauss, president of the Ligue contre la mortalité infantile, and a leading member of the Senate, who argued against Pinard's hardline position in the second chamber. He and his supporters wanted only a restricted number of particularly demanding and dangerous jobs to be closed to pregnant women, their preferred option being to protect maternity rather than to keep pregnant women out of the labour force. It was their view which weighed with the government rather than Pinard's, and in a law of 5 August 1917 employers were required not to discriminate against pregnant women either by refusing them work or by paying them inferior wages. At the same time, they had to make available two periods in the day, mornings and afternoon, when mothers had the right to breastfeed their children without loss of pay.[66]

Nevertheless, the war undoubtedly boosted the pronatalist cause. Anxiety about the decline in the French birth rate over the course of the nineteenth century was widespread in France, especially after the defeat of 1870, and by no means confined to Catholics, conservatives and right-wing nationalists. Republicans, socialists and feminists all expressed concern about *dénatalité* and openly opposed the campaigns in favour of birth control undertaken by the likes of the dissident feminist Nelly Roussel and the neo-Malthusian birth control lobby led by Paul Robin.[67] In the aftermath of the First World War, however, it was the more right-wing elements of the pronatalist movement spearheaded by the Alliance Nationale pour l'Accroissement de la Population Française which seized the propaganda initiative and set the pronatalist agenda. The victory of the conservative Bloc National in the legislative elections of November 1919 was followed by legislation which prescribed imprisonment and fines for the dissemination of information about birth control (Law of 31 July 1920) and tougher anti-abortion legislation (Law of 27 March 1923). The text of the 1920 law was accompanied by a letter to the President of the Republic drawn up by the Minister of Hygiene, Jules-Louis Breton (who as a left-wing and anticlerical Republican was one of the less conservative members of the coalition government). His text recommended the establishment of 'motherhood medals' to be given to the mothers of *familles nombreuses*. The mothers of five children qualified for a bronze medal, while those with eight were to have silver, and those with ten gold.[68] In postwar France, as far as the legislators were concerned, the paramount duty of every woman was to be the mother of as many children as possible. Precisely because the war had exacerbated the demographic crisis, the maternal role assumed even more importance and the public/private divide was reinforced rather than undermined.

Conclusion

In terms of representations of gender, it seems clear that the war did little to transform the gender system and much to reproduce it. Cultural definitions of gender hardened rather than softened. There was no 'crisis of gender relations', though there was certainly a continuation and intensification of the ongoing debate about gender roles in the context of the war. What is striking about this verdict is that, by using the methods of cultural history, one arrives at precisely the same conclusion as that of the social historians of the 1970s who stressed the importance of continuities rather than ruptures in women's situation. Unlike the social historians, however, cultural historians have little or nothing to say about important distinctions of class, region and religion when discussing the operation of gender ideology. 'Watershed' history may have its limitations, but so too does a cultural history which confines itself to the realm of the social imaginary and ignores the material world of real-life experience. To assume, for example, that the discourse of male doctors on the subject of the female labour force in the war factories is of more importance than the work experiences of the women themselves is to replicate, in the guise of cultural history, the condescension of posterity for the lower orders once practised by an elitist political history. As Deborah Thom has reminded us, work, too, needs to be regarded 'as an experience constitutive of gender identity', and requires 'to be built into the history of the history of women and war as much as sexuality, family and consumption'.[69] In any larger history of the Great War and gender relations, room will need to be found not just for the cultural historian's examination of rhetoric but for the social historian's preoccupation with people. Cultural history can enlarge the perspectives of social history but it dispenses with them at its peril.

Notes

1. The debate was launched by the pioneering work of Arthur Marwick. See in particular his *The Deluge: British Society and the First World War*, Macmillan, 1965 and *War and Social Change in the Twentieth Century*, Macmillan, 1974. Different perspectives on the gender dimension emerged in G. Braybon, *Women Workers in The First World War*, Croom Helm, 1981 and J. F. McMillan, *The Effects of the First World War on the Social Condition of Women in France*, unpublished D.Phil.Thesis, University of Oxford, 1976, a

revised version of which was published as *Housewife or Harlot: The Place of Women in French Society 1870–1940*, Harvester Press, 1981. A convenient summary of the debate is A. Marwick (ed.), *Total War and Social Change*, MacMillan, 1988. Important French contributions include F. Thébaud, *La femme au temps de la guerre de 14*, Stock/Laurence Pernoud, 1986; P. Fridenson (ed.), *1914–1918: L'Autre front*, Paris, 1977 and J-J Becker and S. Audoin-Rouzeau (eds), *Les sociétés européennes et la guerre de 1914–1918*, Centre d'Histoire de la France Contemporaine, Université de Paris X-Nanterre, 1990. Thébaud's work can be accessed in English in her chapter 'The Great War and the Triumph of Sexual Division' in F. Thébaud (ed.), *A History of Women in the West*, Volume 5: *Toward a Cultural Identity in the Twentieth Century*, The Belknap Press of Harvard University Press, 1994. See also R. Wall and J. Winter (eds), *The Upheaval of War. Family, Work and Welfare in Europe, 1914–1918*, Cambridge University Press, 1988; J. Winter and J-L Robert (eds), *Capital Cities at War: Paris, London and Berlin 1914–1919*, Cambridge University Press, 1997, and J. Horne (ed.), *State, Society and Mobilization in Europe during the First World War*, Cambridge University Press, 1997.

2. M. L. Roberts, *Civilization without Sexes: Reconstructing Gender in Postwar France, 1917–1927*, Chicago University Press, 1994, 5.
3. Scott's comments are in M. R. Higonnet, J. Jenson, S. Michel and M. C. Weitz (eds), *Behind the Lines: Gender and the Two World Wars*, Yale University Press, 1987, 21–30.
4. S. R. Grayzel, *Women's Identities at War: Gender, Motherhood, and Politics in Britain and France during the First World War*, University of North Carolina Press, 1999.
5. For this and the subsequent paragraph on the 'long nineteenth century', see J. F. McMillan, *France and Women 1789–1914: Gender, Society and Politics*, Routledge, 2000.
6. M. Proust, *A la recherche du temps perdu*, Editions Gallimard, 1999, (especially 'La Prisonnière').
7. M. Prévost, *Les demi-vierges*, Paris, 1894.
8. McMillan, *France and Women*, Chapter 10.
9. These key themes are discussed in a German context in L. Abrams and E. Harvey (eds), *Gender Relations in German History: Power, Agency and Experience from the Sixteenth Century to the Twentieth Century*, UCL Press, 1996.
10. McMillan, *Housewife or Harlot*, 111.
11. Police report in Archives Nationales F7 13226: *La propagande féminine en faveur de la paix: synthèse d'activités des divers groupements*. See also the articles by the leading French feminist Mme Brunschvicg in *Jus Suffragii*, 1 April 1915 and 1 October 1915.
12. Numerous examples are recounted in contemporary literature such as Mme Léa Bérard, *Les décorées de la grande guerre*, 2 vols, Paris, n.d.; Dr Berthem-Bontoux, *Les Françaises et la grande guerre*, Paris, 1915; F. Corcos, *Les femmes en guerre*, Paris, 1917; and A. Capus, *Le personnel féminin des P.T.T. pendant la guerre*, Paris, 1915.
13. Cf. Dr C. Fromaget, *De l'utilisation de la femme comme infirmière en temps de guerre*, Bordeaux, 1916; M. Eydoux-Demains, *Notes d'une infirmière*, Paris, 1915.
14. M. Donnay, *La Parisienne et la guerre*, Paris, 1916, 26.
15. L. Descaves, *La maison anxieuse*, Paris, 1916, 45–6, 48.
16. H. Robert, 'La femme et la guerre', *La Revue*, May 1917, 243–57.
17. Bracke, 'Le suffrage des femmes', *L'Humanité*, 23 June 1917.
18. M. Barrès, *Le coeur des femmes de France: extraits de la Chronique de la Grande Guerre, 1914–20*, Paris, 1928.
19. Marguerite Durand, in *L'Oeuvre*, 2 February 1916.
20. S. Grinberg, 'Le suffrage des femmes', *La Renaissance Politique, Littéraire et Artistique*, 19 January, 2 February 1918.
21. S. Grinberg, *Historique du mouvement suffragiste depuis 1848*, Goulet, 1926, 107–9.
22. The fullest and best account of these debates is in S. Hause with A. R. Kenney, *Women's Suffrage and Social Politics in the French Third Republic*, Princeton University Press, 1984.
23. L. Colliard, 'Le suffrage des femmes', *La Vie Ouvrière*, 11 June 1919
24. Jane Misme and Juliette-Francoise Raspail, *La Française*, 31 May 1919.
25. *Journal Officiel* (Sénat), séance 7 November, 1922.

26. P. Smith, *Feminism and the Third Republic: Women's Political and Civil Rights in France, 1918–1945*, Clarendon Press, 1996, 115 ff., quotation on 124.
27. On French 'singularity', see M. Ozouf, *Les mots des femmes: essai sur la singularité française*, Fayard, 1995. Contrast this with the views of Siân Reynolds in S. Reynolds (ed.), *Women, State and Revolution*, Wheatsheaf Books, 1996 and McMillan, *France and Women 1789–1914*.
28. J. Bourke, *Dismembering the Male: Men's Bodies, Britain and the Great War*, Reaktion, 1996; 'Le corps dans la première guerre mondiale', *Annales HSS*, 1, janvier-février 2000; cf. S. Audoin-Rouzeau, 'Corps perdus, corps retrouvés: trois exemples de deuils de guerre', 47–71.
29. N. Huston, 'The Matrix of War: Mothers and Heroes', in S. R. Suleiman (ed.), *The Female Body in Western Culture*, Harvard University Press, Cambridge, Mass, 1986, 119–36.
30. G. L. Mosse, *Fallen Soldiers: Reshaping the Memory of the World Wars*, Oxford University Press, 1990.
31. Thébaud, *La femme au temps de la guerre de 1914*, 89.
32. L. Huot and P. Voivenel, *Le Courage*, Paris, 1917.
33. Audoin-Rouzeau, 'Corps perdus, corps retrouvés: trois exemples de deuils de guerre', 62ff.
34. N. Offenstadt, *Les fusillés de la Grande Guerre et la mémoire collective, 1914–1999*, Editions Odile Jacob, 1999.
35. A. Becker, 'Guerre totale et troubles mentaux', *Annales HSS*, 1, janvier-février 2000, 135–51.
36. Huot and Voivenel, *Le Courage*, 345.
37. Huot and Voivenel, *Le Courage*, 247–8.
38. Huot and Voivenel, *Le Courage*, 86, 101ff.
39. S. Audoin-Rouzeau, *L'Enfant de l'ennemi*, Aubier, 1995.
40. J. Horne, 'Corps, lieux et nation: La France et l'invasion de 1914', *Annales HSS*, 1, janvier-février 2000, 73–109, esp. 93–95.
41. R. Harris, ' "The Child of the Barbarian": Rape, Race and Nationalism in France during the First World War', *Past and Present*, 141, 1993, 170–206, esp.192.
42. Thébaud, *La femme au temps de la guerre de 1914*, 50; Grayzel, *Women's Identities at War*, 56.
43. Y. Knibiehler (ed.), *Cornettes et blouses blanches: les infirmières dans la société française, 1880–1980*, Hachette, 1984; M. H. Darrow, 'French Volunteer Nursing and the Myth of War Experience in World War I', *American Historical Review*, 101, 1996, 81–106, esp. 86; and the same author's *French Women and the First World War: War Stories of the Home Front*, Berg, 2000.
44. V. Leroux-Hugon, *Des saintes laïques: les infirmières à l'aube de la Troisième République*, Sciences en Situation, 1992.
45. Dr Berthier, *Croix Rouge Française: les devoirs de la femme en vue de la guerre*, Belfort, 1910.
46. Darrow, 'French Volunteer Nursing', 85.
47. L. Abensour, *Les Vaillantes: Héroines, martyres et remplaçantes*, Paris, 1917, 85.
48. Mme Léa Bérard, *Les décorées de la grande guerre*, 2 volumes, Paris, n.d., cited McMillan, *Housewife or Harlot*, 110.
49. L. Narquet, 'La Française de demain, d'après sa psychologie de guerre', *Revue Bleue*, 56, nos. 18–20, September-October 1918; cf. J. Misme, 'Le costume des infirmières', *La Française*, 5 December 1914.
50. Descaves, *La maison anxieuse*, 81.
51. Cf. Mme Tony d'Ulmès, 'Ces dames de la Croix-Rouge', *La Revue de Paris*, 15 November 1915, 414–28.
52. Donnay, *La Parisienne et la guerre*, 33–4; cf. the novel by Jack de Bussy, *Refugiée et infirmière de guerre*, Paris, 1915.
53. Fromaget, *De l'utilisation de la femme comme infirmière en temps de guerre*, 16.
54. Cf. the testimony of Gabriel Perreux in G. Perreux, *Vie et mort des français, 1914–1918*, Hachette, 1962, 229; E. Reibold, *Quatre mois dans un hôpital militaire de Lyon*, Paris, 1915.

55. Eydoux-Demains, *Notes d'une infirmière*, Paris, 1915.
56. Abensour, *Les Vaillantes*.
57. Quoted by Thébaud, *La femme au temps de la guerre de 1914*, 98.
58. Comtesse de Courson, *La femme française pendant la guerre*, Paris, n.d., 41–2.
59. Dr Toulouse, *La réforme sociale: Question sexuelle de la femme*, Paris, 1918, 16, 71–2.
60. M. Prévost, *Nouvelles lettres à Françoise, ou la jeune fille d'après guerre*, Paris, 1925, 37.
61. M. Prévost, *Mon cher Tommy*, Paris, 1920.
62. V. Margueritte, *La Garçonne*, Paris, 1922. For its reception, see A-M. Sohn, '*La Garçonne* face à l'opinion publique: type littéraire ou type sociale des années 20', *Le Mouvement Social*, 80, 1972, 3–27. Cf. McMillan, *Housewife or Harlot*, 163ff. and the discussion in Roberts, *Civilization without Sexes*, 46ff.
63. M. Huss, 'Pronatalism and the popular ideology of the child in wartime France: the evidence of the picture postcard', in Wall and Winter, *The Upheaval of War*, 329–368. For a fuller account, see M. Huss, *Histoires de famille: cartes postales et cultures de guerre*, Noesis, 2000.
64. Examples include C. Duplomb, 'L'emploi de la femme dans les usines', *La Renaissance Politique, Littéraire et Artistique*, August 1917 and M. Gabelle, 'La place de la femme française après la guerre', ibid., 17 February 1917.
65. L. L. Downs, *Manufacturing Inequality: Gender Division in the French and British Metalworking Industries, 1914–1939*, Cornell University Press, 1995.
66. M. Frois, *La santé et le travail des femmes pendant la guerre*, Carnegie Endowment for International Peace, 1926
67. The literature on pronatalism is substantial. The best guide is now S. Pedersen, *Family, Dependence and the Origins of the Welfare State: Britain and France, 1914–1945*, Cambridge University Press, 1993.
68. An English translation of the French decree establishing medals for mothers is given in S. G. Bell and K. M. Offen, *Women the Family and Freedom: The Debate in Documents*, 2 volumes, Stanford University Press, 1983, Volume 2, 308–9.
69. D. Thom, *Nice Girls and Rude Girls: Women Workers in World War I*, I. B. Tauris, 1998, 207.

7

Mental Cases
British Shellshock and the Politics of Interpretation

Laurinda Stryker

What was shellshock? The question has been of concern to a wide range of observers and commentators. During the First World War, specialists variously equated shellshock with hereditary degeneracy, with neurological injury, and with nervous disorders; some military men insisted that it did not exist; and poets at times went so far as to view it as war-induced madness – not merely neurosis, but thoroughgoing insanity.[1] Even at the time, there was a tendency to imbue war neurosis with a metaphorical, symbolic dimension. In recent years, as historical examinations of shellshock have proliferated and as cinematic and literary portrayals of the phenomenon have influenced the popular mind, this tendency has persisted. Perhaps, due to the nature of the disorder, it is inevitable.

As a literary plot device, shellshock serves to raise questions about war, about identity, and about cultural norms. As an object of historical study this is also the case, as can be seen nowhere more clearly than in the work of Elaine Showalter, whose analysis of shellshock – first developed in *The Female Malady* and reiterated in subsequent writings – has had a significant impact on historians of hysteria as well as on writers outside the historical discipline.[2] Showalter's contention – that shellshock is to be understood as having to do above all with the inscription (and attempted rejection) of gender roles – is a decidedly and visibly political one. In this she follows on from Eric J. Leed's discussion of shellshock as an unconscious and implicit protest against industrialised war; it is in fact on his discussion that her own argument is based.[3] In exploring the difficulties of satisfactorily answering the opening question 'what was shellshock?', it is therefore useful to begin with an exposition of the interpretations offered by these two authors, before going on to an examination of related and parallel problems and simplifications of shellshock theorising during the war. Together, the analysis of historiography and of contemporary theory highlight the complexity of determining the causes, significance and meaning of the disorder.

In her writings on the First World War, Elaine Showalter argues that shellshock can best be understood in terms of gender. Wartime Britain emphasised 'manliness'; the trenches, however, contrasted starkly with the masculinist expectations of recruits, and faced with the material realities of the front, men broke down in record numbers. Summarising her thesis, Showalter writes, 'If the essence of manliness was not to complain, then shellshock was the body language of masculine complaint, a disguised male protest not only against the war but against the concept of "manliness" itself.'[4] Men at the front became hysterical, and the gender of the soldiers was no less salient than the conditions of trench warfare.

Although the importance she accords gender is obvious throughout Showalter's examinations of shellshock, the precise nature of this linkage is not entirely clear in her writings. Thus in her first and most extended account of shellshock, Showalter initially notes the frustration some men seem to have felt about the expectation that they respond to the experience of war in 'manly' ways. She quotes from a novel by Ford Madox Ford: 'Why isn't one a beastly girl and privileged to shriek?'[5] Here it appears that Showalter is directing attention to the gendered expectations internalised by the men who went to war. Men in battle believed they must react in manly ways – that, in Showalter's reading of 'manliness', they must not complain. The possible implications of this – that permitting the expression of fear and other emotion in industrialised war might be prophylactic and permit the more efficient prosecution of such wars – is not, however, developed by her; after introducing this issue, Showalter then shifts her attention to other ways in which gender expectations and war neuroses can be seen as bound together.

The starting point for Showalter's primary argument about shellshock and gender is that the war waged on the Western Front revealed the untenability of ideals of manliness in conditions where men have no control over their circumstances. 'In combat,' Showalter notes, 'displays of manly stoicism and heroics were expected and encoded.'[6] Industrialised war gave few opportunities for such displays; instead, the experience of war was one of enforced passivity coupled with terror. In Showalter's words, 'The most masculine of enterprises, the Great War, feminized its conscripts by taking away their sense of control.'[7] Rather than becoming heroic warriors, men were emasculated and found themselves in a situation of powerlessness bearing similarity to that experienced by Victorian women in the domestic sphere.[8]

Showalter's fundamental point, then, is that the experience of the trenches was at odds with the heroic roles prescribed by conventional understandings of masculinity, and that shellshock was a response to the unexpected realities the troops discovered at the front. And yet the precise etiology which Showalter posits for shellshock is unclear. In her discussions she adumbrates two possible causative mechanisms; unfortunately, she does not distinguish sufficiently between them. Basic to each is the inability of some men at the front to cope psychologically with their experience there. One, however, points in a more universalistic direction and thus to some extent undermines her singular emphasis on gender; the other, which she develops more fully and which fits more neatly with her other writings on hysteria, ensconces the disorder within a history of gender but only at the price of some misrepresentation.

Did conditions at the front cause men to break down? Chief among these, as Showalter notes, was the passivity experienced by men in the trenches: although it felt as though the war were being waged upon them, they could not themselves fight back against it. The enemy was usually invisible; there was little one could do to defend oneself against shellfire; one suffered but could only rarely act. It is these features of the First World War that Showalter highlights in suggesting that industrialised warfare in some ways 'feminised' men, and in doing so she seems to be suggesting that what in peacetime was characteristic of the female condition – namely, the lack of control over one's environment and circumstances – was decisive also in engendering the neuroses of war. Without autonomy, humans cannot healthily function; to be forced to surrender human agency is to risk psychic trauma.

Here, then, the emphasis is on conditions rather than on gender roles per se. Any human placed in certain oppressive situations risks breakdown; in Showalter's words, the lesson of shellshock was that 'powerlessness could lead to pathology'.[9] The war neuroses, like women's hysteria, were 'symbolic disorders of powerlessness'.[10] Such an appraisal may lead one to learn another lesson of shellshock: in Showalter's own words, '[w]ar makes people sick.'[11]

This interpretation of shellshock, however, sits somewhat uneasily with the thrust of Showalter's writings on the disorder, where gender construction rather than the institution of war is what is primarily scrutinised. If war makes people sick, where is the importance of the gender of those involved? In her analysis of shellshock in the First World War, Showalter wishes to give great prominence to gender; she repeatedly suggests that it was the clash between constructions of masculinity and the actual realities at the front which caused mental breakdown. In such a reading, though, it is men's psychological and cultural maladaptation for powerlessness rather than the powerlessness itself which is to blame for the disorder. In attempting to understand the significance as well as the causes of shellshock, this distinction is of some consequence; Showalter's failure to separate the issues generates confusion.[12]

For the most part, then, Showalter elaborates an interpretation of shellshock which places masculinity front and centre. Shellshock was 'the body language of masculine complaint'; men who were expected to 'react [to war] with an outmoded and unnatural "courage"' instead 'lost their voices and spoke through their bodies'.[13]

In short, the First World War was 'a crisis of masculinity and a trial of the Victorian masculine ideal'.[14] Faced with the mud of Flanders, that ideal failed, and soldiers broke down psychologically; their mental pathology can best be understood as a 'suppressed rebellion' against the code of manliness.[15] This 'suppressed rebellion', argues Showalter, took forms which further placed shellshock patients outside the bounds of conventional masculinity. War neuroses in the First World War were seen as taking two basic forms: hysteria and neurasthenia. Hysterical soldiers exhibited functional symptoms: their symptoms were predominantly physical, with paralyses, blindness, deafness, mutism, speech disorders and tremors widely occurring. Neurasthenia, in contrast, was largely characterised by mental symptoms: irritability, dizziness, insomnia or nightmares, anxiety. In prewar Britain, both hysteria and neurasthenia had been primarily associated with women. Hysteria in particular was viewed as a disorder rare among men though seen as endemic in the female population. The emotional instability of war neurotics itself, then, might be seen as having something of the 'feminine' about it. Moreover, in Showalter's representation shellshocked men were emasculated in another way. 'Sexual impotence', she writes, 'was a widespread symptom.'[16] It is worth noting that Showalter cites Leed as her reference for this point; Leed himself, however, quotes only from one shellshock theorist – the Hungarian Freudian Sandor Ferenczi.[17] Thus Showalter's assertion concerning *British* war neurotics is unproved, particularly as a comprehensive survey of the relevant British theoretical literature on shellshock reveals silence on this point.[18]

It is, of course, likely that impotence did occur in at least some patients; the issue is of significance primarily in that it highlights the importance of remaining attuned to national variations when citing sources. Neither theory nor treatment was the same in all countries; descriptions of shellshock varied internationally. Whatever the incidence of impotence in the British Army, however, Showalter's fundamental point – that the experience of the trenches and the symptoms of shellshock were at odds with the heroic roles prescribed by conventional understandings of masculinity – can still stand. But does this establish the inextricable, necessary and causal linkage between gender roles and shellshock that Showalter suggests?

Assertions as to what shellshock 'really' was – definitive ascriptions of character, causes and meaning – are necessarily problematic in ways which will be demonstrated. Consequently, Showalter would seem to be on more solid ground when describing reactions to shellshock on the part of the wider society. Whatever the objective relation between shellshock and gender anxiety in its sufferers, those who encountered war neurotics may have viewed them as somehow 'unmanned' by their disorders. This is what Showalter suggests. In making the point, she draws particularly on literature, citing novels including Rebecca West's *The Return of the Soldier* and Virginia Woolf's *Mrs Dalloway*.[19] Shellshocked characters in both of these books are portrayed by the authors as more emotional than is thought proper for men by the wider society; treatment for their war neurosis consists of an attempt to return them to a socially sanctioned, but emotionally barren, masculinity. Of Woolf's character Septimus Smith, Showalter writes, 'Septimus's problem is that he feels too much for a man.'[20] Showalter's point is not simply one about postwar cultural representations of shellshocked soldiers and veterans, however; rather, she uses such portrayals to support her broader contention that shellshocked men were viewed as effeminate during the war as well as afterwards, by the public and by their doctors alike.

Such use of literary representations is, needless to say, problematic: the typicality of what is being portrayed must be independently established, something which Showalter fails to do.[21] Even more problematic, however, are her assertions about the attitudes of doctors to their shellshocked patients. Showalter writes that doctors 'dismissed shell-shock patients as "cowards" and "malingerers"', 'hinting at effeminacy or homosexuality'; she claims that the suggestion that hysteria was a feminine type of behaviour 'is a recurrent theme in the discussions of war neuroses'; she states that soldiers with shellshock 'were treated with the hostility and contempt that had been accorded hysterical women before the war.'[22] In support of these contentions, however, little evidence is adduced – possibly for the simple reason that with regard to British shell-shock theory it does not exist. Rather than dismissing their patients as cowards, malingers or effeminate individuals, medical writers on shellshock were at pains to remark upon the courageous, manly nature of the men who suffered breakdowns in war, and the genuineness of their disorders. Similarly, discussions of the role of homosexuality or other sexual deviance did not occur outside the writings of the small number of orthodox Freudians in Britain, and even here were usually muted.[23] In part, of course, this was due to British antipathy towards Freudianism. Thus one correspondent who, like W. H. R. Rivers himself, accepted certain aspects of Freud's work wrote to Rivers:

> Many thanks for your pamphlet on Freud's Psychology of the Unconscious. I am very glad that you look askance at the pornographic side of the work of Freud & his followers & that you point out the value of his method apart from that ... The psychoanalyst as a rule seems to plumb for the sexual side & I am sure often suggests it to the patient's mind & I have seen this done with disastrous results.[24]

Given the near ubiquity of such views of Freud even amongst the British psychological avant-garde, it would be surprising indeed if Showalter's charges found substantiation in primary sources. Nor do they. Little evidence is offered by Showalter herself; what is put forward is, moreover, often misinterpreted. Thus in stating that shellshock was described by British theorists as 'the product of womanish, homosexual, or childish impulses in men', Showalter misrepresents – or perhaps merely misunderstands – the meaning of 'regression' as used by those three psychologists whose comments on military training and on war neurosis she cites.[25] Similarly, her assertion that the neurologist Charles S. Myers initially argued for a physical etiology for shellshock as a means of avoiding the use of 'the feminizing term "hysteria"' is not only inexplicable given Showalter's portrayal of shellshock doctors' attitudes to their patients but is also unsubstantiated in his own writings.[26]

That the relationship between shellshock doctors and their patients was an antagonistic one is, however, central to the interpretation of shellshock which Showalter offers. Treatment, to her mind, was 'essentially coercive'; it forced patients to resume a 'masculine' identity which had been shattered at the front.[27] For Showalter, all treatments were thus in essence 'disciplinary'.[28]

What Showalter attributes to patriarchy – the blindness of both patients and their doctors to the actual causal basis of the war neuroses – Eric Leed attributes to the military location in which wartime therapy was transacted.[29] For him, too, shellshock treatment was an attempt to force men back into roles they were attempting to abandon: '[w]ithin the drama of therapy the traditional "offensive" soldierly role was clarified and fitted upon those who desperately wished to repudiate it.'[30] While in Leed's reading treatment could, at times, be viewed as a compromise between victims' needs and war's demands, in general it bore the character of domination.[31]

Although Showalter's analysis of shellshock relies upon the research undertaken by Leed – at times failing to distinguish between points primarily concerning French, German and Austro-Hungarian theories and therapies, and those points germane to those of the British – while Showalter highlights gender, Leed highlights the nature of industrialised war. Here too it is the immobility and enforced passivity of men at the front which is the key factor; the moral categories holding soldiers there, however, are identified with the military ethos rather than with codes of masculinity per se.[32] Consequently, although for both writers shellshock assumes moral and political significance, their interpretations of its meaning, as of its nature, differ subtly but importantly. For Showalter, shellshock was 'a disguised male protest not only against the war but against the concept of 'manliness itself'; for Leed, it is the 'human costs of war' – not only the First World War but modern war more generally – which a study of shellshock makes evident.[33]

Yet if one looks at contemporary sources – British theories of shellshock formulated during the First World War – questions about the appropriateness of notions of 'manliness' and questions about the morality of industrialised slaughter are not in fact explicitly raised. British psychologists did not brand their patients as effeminate, homosexual or cowardly, or ponder inherited ideals of masculinity , nor did they engage in ruminations on the justice of modern warfare and its demands on the citizen. Moreover, given the nature of the theories propounded, it is not at all clear that shellshock psychologist themselves became aware of such implications. This in itself requires explanation. How was it that 'meanings' of shellshock which seem so obvious to us today did not enter into shellshock theory – that it apparently did not occur to psychologists to think of the war neuroses as being 'about' manliness or 'about' anti-war dispositions? Simply put, shell-shock theory framed soldiers' breakdowns in ways which served to militate against such understandings and forestall such reflections. To understand how this was so requires one to look, not only at the institutional and social locations of military psychologists and at the nature of the treatments they devised, but at the theories which underlay their practices.

All historians of shellshock agree that the disorder was viewed with great concern by the British military. Military officials worried that a sanctioned escape from the front line through a purely psychological reaction to warfare would undermine morale; they worried, too, that the incidence of shellshock might reach epidemic proportions. In actual fact, it is difficult to ascertain the number of those who broke down with any degree of accuracy. Informed estimates from the immediate postwar period ranged from 80,000 cases, which would include many recurring admissions, to 200,000 cases severe enough to have required discharge from the military.[34] The discrepancy is impossible to resolve satisfactorily. What is clear, however, is that the first cases of shellshock occurred soon after the Battle of Mons, the frequency of cases varied as the fighting changed in nature and intensity, increasing dramatically with the Battle of the Somme, and new cases continued to occur in large numbers even after the Armistice. As a proportion of total casualties, shellshock cases appear to have been relatively low. Although Showalter claims that up to forty percent of combat zone casualties by 1916 were due to shellshock, Macpherson et al., in *Diseases of the War*, drawing on official documents, place shellshock wastage at less than two percent of the troops in action in the three months of battle at Ypres in the autumn of 1917, a figure which accords well with other estimates for the condition's prevalence in the final years of the war.[35] Nevertheless, in a war of attrition all wastage was significant, and the army furthermore feared a blurring of its traditional strictures against cowardice.

Treatment for shellshock varied widely even within the British army, depending as it did on the type of disorder suffered by the patient, the period when it was treated, and the personality and theoretical leanings of the doctor.[36] Most patients were treated by some version of suggestion, which could range from direct verbal persuasion, to suggestion taking the form of faradism – that is, the use of electrical currents – or employing hypnosis, or a light anaesthetic to increase suggestibility. Analytical methods such as those practiced by W. H. R. Rivers were always a minority approach; they aimed at uncovering the anxieties that underlay symptoms rather than simply eradicating the symptoms themselves.[37]

These analytical treatments, however, deserve particular attention. However atypical they were, they form the basis for most recent discussions of shellshock. More than any other approach to shellshock, they seemed to suggest that the experience of trench warfare could cause psychological damage, a position which one might assume has inevitable moral implications. The analytic theories did not, nevertheless, lead to any profound criticism, let alone condemnation, of the war. The reasons for this can best be understood by looking closely at the theories themselves.

Military witnesses to the War Office 'Shell-Shock' Committee feared the effects of classifying shellshock as a disability that was as legitimate as any other; had they fully understood the theories of war neurosis, they might have been reassured. War neurosis as constructed in Britain during the First World War did not undermine ideals common both to the military ethos and to civilian understandings of manliness and masculinity, but rather built upon and upheld these moral values. This was true of psychological no less than commotional theories.[38]

First and foremost, shellshock was viewed as an illness, and as such was not seen as a normal response to the experience of war. Even during the worst battles, only a minority of men broke down psychologically. The questions raised by these cases, then, were less about the conditions of war than about patients' responses to those conditions, and about the possibility of returning them to a normal adjustment. Wider moral and political issues were thus unlikely to be raised.

The illness label applied to shellshock restricted the significance accorded to the war neuroses in another way, for the disorder was viewed as largely curable. Patients sometimes feared that they were mad, that the war had permanently shattered their minds. Doctors taking a matter-of-fact view of the disorder suggested that this was an overestimation of its gravity. E. D. Adrian and L. R. Yealland wrote, '[The patient] may relapse after an equally severe strain, but if his cure has been rapid and complete on the first occasion he will have less reason to fear a relapse and to regard a temporary loss of speech as a serious and intractable condition.'[39] The patient was to take even relapses in his stride, viewing shellshock as of no greater significance than the other illnesses and ailments endemic to the trenches.

Because shellshock was viewed as an illness, recognition of it did not necessarily involve criticism of the conditions in which it arose, or a reappraisal of the values that placed men in those circumstances. Nor did theoretical works link war neuroses with any such questioning within the patients themselves. Shellshock as understood by British psychologists during the First World War was not associated with rejection of duty. In fact, the treatments themselves relied upon the presence of a conventional sense of duty within the patients. This was true even of what are called the 'disciplinary' approaches, usually known in Britain as the Queen Square method after the hospital where its most famous exponent, L. R. Yealland, worked. Such practices were never widespread in Great Britain, despite the emphasis on them in Showalter's writings. That they have received widespread attention, however, suggests the need for a closer examination.[40]

What is commonly held to have been the hallmark of the Queen Square treatment was the use of electric shocks to force the abandon-

ment of functional symptoms or, in the words of its practitioners, to overcome 'negativism'.[41] Adrian and Yealland themselves described their
treatment as 'a little plain speaking accompanied by a strong faradic current'.[42] Leed interprets such practices as 'acts of pure domination', but
the reality was in fact more complex.[43] Most fundamentally, a use of electricity was not in itself equivalent to torture. The basis of faradism was in
most instances suggestion rather than 'persuasion' or punishment. Soldiers were told that the current could cure them; their doctors made use
of the suggestive potential of what was described as 'the paraphernalia of
an apparently complicated noisy machine'.[44] When a doctor was skilful at
suggestion, a very mild current often sufficed. The widespread application of electricity without the use of suggestion, however, meant that
patients on whom it had been used unsuccessfully grew to doubt the efficacy of the treatment. Adrian and Yealland therefore advocated the use of
stronger and consequently more painful currents on these patients,
accompanied by the explanation that the sort of electricity now being
applied was 'more potent' than that previously used elsewhere.[45]

The suggestive potential of electricity was not limited to its placebo
effect, however. In cases of functional paralysis, mild stimulation of the
affected muscles produced contractions which demonstrated to the
patient that an apparently paralysed limb could in fact be moved. Thus
reassured that there was no organic disability, the patient was frequently
able to overcome his hysterical symptoms. Such a use of electricity in fact
became Yealland's preferred method. He wrote:

> But I often reproach myself when I recall to mind the patients who needlessly
> suffered under a method born of one idea – compulsion. The patients to
> whom I here refer were those treated by very strong faradism applied by
> means of a wire brush, the idea being to 'break down the resistance'.[46]

This more punitive use of electricity was born of the idea of negativism,
which as defined by Adrian and Yealland ranged from 'a mere inertia ... to
an active, but not necessarily a conscious, resistance to the idea of recovery'.[47] Because the resistance could be unconscious, it was not a clear-cut
repudiation of the conventional ideals of duty. Moreover, patients' negativism was directed largely toward the likelihood of recovery.[48] Treatment
was resisted because it was thought to be pointless, not because a cure
was feared. The Queen Square method was designed to overcome this
resigned acceptance of symptoms by forcing the patient to recognise that
his disability was functional, that he could move an affected limb or, under
sufficient provocation, was able to speak.

In analysing the Queen Square method, it is wrong to focus too exclusively on the idea of negativism, which was not regarded by Yealland as
characteristic of all patients and was viewed as a result of previously inef-
fective treatment rather than of men's war experiences. It is an even
greater error to see negativism as a conscious rejection of duty on the

patient's part. In reality, a sense of duty in patients was at times directly called upon, even by this method. Yealland opens his book with such a case, which has been recounted frequently in recent writings on shell-shock.[49] When the mute patient indicates that he wishes to leave the treatment room before a cure has been effected, Yealland urges:

> I know you do not want the treatment suspended now you have made such progress. You are a noble fellow, and these ideas which come into your heard do not represent your true self. I know you are anxious to be cured and are happy you have recovered to such an extent; now you are tired and cannot think properly, but you must make every effort to think in the manner charac-teristic of your true self – a hero of Mons.[50]

The man is in the end cured of his mutism, upon which he exclaims, 'Doctor, doctor, I am champion.' Yealland replies, 'You are a hero.'[51]

This history is not typical in its overt references to duty, but it warrants attention because it is the case frequently cited to establish the coercive nature of 'disciplinary' therapy, a type of therapy regarded by Leed and Showalter as enforcing a standard of behaviour that had clearly been repudiated by the patient.[52] Leed, for example, significantly makes no mention of the exchanges quoted above, with their obvious invocation of a surviving sense of duty on the part of the patient. Yet it should be noted that neither here , nor at any other point, does Yealland suggest the neces-sity for a moral re-education of shellshock patients.[53] Men need only be taught how to walk, talk or hear correctly; it is upon this that Yealland's treatment is focused. No complementary effort was directed toward instilling a sense of duty. Its presence is largely assumed.

In this Yealland is representative. British shellshock theorists did not recognise any need to reinforce or correct patients' values. The emphasis in their writings is instead on the removal of obstacles to the fulfilment of duty, which took the form of psychological blocks, variously defined. Treatment did not teach patients what was right; it only enabled them once more to do what they already knew to be right. Theories by and large presumed a conventional moral sense in patients, and even the symptoms themselves could be seen as evidence of this. Thus the sever-ity of most hysterical symptoms – blindness, paralysis, mutism – was cited as proof of a potent underlying commitment to ideals of courage and duty. That the unconscious had to adopt such extreme measures was itself proof of the soldiers' mettle.

Shellshock, therefore, was not necessarily and intrinsically to be seen as a repudiation of conventional standards of manliness and masculinity. Similarly, the fact that psychologists might, through their clinical work, come, in Leed's words, to 'an excruciating awareness of the human costs of the war' did not lead them to a reappraisal of the war itself.[54] In fact, the theoretical framing of the war neuroses precluded such a development.

The theories most likely to generate new views of the war were those that emphasised psychological conflict, counterbalancing military duty with some other element upon which a critique of the war might then be based. For this critique to have been developed, however, the factor that opposed the duty of the soldier must itself be such as to yield an obligation with moral standing at least equal to that of military duty. Thus the conflict that psychologists such as W. H. R. Rivers identified as central to shellshock – an instinct of self-preservation versus a duty to serve – was patently inadequate, given that opposition to war rooted solely in a regard for the self is, even today, considered craven. Self-preservation is at best amoral; at the time, its conflict with duty was unambiguous from a moral perspective. It was this conflict, however, that analytic shellshock theory regarded as fundamental to the nervous disorders, to the extent that all other factors opposing duty were collapsed into fear. As a result, difficult questions about the war were simply not raised.

At the front, men saw things that human beings should not see. Such sights produce both horror and fear. The mix of emotions which are engendered, however, is crucial. Fear is generally viewed as a response to be overcome. But if horror rather than fear becomes the main factor antithetical to a sense of military duty, then the moral significance of shellshock is altered. Horror *can* lead to a reappraisal of the war itself, for horror is qualitatively different from fear. One book on shellshock stated it thus:

> Horror differs both from fear and terror … It is superior to both in this, that it is less imbued with personal alarm. It is more full of sympathy with the sufferings of others than engaged with our own.[55]

Horror suggests duties of altruism that may counterbalance the duties of warfare. Under its influence one can seek to alleviate suffering, or at least do no additional harm. It can therefore can provide potential grounds for re-evaluating a war's propriety. Case histories treating horror as an independent factor were rare in British writings, however.[56] In general, the relation of a sense of military duty to pity and sympathy was not examined, for horror was almost universally treated as a subspecies of fear in shellshock theory. Shellshocked soldiers, then, were those who through no fault of their own were no longer able to overcome their terror.

This redefinition of horror was usually accomplished obliquely. A mention of horror as an etiological factor in shellshock would be followed by a discussion of fear alone, or horror would be written about in language more suited to analyses of courage. Because of this process, shellshock theory lost one path by which it might have reached a critique of the war. Furthermore, since treatments were based on these theories, patients also tended to lose this basis for criticism of the war. The apparently unconscious confusion of horror and fear occurred not only in journal articles and books but also in therapy. Usually veiled, occasionally this process of redefinition was more or less overt. Thus the psychologist M. D. Eder described a former groom who had developed nervous symptoms including nightmares about the mistreatment of transport animals at the front:

He wept profoundly when talking to me of the sufferings experienced by the wounded mules in Gallipoli, and when I suggested that human beings suffered more he would not have it so. Animals could not talk. No animals should have been allowed there he said.[57]

Eder did not believe that the patient's anxiety was in fact about horses, however. Instead, he asserted that the patient identified with the injured horses: pity for them was pity for himself. 'Soldierly instincts' precluded the direct expression of his fear, and so it emerged veiled.

Eder's interpretation is plausible, but it is not the only possible reading. More than a half million animals on the British side alone died in the First World War; in a man who cared deeply about animals a reaction of horror might be expected.[58] In the end, the question of the origin of shellshock in this case, as in others, cannot be answered definitively. Perhaps the patient's response was indeed one of fear, or perhaps it was horror; perhaps it was a combination of the two, or was something else entirely. One must, however, be wary of accepting Eder's interpretation too readily even if it did, in the end, prove persuasive to the patient.[59] Suggestion plays a prominent role in all psychotherapy. Patients are led to think in certain ways, and they answer the questions that they are asked. Shellshock theory as it was developed in the First World War meant that certain questions, and among them those that might most subvert conventional ideals, were unlikely to be raised. What is significant about Eder's case, then, is not its intrinsic meaning (which if it exists is undiscoverable) but the very way in which the case was framed at the time. The patient's concern for horses was read as a concern for the self: it was not a concern for animals, and equally not a concern for other human beings. Horror therefore completely vanished; fear, less morally ambiguous by far, became the sole etiological factor. The subsumption of horror under fear made treatment relatively straightforward; it also permitted an unequivocal response to the underlying conflict on the part of the doctor, and probably the patient as well.

If horror was inadequately dealt with in shellshock theory, however, guilt was almost completely ignored. The vast majority of writers on war neurosis did not mention guilt as a possible etiological factor, and the only extensive attention given to it, and to the general psychological significance of killing, was in the writings of John T. MacCurdy and Ernest Jones.[60] Even more than horror, guilt is directly related to moral doubt about an enterprise. Its neglect in the psychology of shellshock meant that the scope of the questions raised by the incidence of the disorder, and considered in its treatment, was further limited. A moral conservatism prevailed even amongst the most radical of the Freudians; the potential political and ethical implications of shellshock theory were overwhelmed by the pull of conservative values which were shared by psychologists and their patients alike.

The conclusions about shellshock which British psychologists reached, and the interpretations offered by recent historians such as Eric Leed and Elaine Showalter, are very different. Whereas analytical psychologists posited a straightforward conflict between the ideal of courage and instincts of self-preservation, Showalter interrogates the basis of the moral code to which both soldiers and psychologists adhered, and Leed articulates questions about the situations in which adherence to this code was demanded of them. In interpreting shellshock, both writers examine the context in which the disorder was theorised; in doing so, they raise questions about the adequacy of the psychologists' approach.

And yet problems remain. If the psychologists' understandings of shellshock were in some ways blinkered, in other ways incomplete, this does not in itself mean that either Showalter or Leed succeeds in defining, once and for all, the nature of the disorder. Rather, their interpretations – like those of the shellshock psychologists – in turn raise new questions and suggest further complexities.

Showalter argues that the incidence and treatment of shellshock should be understood with reference to the behavioural, gendered ideals of a patriarchal society. Shellshocked soldiers were in unconscious, implicit rebellion against the codes of manliness and masculinity in which they had been socialised. Behaving in a manly way – not complaining and not showing fear – proved dysfunctional or untenable for men placed in the conditions of a static, industrialised war.

Showalter's conception, it should be noted, does not necessarily imply a critique of war as an institution, or of soldiering as an occupation. Only if one posits an invariable and necessary link between a certain set of gender ideals and the prosecution of war will one be required to condemn the latter in criticising the former. If Showalter's understanding of shellshock is correct, various strategies can be devised to make it less psychologically damaging to fight a war. Something of this was suggested even in the immediate aftermath of the First World War. Thus one witness to the War Office Committee of Enquiry into 'Shell-Shock' stated, 'I think in training it would be a very good thing if it could be explained to the men that they will be afraid and that they are liable to develop neurosis by repressing that fear, but explain that everybody does feel afraid.'[61] It has been argued, in fact, that the lower incidence of permanently debilitating shellshock in the Second World War, as compared with the First World War, was in part due to soldiers' willingness to express their anxieties and show their fear in the more recent conflict.[62]

Nevertheless, Showalter's interpretation of shellshock is convincing because it seems plausible, particularly when one looks exclusively at the events of the First World War, and the assumptions of society at the time. In recently equating Gulf War Syndrome with the shellshock of the First World War or with other instances of war neurosis, however, Showalter seems to suggest that Leed's privileging of the conditions and experience of combat as determinant of war neuroses may be correct, and that her focus on the gender of combatants must be reconsidered. Women, as well as men, report that they suffer from Gulf War Syndrome; in her explanation of the disorder, Showalter highlights the anxieties and uncertainties experienced by troops on active duty in that war as sufficient cause for its onset.[63]

Perhaps, then, it is the nature of war itself rather than specific gender expectations which produces psychopathology in soldiers? In her discussion of Gulf War Syndrome, Showalter focuses on the fear felt by combatants in all wars. In this she mirrors the thinking of the analytical psychologists of the First World War. Participation in war involves more than simply suffering from its effects, however; war involves killing as well as dying, and killing too can be psychologically damaging.[64] If war causes shellshock, perhaps it is the very nature of war – that is, institutionalised killing as well as dying – that is to blame.[65]

The phenomenon of war neurosis, therefore, can lead one to be critical of gender conditioning, or to question the supportability of war itself. The interpretation of shellshock is pivotal; moreover, any such interpretation has its political implications. This is true no less of the equation of shellshock with Post-Traumatic Stress Disorder (PTSD) by the American Psychiatric Association, than of the way in which shellshock doctors framed the disorder in terms of fear versus self-preservation during the First World War. If shellshock may be seen at root as due to an insistence on 'manliness', or may be seen as a consequence of fear, horror or guilt, it can also be seen as simply a response to trauma, including natural disaster or crime. This, despite appearances, is not an apolitical interpretation: to equate the results of armed participation in a war with the experience of victims of genocide , or the feelings of those who have survived a tornado, is a profoundly important move. The history of the categorisation of PTSD bears this out, being rooted in compromises stemming from the political divisiveness of the Vietnam War in America.[66]

So what, then, was shellshock? An historiographical inquiry in the end reveals its political dimensions. In many ways, shellshock has been a screen upon which responses to current events, to war, and to gender issues have been projected. And yet it was not only that. Shellshock, although used as a political metaphor which seemingly evades objective, final definition, was also a disability which affected real lives and caused lasting damage. For those who suffered it, shellshock was an inability to speak, or to walk, or to eat, or to see. These disabilities, moreover, often persisted long after the end of the war. Yet successful treatment in time of war, then and now, returns soldiers to the front just as surgery, which extracts bullets and minimises physical damage, is intended to do.

To understand shellshock, then, may require that historians do more than analyse theories, treatment strategies and statistical returns. In proposing interpretations, historians no less than psychologists, should be responsible for making overt the political import of their interpretations. They must also acknowledge that the experience of shellshock was, in the end, something *apart* from the meanings accorded to the disorder. Shellshock, however useful as a metaphor and as an element in political contention, must not be seen only as such. The 'mental cases' described by Wilfred Owen, who accused the civilian world of having 'dealt them war and madness', are a rebuke to easy answers.

Notes

1. For an account of the range of medical and military opinion, see Ted Bogacz, 'War Neurosis and Cultural Change in England, 1914–22: The Work of the War Office Committee of Enquiry into "Shell-Shock"', *Journal of Contemporary History*, 24, 1989, 227–56; for an example of a contemporary literary equation of shellshock with insanity, see Wilfred Owen's poem 'Mental Cases', C. D. Lewis (ed.), *The Collected Poems of Wilfred Owen*, Chatto and Windus, 1963, 69.
2. Elaine Showalter, *The Female Malady: Women, Madness and English Culture, 1830–1980*, Virago, 1987, 167–94; see also her 'Rivers and Sassoon: The Inscription of Male Gender Anxieties', in M. R. Higonnet, J. Jenson, S. Michel and M. C. Weitz (eds), *Behind the Lines: Gender and the Two World Wars*, Yale University Press, 1987; also her essay 'Hysteria, Feminism, and Gender', in S. Gilman, H. King, R. Porter, G. Rousseau and E. Showalter (eds), *Hysteria Beyond Freud*, California University Press, 1993, 320–27; and the briefer discussion of her position in *Hystories: Hysterical Epidemics and Modern Media*, Columbia University Press, 1997, 72–75. For Showalter's role in hysteria studies, see Mark S. Micale, *Approaching Hysteria: Disease and Its Interpretations*, Princeton University Press, 1995, 75–77, 166–68; for her impact on one fiction writer, see Pat Barker, *Regeneration*, Penguin, 1991, 252.
3. Eric J. Leed, *No Man's Land: Combat and Identity in World War I*, Cambridge University Press, 1979, 163–92.
4. Showalter, *The Female Malady*, 172.
5. From Ford Madox Ford's *Parade's End*, quoted Showalter, *The Female Malady*, 173.
6. Showalter, 'Hysteria, Feminism, and Gender', 325.
7. Showalter, *The Female Malady*, 173.
8. The comparison is Sandra Gilbert's; it is quoted approvingly by Showalter in *The Female Malady*, 174.
9. Showalter, *The Female Malady*, 190.
10. Showalter, 'Rivers and Sassoon', 62.
11. Showalter, *Hystories*, 75.
12. At times, the issue is even more confused. Thus in *The Female Malady* Showalter writes, 'The heightened code of masculinity that dominated in wartime was intolerable to surprisingly large numbers of men', 172. Here it is suggested that it is the code itself – and not just its discordance with the role of the front soldier – that underlies the disorder.
13. Showalter, 'Rivers and Sassoon', 64.
14. Showalter, *The Female Malady*, 171.
15. Showalter uses the term 'suppressed rebellion' in discussing women's hysteria and its relation to feminism; shellshock, she then notes, was a 'disguised male protest' against manliness itself. Showalter, *The Female Malady*, 147, 172.
16. Showalter, *The Female Malady*, 172. See also Showalter, 'Rivers and Sassoon', 62.
17. Leed, *No Man's Land*, 182.
18. In a study of British shellshock theory, I examined the publications of eighty-six theorists as well as other discussions published as books or as articles in the *British Journal of Psychology, British Medical Journal, Journal of Mental Science, Journal of the Royal Army Medical Corps, Lancet* and the *Proceedings of the Royal Society of Medicine* during the war and in the immediate postwar period. Impotence is not cited as a symptom in these discussions. See Laurinda S. Stryker, 'Languages of Suffering and Sacrifice in England in the First World War: Chaplains, Psychologists, and Poets', unpublished Ph.D. Thesis, University of Cambridge, 1992.
19. Showalter, *The Female Malady*, 191–94.

20. Showalter, *The Female Malady*, 193.
21. This point, which relates more generally to Showalter's overall approach to the history of hysteria, is made by even one of her most enthusiastic supporters. See Micale, *Approaching Hysteria*, 77.
22. Showalter, *The Female Malady*, 172; 'Hysteria, Feminism, and Gender', 324, 322.
23. Showalter's own discussions of Freudian sexual etiologies for shellshock cite Karl Abraham, who was a German rather than a British psychoanalyst, as well as David Eder, David Forsyth and Ernest Jones. See *The Female Malady*, 172 and 'Hysteria, Feminism, and Gender', 324. The confusion here as elsewhere may derive in part from her reliance on Eric Leed, who deals with Continental as well as British shellshock theory.
24. Robert Percy Smith to W. H. R. Rivers, July 1917, Cambridge, Experimental Psychology Archives, Papers of W. H. R. Rivers. This collection contains a number of letters to Rivers that express opinions about his assessment of Freud.
25. Showalter, 'Hysteria, Feminism, and Gender', 323–24.
26. Ibid., 321. Cf. Charles S. Myers, 'Contributions to the Study of Shell Shock.' *Lancet*, 13 February 1915, 316–20; 8 January 1916, 65–69; 18 March 1916, 608–12; 9 September 1916, 461–67; 11 January 1919, 51–54; Charles S. Myers, *Shell Shock in France 1914–18: Based on a War Diary*, Cambridge University Press, 1940.
27. Hence her interest in Rebecca West's novel. See *The Female Malady*, 191.
28. The term, first used by Leed, refers to punitive treatments. These will be discussed in the British context below. For Showalter's views of treatment, see *The Female Malady*, 178.
29. Showalter, *The Female Malady*, 194; Leed, *No Man's Land*, 169.
30. Leed, *No Man's Land*, 165.
31. Leed, *No Man's Land*, 179.
32. Leed, *No Man's Land*, 180–86.
33. Showalter, *The Female Malady*, 172; Leed, *No Man's Land*, 180.
34. W. G. MacPherson, W. P. Herringham, T. R. Elliott and A. Balfour (eds), *History of the Great War Based on Official Documents: Medical Services: Diseases of the War*, London, 1923,Volume 2, 7; Martin Stone, 'Shellshock and the Psychologists', in R. Porter, W. F. Bynum and M. Shepherd (eds), *The Anatomy of Madness*, London, 1985, Volume 2, 249.
35. Showalter, *The Female Malady*, 168; 'Rivers and Sassoon', 63; 'Hysteria, Feminism, and Gender', 321. Cf. W. G. MacPherson et al., *History of the Great War Based on Official Documents*, Volume 2, 7. Showalter cites Stone, 'Shellshock and the Psychologists', 249 as her source. There Stone attributes this figure to an observer who was speaking of casualties from heavy fighting zones; his citation, which gives the wrong page number, is to Emanuel Miller (ed.), *The Neuroses in War*, Macmillan, 1940. In that volume a contributor, summarising statistics from the *History of the Great War*, states, 'On occasion neuroses made up 40 per cent of the casualties evacuated home', Miller, 8. Although it is possible that at particular times high numbers of psychological casualties did occur, the figure of two to three percent seems roughly consistent with figures derived from admissions for sickness in Casualty Clearing Stations of the Second Army through 1917 and with the less than two percent wastage from shellshock during the heavy fighting in Ypres in autumn 1917 as suggested by MacPherson, above. Such a figure also accords with an analysis of a sample 1,043,653 British casualties admitted to medical units from 1916 to 1920. See T. J. Mitchell and G. M. Smith (eds), *History of the Great War Based on Official Documents: Medical Services: Casualties and Medical Statistics of the War*, London, 1931, 305. For discussions of statistical evidence regarding shellshock, see Stryker, 'Languages of Sacrifice and Suffering', 2–4, and Peter John Lynch, 'The Exploitation of Courage: Psychiatric Care in the British Army, 1914–1918', unpublished M.Phil. Dissertation, University College, London, 1977, 123–25.
36. Showalter contends that the principle determinant of shellshock treatment was the rank of the patient: officers were 'usually given various kinds of psychotherapy' while other ranks were 'subjected to disciplinary treatment, quick cures, shaming, and physical retraining', 'Rivers and Sassoon', 65; see also 'Hysteria, Feminism, and Gender', 322–23. She does not, however, provide evidence for these categorical statements. It is

moreover somewhat ironic that one of the principal psychologists whom she discusses is W. H. R. Rivers, who worked with soldiers at Maghull before treating officers at Craiglockhart. Many of the analytic doctors were, in fact, based at Maghull at some stage of their wartime careers; these include William Brown, who like Rivers was a prominent advocate of analytic approaches to the treatment of war neuroses. See Peter Jeremy Leese, 'A Social and Cultural History of Shellshock, with Particular Reference to the Experience of British Soldiers During and After the Great War', unpublished Ph.D. thesis Open University, 1989, Chapters 6 and 7 for an accurate and thorough account of other ranks' and officers' treatment, and Lees, 'Problems returning home: the British Psychological casualties of the Great War', in *Historical Journal*, 40 (4), December 1997.

37. For a fuller discussion of the treatment of shellshock and the associated theoretical explanations, see Stryker, 'Languages of Sacrifice and Suffering', Chapter 3.

38. Bogacz, in 'War Neurosis and Cultural Change in England, 1914–22' and Leed, in *No Man's Land*, identify the challenge to the traditional moral values as arising from the psychological theories, which in part accounts for my own emphasis. Questions raised by approaches that stressed commotion or a neuropathic predisposition were clearly less far-reaching than those arising out of psychological theories.

39. E. D. Adrian and L. R. Yealland, 'The Treatment of Some Common War Neuroses', *Lancet*, 9 June 1917, 872.

40. See Leese, 'A Social and Cultural History of Shellshock', 99–114; for an examination of treatment in the Central Powers, see José Brunner, 'Psychiatry, Psychoanalysis and Politics during the First World War', *Journal of the History of the Behavioral Sciences* 27, October 1991, 352–365. Showalter's reliance on Leed, who discusses such therapies without distinguishing between Britain and the Continent where they were not only more common but more overtly punitive, may have misled her. As a consequence, she discusses 'disciplinary' therapy at length without making clear its atypicality in the British context; it also figures prominently in Barker's novel *Regeneration*. Showalter, *The Female Malady*, 175–78; Barker, *Regeneration*, 223–39.

41. See Adrian and Yealland, 'The Treatment of Some Common War Neuroses', 868.

42. Adrian and Yealland, 'The Treatment of Some Common War Neuroses', 869.

43. Leed, *No Man's Land*, 165.

44. Wilfred Harris, *Nerve Injuries and Shock*, Oxford War Primers, 1915, 121.

45. Adrian and Yealland, 'The Treatment of Some Common War Neuroses', 869. See also 871.

46. L. R. Yealland, *Hysterical Disorders of Warfare*, Macmillan, 1918, 74. It is difficult to square this statement with Showalter's contention that Yealland wrote in this book with 'complacent pride'. Showalter, *The Female Malady*, 176.

47. Adrian and Yealland, 'The Treatment of Some Common War Neuroses', 868. The acknowledgement of the possibility that a patient's negativism was unconscious did not, however, stop them from using moralistic language to describe some cases, for example writing, 'The current can be made extremely painful if it is necessary to supply the disciplinary element which must be invoked if the patient is *one who prefers not to recover*' [emphasis added], Ibid, 869. However, a similar lack of consistency occurs in Leed himself, upon whom Showalter's own account is largely based; it is in fact basic to his argument that all shellshock treatments were instances of coercion (see Leed, *No Man's Land*, 179). He accepts the idea of war neurosis as an unconscious 'flight into illness' but also repeatedly seems to suggest that the neurosis was a conscious choice on the part of the affected individual. He writes, for example, of the traditional soldierly role as one which 'common sense and a familiarity with the realities of war had caused him [the patient] to reject' (170) and describes therapy as fitting the soldier's role 'upon those who desperately wished to repudiate it' (165). Both statements imply volition.

48. This attitude is common to the majority of cases described in Yealland, *Hysterical Disorders of Warfare*.

49. See Leed, *No Man's Land*, 174–75; Showalter, *The Female Malady*, 175–78; Barker, *Regeneration*, 223–39.

50. Yealland, *Hysterical Disorders of Warfare*, 12.

51. Yealland, *Hysterical Disorders of Warfare*. In portraying the Queen Square method as unambiguously coercive, both Showalter and Barker omit the final words spoken to Yealland by the patient in this case history: 'Why did they not send me to you nine months ago?' Yealland, *Hysterical Disorders of Warfare*, 10. Instead, Showalter asserts that the man was 'required' to say 'thank you'. Showalter, *The Female Malady*, 177.
52. See Leed, *No Man's Land*, 174–75.
53. Adrian and Yealland do posit a disciplinary role for their treatment in certain cases, but there is no subsequent reeducation mentioned. Once the patient's negativism is overcome, he is fit for duty, and his acceptance of this role even after he has left the hospital, without further 'persuasion' or other retraining, is evidently taken for granted.
54. Leed, *No Man's Land*, 170.
55. Sir Charles Bell, quoted in F. W. Mott, *War Neuroses and Shell Shock*, Oxford Medical Publications, 1919, 120. Mott himself, however, subsequently collapses horror into fear.
56. For one rare case, see J. T. MacCurdy, *War Neuroses*, Cambridge University Press, 1918, 42–43. That the patient himself viewed his horror as neurotic suggests that pacifism was not the inevitable result of horror. Other values could prove stronger.
57. M. D. Eder, 'The Psycho-pathology of the War Neuroses,' in the *Lancet*, 12 August 1916, 266.
58. There is ample evidence that many men were horrified by the fate of animals in the war. See, for example, Robert Graves, writing about the Somme: 'The number of dead horses and mules shocked me; human corpses were all very well, but it seemed wrong for animals to be dragged into the war like this.' Robert Graves, *Goodbye to All That*, revised 2nd edn, Doubleday Anchor Books, 1957.
59. As Eder based his apparently successful treatment of the case on this interpretation, one must assume that the patient did accept it.
60. See MacCurdy, *War Neuroses*; Ernest Jones, 'War and Individual Psychology', *The Sociological Review*, 8, 1915, and his article 'War Shock and Freud's Theory of the Neuroses', *Proceedings of the Royal Society of Medicine (Sect. of Psychiatry)*, 11, 1918, 21–36. For a detailed discussion, see Stryker, 'Languages of Sacrifice and Suffering', 131–40.
61. F. A. Hamilton, quoted in *Report of the War Office Committee of Enquiry into 'Shell-Shock'*, London, 1922, 59. Hamilton had served as a medical officer during the war, gaining firsthand experience of shellshock patients.
62. Hans Binneveld, *From Shell Shock to Combat Stress: A Comparative History of Military Psychiatry*, translated by John O'Kane, Amsterdam University Press, 1997, 94.
63. Showalter, *Hystories*, 138–43.
64. Modern military psychiatry recognises this. For a thought-provoking discussion of the psychological effects of killing, see Dave Grossman, *On Killing: The Psychological Cost of Learning to Kill in War and Society*, Little, Brown, 1995.
65. Members of the Einsatzgruppen, responsible for shooting Jews behind the Eastern front in the Second World War, also suffered psychological problems although not themselves in any way endangered.
66. For a concise summary of this history, see Binneveld, *From Shellshock to Combat Stress*, Chapter 10.

8

Food and the German Home Front

Evidence from Berlin

Keith Allen

Focusing on the management of food supplies in the German capital, this essay considers the social consequences of war. Specifically, in the realm of food policy I show how German civil authorities between 1914 and 1918 forged alliances with segments of the urban public. This perspective allows me to challenge interpretations that attribute Germany's loss in the First World War to the nation's ostensibly undemocratic political culture.

This essay draws attention to the paradoxical effects of wartime scarcity. As a diverse group of scholars have rightly insisted, hard times in wartime Germany engendered conflict. The inability of the German government to provide citizens with foodstuffs at reasonable prices led to the explosion of black markets and greatly exacerbated tension between town and country, producers and consumers and, of course, social classes. These tensions have encouraged historians to judge Germany's food supply system a failure, and the bureaucrats who managed it inept.[1] According to Gerald Feldman, the inability of authorities to cope with the problems of modern war not only hurt ordinary citizens. 'Slow moving, ponderous and bureaucratic', the German wartime governments' 'absence of adequate leadership' contributed to illiberalism's postwar ascendancy.[2]

First articulated in the mid-1960s, Feldman's account continues to influence historians. Most recently, Thierry Bonzon and Belinda Davis have argued that '... [from late 1915 on] authorities [in Berlin] seemed to have breached the pact between society and state, a social contract of loyalty and sacrifice in return for adequate and fairly apportioned food supplies. The rupture of this informal but palpable understanding undermined the authority and legitimacy of the state.'[3] 'Problems of food supply and distribution,' Bonzon and Davis conclude, 'clearly played a decisive role in the unravelling of the German war effort in the last two years of the war.'[4] Bonzon and Davis agree that the unwillingness of wartime authorities to embrace reform was a determining factor in the collapse of state authority in 1918.

In fact, the line of conflict carefully drawn by Feldman between army, industry and labour on the one side, and an isolated, inept imperial bureaucracy on the other, never fully characterised wartime policy towards food in Germany's largest city.[5] Rather, in Berlin, wartime coalitions of particular interests – local bureaucrats, trade union leaders, women's groups and favoured consumers – promoted cooperation during the 1914–1918 European conflict. Notwithstanding the glaring deficiencies of the rationing system, when faced with the choice of supporting the central authority or looking out for themselves, large numbers of Berliners ultimately favoured cooperation over autarky.[6]

This essay focuses on two elements of Berlin's wartime rationing network: the creation of municipal kitchens and the rationing of Germany's most important foodstuff, bread. It begins with the origins of the smaller of the two programmes, an unprecedented initiative to prepare meals for the masses at the expense of the state.

1. From Advice-Giving to Communal Dining

While virtually all contemporaries quickly registered the unprecedented scope of the nation's nutritional problems, initial responses to the challenges of food shortage bore a clear resemblance to prewar initiatives. In the first months of war, women's education in the domestic arts was eagerly promoted in order to keep the German household – and therewith the German war machine – running smoothly.[7] Women's groups, most prominent among them a new organisation, the German Federation of Housewives (*Reichsverband deutscher Hausfrauenvereine*), assembled listeners for travelling cooking courses, exhibitions and, above all, public lectures.[8] Even Germany's Social Democrats, long a thorn in the side of the nation's economic and political elite, rushed to spread the word about wartime nutrition.[9] For those unable to attend public lectures, the national umbrella organisation for most prewar feminist associations, the Federation of German Women's Organisations (*Bund deutscher Hausfrauenvereine*) summarised nutritionists' speeches in bulletins, published them in a new journal devoted to wartime nutrition, and distributed them to both local and regional newspapers.

Feminists' efforts provided nutritional experts with unprecedented opportunities to disseminate the collected wisdom of their youthful discipline. Max Rubner, the most important nutritionist of the era, harangued the nation for its overconsumption. Rubner insisted that Germans – particularly urban Germans – ate too much fat, drank too little milk and con-

sumed too few vegetables. The first step toward a healthy diet and economic self-sufficiency, argued Rubner, was to restrict meat consumption
to the warm, midday meal. Under no circumstances should families eat
meat for either breakfast or supper. The 'evening bread,' as northern Germans called the meal, should be a Spartan affair of wheat or especially
home-grown rye bread, as well as vegetables served without meat or
other animal fats.[10]

As Rubner and other contemporaries had noted in the decades preceding the war, the confluence of four factors – the rise of the wage economy,
the growing distance between residence and workplace, the adoption of
modern time-work discipline (especially the implementation of shorter
lunch breaks) and the perception that greater numbers of women were
working outside the home – created a new, and distinctly urban, diet. By
1914, working Berliners had traded the traditionally large, warm, vegetable-
centred midday meal for concentrated, easily digestible, cold, meaty and
fatty units of food known locally as *Stullen*, or open-faced sandwiches on
white bread.[11] So long as women worked at home, the possibility of a set
table at noon remained a possibility. The wartime division of families and,
in particular, the reality of women's paid labour in factory jobs began to
dampen criticism of the public consumption of foodstuffs.

In early 1915, the élan of the first war months had clearly waned, and the
tolerance of authorities for public assembly declined accordingly. Large
gatherings devoted to raising housewives' sense of responsibility vis-à-vis
the Fatherland often raised more questions than they answered, as some
speakers, particularly Social Democrats, refused to restrict their comments
to the subject of nutrition.[12] As times got harder, civic leaders shifted
resources from the pulpit to the printing press. Especially during the winter
of 1915 to 1916, articles in important German dailies[13] and the nation's leading welfare journals[14] sang the praises of an unlikely set of wartime heroes:
the creators and sustainers of public dining institutions.

As the state subsidised advice-giving and, above all, sought to regulate
the nation's food consumption through household rationing, communal
charitable organisations demonstrated their fealty to the Fatherland
through the public provision of meals. The oldest such charity in Berlin
was Lina Morgenstern's Society for Public Kitchens, an organisation
whose efforts had begun fifty years earlier during the Austrian-Prussian
War. In 1916, Morgenstern's organisation made headlines with the introduction of 'travelling kitchens', horse-drawn carriages which delivered
large kettles of soup to workingclass neighbourhoods. The Society's deliv-
eries of soup to the hungry were cited with approval by imperial civilian
and military authorities, including the Supreme Commander of the Borderlands, Gustav Kessel.[15]

The largest and best known philanthropic meal provider in Berlin was
Hermann Abraham's Society for Children's Public Kitchens (*Verein für
Kindervolksküchen*). By 1916, Abraham's society was feeding over 25,000
schoolchildren a free meal at lunch; in the autumn of the same year, Abra-

ham had shifted his resources to preschoolers, an equal number of whom received warm nourishment from the Society during the last two years of the war. Abraham's largesse also expanded during the war to include adults. Drawing inspiration from similar initiatives in Frankfurt, Abraham created in Berlin during the first months of the war a new genre of public dining, 'middleclass kitchens', eateries that in fact served a broad spectrum of skilled labourers, as well as members of the lower-middleclass. In August 1918, Abraham's Society boasted over 40,000 members, over 140 dining halls, and had served more than 40 million meals. His was the largest organisation of its kind in Germany, perhaps in all of Europe.[16]

Amongst Abraham's prewar opponents, midday feeding in the capital, as elsewhere in Central Europe, suffered the stigma of poor relief. Since 1800 another quasi-public organisation, the Food Relief Centre for the Poor (*Armen-Speisungs-Anstalt*), had provided warm, midday meals to needy adults.[17] Like the volunteers, the unpaid city bureaucrats who ran the Centre were careful of who they fed. In order to receive a meal coupon, individuals had to retrieve forms from the community poor relief office, return the application to the proper authority, and then submit themselves, family members, and often neighbours, to regular visits from volunteer state servants. Berlin's rapid growth in the years prior to 1914 sent the sick, the infirm, the aged and the poor in droves to the Centre. One example, taken from a 1906 report prepared by a poor relief official about one of the Centre's fifteen kitchens, must stand for many:

> The crowd this past winter was really something else. A fourth of the coupon holders, men and women, were almost always drunk – so drunk in fact that I had to deny them food. Of course this caused a scandal, and a policeman had to remove the troublemakers from the premises. I simply don't understand why managers give such people coupons. It is just dreadful when such a character leaves the building with a pot or bucket of stew. I mention this again because I just couldn't bear these people any longer in my kitchen. A minute after I had shown them the door, I found their soup spilled all over the street. Also, there are always problems when we cook millet, rice, or pearl barley. On these days, only half the people come to collect their meals, while the other half wait outside to see what's being served. If it's one of the accursed grains I mention above, the early birds turn around and give their coupons to those waiting below, or anyone in the vicinity. I have noted this phenomenon, and I have recorded the coupon numbers. I have spoken to those in charge about the matter, but they simply do not take it seriously.[18]

Military gridlock, chronic shortages of wood, coal and many other items, as well as reports of dangerously poor health amongst children and infants, further encouraged civilian, and particularly military, officials to ponder the economics of scale offered by the public provision of meals. In particular the shift in emphasis of women's work from non-industrial occupations, such as domestic service to work in armaments factories, further encouraged efforts to adopt a system of benefits for wage-earning women and their dependants.[19] By the spring of 1916, supplements for industrial workers, the needs of the military, and growing concern about the black market had further encouraged high-ranking civilian leaders to embrace the long-stigmatised act of public feeding (*Massenspeisung*). Berlin's city officials were under greater pressure than many of their colleagues, for in the eyes of the military Germany's largest city had extensive experience with mass feeding initiatives.[20] Generous public subsidy from the Prussian Interior Ministry and the Imperial War Nutrition Office (KEA), if not new foodstuffs, was to lay the foundation for new urban public feeding initiatives.[21]

On 10 July 1916, Berlin city officials opened the first kitchen, and thereafter they established a new kitchen every week. By the end of September, eleven municipally-sponsored restaurants and seventy-seven distribution centres sought to meet the basic nutritional needs of Berliners.[22] Unlike the smaller cities of Westphalia, where authorities established cooking facilities within the new restaurants, Berlin's administrators converted empty market halls into mass kitchens.[23] Large cellars held the stores. Above ground, giant electrical appliances rinsed, peeled and sliced hundreds of pounds of vegetables per hour, while stew simmered in 200, 300, and 600 kilogram iron-forged kettles. No citizen, town leaders announced with pride, had to walk more than twelve minutes to retrieve a hot midday meal. Within ten weeks, the city had assembled the kettles, cooks and storage space to create a quarter million quarts of soup per day.

So how did Berlin's meal distribution system work? Between Monday and Thursday, those citizens who wanted a weekly meal pass visited their local rationing centre, known to contemporaries as the Bread Commission Office. There, they traded a week's worth of meat and potato ration cards for a weekly meal pass. Patrons brought their pass and containers to their nearest distribution centre, and in return, they received a bowl of warm stew. In larger kitchens, solid oak benches lined each side of the entrance. Here, visitors could lunch in peace. As city fathers intended, however, most ordered their stew to take away. 'The meal should be eaten at home,' they piously proclaimed, 'in order to protect domestic family life.'[24]

The municipally-sponsored restaurants differed from the traditional soup kitchen in important respects. First and foremost, citizens were not required to establish their indigence to receive a pass.[25] Indeed, town fathers encouraged all Berliners, regardless of economic status, to make use of the city meal programme. As authorities emphasised in a 1916 report, 'the city's meal programme has absolutely nothing in common with poor relief or charity. On the contrary, the programme is intended to meet the needs of all citizens. This principle lead us to charge a price that cover only the costs of production.'[26] The new lunch halls remained open almost every day of the year, except for a few days before and after Christmas and New Year.

The city's claims were too strident not to be met with a certain degree of scepticism. Town fathers knew that many aspects of their new enterprise – the weekly-sign up, the 'cash and carry' service, and, above all, the fare – reminded citizens of the city's sixteen soup kitchens.[27] Thus, when the time came for the city to choose a leader for the new welfare endeavour, Berlin officials overlooked the poor relief office's long list of qualified male candidates, and chose a female philanthropist instead: Hedwig Heyl.

Heyl's personal and professional qualities made her an ideal candidate in the eyes of municipal bureaucrats as well as state and imperial authorities. As Gertrud Bäumer, the writer and feminist thinker, described her, Heyl was 'worldly-wise in the feminine sense'. Heyl knew, as Bäumer put it, 'better than to drill at the hardest point in the board'.[28] When Dr Georg Reicke, mayor of Charlottenburg (then an independent city, today a district of the city in the west), asked the most distinguished living Fröbellian to 'lend the guiding hand' to the city's new enterprise, Heyl reportedly answered with a 'friendly, unassuming "Yes".' As the conversation turned to the 'thousands, hundreds of thousands' involved, Heyl, according to Mayor Reicke, rushed to catch her breath. Suddenly serious, she put her hands to her head and exclaimed: 'Oh God, my dear mayor, what are you asking of me! Yes, but it must be done! But it shall require great resources! And volunteers! My ladies would help. Dear Lord, but we simply have to succeed!' Much to the satisfaction of her male colleagues, she worked long hours, devoted her considerable energies to the smallest detail and, as Reicke later noted, proved invaluable in the city's ongoing efforts to curry favour with provincial and imperial authorities.[29]

An accomplished public speaker, domestic science expert and self-taught nutritional scientist, Heyl had mastered skills that served her well in her new capacity. Heyl's wartime credentials were impeccable. She had been among the select list of speakers at the first national conference on wartime nutrition in the capital in January 1915. She held numerous public lectures during the nation's short-lived lecture series. When authorities favoured the pen over public assembly, Heyl devoted an essay to the humble potato. When Germans' cherished fatty foods grew scarce, Heyl wrote a pamphlet entitled, 'The Low-Fat Kitchen'. When sugar disappeared, she invented marmalade from available materials. And as Berlin's leading prewar proponent of home cooking, Heyl was detached from any association with poor relief. As Berlin's wartime Lord Mayor, Adolf Wermuth, later noted, 'Germany's ideal housewife, Hedwig Heyl, swung the first enormous cooking kettle like a victor on the battlefield.'[30] Heyl, however, hardly laboured alone. In the summer of 1916, she was joined by a staff of two hundred female volunteers, most of them graduates of her own cooking course. Hundreds more would follow.[31]

The women's first task was to ensure that their efforts reached the largest possible number of Berliners. To this end, the municipality invited entire factories and branches of government to join the new stew network.[32] By the end of the year, the programme delivered meals to over one hundred factory canteens city-wide. The Imperial Office for War Nutrition, or *Kriegsernährungsamt*, a new ministry created in May 1916, was pleased with the new system, for it ensured that workers in armament industries would receive at least one warm meal a day. The Office encouraged Prussian authorities to allocate prized frozen meat supplies to Berlin's feeding experiment. In turn, the city offered industrial workers stew with an extra 350 gram portion of meat at the reduced price of seventy-five pfennig. As the example indicates, the city's new network of municipal dining halls enjoyed the financial support of state and imperial authorities.

The story of mass feeding in Berlin was in some respects successful.[33] Except for the brief interruption of the Kapp Putsch in 1920, when water, gas and electricity were shut off city-wide, the municipal kitchen staff served the city's neediest a warm lunch every day of the week for almost six years. Berlin's women volunteers not only showed up for work every day, they alerted town fathers to the new plan's shortcomings, and their suggestions led to a number of improvements. After an initial trial period, citizens were allowed to bypass the cumbersome registration at their local bread commission office in favour of signing-up at their local distribution centre.[34] Registration was also made easier for those who lived outside of the city's centre. Heyl and her colleagues worked to eliminate distinctions between central Berlin and the suburbs, making where one worked and, by implication, where one ate, the guiding principle of meal distribution.

Many of the problems Heyl and her staff faced were beyond their control. Trouble began with the unpopular fare. In place of the three-course meals offered at Abraham's popular 'middleclass' restaurants, the new city programme only offered stew.[35] In Dortmund as in Berlin, labourers insisted they deserved better than the 'messes' of old, demanding that their hard work earned them the right to truly nourishing food.[36] Quantity cooking at reasonable prices demanded that the city's cooks cut the occasional corner. When it came to the availability of comestibles, Heyl and her staff took what they were given and threw it in the kettle.

The guardians of Berlin's feeding enterprise also missed opportunities to advance their cause. Unlike organisers in Dortmund, where war restaurants operated in close cooperation with consumer groups, Heyl and her supporters at City Hall chose to ignore offers of assistance from philanthropic meal providers such as Abraham.[37] Indeed, the oversupply of soup in the first weeks of the new kitchens' operation led authorities to assume control of Abraham's hitherto voluntary school lunch programme, a decision Abraham, reasonably enough, viewed with suspicion.[38] In Hamburg, where a successful charity was merged with the city's own feeding programme, results were markedly better.[39] In October 1918, for example, nearly 20 percent of city's population took advantage of Hamburg's kitchen network on a daily basis.[40]

Worse still, authorities in Berlin made little effort to accommodate popular wishes, much less popular tastes. Citizens were wary of trading a week's worth of meat and potato cards for a meal pass. Why not, as some suggested, simply introduce a separate rationing card for the kitchens themselves? As one city councillor put it in the summer of 1916, 'I don't consider the weekly meal cards that the city is now introducing a way to alleviate people's suffering, but instead a way of scaring them off. I mean, the public has to go the kitchen every day without knowing what they'll get. The truth is that the rise and fall of customers is the best barometer we have as to whether the food is any good or not.'[41] City officials turned a deaf ear to this request. As the Social Democratic daily, *Vorwärts*, had warned, 'thousands of women will greet the establishment of kitchens that produce and distribute tasty, nutritious, and reasonably-priced meals.' If, however, these modest demands were not met, citizens will regard it as merely another 'bureaucratic institution and a soup kitchen unworthy of their patronage.'[42]

In truth, even enthusiasts found it difficult to register popular support for the public dining halls. The city never came close to its projected quarter million customers. At the beginning of 1916, when construction was finished, the city fed a mere 55,000 thousand citizens. The unusually harsh winter of 1916–17 improved the kitchens' fortunes somewhat, as the number of citizens who received meals rose to 152,000 in February of the next year. In April, when potatoes reappeared on grocery shelves, the kitchens lost 35,000 customers. In October 1918, the number had shrunk to 48,000, and even during the worst of the winter of 1919, the city's kitchen network drew in a mere 42,000 souls. A year later, demand hovered somewhere between ten and twenty thousand people; even normally rigorous Prussian statisticians had lost interest in the exact fate of the experiment. By spring 1920, only two central kitchens and a handful of distribution centre remained.[43]

It is, as Jay Winter has noted, commonplace to speak of the expansion of the European state in wartime.[44] Particularly in the realm of social reproduction the wartime state is believed to have aggressively intervened in the home lives of German men, women and children.[45] In my examination of the most important daily act of physical production, eating, I find limited evidence to support these claims. Wartime innovations brought entire industries under state control and reconfigured the labour force; they did not, however, challenge the balance of power at the dinner table. In the midst of 'total war', civilian (though not military) leaders, nutritional experts, and central figures within the women's movement only reluctantly embraced the concept of public eating, instead offering hungry citizens advice, foodstuffs and, only as a last resort, prepared meals.

More than a tale of the expansion of the wartime state, the story of Berlin's wartime take-away meal allows one to discern a limit to the German nation's ability to mobilise resources for war. Virtually all contemporary prescribers of social policy and personal lifestyle acknowledged that centralised production saved labour, time and, above all, food. It also seemed to offer an effective means to ensure that citizens received minimum daily nutritional requirements. And yet, before investing in the municipally-sponsored kitchens, Berlin's city government had spent millions of marks on programmes designed to promote the production of meals *within the household*. These included cookery courses, nutritional bulletins and, above all, rationed foodstuffs, particularly flour and bread.[46] The arrangements of rationing confirmed, not challenged, the prewar ideal of domestic reproduction.[47] Although the nation's most extensive endeavour in public dining, Berlin's municipal meal programme after 1916 nevertheless remained a neglected sibling to the city's exponentially larger programme of foodstuff rationing. On the other hand, analysis of the provision of households in the capital with bread – the cornerstone of the German home meal during the war – supports Ute Daniel's contention that local governments (in spite of losses due to conscription) largely met the unprecedented administrative challenges presented by the wartime scarcity of foodstuffs.[48]

2. The Rationing of Breadstuffs

Municipal efforts to subsidise the home production of meals began very early, more than a year and a half prior to the establishment of city's first municipal kitchen. In December 1914, German civil authorities assumed responsibility for the price, quantity and quality of grain stores.[49] In Berlin, a municipal war commission, including representatives from the city's upper and lower chambers of government, consumer cooperativists, captains of local industry, leaders of the local bakers' federation, and organised labour created a Bread Commission Office (*Abteilung für Brotversorgung*). Staffed by ten city councillors and five representatives from the mayor's office, the 'Mixed Deputation for the Supply of Berlin with Foodstuffs' acted largely independently of the government that created it. Based on the example of bread distribution, at the end of two years of war virtually every imaginable food product was rationed at the local level.[50]

Every city in Germany had a somewhat different ration, depending on such considerations as its size, proximity to rural areas and municipal competence.[51] In Berlin, in accordance with guidelines established by imperial authorities, the city's Bread Supply Office initially gave people over the age of eighteen coupons that permitted them to buy 1,950 grams of bread, or the equivalent amount of flour, each week. The Office distributed ration cards on a weekly basis, usually on the Thursday before the start of the next rationing week. Beginning on the following Monday, consumers could exchange coupons at bakery and pastry shops, paying 80 pfennig for either a ration of bread or an equivalent amount of flour. Most preferred bread to flour.

To the bakers fell most of the responsibility for making the new commercial regime work. They were required to submit new ration coupons weekly, along with an itemised flour inventory book, to their local bread commission office. While the breadmaker watched, an official weighed his burlap coupon sacks. If the scale confirmed that he had traded virtuously, the baker received flour for the coming week. Restaurateurs had it easier, at least at first. Much to the chagrin of pastry makers, the owners of the city's restaurants, cafés and hotels could serve customers without the bother of using cards. Proprietors were merely required to record purchases of bread. By October 1916, however, most purveyors of prepared foods had to meet the strict rationing regulations.

Few people in 1914 predicted a long war, and virtually no one expected the hardship to last an entire year, much less two, three and four. No plan existed to replace the intricate network of shops, warehouses and processing facilities that had delivered bread to the peacetime masses. The new rationing measures exacerbated strained relations between city and countryside, as farmers were unable to grow enough to compensate for Germany's basic dependency on foreign foodstuffs.[52] When farmers hid stores, refused to slaughter animals, or sold grain on the black-market, urban bureaucrats were forced to improvise.[53]

Much like their counterparts on the General Staff, the officials of the city's bread commissions were forced to learn by doing, with predictable results. After a reasonably harmonious first twelve months, the second year brought attempts to prescribe the sizes, shapes, weights and ingredients of pastries and other bread stuffs. The Bread Office issued instructions not to mix foreign with domestic flours. In cases where the grains had nonetheless been combined, pastry makers were instructed to place a sign in the window warning customers that the proprietor offered 'baked goods made from foreign flour'. [54]

The most dire days for those in charge of rationing came during the harsh winter of 1916–17. The harvest of 1916 was a poor one in much of Europe. In Paris, food riots led by women workers forced the municipal government to introduce a comprehensive series of food controls. Even in London, where food rationing (with the important exception of bread) did not begin until February 1918, *The Times* reported long lines in front of East End food shops.[55] In Berlin, matters were far worse, as potato flour initially replaced flour made from grain, and the weekly bread ration dipped to an all-time low of 1,600 grams. From the first week of February to the beginning of April, the lord of the city's granaries searched his delivery list each morning for a train car of potatoes. In its place, he found turnips. As it became clear that the bloodless beet had assumed a place of prominence in the unholy trinity of wartime hunger, townspeople took to the streets.

Bonzon and Davis insist that 'bureaucratic foul-ups were inevitable given the structure of civil administration in Berlin.'[56] Still, it is worth noting that when Berlin's hunger victims converged on the citadel of city power, the *Rathaus*, the city's Lord Mayor, Adolf Wermuth, emerged to listen.[57] After hearing their demands, Wermuth invited representatives to join him to discuss the city's food supply. The next morning, the elected officials joined Wermuth, Georg Michaelis, the Prussian Food Commissar, and Adolf von Tortilowicz Batocki, President of the Imperial War Nutrition Office, in the *Rathaus* ballroom.[58] During the next three and a half years, Wermuth met with labour leaders each Saturday morning. The atmosphere was not always cordial, and many a patrician's heart beat faster, as Heyl later put it, to hear the Lord Mayor 'scolded like a mere schoolboy.'[59] Still, the sessions paid dividends. An initial concession was a decision to compensate for the harsh winter by doubling summer meat rations. In return, Wermuth solidified the city's claim to represent the urban labouring classes before the provincial and imperial governments, as well as the army.[60]

As Davis has argued, 'by failing to take decisive control of the food question, however, they [imperial authorities] ceded this authority to others.'[61] True, the inability of civilian officials, particularly at the level of provincial and Imperial government, encouraged Berliners of lesser means to provision themselves via the black market, a state of affairs condoned – and, in some cases, actively promoted, by local governments. In retrospect, national attempts to provide bread stuffs and other important food items to households seem doomed to failure. In contrast to the Austro-Hungarian and Russian monarchies, which in peacetime produced more than enough food to feed their populations, Germans imported almost six million tons of fodder, mostly grain, annually in the years before 1914. In fact, the shortfall was larger still, since much of the rye cultivated on German farms was used as animal fodder, while bread was baked from three million tons of imported wheat. The British embargo meant that during the war years comparable amounts of rye were diverted from animals to breadmaking.[62]

City rationing authorities certainly had their hands full. As if keeping citizens, soldiers and bakers happy was not enough, they also had to answer to their superiors in provincial (especially the Prussian war and interior ministries) and imperial agencies (such as the War Nutrition Office), the Bundesrat (federal council), as well as the less influential Reichstag. Beginning on 1 February 1915, the Bread Commission of Berlin, and its counterparts elsewhere in Germany, received shipments of wheat, barley, oats and rye exclusively from an imperial allocation office. Berlin's authorities welcomed this decision, for it ended precautionary hoarding, price fluctuations, and the speculation of the first weeks of the war. The new order returned urban officials to a more familiar form of town rivalry, as local civilian and military authorities honed their skills at portraying the nutritional state of their charges in the direst terms. Arbitrary seizures of grain never disappeared completely. Military interference (particularly after the summer of 1916) took on a new guise, when the army successfully pushed provincial and imperial authorities to allow it to supply bread, other foodstuffs and, less often, meals directly to 'war' factories.[63] In the meantime, however, the new regulatory system limited the involvement of the army long enough to halt the ruinous intra-municipal competition that threatened to devour city grain stores.

The subjection of bread distribution and processing to a single system of supply/control should have enabled the municipalities to regulate demand. Unfortunately for city officials, those who made the rules which governed food distribution frequently chose to break them. The more desperate military leaders became, the greater was their willingness to tinker with the home front's local food markets. Imperial and provincial authorities could not prevent General Erich Ludendorff, quartermaster-general of the army and second in command to Field Marshal von Hindenburg (he received his appointment to head the Third Supreme Army Command after the disasters of Verdun and the Somme in August 1916), from seizing precious grain resources.[64]

Like the bakers they sought to control, municipal authorities were caught in a double bind. Both pastry cooks and policymakers had to accept the flour given to them whatever the quantity. Both groups were forced to adjust to a constant stream of regulations and had to explain to customers why some grains were available while others were not: neither group exercised influence over the country's powerful agricultural lobby, a strong voice at court and in the Imperial government.[65] Of course, the plight of bureaucrats and bakers paled in comparison to that of most Berliners, the majority of whom belonged to workingclass families that had been stripped of their wage-earning male members. The long wait for life's necessities that began early each morning and often extended well until the evening gave many women plenty of time to reflect upon the miserable state of their affairs. The growing number of Berlin women engaged in paid labour fared even worse. From early 1915 to the end of 1917, the number of women employed in Berlin's factories expanded dramatically. Holding down a job outside of the home while raising a family was hard enough before 1914. The war made it virtually impossible. The dangerous and often poorly-paid hours at the factory, followed by the endless wait at the shops, plagued many Berlin women. The fear that the wait would end, as so many had before, with an empty-handed walk home to hungry dependants was nearly unbearable.[66]

Popular resentment of privilege focused on City Hall, though it also had class dimensions. As Carl Timm, physician from the district of Prenzlauer Berg noted,

> ... housewives (let's be honest, their servants) in the city's western suburbs merely display their rationing coupons and receive their goods without any hassle. That's a lot different than how things are in the city's northern and eastern districts, where municipal authorities really throw up obstacles. First, they pronounce with full fanfare how much of each good, at what weight, each citizen shall receive. Next, citizens exchange their wait number for a ration card. At this point, the nonsense truly gets under-way. In vain, our women here in the North and East try to find out just what exactly they can expect to receive in exchange for their 'coupons'. And so it goes, day in, day out, until finally the commissioners have got rid of consumers and shopkeepers alike.[67]

Rationing in Berlin was never popular, as this and many other letters make abundantly clear. Nonetheless, at the local level cooperation among local political actors never dissipated altogether. In sustaining the war effort, the city's government called upon – and received – public participation in the delivery of basic foodstuffs to individual households. In order to fulfil their day-to-day obligations to customers, the city government enlisted the support of able bureaucrats, loyal bakers, members of organised labour and representatives of the women's movement.

Berlin's rationing system created conflicts between consumers, planners and merchants, but it also contained mechanisms to ensure that tempers did not reach a boiling point. Pressures notwithstanding, the bakers and bureaucrats worked together in a court of appeals to adjudicate bread producers' grievances. The new body represented both master artisans and senior civil servants. Members of the pastry makers' federation and civil servants also sat together in a special division of the Bread Office established to catch falsifiers and to eliminate black market activity. When Berlin's government levelled charges of unfair trading practices against bakers, it did so with the approval of at least three of the city's master bakers.

In both provincial and imperial ministries, the municipal government was far from isolated. Berliners, particularly city officials, were well represented in the agencies charged with the national and provincial distribution of meat, fruits and vegetables, potatoes and bread. Moreover, the lord mayor, Wermuth, until 1912 imperial secretary of the treasury, was on close terms with a number of well-placed national government officials, including the Kaiser, Prime Minister Theobald von Bethmann Hollweg, General Ludendorff and Gustav von Kessel, the territorial commander of the province of Brandenburg and Berlin.[68] When Georg Simonsohn, Wermuth's most important deputy, disobeyed orders, he did so with the full concurrence of Wermuth, who then turned to his superiors and proclaimed his ignorance, all the while shielding the Bread Office's day-to-day operations from provincial and imperial intervention.[69]

German wartime rationing succeeded to some degree because a not insignificant number of consumers supported it. Gestures of conciliation did not have to be large to be meaningful. Simonsohn knew that the bread scheme worked only when communal authorities took the time to respond promptly to customers' seemingly endless questions. He appears to have understood that the art of civil service lies in the ability to refuse without offending. While anxious to keep the peace within his expanding department, Simonsohn nonetheless refused to tolerate rudeness from communal rationing authorities. Responding to press complaints that citizens were not being treated with the proper respect, Simonsohn instructed local managers that 'office staffers must meet all public requests with politeness'.[70] Simonsohn, the city's de facto bread chief, helped ensure that professionalism mollified the city's sceptical citizenry.

The Bread Office's gestures of goodwill involved still other, more substantial, concessions to the public. In response to consumer requests, Simonsohn extended local commissions' hours, from 5 p.m. to 8 p.m. on weekdays and added another two hours on Saturday. They also allowed the city's few vegetarians to substitute meat rations for extra barley, semolina, rolled oats and pasta, as well as provided Jewish citizens with matzos for Passover.

Enlightened self-interest guided the bread lords' decisions. Keeping managers at their desks well into the evening helped prevent frequent break-ins; providing vegetarians with alternatives ensured that more meat was available to the rest of the population; and allowing commuters to draw on the inner city's reserves meant that they too had a stake in the system's successful operation.

Other gestures to the city's hungry poor are not easily explained in terms of narrow-minded self-interest. The provisions established for the city's Jewish population fall in this category, as did the municipal government's efforts to ensure that domestic servants received their own full rations. In a dramatic break with precedent, the Bread Office instructed local newspapers to inform heads of households that domestics had a right to receive bread ration-cards. Those who failed to meet their obligations to their servants, Simonsohn warned, faced the possibility of fines or imprisonment. True to its word, the city government tried three cases within the first three months of rationing.

Personal contacts, decent service, enlightened self-interest and patriotism were among the most important elements of Berlin's rationing programme. A less obvious, though no less important, source of social consensus was agreement on whose hunger pangs should be eased first. The ultimate justification for the people's sacrifices was the shared sentiment that those at the front should receive the best food available. As Edwin Schuster, member of Bavarian Engineering Company Number 8, testified, the common foot soldier had considerably more food, in particular bread, than he needed.

> No difference is more glaring than the paucity of foodstuffs at home and their waste here in the battlefield. The squandering begins immediately. During the transport, men receive a number of warm meals, and upon arrival at the Front, each soldier obtains four pounds of bread, sausages, and an additional pound and a half of red meat. These provisions are fully superfluous, for virtually every man receives in care packages from home enough foodstuffs to keep himself stuffed. We have no idea what to do with all the bread we receive, the Home Front's most important foodstuff. As soon as we arrived at the battle field, we also get an entire week's ration of bread. Many throw the rock-hard loaves away. Others feed them to the horses.[71]

Schuster's testimony illustrates that wartime rationing was based upon a policy that held army rations above civilians' dietary needs. When authorities felt least assured of popular support, they invoked sacrifice in terms of military exigency. By and large, civilians agreed to pay the price. The irony was, as Schuster noted, that food packages from home not only endangered the lives of loved ones, they also added to the front's abominable rat plague.

The willingness of ordinary Germans to keep the home fires burning also rested upon their belief, sometimes shaken but often confirmed, that their leaders were doing their best to help those civilians who sacrificed the most. The first group to receive the recognition of the authorities were workers whose jobs involved unusual physical strain. Acting on instructions from the Imperial government (the War Wheat Commission), Berlin's city government moved in the spring of 1915 to provide supplemental bread rations to workers over twenty-one years of age who were engaged in heavy labour. Soon thereafter, qualified labourers received an extra 450 grams of bread per week.[72]

Simonsohn and Wermuth pushed the imperial authorities to cover many more people than their plan originally envisioned. Simonsohn's most important deputy, Erich Simm, instructed local commissioners that they should not, as the food administrators from the War Wheat Commission prescribed, ask workers to submit a letter of approval from their employers. 'It is self-evident,' Simonsohn added, that 'the applicant's entire economic status must be considered, above all the number of children in his household.'[73]

In the ensuing months, Simonsohn and his subordinates ensured that every Berlin household received an application for a supplemental bread card. By the end of 1915, the city had issued over 625,000 cards, and by the end of 1916, the number of supplemental cards distributed weekly had reached 600,000. During the winter of 1916–1917, at the insistence of Prussian and imperial authorities, the city government trimmed the number of cards to 400,000 per week. The cuts, which coincided with a reduction of the supplemental ration from 450 to 350 grams, were ill-timed, and Berlin's municipal authorities protested to their superiors.

The city government nonetheless supplied a spectrum of workers with supplemental bread coupons throughout the war. Many of these occupations were essential to the war effort, and included workers on Berlin's rail and waterways, as well as munitions workers. The labour of other Berliners, such as nightshift workers, textile workers, street cleaners, or construction workers was, however, probably not so essential to waging war.[74] The Office's commitment to the labouring classes earned it the grudging praise of critics. As an otherwise disgruntled anonymous 'member of the majority party' (the German Social Democratic Party) acknowledged to trade union bosses, 'if work is demanded, then you all [trade union leaders and municipal rationing authorities] step in and make sure labourers receive an adequate diet.'[75]

The bread card supplement acknowledged the special importance of skilled labour, the rank-and-file members of the German Social Democratic Party and the party-affiliated Free Trade Unions. Beginning in early 1915, the socialists were regularly consulted on the division of the country's meagre grain reserves among the labouring classes. During the difficult year of 1917, Adolf Cohen, head of the metalworker union of Greater Berlin, and Alvin Körsten, a Social Democratic delegate in the Reichstag, attended numerous meetings, private and public, with Simonsohn and Simm. Acting on their constituents' wishes, Cohen and Körsten asked that supplemental cards be distributed to any worker who held sickness insurance, that is, to virtually everyone (both men and women) who worked outside of the home. Simonsohn and Wermuth agreed. Labour leaders rewarded this gesture by joining municipal authorities in the renunciation of Prussian government demands to raise the weekly supplemental bread ration to its previous level of 500 grams. Supplemental bread cards certainly helped ease the hunger pangs of labourers. They also signified social worth. The provision of extra food to men waging war, or to those who produced the material necessary to supply the front, not only reflected planners' priorities, but also elicited the support of the city's labouring classes.

The war brought about dramatic changes in the nature of production, as Berlin's workers left the light-manufacturing sectors of the economy to accept employment in heavy industry. Higher rates of migration, coupled with mass conscription, seemed to ensure that the city's labouring classes in the postwar era would be younger, less skilled and include more women.[76] Berlin's Social Democratic leaders noticed these changes. While acknowledging the wish of provincial and imperial authorities to favour workers in armaments industries, Cohen and Körsten nonetheless aligned themselves with policies that profited *all* workers, regardless of age, sex or skill level. In this decision, labour found an important but unlikely ally in the Office for Bread Supply.

On 1 October 1915, Simonsohn proposed that a supplemental bread ration card be distributed to young people between the ages of nine and twenty-one. In his view, this supplemental bread ration would recognise the contribution of youth to the war effort, though he emphasised that it was more than merely another reward to hungry labourers. All young people, he insisted, regardless of economic class, were to be included in the programme.

The Prussian and imperial authorities initially agreed to make young people's diets a priority, though they successfully lobbied to limit supplements to those between the ages of twelve to seventeen. By the summer of 1917, however, Prussian authorities sought to reverse their decision, arguing that the desperate military situation justified eliminating the measure in favour of increasing rations to metalworkers. Simonsohn, Simm, Cohen and Körsten refused.[77] Since labourers in armaments factories were already receiving higher wages and working longer hours than their comrades who produced foodstuffs and textiles, Cohen and Körsten argued against further benefits to workers engaged in wartime production.[78] Berlin's bureaucrats and labour leaders together faced the opprobrium of their superiors. Batocki and Michaelis attacked the Office for Bread Supply in the imperial and provincial parliaments, and Berlin's civilian leaders and their Social Democratic allies responded in kind in the city assembly and in the national organisation of cities, the *Städtetag*. The Berliners refused to budge. In the last months of the war, provincial and imperial authorities tried again to bring the capital's administrators to heel, decreeing that the de facto reward system for youth go instead to pregnant women.[79] Only the end of the war cut short the renewal of further hostilities.

Friendly service, reasonable prices and the cooperation of organised labour help explain the relative success of Berlin's bread rationing programme. Yet in order to fulfil their day-to-day obligations to customers, the city government again needed shock troops. It found them in the Berlin branch of the Women's National Service, or *Nationaler Frauendienst,* the umbrella organisation for all women's associations during the war.[80] On 1 August 1914, Heyl and Gertrud Bäumer had presented the Prussian Interior Ministry with the plan for this distinctly German service organisation intended to replace international relief agencies, such as the Red Cross. At the Berlin branches, tens of thousands of women handed out bread rations, cooked and delivered meals to school children, delivered lectures on domestic science, offered travelling cooking courses, and distributed bread rations to wounded soldiers at city train stations. Without their energy and ingenuity, Berlin's rationing scheme would not have survived the first difficult months, much less the break-ins, the Turnip Winter and demobilisation.

Maintenance of local rationing schemes therefore hinged upon the participation of women's charitable organisations. One of the central problems for Simonsohn and his staff was keeping tabs on the city's bakers, and to this end women's groups rendered invaluable services. Responding immediately to the government's request for help with 'the confidential supervision of the bakeries', Josephine Levy-Rathenau, founder of Berlin's first women's employment bureau, instructed her charges to 'present yourselves as consumers at bakeries during their busiest hours and record whether merchants observe the city's regulations'.[81]

By keeping bakers honest, citizens satisfied and bureaucrats vigilant, the new guardians of shortage advanced the work of rationing. Women's efforts as overseers were so indispensable that they came to work not only for Simonsohn's department, but also for his Prussian and imperial counterparts. Herein lay the roots of conflict. Initially charged with helping Berlin's municipal authorities to spy on the bakers, the women's organisations ended up caught between the bureaucratic fronts. Frau Ilse Müller-Öestreich, member of the Women's Advisory Food Council, established by the Reichstag in January 1916 to oversee the War Nutrition Department's efforts, repeatedly chastised Berlin's city government for its handling of investigations initiated by evidence her zealous volunteers had gathered. In a 1918 letter to Simonsohn's superiors, Müller-Öestreich explained that in many cases 'it is hardly worth the effort of submitting a report'.[82] After outlining two cases where the city government had failed to follow up on two leads, Müller-Öestreich turned the ethos of civil service to her own advantage. 'You will understand that my time is too precious to waste on reports no one reads. I will assume that you do not intend to call my credibility into question. The effect, however, is the same.' Müller-Öestreich threatened to direct 'future observations to other authorities', a thinly-veiled reference to Simonsohn's foes in the Imperial government.[83] Careful not to provide his many opponents with an excuse to eliminate his office, Simonsohn responded cautiously, stating his willingness 'to continue the work we began together' while nonetheless pinning the blame for the sorry state of relations 'solely' on the advisory council's 'method of communicating individual cases' instead of, as the food director insisted, 'establishing common principles for meaningful, long-term co-operation.'[84]

Simonsohn's expressed desire to 'establish common principles' with the women's organisation was cynical enough to be mistaken for irony. In the course of gathering information about the availability of foodstuffs and their price, leaders of the women's movement entertained hopes that their service to the nation would yield postwar dividends. At each opportunity, Berlin's bread commissioners blocked their progress. As early as 1916, Levy-Rathenau, Bäumer and other leaders of the women's movement asserted their claim to participate in the formation of municipal bread policy. In each instance, the commissioners defended their decision-making prerogative tooth-and-nail, arguing that 'the inclusion of women in planners' decision-making bodies would destroy their character as administrative organs of the state.' For this reason, they insisted, women's participation at the highest levels of governance 'cannot be justified'.[85] In the face of male resistance, women volunteers were unable to use their devotion to the Fatherland as a means of levering themselves into greater political participation.

In early October 1918, the German Army High Command urged the Kaiser and Germany's new civilian leadership to request an armistice based on U.S. President Woodrow Wilson's 'fourteen points' of January 1918. In later years, many Germans – and historians – would come to share Ludendorff's view that the Home Front had stabbed the army in the back. In truth, as C. Paul Vincent has put it, 'the general [and many later commentators] overlooked the fact that the army had fashioned the knife.'[86] The shattering news of defeat on the battlefield made the sacrifice of all German citizens appear tragically wasted; suffering, as many civilians bitterly concluded, had lost its point.

'In Berlin,' Bonzon and Davis insist, 'the authorities' inability to gain a hold on the [food] situation was an essential element in the erosion of the authority of the state.'[87] In fact, in Berlin the war's revolutionary finale did not end the municipal rationing coalition. Instead, the wartime liberal-socialist alliance, with its tested policy of conciliation among the local political class and active exclusion of left-wing elements, prevailed. Just as they had done during the long war years, Social Democratic labour representatives continued to join Lord Mayor Wermuth every Saturday morning to discuss food policy. With Wermuth's acceptance, the postwar council for the provision of foodstuffs eliminated the supplement to 'hard working' and 'hardest working' industrial labourers, an initiative championed by Imperial authorities and the military, and raised the overall bread ration to 2,350 grams per citizen per week.[88]

Wermuth's presence at the council's meeting demonstrates the lines of continuity between the war and the new Republic. Even in the heady days of Berlin's revolutionary November, the soldiers' and workers' councils acceded to Simonsohn's wishes, agreeing to deny efforts to obtain bread by merely presenting an identity card.[89] At the local level, the unity of the political class mitigated ideological allegiances. The transfer of control over Berlin's food supply to local authorities laid the foundation for consensus among Berlin's Majority Socialists, the bourgeois democratic bloc, and monarchists through both war and revolution.[90]

Price controls that the Office of Bread Supply had created during the years of war remained in place during the lean years of peace. Ties to segments of the organised labour movement, firm since the April 1917 uprising, were strengthened, as city food authorities enlisted representatives of Social Democracy, liberal unions and Christian workers' organisations in the struggle against black market activity. Women's organisations, the backbone of the Department's surveillance efforts, remained an integral part of the postwar supervision of bakeries.

Precious little changed in the management of the city's bread resources, save a thick, black pencil line on the stationary masthead through the words 'Royal Residence'. Wermuth remained in office until the end of 1920. It was not the socialists, the left-wing 'independent' Social Democrats, or the centrist majority who left the lord mayor in a lurch, but his former monarchist allies instead. Much to the surprise of many contemporaries and later historians, neither the First World War's deprivations (which, particularly in terms of children's public health, were real and longlasting)[91] nor the postwar uprising of Spartacists and other left-wing radicals (many of whom had hoped that hunger would pave the way for a coup) brought about a reconstitution of social relations in Berlin. In the immediate postwar era, the continued Entente blockade promoted further collaboration between the forces of parliamentary democracy and repression against opponents on the left.

The Inflation, not the war or revolution, terminated wartime rationing in Germany.[92] Despite all the deprivations they suffered during the war, many reported that really hard times set in after the Armistice and continued until December 1923 with the consolidation of the new Rentenmark.[93] The mounting insolvency of Germany's largest municipality took many faces; among the first signs of deterioration was a dramatic rise in the number of break-ins. Burglaries at bread commission offices were so common in March of 1919 that the entire batch of cards had to be declared invalid. As the troubles worsened in the succeeding months, bakers in the city's north and east closed on Friday and Saturdays, leaving customers with empty stomachs and a lot of time on their hands to consider their predicament.[94] In spring 1920, hundreds of women led protest marches on the now-socialist City Hall with banners reading: 'Down with the Food Profiteers' and 'Give us Cheap Bread'.[95] Mass plundering of bakeries ensued, led neither by socialists nor communists, nor by armed paramilitary bands, but instead by the city's women and young men, during the next three years.[96] Rising prices and the explosion of the black market had made impossible what had always been a Herculean task: promoting relative equity in the distribution of basic foodstuffs among citizens of dramatically unequal incomes.

Years of scarcity had pitted bakers against planners, city against countryside, and households against rationing officials. Nonetheless, growing dissatisfaction did not lead a collapse of the home front in 1918. Hardship neither brought to a boil social tensions nor unravelled the nation's (admittedly extremely frayed) social fabric. Consideration of the two pillars of wartime food rationing – public provision of meals in municipally-sponsored kitchens and the domestic supply of foodstuffs to individual households – draws us into a narrative that begins to explain how, for four long years, the links in a chain of active endurance between the capital and the front were forged and maintained.

Notes

For their helpful comments on versions of this essay I wish to thank Gail Braybon, Deborah Cohen, Gerald Feldman, Karl Christian Führer, Donna Harsch, Mary Lindemann, Christine von Oertzen, Jean Quataert, Patrice Poutrus, Peter Stearns, Hans Jürgen Teuteberg, Ulrike Thoms, Martin Vogt, Jonathan Wiesen, Christine Worobec and Tetsuya Yamane.

1. See, for examples, Jürgen Kocka, *Facing Total War: German Society, 1914–1918*, Berg, 1984, 160; Robert Moeller, *German Peasants and Agrarian Politics, 1914–1924: the Rhineland and Westphalia*, University of North Carolina Press, 1986, 53; Avner Offer, *The First World War: An Agrarian Interpretation*, Clarendon Press, 1989, 58.
2. Gerald Feldman, *Army, Industry and Labor*, Princeton University Press, 1966, 503. See also 3–27; 97–135; 283–91.
3. Thierry Bonzon and Belinda Davis, 'Feeding the Cities', in Jay Winter and Jean-Louis Robert (eds), *Capital Cities at War: Paris, London, Berlin 1914–1919*, Cambridge University Press, 1997, 339.
4. Bonzon and Davis, 'Feeding the Cities', 308.
5. Greater Berlin had a population of around 4 million in 1914.
6. The analogy is borrowed from Lars T. Lih. His excellent book on grain procurement in Russia during the period 1914 to 1921 is *Bread and Authority in Russia, 1914–1921*, University of California Press, 1990; see 231–3, 246, 247.
7. See Geheimes Staatsarchiv Preußischer Kulturbesitz, Berlin-Dahlem (Hereafter referred to as GsSta, Berlin), Der Minister des Innern, 22 January 1915, Rep. 197A, Preußischer Staatskommisar für Volksernährung, It Volksaufklärung, 1d Rednerkursus in Volksernährungsfragen.
8. See Renate Bridenthal, '"Professional" Housewives: Stepsisters of the Women's Movement', in Renate Bridenthal, Atina Grossmann and Marion Kaplan (eds), *When Biology Became Destiny: Women in Weimar and Nazi Germany*, Monthly Review Press, 1984, 153–173; Kirsten Schlegel-Matthies, '*Im Haus und am Herd': Der Wandel des Hausfrauenbildes und der Hausarbeit, 1880–1930*, Franz Steiner, 1995, especially 134–48.
9. GsSta, Berlin, An das Königliche Polizeipräsidium Berlin, Verband der sozialdemokratischen Wahlvereine Berlins und Umgegend, 6 February 1915, Rep. 197 A Preußischer Staatskommisar für Volksernährung, It Volksernährung, 1 e, Abhaltung öffentlicher Versammlungen in Volksernährungsfragen.

10. Max Rubner, 'Grundfragen der Volksernährung', *Blätter der Zentralleitung für Wohltätigkeit in Württemberg*, 68 (47), 20 November 1915, 189–92.

11. Max Rubner, 'Die Volksernährung im Kriege. Sonderdruck der deutschen medizinischen Wochenschrift', 40, 1914, 12–15; Alfred Grotjahn, 'Über Wandlungen in der Volksernährung', *Staats- und sozialwissenschaftliche Forschungen*, 20 (2), 1902, 16–21; 64–72.

12. GsSta, Berlin, Regierungsrat von Bergen, Betrifft die gestrigen öffentlichen Volksversammlungen des Verbandes der sozialdemokratischen Wahlvereine Berlins und Umgegend und der Berliner Gewerkschaftskommissionen v. 23.2.1915, Rep. 197A/1t; Oberkommando in den Marken an das stellvertretende Generalkommando in Stettin v. 10 März 1915, GStA Berlin (Geheimes Staatsarchiv Preussischer Kulturbesitz, Berlin-Dahlem), Rep. 197A/1e.

13. In Prussia, the creation of a 'News Office for Nutritional Questions' (*Nachrichtendienst für Ernährungsfragen*) in November 1915 ensured that local, regional and national newspapers received a steady flow of articles on nutrition which reflected the views of Prussian and imperial rationing authorities. See, Brief von dem Minister des Innern an sämtliche Herren Staatsminister v. 12.11.1915, GStA Berlin, Rep. 197A, Nr. 1h.

14. See for example, the following article written by the director of Hamburg's office of poor relief: Dr Lohse, 'Die Volksspeisung im Kriege', in *Blätter der Zentralleitung für Wohltätigkeit in Württemberg*, 68 (45), 6 November 1915, 180–2. His article was originally published in *Soziale Praxis*, the most important German welfare journal of the era.

15. 'Goulashkanonen. Die ersten rücken in den Strassen von Berlin vor', *Berliner Tageblatt*, 29 March 1916. See also, Rudolf Ziege, 'Die Volksspeisung der Stadt Berlin', in *Berliner Wohlfahrtsblatt. Beilage zum Amtsblatt der Stadt*, Berlin, 5 (11), 26 May 1929, 101. Charitable goulash canons ran in other cities as well – Cologne, Frankfurt am Main, Göttingen, Heidelberg, Magdeburg, Mannheim, Münster, Posen und Würzburg. See Stadtverteilungsstelle Breslau an den Berliner Magistrat von 7.6.1916, betr. Fahrbare Küchen (sogennante Goulaschkanonen), LA-B, Rep. 142/1, Nr. 3167.

16. See Chapters 2 and 4 of my book, *Hungrige Metropole. Essen und Wohlfahrt in Berlin*, Ergebnisse, 2002; on charity and the municipal welfare state in Berlin generally, Meinolf Nitsch, *Private Wohltätigkeitsvereine im Kaiserreich. Die praktische Umsetzung der bürgerlichen Sozialreform in Berlin*, Nicolai, 1999.

17. [Author unknown], *Denkschrift zur hundertjährigen Jubelfeier der Armen-Speisung-Anstalt*, Berlin 1900; [Author unknown], *Geschäftsbericht des Vereins Armenspeisungsgesellschaft zu Berlin für das Geschäftsjahr 1930*, Berlin, 1931, 3; Dietland Hüchtker, *Elende Mütter und 'liederliche Weibspersonen'. Geschlechterverhältnisse und Armenpolitik in Berlin*, Westfälisches Dampfboot, 1999, especially 125–128.

18. LA-B, Mandel, 23 April 1906. Fragebogen für die Küche Lychenerstraße 106, Rep. 03 Armendirektion, Nr. 31 Mißstände in Armenspeisungsanstalten (1895–1925).

19. This shift in women's paid labour was in many cases more of a perception than a reality: in particular, efforts to bring new women into the workforce were largely unsuccessful, and employers generally sought to exempt skilled workers from conscription and/or to supplement the skilled work force with (especially after 1916) male foreign labourers or prisoners of war. See Ute Daniel, *Arbeiterfrauen in der Kriegsgesellschaft: Beruf, Familie und Politik im Ersten Weltkrieg*, Vandenhoeck and Ruprecht, 1989, 36–100, 259–65. (Her work is also available in English as *The War From Within: German Working Class Women in the First World War*, translated by Margaret Ries, Berg, 1997.) On the inferences contemporaries drew concerning women's paid labour outside the home from the occupational surveys, see Christina Benninghaus, *Die anderen Jugendlichen. Arbeitermädchen in der Weimar Republik*, Campus, 1999; Kerstin Kohtz, 'Die Jugendwohlfahrtsgesetzgebung von 1922 und die Behandlung von Mädchen in Fürsorgeerziehungsverfahren in der Weimar Republik', in Ute Gerhard, (ed.) *Frauen in der Geschichte des Rechts. Von der Frühen Neuzeit bis zur Gegenwart*, C. H. Beck, 1997, 759–71.

20. Adolf Wermuth, *Ein Beamtenleben*, A. Scherl, 1922, 380; Kaeber, *Berlin im Weltkriege. Fuenf Jahre Staedtischerm Kriegsarbeit*, de Gruyter, 1964, 144.

21. August Skalweit, *Deutsche Kriegsernährungswirtschaft*, DeutscheVerlag-Aktiengesellschaft, 1927, 43–8; H. Krüger and M. Tenius, *Massenspeisungen*, Hobbing, 1917, 5–10;

Martin Gasteiger, *Die städtische Volksspeisung in München. Ein Kriegsbericht von der Heimatfront*, Hardenburg, 1918, 16.

22. [Author unkown], *Die städtische Volksspeisung in Berlin [im Kriegsjahr 1916]*, Berlin, 1916, 9.
23. Anne Roerkohl, *Hungerblockade und Heimatfront. Die kommunale Lebensmittelversorgung in Westfalen während des Ersten Weltkrieges*, Franz Steiner Verlag, 1991, 230.
24. *Die städtische Volksspeisung in Berlin*, 3; see also, *Berliner Tageblatt*, no. 354, 13 July 1916 and Agnes von Harnack, *Der Krieg und die Frauen*, Berlin, 1917, 29.
25. BLHA (Brandenburgisches Landeshauptstadt Archiv), Potsdam. Magistrat der Königlichen Haupt- und Residenzstadt, Wermuth, Bekanntmachung. Städtische Volksspeisung, 30 June 1916, Rep. 30 Bln C Polizeipräsidium, 20269 Die städtische Volksspeisung.
26. *Die städtische Volksspeisung in Berlin*, 12.
27. See Lord Mayor Wermuth's comments to this effect in 'Städtische Massenspeisung', *Berliner Tageblatt*, 7 July 1916.
28. Gertrud Bäumer, *Gestalt und Wandel. Frauenbildnisse*, F. A. Herbig, 1939, 703. On Bäumer generally, see especially Angelika Schaser, *Helene Lange und Gertrud Bäumer. Eine politische Lebensgemeinschaft*, Böhlau, 2000.
29. Georg Reicke, 'Die Massenspeisung in Berlin während des Krieges', in Elise von Hopffgarten (ed.), *Hedwig Heyl. Ein Gedenkblatt zu ihrem 70. Geburtstage, dem 5. Mai 1920 von ihremn Mitarbeitern und Freunden*, Berlin, 1920, 127.
30. Adolf Wermuth, *Ein Beamtenleben*, 380, 381.
31. Bundesarchiv Berlin-Lichterfelde (hereafter cited as BA Berlin), Niederschrift über die Sitzung des Frauenbeirats am 8. November 1916, Rep. 3601 Reichsministerium für Landwirtschaft 30 Kriesernährungsamt, Frauenbeirat.
32. Kaeber, *Berlin im Weltkriege*, 150.
33. Supporters and detractors of the public kitchen on both sides of the issue were remarkably vocal. While Agnes Harnack insisted (in retrospect) that the kitchens injured the pride of workingclass women, August Skalweit described the idea of '… publicly feeding the entire nation an utopia, grown out of a war psychosis, blowing remarkably hot air off the brains of doctrinaires and fanatics.' Skalweit, *Die Kriegsernährungswirtschaft*, 45; von Harnack, *Der Krieg und die Frauen*, 29. The strongest proponents came from the military and Social Democracy; for the latter, see, Richard Calwer, *Die Ernährung der städtischen Bevölkerung*, Böhlau, 1919, and especially Elisabeth Engelhardt, *Die Zentralisation der städtischen Haushaltungen*, Parcus, 1916. Skalweit's highly negative statistical assessment of public meal ventures in Berlin and elsewhere in Germany should be considered with this view in mind. See especially Skalweit, *Die Kriegsernährungswirtschaft*, (for Berlin) 31, (for urban Germany as a whole), 51.
34. BLHA, Potsdam, Wermuth, 'Bekanntmachung'. Städtische Volksspeisung, 19 October 1916, Rep. 30 Berlin C Polizeipräsidium, 20269 Die städtische Volksspeisung.
35. A similar card system was not introduced in commercial restaurants. As the director of the municipal feeding programme in Munich, Baron Horn, noted, better-off citizens could thus avoid the public feeding centres in favour of for-profit eateries. See, BA Berlin, Niederschrift über die Sitzung des Frauenbeirats am 8. November 1916, Rep. 3601 Reichsministerium für Landwirtschaft 30 Kriesernährungsamt, Frauenbeirat.
36. Roerkohl, *Hungerblockade und Heimatfront*, 250.
37. Roerkohl, *Hungerblockade und Heimatfront*, 250–1.
38. Kaeber, *Berlin im Weltkriege*, 146–50; Allen, *Hungrige Metropole*, Chapter 2.
39. On the relative success of philanthropic eateries in Hamburg, Keith R. Allen, 'Weiche Drinks für harte Kerle. Die Geburtsstunde der öffentlichen Massenspeisung in Deutschland', in *WerkstattGeschichte*, 11 (31), Summer, 2002, 5–25.
40. Gaststeiger, *Städtische Volksspeisung*, 11; Skalweit, *Deutsche Kriegsernährungswirtschaft*, 48.
41. [Author unknown], Praktische Durchführung von Massenspeisung. Außerordentliche Tagung der Zentralstelle für Volkswohlfahrt in Gemeinschaft mit dem Zentralverein für das Wohl der arbeitenden Klassen im Reichsitzungssaal zu Berlin am 3. und 4. Juli 1916, Nicolai, 1916, 8.

42. [Author unknown], 'Aus Groß-Berlin. Speisegemeinschaften', Vorwärts, 17 November 1917.
43. Kaeber, *Belin im Weltkriege*, 150–1.
44. Jay Winter, 'Some Paradoxes of the First World War', in Richard Wall and Jay Winter (eds), *The Upheaval of War: Family, Work, and Welfare in Europe, 1914–1918*, Cambridge University Press, 1988. See also, Jean-Louis Robert and Jay Winter, 'Conclusions: Toward a Social History of Capital Cities at War', in Winter and Robert, *Capital Cities at War*, 547; Susan Pedersen, *Family, Dependence, and the Origins of the Welfare State: Britain and France, 1914–1945*, Cambridge University Press, 1993, 79. See also, M. R. Higonnet, J. Jenson, S. Michel and M. C. Weitz (eds), *Behind the Lines: Gender and the Two World Wars*, Yale University Press, 1987.
45. Elisabeth Domansky, in 'Mobilization and Reproduction in World War I Germany', in *Society, Culture, and the State in Germany, 1870–1930*, The University of Michigan Press, 1996, asserts that 'the family ceased to exist for the duration of the war as a unit of social and economic power and, beyond the war's end, as the site of society's social and biological reproduction', 428. This remains contentious.
46. On wartime regulations and their effect on women, Angelika Tramwitz, 'Vom Umgang mit Helden. Kriegs(vor)schriften und Benimmregeln für deutsche Frauen im Ersten Weltkrieg', in Peter Knoch (ed.), *Kriegsalltag. Die Rekonstruktion des Kriegsalltags als Aufgabe der historischen Forschung und der Friedenserziehung*, J. B. Metzler, 1989, 84–113; for Berlin, Christiane Eifert, 'Frauenarbeit im Krieg. Die Berliner "Heimfront" 1914–1918', *Internationale Wissenschaftliche Korrespondenz zur Geschichte der deutschen Arbeiterbewegung*, 21, 1985, 281–95.
47. For similar set of impulses after the war, see Susanne Rouette, *Sozialpolitik als Geschlechterpolitik. Die Regulierung der Frauenarbeit nach dem Ersten Weltkrieg*, Campus, 1993.
48. Daniel, *Arbeiterfrauen*, 213.
49. Preliminary steps toward the establishment of price ceilings were taken in the last days before the war, with the promulgation of decrees which prohibited the export of important foodstuffs and the concurrent lifting of tariffs on the same.
50. On the complex relationship between imperial purchasing agents and municipal distribution of foodstuffs see Daniel, *Arbeiterfrauen*, especially pages 190–1, 205–7.
51. Skalweit, *Die deutsche Kriegsernährungswirtschaft*, 146–224.
52. Skalweit, *Die deutsche Kriegsernährungswirtschaft*, 235–9.
53. See especially, Moeller, *German Peasants and Agrarian Politics*.
54. LA Berlin, Simonsohn, 'Auslandsmehl!,' June 3, 1916, Rep. 13–01 Deputation für das Ernährungswesen, 15263 Verordnungen. See also, Annette Godefroid, 'Neun Jahre Kommunale Mehl- und Brotversorgung (1914–1923)', *Berliner Geschichte und Gegenwart* , 1999, 48–72, here 48–49, 52
55. Bonzon and Davis, 'Feeding the Cities', 330.
56. Bonzon and Davis, 'Feeding the Cities', 341. See also, Belinda J. Davis, *Home Fires Burning: Food, Politics, and Everyday Life in World War I Berlin*, University of North Carolina Press, 2000, especially, 99–103. Davis ignores the central individuals involved in the *municipal* distribution network in Berlin, dealing instead with the well-covered terrain of Prussian and imperial politics. In discussion of the impact of imperial and Prussian policies on the capital, Davis draws heavily upon spy reports (*Stimmungsberichte*) supplied by undercover police agents. See Davis, 'Geschlecht und Konsum: Rolle und Bild der Konsumentin in den Verbraucherprotesten des Ersten Weltkrieges', *Archiv für Sozialgeschichte*, 38, 1998, 119–39. Published excerpts of undercover police reports (many of which Davis cites extensively in this essay and her monograph) may be found in Ingo Materna and Hans-Joachim Schreckenbach, (eds) (with the assistance of Bärbel Holtz), *Dokumente aus geheimen Archiven. Band 4 1914–1918. Berichte der Berliner Polizeipräsidenten zur Stimmung und Lage der Bevölkerung in Berlin 1914–1918*, Weimar, 1987. Published in the GDR, the portrayal of wartime life offered in this particular selection of reports is unfortunately not examined in her volume in this (additional) historical context. For the 'problem-orientation' of secret police reports, see Richard

Evans, *Kneipengespräche im Kaiserreich. Stimmungsberichte der Hamburger Politis-chen Polizei 1892–1914*, Rowohlt, 1989, 16–18. Reports submitted to Berlin's chief of police were often forwarded to his de facto superior, the Prussian Minister of the Inte-rior; rationing in the capital was subjected to uncommon scrutiny. See here Linden-berger, *Straßenpolitik*, 75. A more nuanced account of conflicts surrounding food rationing in the *city of Berlin* – one that uses extensively sources from the city's exten-sive archival holdings on rationing in the capital – is Robert Scholz, 'Ein unruhiges Jahrzehnt. Lebensmittelunruhen, Massenstreiks und Arbeitslosenkrawalle in Berlin 1914–1923', in *Pöbelexzesse und Volkstumulte in Berlin. Zur Sozialgeschichte der Straße, 1830–1980*, Euröpische Perspeckitven, 1984, 79–123. Historians in Germany have drawn considerable inspiration from E. P. Thompson in their considerations of the relationship between food and conflict. See especially the excellent essay by Manfred Gailus and Thomas Lindenberger, 'Zwanzig Jahre "moralische ökonomie". Ein sozialhistorisches Konzept ist volljährig geworden', *Geschichte und Gesellschaft*, 20, 1994, 469–477.

57. According to Kocka, some 200,000 workers, particularly munitions workers, took part in the April strikes. See Kocka, *Facing Total War*, 49, 61. The number of strikes in the face of significant repression increased in each war year except the last.

58. *Ein Beamtenleben*, 373–8. See also, George L. Yaney, *The World of the Manager*, Peter Lang, 1994, 134–41; Godefroid, 'Neun Jahre Kommunale Mehl- und Brotversorgung', 59–62; on the creation of the Imperial War Nutrition Office (Kriegsernährungsamt), Skalweit, *Deutsche Kriegsernährungswirtschaft*, 179ff and Daniel, *Arbeiterfrauen*, 192. After Michaelis' appointment to chancellor in August 1917, the Lord Mayor of Cologne, Wilhelm von Waldow, assumed responsibility for the Prussian and the Imperial offices.

59. Hedwig Heyl, *Aus meinem Leben*, C.A. Schwetschke,1925, 155.

60. Kaeber, 'Die Oberbürgermeister Berlins seit der steinischen Städteverordnung', 94.

61. Davis, *Home Fires Burning*, 92.

62. Offer, *The First World War*, 63. Shortages of coal, locomotives, rolling stock, spare parts, and labour further curtailed Germany's ability to deliver grains to the cities. See Feld-man, *Army, Industry and Labor*, 254–9; Offer, *The First World War*, 341. On prewar ten-sions surrounding foodstuffs, particularly meat, see Christoph Nonn, *Verbraucherprotest und Parteiensystem im wilhelmischen Deutschland*, Drost, 1996; for Berlin in particular, see especially Thomas Lindenberger, 'Die Fleischrevolte am Wedding' in Manfred Gailus and Heinrich Volkmann Opladen (eds), *Der Kampf und das tägliche Brot. Nahrungsmangel, Versorgungspolitik und Protest 1770–1990*, Westdeutscher Verlag, 1994. Although Britain itself imported still more wheat, with about four-fifths of its total bread grains coming from abroad, the Royal Navy ensured that Manitoba's wheat con-tinued to reach Manchester's masses; L. Margaret Barnett, *British Food Policy during the First World War*, Allen and Unwin, 1985. For the long-term effects of the blockade see also F. Aereboe, *Der Einfluß des Krieges auf die landwirtschafliche Produktion in Deutschland*, Deutsche Verlags-Anstalt, 1927.

63. Daniel, *Arbeiterfrauen*, 198–200; Davis, *Home Fires Burning*, 174.

64. See Skalweit, *Deutsche Kriegsernährungsamt*, 47ff; Daniel, *Arbeiterfrauen*, 200–1; Krüger and Tenius, *Die Massenspeisungen*, 9; On the Hindenburg-Program see espe-cially Feldman, *Army, Industry and Labor*, 154ff.

65. Kocka, *Facing Total War*; M. Schumacher, *Land und Politik. Eine Untersuchung über politische Parteien und agrarische Interessen 1914–1923*, Droste, 1978.

66. Reliable statistics for women's paid labour outside of the home are very difficult to obtain for the entire wartime period (but especially before September 1916). See Chris-tiane Eifert, 'Frauenarbeit im Krieg. Die Berliner "Heimatfront" 1914 bis 1918', 282, 283. Citing the example of a single firm in the electronics industry, Eifert shows that the per-centage of women employed grew from 35.72 percent in March 1915 to 56.11 percent in December 1915 to 64.88 percent in September 1916. On women's paid labour outside of the home after the 1914–1918 war, Rouette, *Sozialpolitik als Geschlechterpolitik*, esp. 53–130; Karin Hagemann, *Frauenalltag und Männerpolitik: Alltagsleben und gesellschaftliches Handeln von Arbeiterfrauen in der Weimarer Republik*, Bietz, 1990,

esp. 430–65; Richard Bessel, '"Eine nicht allzu große Beunruhigung des Arbeitmarktes."' Frauenarbeit und Demobilmachung in Deutschland nach dem Ersten Weltkrieg', *Geschichte und Gesellschaft*, 6, 1988, 20–34.

67. LA Berlin, Carl Timm, 10 April 1917, Rep. 13–01 Deputation für das Ernährungswesen, 9066 Die Zuteilung von Milch an Kranke, 133. On war sentiment among workingclass women generally, Daniel, *Arbeiterfrauen*, especially 234–40.

68. See Yaney, *The World of the Manager*, 89f.

69. In addition to being a member of the Magistrat (Stadtrat), Simonsohn was Vorsitzender der Abteilung für Brotversorgung, one of the three chairmen of the important Lebensmitteldeputation, as well as the Fettstelle Groß-Berlin and the Lebensmittelverband Groß-Berlin. Finally, he shared chairmanship of the Mehlverteilungsstelle with another member of the city's Magistrat. See, Personalnachweisung der Berliner Gemeindeverwaltung und der mit ihr in Verbindung stehenden Verwaltungen und Anstalten. Amtlich herausgegeben vom Magistrat der Stadt Berlin, Berlin, 1920, 2, 11, 502, 504, 505, 509, 510.

70. LA Berlin, Simonsohn, An sämtliche Brotkommissionen, 12 December 1916, Rep. 13–01 Deputation für das Ernährungswesen, 15109 Rundschreiben an die Brotkommissionen.

71. GStA., Abschrift V 9611. An das Ministerium des Innern (Zentralstelle der Lebensmittelversorgung), Betreffend: Verbot von Lebensmittelsendungen ins Feld, Priv. Doz. Pionier i. d. Bayer. Pion. Park-Komp. Nr. 8, Im Felde, 7 April 1916, Rep. 197 A Preuß. Staatskommissar für Volksernährung, Io Ausschreitungen, Ausstände.

72. LA Berlin, Wermuth, 'Verordnung über Zusatzbrotkarten', 15 June 1915, Rep. 13–01 Deputation für das Ernährungswesen, 14065 Verordnungen des Magistrats.

73. LA Berlin, Simonsohn, 7 July 1916, Rep. 13–01 Deputation für das Ernährungswesen, Nr. 15109 Rundschreiben an Brotkommissionen.

74. LA Berlin, Unsigned, 29 November 1916, Rep. 13–01 Deputation für das Ernährungswesen, Nr. 11842 Verordnungen und Verfügungen betr. Zustatzkarten.

75. LA Berlin, An den Gewerkschaften Berlin, 25 January 1917, Rep. 13–01 Deputation für das Ernährungswesen, Nr. 8544 Das Einheitsbrot.

76. Kocka, *Facing Total War*, 17–9, 48–9; Ute Daniel, *Arbeiterfrauen*, 98.

77. BLHA, Allgemeine Angelegenheiten der Abteilung I Lebensmittel, Rep. 1A, Staatliche Verteilungsstelle für Groß-Berlin, No. 29.

78. Primarily because of conscription, SPD membership rolls declined dramatically during the War. See Kocka, *Facing Total War*, 52.

79. LA Berlin, Unsigned, An das Preußisches Landes-Getreide Amt. Betrifft: Verbrauchsregelung im Erntejahre 1918, Rep. 13–01 Deputation für das Ernährungswesen, 12631 Die Versorgung der Jugendlichen alten Leute, Schwangeren, und Wöcherinnen.

80. See Schaser, *Helene Lange und Getrud Bäumer*, 156–64; Catherine Elaine Boyd, *Nationaler Frauendienst: German Middle Class Women in Service to the Fatherland, 1914–1918*, University of Georgia Press,1979.

81. LA Berlin, Josephine Levy-Rathenau, An Herrn Stadtrat Simonsohn, Rep. 13–01 Deputation für Ernährungswesen, 1201 Einrichtung der Brotkommission.

82. LA Berlin, Frau Ilse Müller-Öestreich, Sekretariat des Frauenbeirats des Reichs-Ernährungs-Ministeriums, An Lehmann, 5 June 1919, Rep. 22–02 Lebensmittelverband Groß-Berlin, 2381 Schleich- und Kettenhandel.

83. LA Berlin, Frau Ilse Müller-Öestreich, Sekretariat des Frauenbeirats des Reichs-Ernährungs-Ministeriums, An Lehmann, 5 June 1919, Rep. 22–02 Lebensmittelverband Groß-Berlin, 2381 Schleich- und Kettenhandel.

84. LA Berlin, Simonsohn, 11 July 1919, Rep. 22–02 Lebensmittelverband Groß-Berlin, 2381 Schleich- und Kettenhandel.

85. LA Berlin, Simonsohn, Runge, Lehmann, Gordon, Henshel, Simm, Kamnitzer, Fischer, 22 October 1918, Niederschrift über die Sitzung des Lebensmittelausschusses, Rep. 13–01 Deputation für das Ernährungswesen, 13208 Verordnungen und Bekanntmachungen der Abteilung für Brotversorgung.

86. C. Paul Vincent, *The Politics of Hunger: The Allied Blockade of Germany, 1915–1919*, Ohio University Press, 1985, 23.

87. Bonzon and Davis, 'Feeding the Cities', 341. The formulation in Davis's monograph reads as follows: 'Authorities' own recognition of their ability to provide for Germans' basic needs was an important part of the government's retreat from authority in October 1918', Davis, *Home Fires Burning*, 219. Simonsohn, the central actor in Berlin's bread rationing scheme, goes unmentioned in Davis's work.
88. LA Berlin, Verordnung über Brotmenge sowie den Fortfall der Zusatzbrotkarten, Wermuth, 27 November 1918, Rep. 13–01 Deputation für das Ernährungswesen, 16149 Verordnungen und Bekanntmachungen der Abteilung für Brotversorgung.
89. LA Berlin, Simonsohn, An sämtliche Brotkommissionen, 13 November 1918, Rep. 13–01 Deputation für das Ernährungswesen, 15132 Rundschreiben an die Brotkommissionen.
90. Relations between workers' councils and more traditional agents of city government were however contentious elsewhere in Germany. See, for example, Helmut Paulus, 'Volks- und Wuchergeschichte – die ersten Bayreuther Sondergeschichten in der Notzeit nach dem Ersten Weltkrieg', *Archiv für die Geschichte von Oberfranken*, 79, 1999, 369–374. I would like to thank Karl Christian Führer for drawing this essay to my attention. For Munich, see Martin Geyer, 'Teuerungsprotest, Konsumentenpolitik und soziale Gerechtigkeit während der Inflation, München 1920–1923', *Archiv für Sozialgeschichte*, 30, 1991, 181–215; Klaus Tenfelde, 'Stadt und Land in Krisenzeiten. München und das Münchener Umland zwischen Revolution und Inflation 1918 bis 1923', in Wolfgang Hardtwig und Klaus Tenfelde (eds), *Soziale Räume in der Urbanisierung. Studien zur Geschichte Münchens im Vergleich 1850 bis 1933*, Beck, 1990, 37–57.
91. See, for example, Roerkohl, *Hungerblockade*, 305–12; F. Bumm (ed.), *Deutschlands Gesundheitsverhältnisse unter dem Einfluß des Weltkrieges*, Vols. 1–2, Deutsche Verlags-Anstalt, 1928; Offer, *The First World War*. I consider philanthropic efforts, led by English and American Quakers, to feed German schoolchildren after the war in Allen, *Hungrige Metropole*.
92. Gerald Feldman, *The Great Disorder: Politics, Economics, and Society in the German Inflation, 1914–1923*, Oxford University Press, 409; 561–4; 622, 637–8; 701–2; 705–7; 768.
93. Joshua Cole has argued that the inflation had a particularly detrimental effect on the governance of the German capital, where a very large number of unemployed labourers were dependent upon municipal support at low fixed rates. The result, he notes, was an increasingly volatile political environment in Berlin, less so in the rest of Germany. See his essay, 'The Transition to Peace, 1918–1919', in Winter and Robert, *Capital Cities at War*, 196–226; see also, Kaeber, *Berlin im Weltkriege*, 364–5; 367.
94. LA Berlin, Müller, Obermeister, Bäcker-Zwangsinnung in Berlin, An den Magistrat Berlin, Rep. 13–01 Deputation für das Ernährungswesen, 10175 Brotknappheit in den Bäckereien. See especially, Alf Lüdtke, '"Ihr könnt nun wissen, wie die Glocken eigentlich leuten sollen". Brotration und Arbeiter-(¨Über) Leben im Sommer 1919 – ein Beispiel aus Bochum', *Geschichtswerkstatt*, 12, 1987, 27–33.
95. *Vorwärts*, no. 323, 28 June 1920; *Vossische Zeitung*, no. 322, 29 June 1920. On women's leadership in food strikes in Berlin before the war, Thomas Lindenberger, 'Die Fleischrevolte am Wedding', in Gailus and Opladen, *Der Kampf und das tägliche Brot*. Conflict surrounding the price of foodstuffs in the years before the 1914–1918 war revolved primarily around meat (primarily pork), not bread, a clear indication of the relative affluence of late Wilhelmine Germany.
96. See, Andrea Lefèvre,'Lebensmittelunruhen in Berlin 1920–1923', in Gailus and Opladen, *Der Kampf um das tägliche Brot*, 346–60. Lefèvre's interesting account is unfortunately based entirely on one source, newspaper accounts. The peak of the protest movement came in the autumn of 1923, where, as Lefèvre argues, broad segments of the public joined the protest. In November 1923 a pogrom ensued in the city's 'Scheuenviertel'; on the relationships between the pogrom and food protest, see Scholz, 'Unruhiges Jahrzehnt' in *Pöbelexzesse und Volkstumulte in Berlin*. 105; Geyer, 'Teuerungsprotest und Teuerungsunruhen 1914–1923', 331–2, 335–6, 343; Lefèvre, 'Lebensmittelunruhen', 352–3, 358. On anti-Semitic expressions during the war, see also Davis, *Home Fires Burning*, 132–5.

9

The Epic and the Domestic:
Women and War in Russia, 1914–1917

Peter Gatrell

In her excellent recent collection of essays on gender and identity in war and peace, Billie Melman urges historians to transcend conventional views concerning the emancipatory potential (or otherwise) for women of total war, and to focus instead on contextualised discourses of gender. Such an approach, she maintains, will yield fresh insights into the ways in which the experiences of women were depicted in relation to those of men. In particular, it will encourage historians to elaborate the ways in which wartime discourse was connected to broader contemporary anxieties, notably about nation and 'race'.[1]

Whatever opinion one holds of the centrality or otherwise of discursive practices (and this volume contains several sceptics), the fact remains that war was a moment of truth in which underlying assumptions about gender roles and boundaries were sorely tested.[2] As wartime opportunities for employment expanded, women were able to mount a challenge to economic spheres which working men dominated. Nor was this the only form of 'dilution'. The mass mobilisation of men enabled women to substitute for their husbands' control over household affairs and often required that they enter negotiations with officialdom in a manner that had scarcely been possible hitherto. For some women, then, the war opened up new possibilities for self-realisation. Yet existing gender hierarchies were difficult to subvert, and such gains as were made in employment or civic involvement proved difficult to defend as war came to a close.[3]

At first sight, no such difficulty arose at the front, where fighting and killing 'belonged' to men. Yet the image of a fixed front, conceived as a masculine domain, became increasingly difficult to sustain during the First World War. Neatly gendered dichotomies tended to dissolve on closer inspection.[4] For one thing, changing military fortunes ensured that 'front' could become 'rear' and vice versa. Occupation by the enemy brought the front into spaces hitherto occupied by civilians, forcing civilian women (and men) to confront warfare at close quarter. This was particularly true of a large proportion of the civilian population in Belgium, Poland, the Baltic lands, Galicia, Ottoman Armenia and Serbia, who experienced the war as involuntary displacement and who, male and female alike, were directly exposed to military action.[5]

These reflections are an appropriate starting point for historians who seek to bring Russia's First World War into the mainstream of modern historiography. The First World War has been a largely forgotten episode in modern Russian history, serving as merely a backdrop to the compelling events of 1917. Soviet historians wrote little on the impact of the war, because the officially sanctioned historiography found the origins of the Bolshevik revolution to lie deep in the socio-economic structures of imperial Russia. The ensuing revolution and bitter civil war – described by Sheila Fitzpatrick as a 'formative experience' for an entire generation – all but obliterated the collective and official memories of the 1914–1917 conflict.[6] This is not in itself surprising, but it does deserve at least passing comment, in view of the extraordinary degree to which the Second World War was (and is) commemorated.[7] Largely for these reasons, a full account of the First World War in Russia is some way off.[8] In the meantime, the present essay is offered as a contribution to that project and to the burgeoning interest in the global and comparative history of the First World War. In keeping with one of the major themes of this volume, the main focus is on the lived experiences of women and the representation of those experiences in wartime.

It seems clear enough that historians of the war will miss much of significance if they fail to set wartime developments in a broader chronological perspective. This is certainly true of social and cultural processes in Russia, where debates before 1914 about the appropriate role and behaviour of the Tsar's male and female subjects had a particular intensity that helps to shed light on the impact of war. As Laura Engelstein has shown, these debates were heavily politicised. The autocratic impulses of the tsarist state expressed themselves in a heavily regulated approach to social and sexual behaviour, but by the turn of the century an emerging Russian liberal and professional elite could couch its opposition to tsarist authority in terms of the primacy of the rational and self-governing subject, whose private life was deemed immune from bureaucratic intervention. The revolution of 1905 to 1906 prompted anxieties from bureaucrats and professionals alike about public order and civic involvement; those concerns were frequently portrayed in terms of sexual conduct and appetite. Threats to social stability were of course also expressed in terms of political dissent and radical protest, but these were accompanied by a pervasive discourse that raised disturbing questions about loss of self-control, coupled to a lack of respect for established domestic authority. The issue of public crime and disorder assumed prominence after 1905, with the added spice of concern for the 'vulnerable' female citizen: according to Joan Neuberger, hooligans on the streets of Russia's capital city asserted their claims to appropriate space reserved for 'respectable' people by making women specific targets of aggression. In due course, some professionals came to regret both revolutionary excess and what it appeared to imply about self-indulgence and mob behaviour. They were disposed at first to look favourably upon a war that promised to rekindle a sense of commitment to civic purpose, national integrity and self-control. Put another way, without discipline in the domestic sphere, the epic struggle would be unlikely to succeed.[9]

Other changes seemed no less threatening to the status quo. As is well known, one hallmark of Russia's social and economic transformation during the later nineteenth century was the mass migration between town and country. This gave rise to a growing sense of social disturbance, of which concerns about health, family breakdown and prostitution were especially prominent. Prostitution appeared to challenge the accepted cultural norms that required a father or husband to 'protect' his daughter and his wife; whether coerced into or making a voluntary decision to engage in commercial sex, it was (in Barbara Engel's words), 'the freedom from patriarchal authority that seemed to trouble officials most.'[10] Official intervention was designed to encourage prostitutes to form a stable conjugal union, in order to escape the economic and social pressures that drove them to prostitution in the first place. Women who challenged the norms of tsarist officialdom or of educated society were liable to the capricious harassment of the police and the intrusive scrutiny of doctors and social investigators.[11] As we shall see, wartime movements of refugee women complicated official attempts to monitor the activities of prostitutes, casting renewed doubt on the efficacy of administrative practice. Other anxieties assumed a somewhat different guise. Most instances of perceived cultural crisis revealed fundamental uncertainty about the resilience of existing social distinctions and gendered hierarchies.

Redefining the 'Home Front' and 'Front Line'

To be sure, war was not just a moment of cultural anxiety. It was also a time of opportunity. Here too, however, we need to tread cautiously, particularly where Russian rural society is concerned, lest we draw too clear a line between war and peacetime developments. Contrary to received wisdom, many Russian peasant women already exercised some responsibility for household management before the war and engaged in village affairs to a greater extent that is often realised. For example, they assumed primary responsibility for the peasant family farm when their husbands left in order to work away from home, as many did in the textile towns in Russia's Central Industrial Region from the 1880s onwards. Furthermore, the individual acquired a higher level of literacy than the adult female norm, enabling her 'to deal with local authorities, to run her household, and to fulfil other responsibilities in her husband's absence, such as renting out land and hiring workers'. In these circumstances, marriage became more of a partnership than a condition of female subordination to patriarchal authority. As a result, according to Barbara Engel, women 'breathed more freely' in the generation before the First World War.[12]

This 'freedom' appears all the same to have been greatly magnified by the impact of wartime conscription on the world of the peasantry. By 1916 women outnumbered men in the Russian village by 60 percent. According to Tikhon Polner, the peasant woman 'found herself acquiring a new importance in the eyes of the community and was getting for the first time (sic) in her life into personal contact with the authorities.' She 'began to develop a new consciousness of the value of her own work, a sense of personal dignity, and a jealous regard for her rights.' Polner also acknowledged the 'surprising discovery ... that the peasant women were less conservative than the men; spurred on by necessity, they showed themselves quite ready to welcome new methods of farming (and) saved the farms of the peasantry from total collapse' during the war.[13] Contemporary sources testified to the interest that peasant women showed in acquiring new skills.[14] It remains unclear what impact this had on Russian farming methods after the war. What is clear is that non-rural observers easily lapsed back into the patronising attitudes towards peasant women that were typical of prewar Russia. Just as rural Russia remained the prime site of economic backwardness, whatever the signs of technical progress, so its womenfolk were depicted as socially inferior, culturally inept and incapable of independent action.[15]

Women were consumers as well as producers. Nuanced accounts are now being offered of women who entered into negotiation with tradesmen and with the administrators who were responsible for food supply in wartime. Barbara Engel's recent work on food riots draws attention to an expanded sphere of female participation in political life, suggesting that the well-known activism of women in St. Petersburg during the days preceding the overthrow of the Tsar in February 1917 followed a long line of direct engagement with merchants and state officials. Frequently describing them as 'women's riots' (*bab'i bunty*), contemporaries dismissed these protests as the result of 'spontaneous' or elemental behaviour, rather than the 'conscious' deliberation that appeared to speak of revolutionary intent. But this discourse – crucially revealing assumptions of appropriate (male) and inappropriate (female) behaviour – failed to take account of the way in which women's subsistence riots expressed a longing for social justice and equality of entitlement. Also important was the transformation of several million women into soldiers' wives (*soldatki*), whose 'more modern sense of entitlement derived from their connection to men at the front'. This had explosive implications for the old regime since, as Engel suggests, Russian troops were reluctant to suppress riots in which the wives and mothers of fellow soldiers were prominent participants. The 'home front' was thus deeply intertwined with the front line.[16]

The war also demonstrated female capacity to enter directly the military terrain, in ways that both liberated women and disturbed current convention. Military nursing is the obvious example. Interesting possibilities are opened up by the work of Margaret Higonnet and her colleagues, who argue that we must attend to language as a means of articulating a place for women in the First World War, of justifying their own purpose and of showing that women's bodies, not just those of men, were 'at stake in war'. Women placed themselves at risk, not by virtue of their direct exposure to shrapnel or liability to gangrene, but by acquiring or being forced to undertake tasks that challenged accepted norms. Military nurses provided care and comfort, yet at the same time saw men at their most vulnerable.[17]

There are as yet no studies of the Russian nursing profession or of the ways in which it was transformed by war.[18] We do, however, have a powerful account of wartime experience on the Russian front, written by an English nurse, Violetta Thurstan. Attached to a Red Cross unit, Thurstan vividly described her efforts to attend to wounded and dying Russian and Cossack soldiers in the midst of the great retreat in 1914 to 1915. She spared few details of the strain under which the nursing staff worked and of the terrible wounds suffered by soldiers and civilians:

> In the largest ward where there were seventy or eighty men lying, there was a lavatory adjoining which had got blocked up, and the stream of dirty water trickled under the door and meandered in little rivulets all over the room. The smell was awful, as some of the men had been there already several days without having had their dressings done ... A little child was carried in with half its head blown open, and then an old Jewish woman with both legs blown off, and a terrible wound in her chest, who only lived an hour or two ...[19]

As this account implies, the war manifested itself as a surreal experience. Finding herself amongst the wounded soldiers billeted in the court theatre attached to the Radziwill castle west of Warsaw, she recounts that 'the scenery had never been taken down after the last dramatic performance played in the theatre, and wounded men lay everywhere between the wings and the drop scenes. The auditorium was packed so closely that you could hardly get between the men without treading on someone's hands and feet as they lay on the floor.'[20] At other moments, Thurstan emphasised the thrill and excitement of war. Her encounters with the scarred, suffering or dying victims of battle did not prevent her from suggesting that 'even the returning wounded in the evening did not seem altogether such a bad thing out there.'[21] She was at pains to emphasise the gulf between the male victims of battle and the ministering female servant. But she was simultaneously able to bask in the exploits of war, as the following account of an off-duty visit to the front reveals:

War would be the most glorious game in the world if it were not for the killing and wounding. In it one tastes the joy of comradeship to the full, the taking and giving, and helping and being helped in a way that would be impossible to conceive in the ordinary world ... (O)ne could see the poetry of war, the zest of the frosty mornings, and the delight of the camp-fire at night, the warm, clean smell of the horses tethered everywhere, the keen hunger, the rough food sweetened by the sauce of danger, the riding out in high hope in the morning; even the returning wounded in the evening did not seem altogether such a bad thing out there. One has to die some time, and the Russian peasants esteem it a high honour to die for their 'little Mother' as they call their country. The vision of the High Adventure is not often vouchsafed to one, but it is a good thing to have had it – it carries one through many a night at the shambles. Radzivilow [a village in Poland] is the only place it came to me. In Belgium one's heart was wrung by the poignancy of it all, its littleness and defencelessness; in Lodz one could see nothing for the squalor and 'frightfulness'; in other places the ruined villages, the flight of the dazed, terrified peasants show one of the darkest sides of war.[22]

Although she does not overtly interpret her experiences, Thurstan's memoirs imply that military battles were mirrored in her own personal struggle to contend with inadequate facilities and supplies. From this point of view, there was nothing to distinguish her contribution from that of the ordinary soldier. Like them, she wore a uniform. Like them, she risked her life. Like them, she sustained the faltering Russian war effort. As a member of progressive opinion in Britain, Thurstan was also likely to have been conscious of a link between her own struggle for self-emancipation and the project for a renewed, democratic Russia. But the references to such an association are at best oblique. What lingers instead is the idea of experience 'sweetened by the sauce of danger'; of an epic that had overtaken the domestic.

War, Women and Refugees

In Thurstan's passionate rendering, gender differences are dissolved in the company of like-minded adventurers. At the same time, her account draws attention to a crucial, but often overlooked dimension of Russia's war, and one in which gender came to play its part. This concerns the extraordinary displacement of around six million civilians from Poland, the Baltic lands, western Ukraine, and the Caucasus. Whether caused by Russian generals who wanted to clear the front line of supposed fifth-columnists (Jews and Poles being the most harshly targeted minorities), or by enemy troops who threatened the livelihood and lives of the Tsar's subjects, displacement had profound consequences. Here was another aspect of war as epic.[23]

The constitution of refugeedom entailed several implications for notions of gender in late imperial Russia. Although the fact attracted scarcely any direct comment, relatively few refugees were able-bodied men, many of whom had already been conscripted into the Russian army.[24] By implication, patriarchal forms of authority were called into question from the very moment of displacement. It fell to the adult women amongst their number to attend to the immediate needs of the refugee population, many of whom were directly dependent upon them. At the same time, the war presented opportunities for other women. Educated women, who had slowly begun to enter Russia's public sphere, were allowed to claim a particular duty to care for refugees – men, women and children – who entered the Russian interior. Since feminine duty was deemed to lie in the care and treatment of wounded soldiers, it was but a short step towards the assertion of feminine obligation towards other victims of war. The articulation of concern for family integrity also implied the partial feminisation of public discourse.[25] Russian women asserted the right to get involved, precisely because issues of household collapse and reconstitution were at stake. So, too, were the care and rehabilitation of orphans, for whom special provision had to be made. This suggests the elaboration of a range of claims to specifically feminine responsibilities, some of which had no precedent in imperial Russia.[26] As noted earlier, new employment opportunities in the expanding war economy gave a new impetus to the prewar pattern of migration, leading to an increase in the female proportion of the labour force. But the implications were quite different for refugee women, who were often obliged to travel with their dependants and whose primary obligation was towards them. From this point of view, refugeedom did not reinforce the sense of liberation associated with geographical mobility; rather, it served to remind women of their 'domestic' responsibilities, now transferred into the realm of refugeedom (*bezhenstvo*). The contemporary portrayal of the refugee catastrophe tended to emphasise conventional motherhood, as if to combine the epic drama of displacement and the familiar trope of domesticity. Much of the impressive refugee relief efforts were accordingly directed along maternalist lines. As we shall see, this emphasis upon the preservation of family and reproductive duties corresponded to broader concerns that were articulated by the self-appointed leaders of tsarist Russia's national minorities.

Violetta Thurstan, author of a unique book on refugees in the Russian empire, displayed a keen awareness of distinctions of gender. Thurstan was at pains to highlight the plight of female refugees, dragged from their familiar surroundings: 'the old men can be made content with a little tobacco and the company of their old cronies; perhaps, too, they are a little more used to travelling and mixing with the outside world than the women, who seem to miss terribly their accustomed seat near the stove among their familiar household goods.'[27] Distinctive needs justified differential treatment. Hence it was vital to restore a sense of purpose amongst the female refugees, by giving them 'household' tasks in order to restore a commitment to domesticity. Women were given tiny allowances to enable them to buy food for their dependants; what mattered, according to Thurstan, was not the amount or the fact that food could have been prepared more efficiently by communal kitchens, but rather the opportunity given to women to remain active and to retain the dignity that went hand in hand with domestic tasks. Thus the management of this tragedy of epic proportions entailed the assertion of domestic responsibilities and norms.[28]

The children's colonies organised by refugee relief committees, such as the Tatiana committee (named after the Tsar's second daughter) reproduced similar distinctions. For a start, the sexes were rigorously segregated. In the provincial town of Voronezh, girls were instructed to make their own beds and to maintain the cleanliness of their living quarters. Outdoor activities were neither neglected nor left to chance: older girls gathered berries on behalf of local peasants, who paid them modest sums for an eight-hour working day. Boys were supplied with fishing rods, because 'fishing ... is their favourite occupation'. Nothing was said about the domestic chores that might be found for them.[29]

Inevitably, refugee women faced other kinds of stereotype. Offers of work made it clear that they were regarded chiefly as a source of domestic service. Opportunities of this kind presented themselves in towns across Russia. In the village, on the other hand, refugees found it difficult to secure work, especially during the winter months, except as washerwomen.[30] Welfare workers pointed out that many refugees were likely to find such a position demeaning, by virtue of their social status (the wartime literature on refugees devoted some attention to the theme of downward social mobility). In such cases refugee women were persuaded instead to join sewing circles or to spin and weave at home; many had to be taught how to perform these tasks.[31] Exhibitions of refugee crafts made great play of the fact that customers could examine and purchase 'items of women's work: pressed flowers, hats, caps, shoes, slippers and all manner of beautiful handicrafts'.[32] But these suggestions did not correspond to the needs and meet the wishes of all women, particularly those from a workingclass background, who expressed a preference for paid work in factories producing confectionery, matches or tobacco, where they hoped to have an opportunity to socialise more freely.[33]

The short stories written by the Russian naturalist Evgenii Shveder reveal something of the gendered narrative of refugeedom. In one story a refugee woman in great distress recounts how she had lost everything she possessed, including her beloved cat. Her past is tragic, her future insecure: she has no idea of her final destination. Suddenly her husband breaks in, proudly flexing his muscles and announcing that the family would be able to survive thanks to his physical prowess. In the next episode a young mother assures her anxious child that, although evil people had seized their home, they would eventually be able to return. This theme is developed in the next story, where a mother tells her daughter that their flight provides an opportunity to explore new places; the lights of the big city make an overwhelming impression on mother and daughter. In other stories Shveder resumes the subject of the distraught woman, struggling to cope in the face of disease and inadequate medical care. 'So many tears, so much woe – why have you not looked kindly upon us?', is the question put to God by one mother as her child lies dying in her arms.[34]

Shveder was not alone in establishing a hierarchy of helplessness along gender lines. Refugees themselves drew upon personal experience to show how prescribed gender roles might be preserved amidst social upheaval. A short story by a Russian priest, Vetlin, told of the reassurance offered a young girl ('I'm scared') by her brother, who guided her to safety across a river. The boy is brave, determined and responsible; the girl is vulnerable, innocent and trusting.[35] A young Armenian peasant farmer, Mikhail Zaituntsian, described how the Turks in Ottoman Armenia had tormented him. Mikhail wanted to cry, 'but I pulled myself together and refused to shed tears; I realised that this was the women's way, and that I had to cope differently.' He therefore went out and promptly killed a Turkish soldier who was holding women and children hostage. Melodramatic accounts such as these helped to restore confidence in the integrity of gender boundaries.[36]

Other narratives told a yet more terrible tale. A report from Ruzskii uezd, Moscow province, told of a woman who had been separated from her young baby during the flight east: 'this occurrence had unsettled her so much that she dropped everything and went off in an unknown direction.'[37] What might, in the circumstances, have been portrayed as a perfectly understandable action served instead to foster a belief in the essential frailty and unpredictability of women. Not surprisingly, stories from the Caucasus exerted a particularly horrific effect. Not sparing the sensibilities of his readers, a young doctor spoke of seeing the graves of Armenian women whose breasts had been cut off. He also described how one Armenian woman went mad, after being forced to witness Kurdish soldiers smash the skulls of her children on the wall of her house.[38]

This brings us to the issue of feminine loss, masculine incapacity and national deprivation. At times the association was quite oblique, but it could also become a clear device to bolster projects for 'national' renewal. Violation of the female subject served as a metaphor for the traumatic invasion of territory by German or Turkish troops; and at the same time it emphasised that national security and integrity required a more robust manhood. Jewish and Armenian males – belonging to minorities with a perceived penchant for trade and a supposedly inherent proclivity to be 'rootless' – found themselves a particular focus for opprobrium.[39] Stories gathered by the tsarist police and corroborated after the war spoke of attacks by Cossacks on Jewish women in and around Vilno and Minsk, and although these were concealed from the Russian public they were familiar to local Jewish dignitaries.[40]

Armenian victims of Ottoman atrocities attracted a great deal of sympathetic comment. 'Armenian women have, against their will, become victims of the animal instincts of men who pursue them without any shame, like a hunter in pursuit of its prey.'[41] A contemporary report from the provincial town of Erzindzan told of 'countless' Armenian women who had been raped by Turkish troops. Most of those who had become pregnant could not bear the humiliation and sought an abortion. In desperation one young mother had smothered her new-born infant.[42] 'Those who are unfamiliar with the history and psychology of the Armenian people will regard this behaviour as fanatical and barbaric, but those of us who have seen the hatred instilled in the hearts of Armenian women towards Muslims understand that it is connected to the wish to be rid of all contact with their former captors.'[43] Armenian reporters also drew attention to the predatory and outrageous behaviour of the Kurdish population of western Armenia, who held captive thousands of women and children in appalling conditions where sexual exploitation was rife: 'pretty girls and women were shared out amongst Kurdish beys and Turkish officials.'[44] Contemporaries asked their readers to understand why, in these circumstances, some Armenian women should commit suicide: 'this is not surprising when one takes into account the religious and moral upbringing of Armenian womanhood. The outrage inflicted on her honour and dignity is not just a huge crime but an earthly catastrophe', to which death was the only response.[45] By implication, Armenian men were called upon to avenge those crimes; in short, to demonstrate their prowess and thus their readiness to embark upon the epic task of national reconstruction.

Women's Welfare and Refugeeness

The process of 'victimising' displaced persons paved the way for various projects of voluntary and state intervention in the lives of refugee women. For young married women, in particular, the main task was to improve their mothering abilities. A frequent refrain of contemporary commentaries was that displacement had undermined maternal care, giving rise instead to pathological behaviour. Narratives of refugeedom were riddled with tales of desperate mothers who had been unable to prevent the progressive malnutrition of their children, who had failed to prevent the death of their children from infectious disease, or – most shocking of all – had deliberately murdered their starving or sick children in a fit of madness. Once the refugee population became more settled an opportunity arose to address the vexed issue of infant mortality, for so long a matter of profound concern to the Russian medical profession. Pregnant women were offered places at the Petrograd 'School for Mothers' where they received instruction in childcare, in the hope that they would learn the need for proper neo-natal care and thus enhance the prospects for the next generation of Russian subjects.[46] In this way, refugee relief was harnessed to self-improvement and eugenics.[47]

More frequently, female refugees were deemed to stand in need of protection, not from the enemy or from tsarist officials, but rather from unscrupulous and mercenary or lustful individuals. By virtue of their sex, women were believed to be exposed to specific dangers.[48] The hazards began at the moment refugees left their homes and travelled to the Russian interior. Refugee women turned to prostitution out of a desperate need to feed themselves and their dependants; sometimes their husbands or fathers forced them to sell their bodies for sex.[49] The train journey was invested with particular risks:

> Attention female refugees! The editor of *Iugobezhenets* ['Southern Refugee', a refugee newspaper] considers it his duty to make refugee women aware of the need to be extremely careful when dealing with men who offer their services and protection during the journey. These people move in groups through trains where they make the acquaintance of young refugee girls, passing themselves off as respectable citizens. But when the train reaches its final destination they demonstrate their cunning by leading their victims to dens of iniquity.[50]

Leading lawyers such as A. F. Koni advocated the creation of a team of refugee guardians, employed on the railways and specially trained to keep an eye on refugee women who might be the subject of unwelcome advances by pimps when the train stopped at a station – who might, in the colourful euphemism of the time, become the target of unscrupulous men engaged in the 'recruitment of live goods.'[51]

Graphic stories also reached the government's Special Council for Refugees of the vulnerability of refugee girls to the temptations of the urban milieu. Their protection from 'lascivious actions' and sexual abuse required vigorous and urgent intervention, for example by the Russian Society for the Protection of Women.[52] Predatory brothel keepers reportedly scoured the ranks of refugees in Petrograd for potential prostitutes. Welfare workers commented upon the depressing ease with which grasping madames gained access to women's refuges.[53] Violetta Thurstan paid particular heed to the moral condition of young refugee women. She applauded the intervention of female students in Petrograd who 'have done admirable work in keeping the young girls straight and out of temptation.'[54] Overcrowding posed moral as well as physical dangers. Where numbers could not be reduced, it mattered that refugees should at least be segregated according to sex.

Yet there remained some ambiguity about the link between refugeedom and prostitution. Not all contemporaries pinned the blame on those who organised commercial sex. There was also some suspicion that young women offered themselves all too willingly to prospective customers, choosing 'debauchery' as a means of economic survival.[55] The chief means of deterrence – salvation from commercial sex – and of moral improvement was, first and foremost, to learn a trade. If women could not or would not marry in wartime, at least they could be encouraged to acquire some legitimate money income and avoid the temptation to sell their bodies. Young girls could be taught to sew and cook, allowing them to acquire a sense of self-respect.[56] Wherever possible, young women were to be housed either in sheltered accommodation or with their parents. But it was easier to make this recommendation than to give it practical effect. The government's advisers were well aware that the housing problem was likely to get worse. One solution was to promote the building of more workhouses and rural 'colonies' where young women might live in greater seclusion. In addition, they could learn the virtues of hard work and receive appropriate training, enabling them to ply a craft or to work in cottage industry when they left.[57]

Middleclass women monitored the sexual conduct and physical well-being of refugees in their care.[58] They also extended the scope of charitable activity in which they had engaged before the war. The war inspired a multitude of 'ladies' committees' and 'maidens' societies' (in the Caucasus) which collaborated with other agencies, such as the Tatiana committee, and arranged programmes of welfare and work on their own account. In Tver', the ladies' circle set up kitchens and canteens, helped refugees to find somewhere to live, and created sewing circles to keep female refugees occupied. Its leading light, Sofia Mikhailovna Biunting, had a background in good works, having chaired for several years the long-established local charity, *Dobrokhotnaia kopeika* (literally, 'Obliging kopeck'). The chronicler of all this hectic activity felt it necessary to emphasise that the volunteer workers not only showed sympathy towards refugees but also feminine qualities of 'tenderness and love'.[59] E. V. Kolobova, wife of a local official in Ekaterinoslav, set up a refugee committee, in part with funds donated by white collar workers at the South Russian Dnepr metallurgical company.[60] From the Urals town of Ekaterinburg came a report of the devoted work of Nina Vladimirovna Smirnova who found housing for a hundred refugees at the local copper mine and never missed an opportunity to assist refugees. In Novgorod, the local Tatiana committee encouraged women to volunteer as assistants whose task would be to supervise workshops, inspect accommodation, check the financial status and needs of refugees, and organise collections of money. Once again, the correspondent judged it insufficient to catalogue the practical steps that women had taken on behalf of the refugee population. The 'female element' had developed a 'sensitive and compassionate relationship' with the refugee population.[61] In the Caucasus, several 'maidens' societies' had been active since the winter of 1914, calling upon 'all Armenian girls to offer material and moral support to refugees'.[62] Parties of girls went from house to house at Christmas, singing hymns and collecting money in aid of 'homeless, helpless and hopeless little children'.[63]

Several diocesan committees joined in the celebration of feminine public activism. In Simbirsk, the aptly named Anna Nikolaevna Benevolenskaia – the widow of a priest who lived opposite the railway station – was praised for her readiness to alert the local committee to the immi-

nent arrival of trainloads of refugees. This 'elderly, energetic and cultivated woman' was held up as an example to all readers of the diocesan
journal.[64] She appears to have answered the call for women to frequent
railway depots and see for themselves the plight of refugees: 'Go to them
and extend a friendly hand of assistance; give them not only a piece of
bread, clothing, and shelter, but also love and tenderness. Who, if not
women, can understand the suffering of the mother ...?'[65] Orphaned,
homeless children deserved particular care: 'the world is full of kind people, and it is to be hoped that our mothers, looking at their own children,
will not forget those who stand in need of a mother's tenderness, as well
as food and shelter.'[66]

This level of commitment did not satisfy Russian nationalist opinion.
One jaundiced commentator drew a distinction between the energetic
enthusiasm of Polish and other non-Russian female volunteers and Russian women. 'There (in the Polish national organisation in Petrograd) is no
shortage of kind-hearted welfare workers ... when one Russian woman
volunteered her services she was turned away by the Poles because large
numbers of Polish women were willing to contribute to the welfare of
refugees.' Once again, it was difficult to separate gendered responsibilities from perceived national shortcomings.[67]

Conclusions and Further Reflections

This essay has highlighted aspects of women's experience in wartime
Russia, particularly that of involuntary population displacement, and has
concentrated on some of the ways in which the war magnified prewar
anxieties and produced fresh apprehension. Concerns about sexual
behaviour and the transmission of venereal disease had been linked to
massive migration from country to town. During the war, however, the
danger was much more extensive; to fail to exercise sufficient vigilance
was to expose Russia's towns and villages to an influx of sexually active –
maybe also uninhibited – refugee women, as well as to the predatory
actions of pimps and brothel owners. From this point of view, rules about
sexual segregation, conduct and hygiene also revealed underlying fears
about threats to the security of other boundaries in the Russian empire:
that is, about the consequences of the abrupt shift from fixed to 'scrambled categories' of social demarcation.[68]

The war prompted a flurry of activity amongst middleclass Russian
women. Yet, for all their commitment to the tasks of refugee welfare, Russia's women did not achieve much prominence. Although they figure in
the historical record as clerical staff, actively engaged in registering
refugees, handling requests to trace missing persons or (like Lenin's sister) helping them to find lost luggage, they remain in the shadows, dutiful
yet anonymous assistants to male officials. No women sat on the central
Tatiana committee in Petrograd, at least not until after the February revo-

lution, and even then the democratic impulses it unleashed did not raise their profile. Energetic fundraising or social work did not qualify women for anything other than subordinate status on the home front. For the most part, educated women were employed as volunteer workers whose role (like that of the military nurse) might be liberating in a personal sense but which was accommodated within the existing conventions of gender.[69]

A fuller account of gender and war would have to take account of other issues and vocabularies that surfaced at this time. One obvious focus might be on adult male behaviour, as workers (responding to the challenge of new kinds of work and of employment regime, including the feminisation of some work processes); as soldiers (training, joking, shirking, drinking, raping, killing, etc.); as prisoners (languishing, fantasising, bonding through boredom); and, as in this essay, as refugees who managed to conceal their incapacity. These are matters that still await the proper attention of historians of wartime Russia.

Although much of the focus of this essay has been upon one aspect of social upheaval, we should not overlook the way in which gender history affords the opportunity to rethink the process and meaning of the revolutionary transformation in Russia. One means of thinking about this is to point out how Russia's new rulers sought after 1917 to transform the domestic sphere, through projects designed to socialise menial household chores and to provide socially regulated child care – projects that rapidly foundered on the rock of spending constraints, forcing the Bolsheviks to acknowledge the place of the family in the new society. Thus the new regime ended up embracing the conventional household as the basis for social wellbeing: in practice, the domestic underpinned the state-building epic.[70]

Yet there are other aspects to consider as well, including the discourse of revolution. Here, the epic struggle was conceived in terms that corresponded to a purported contrast in gender attributes. The Bolsheviks called for iron discipline (less 'squabbling'), strong organisation and the pitiless prosecution of their opponents. That project emanated in part from the twin traditions of Marxist socialism and anti-tsarist conspiracy politics. Combined with those traditions was a tendency to describe the revolution itself as a fundamentally masculine project. In so far as they were called upon to take part at all in revolutionary politics, women who became involved in political activity were expected to conform to a standard of behaviour that was established by male revolutionaries, lest the revolution be domesticated and – by extension – enfeebled. To be more precise, what many of its most fervent adherents feared was 'spontaneity' (*stikhiinost'*), the uncontrolled flow of 'elemental' force that undermined consciousness and compromised 'rational' action. 'Female' virtues were seen as a liability in the epic struggle of revolution. Consequently, in the grand narratives of revolution, if not in the practices of everyday life, there was never likely to be any other outcome but the marginalisation of the domestic in favour of the epic.[71]

212 | *Peter Gatrell*

Notes

I should like to thank Billie Melman (Tel Aviv University) and Linda Edmondson (University of Birmingham) for their helpful comments on an earlier version of this essay, as well as the British Academy and the University of Manchester for supporting the research on which parts of it are based.

 1. Billie Melman (ed.), *Borderlines: Genders and Identities in War and Peace, 1870–1930*, Routledge, 1998, esp. 1–25. See also M. R. Higonnet, J. Jenson, S. Michel and M.C Weitz (eds), *Behind the Lines: Gender and the Two World Wars*, Yale University Press, 1987.
 2. A recent volume that concentrates on women's 'lived experiences', without treating women solely as 'victims', is Ronit Lentin (ed.), *Gender and Catastrophe*, Zed Books, 1997. For a stimulating treatment of some of the complex issues involved in representing femininity and masculinity in wartime, see Jean Bethke Elshtain, *Women and War*, Harvester, 1987.
 3. Anna Bravo, 'Italian Peasant Women and the First World War', in Paul Thompson (ed.), *Our Common History*, Pluto Press, 1982, 157–70.
 4. But see Laurinda Stryker's contribution to this volume for a critical discussion of male hysteria, as depicted in Elaine Showalter, *The Female Malady: Women, Madness and English Culture, 1830–1980*, Virago, 1987.
 5. Some graphic eye-witness material was presented in the collection *Bezhentsy i vyselentsy*, Moscow, 1915. See below for a fuller discussion of population displacement in the Russian empire.
 6. Sheila Fitzpatrick, 'The Legacy of the Civil War', in Diane Koenker, W. G. Rosenberg and R. G. Suny (eds), *Party, State, and Society in the Russian Civil War*, Indiana University Press, 1989, 385–98. The Moscow City Brotherly Cemetery (*Moskovskoe gorodskoe bratskoe kladbishche*) opened in February 1915 as a place for the burial of military personnel killed in the war, but by 1918 the Cheka chose it as a site to dispose of its victims; during the 1930s it was turned into a thoroughfare. In the 1950s the Soviet authorities built a cinema ('Leningrad'). I owe this information to an unpublished paper by Dan Orlovsky.
 7. Nina Tumarkin, 'The War of Remembrance', in Richard Stites (ed.), *Culture and Entertainment in Wartime Russia*, Indiana University Press, 1995, 194–207.
 8. The editor of a recent collection bemoans the absence of Russia from his volume. John Horne (ed.), *State, Society and Mobilisation in Europe during the First World War*, Cambridge University Press, 1997. A conference on Russia's First World War took place in St. Petersburg and the proceedings were published in 1999. See Peter Gatrell, 'Refugees and gender' (in Russian), in N. Smirnov (ed.), *Rossiia i pervaia mirovaia voina*, Dimitri Bulanin, 1999, 112–28.
 9. Laura Engelstein, *The Keys to Happiness: Sex and the Search for Modernity in Fin-de-Siècle Russia*, Cornell University Press, 1992 is the outstanding treatment of prewar anxieties; on hooliganism see Joan Neuberger, *Hooliganism: Crime, Culture and Power in St. Petersburg, 1900–1914*, University of California Press, 1993, 32–33.
10. Barbara Engel, *Between the Fields and the City: Women, Work, and Family in Russia, 1861–1914*, Cambridge University Press, 1994, 197.
11. Laurie Bernstein, *Sonia's Daughters: Prostitutes and Their Regulation in Imperial Russia*, University of California Press, 1995.
12. Engel, *Between the Fields and the City*, 50–1. See also Christine Worobec, 'Victims or Actors? Russian Peasant Women and Patriarchy', in Esther Kingston-Mann and Timothy Mixter (eds), *Peasant Economy, Culture, and Politics of European Russia, 1800–1921*, Princeton University Press, 1991, 177–206. This is not to overlook manifestations of cruelty and oppression within the peasant household, which of course continued to surface after 1917 as well.
13. T. J. Polner, *Russian Local Government during the War and the Union of Zemstvos*, Yale University Press, 1930, 157–58.

14. *Izvestiia Kostromskogo gubernskogo zemstva*, 7, July 1915, 74.
15. A peasant youth, writing in 1927, maintained that rural women could only play a subordinate role in the countryside by virtue of their 'illiteracy and fearfulness', although there were instances of 'participation in various kinds of uprising under Kerensky.' I. V. Igritskii (ed.), *1917 god v derevne*, Politizdat, 1967, 62–3.
16. Barbara Engel, 'Not by Bread Alone: Subsistence Riots in Russia during World War One', *Journal of Modern History*, 69, 1997, 696–721; Steve Smith, 'Class and Gender: Women's Strikes in St. Petersburg, 1895–1917 and in Shanghai, 1895–1927', *Social History*, 19, 1994, 141–68.
17. M. Higonnet, 'Not So Quiet in No-Woman's-Land', in Miriam Cooke and Angela Woollacott (eds), *Gendering War Talk,* Princeton University Press, 1993, 205–26.
18. On military nursing during the war see Alfred G. Meyer, 'The Impact of World War One on Russian Women's Lives', in Barbara E. Clements, Barbara A. Engel, and Christine D. Worobec (eds), *Russia's Women: Accommodation, Resistance, Transformation*, University of California Press, 1991, 220. Meyer notes that the Russian army was inundated with offers from prospective military nurses. It would be interesting to contrast women's role in military nursing with their 'traditional' role as village healers, for which see Rose L. Glickman, 'The Peasant Woman as Healer', in *Russia's Women: Accommodation, Resistance, Transformation*, 148–62. For the Bolshevik approach to 'Red nursing', see Elizabeth Wood, *The Baba and the Comrade: Gender and Politics in Revolutionary Russia*, Indiana University Press,1997, 57–59.
19. V. Thurstan, *Field Hospital and Flying Column: Being the Journal of an English Nursing Sister in Belgium and Russia*, G. P. Putnam's Sons, London, 1915, 133, 135.
20. Thurstan, *Field Hospital and Flying Column*, 153.
21. Thurstan, *Field Hospital and Flying Column*, 175.
22. Thurstan, *Field Hospital and Flying Column*, 171–4.
23. Peter Gatrell, *A Whole Empire Walking: Refugees in Russia during the First World War*, Indiana University Press, 1999. This figure translates into something equivalent to five percent of the population of the prewar Russian empire.
24. Latvian political leaders did (in vain) protest the deportation of civilians from Kurland: 'old men, youths and women with young children – none of these groups serve any military purpose and cannot render assistance to the enemy.' Latvijas Valsts Vestures Arhivs (Latvian State Historical Archive), f.5626, o1, d.82, l.5, 16 August 1915.
25. In this connection it is also worth reminding ourselves that 'mother Russia' was often invoked as the inspiration for humanitarian action. See, for example, *Moskovskie vedomosti*, 234, 11 October 1915: 'the Russian interior has taken the devastated borderlands to its heart in a maternal fashion.' For a general discussion of women and the public sphere before the war, see Richard Stites, *The Women's Liberation Movement in Russia*, Princeton University Press, 1978.
26. Meyer, 'The Impact of World War One'. The role of women in charitable activities before the war is discussed in Adele Lindenmeyr, *Poverty Is Not A Vice: Charity, Society and the State in Imperial Russia,* Princeton University Press, 1996, 13–16, 125–9.
27. Violetta Thurstan, *The People Who Run: Being the Tragedy of the Refugees in Russia*, G. P. Putnam's Sons, 1916, 38. Thurstan's presence in Russia was facilitated by the National Union of Women's Suffrage Societies (NUWSS).
28. Thurstan, *The People Who Run*, 59.
29. *Izvestiia Komiteta Ee Imperatorskogo Velichestva Tatiany Nikolaevny*, 10, 15 October 1916, 14–15. Hereafter *Izvestiia KTN.*
30. *Zinojums*, 4, 28 January 1916, revealing that Latvian women 'cannot and will not wash clothes at a hole in the ice, (yet) the Russian peasant expects his servants to work in this way.'
31. *Komitet Ee Imperatorskogo Vysochestva Tatiany Nikolaevny*, Petrograd, 1916, Volume one, 421.
32. *Vestnik Vserossiiskogo Obshchestva Popecheniia Bezhentsev*, 47–48, 29 January 1917, 13. Hereafter *Vestnik VOPB.*

33. *Birzhevye vedomosti*, 15031, 17 August 1915; *Izvestiia KTN*, 6, 15 August 1916, 7. However, refugee women in Simbirsk refused to work as weavers unless they were given a loom for domestic use. They had no wish to work 'in a common place'. *Simbirskie eparkhial'nye vedomosti*, 3, January 1917, 44. Similar comments were made by and about Latvian women who 'prefer to be independent'. See *Zinojums*, 29, 21 July 1916.
34. E. Shveder, *Bezhentsy*, Zikhman, 1915, 4–7, 11, 24.
35. Sviashchennik Vetlin, *Bezhentsy: rasskaz*, 'Tver'skie eparkhial'nye vedomosti, Tver', 1916. The story has a tragic end; brother and sister are both killed by German bullets: 'and the last thought Vania had was that they had at last managed to get away from the enemy. They were saved.'
36. *Kak i pochemu stali my ubiitsami i grabiteliami*, izdanie Armianskogo natsional'nogo biuro, Moscow, 1917, 6.
37. *Izvestiia Moskovskoi gubernskoi zemskoi upravy*, 10–12, October-December 1915, 63–4.
38. L. Ia. Osherovskii, *Tragediia armian-bezhentsev*, Piatigorsk, 1915, 6–7.
39. Billie Melman writes that 'the pogroms occupied a central place in a collective memory in which the violated Jewish woman and her corollary, the impotent Jew unable to defend her, became predetermined metaphors for the degeneration of the nation.' See Melman 'Re-Generation: Nation and the Construction of Gender in Peace and War, Palestine Jews 1900–1918', in *Borderlines*, 121–40 (here 125).
40. 'Iz "chernoi knigi" rossiiskogo evreistva', *Evreiskaia starina* 10, 1918, 283–5, 292–5. One story concerned a woman whose 'reward' for having concealed Cossack soldiers from the Germans was to be raped and beaten by Cossack troops when they returned to her village. The editor of these documents drew attention to particularly serious 'mass assaults' in several towns. Wealthier Jews purchased the freedom of their womenfolk; the poor were most at risk. Many rapes took place in full view of family members. In Lemeshevichi 'defenceless women, separated from their husbands and fathers, were at the mercy of a wild Cossack horde'. Ibid., 294.
41. 'Polozhenie turetskikh armianok', *Armiane i voina*, 7, September 1916, 105. There is some ambiguity about this comment; it is not clear if the author has in mind Turkish or Armenian men, or both.
42. *Armianskii vestnik*, 35, 25 September 1915, 10.
43. *Armianskii vestnik*, 6, 5 February 1917, 19; Osherovskii, *Tragediia armian-bezhentsev*, 8. An analogy was drawn in the same article with German troops' sexual assault of French women on the western front, a subject discussed by Ruth Harris, '"The Child of the Barbarian": Rape, Race, and Nationalism in the First World War', *Past and Present*, 141, 1993, 170–206.
44. *Armianskii vestnik*, 6, 5 February 1917, 18; N. I. Ananov, *Sud'ba Armenii*, Zadruga, 1918, 21.
45. Osherovskii, *Tragediia armian-bezhentsev*, 8.
46. Thurstan, *The People Who Run*, 66–68, 74–5.
47. For a general treatment, see Mark B. Adams, 'Eugenics as Social Medicine in Revolutionary Russia: Prophets, Patrons, and the Dialectics of Discipline-Building', in S. G. Solomon and J. F. Hutchinson (eds), *Health and Society in Revolutionary Russia*, Indiana University Press, 1995, 200–23.
48. 'Pomoshch' bezhentsam', *Trudovaia pomoshch'*, 9, 1915, 364.
49. The veteran zemstvo physician Dmitrii Zhbankov also commented that 'for want of a piece of bread hungry refugee women are drawn into debauchery.' *Trudy vneocherednogo Pirogovskogo s"ezda*, Petrograd, 1917, 62, 77.
50. *Iugobezhenets*, 4, 23 November 1915, 4. Virtually the same language was used in a guide issued on behalf of refugees in 1916, warning young women of the risks of being seduced by smooth-talking men. *Sputnik bezhentsa*, Petrograd, 1917, 17. Linda Edmondson has pointed out to me that similar warnings had been issued in Russia from the beginning of the railway era.
51. RGIA f.1322, op.1, d.23, 1.4. See also *Trudovaia pomoshch'*, 1, 1916, 51–2 for Koni's remarks about the evacuation of 'houses of ill-repute'.
52. Twenty-first sitting of the Special Council for Refugees, 26 November 1915, in RGIA f.1322, op.1, d.1, ll.61–63ob. The Society had been established in 1901.

53. *Birzhevye vedomosti*, 15011, 7 August 1915. See also *Rech'*, 214, 6 August 1915.
54. Thurstan, *The People Who Run*, 64. Contrast the remarks of St. Petersburg's sole female guardian of juveniles, that 'all their stories are so simple and at the same time so awful; but how to help them and what to do, I do not know.' Quoted in Neuberger, *Hooliganism*, 205.
55. A Russian general appeared to support this view: Igel'strom to Evert, 4 July 1915, RGVIA f.2020, op.1, d.131, ll.131–4.
56. Thurstan, *The People Who Run*, 69–72. Some reformers also called for boys to be taught a trade, such as tailoring or carpentry, in order to deter them from street crime. Thurstan met a young man who advocated the wider dissemination of the 'Boy Scout principle'.
57. *Vestnik VOPB*, 3, 10 January 1916, 13. A Ukrainian refugee organisation also complained that 'despair and need' drove many women, 'and children as young as seven or eight years of age', to prostitution. RGVIA f.13273, op.1, d.27, l.11.
58. Aristocratic women, especially in Moscow, acted as patrons of refugee relief. Violetta Thurstan, *The People Who Run*, 89–90, cites the work undertaken by Countess Bobrinskii. The most exalted role, of course, belonged to Grand-Duchess Tatiana who was praised for attending and chairing sessions of the committee that bore her name. An eye-witness could not resist adding that Tatiana was 'most winning with her vivacity and the mischievous sparkle in her eyes.' A. Russian (sic), *Russian Court Memoirs 1914–1916*, H. Jenkins, 1917, 159.
59. *Komitet Ee Imperatorskogo Vysochestva*, Volume 1, 417. For similar activity in Saratov see *Saratovskie eparkhial'nye vedomosti*, 1–2, 1–11 January 1916, 26–30.
60. *Ekaterinoslavskaia zemskaia gazeta*, 28 July 1915; *Ekaterinburgskie eparkhial'nye vedomosti*, 50, 13 December 1915, 851.
61. *Komitet Ee Imperatorskogo Vysochestva*, 260.
62. Quoted in *Mshak*, 4, 1915, 1; see also *Gorizont*, 180, 12 August 1915, 3.
63. *Gorizont*, 5, 9 January 1915, 2.
64. *Simbirskie eparkhial'nye vedomosti*, 23, December 1915, 923.
65. 'A woman', writing in *Zhenskoe delo*, 18, 15 September 1915, 2. The following issue publicised the efforts of Moscow women to attend at railway stations and to serve hot meals. Ibid., 19, 1 October 1915, 1–2. This brief report appears to have exhausted the journal's interest in refugee welfare.
66. *Iugobezhenets*, 6, 7 December 1915, 1.
67. *Vestnik VOPB*, 6, 8 February 1916, 5.
68. Gatrell, *A Whole Empire Walking*, Conclusion, for a discussion of social categorisation in wartime. The phrase 'scrambled categories' belongs to Ann Stoler, as cited in Antoinette Burton, *At the Heart of the Empire: Indians and the Colonial Encounter in Late-Victorian Britain*, University of California Press, 1998, 23.
69. Alfred Meyer observes that *Zhenskoe delo* sought to 'reassure the warrior in the field that the home front was well taken care of and that the domestic hearth he was protecting was in good shape', but that 'by the end of 1916, if not before, such morale-building letters had been replaced by letters in which women complained about their difficult lives, their loneliness, their tiredness, and their despair.' Meyer, 'The Impact of World War One', 224.
70. Some dimensions are explored in Wendy Z. Goldman, *Women, the State and Revolution: Soviet Family Policy and Social Life, 1917–1936*, Cambridge University Press, 1993.
71. That is, until the Communist Party under Stalin embraced a programme designed to restore family life; even then, during the 1930s, the main struggles continued to be conceived in epic terms ('construction of socialism', 'mastery of nature', etc.). For women as 'elemental' and thus in need of revolutionary mobilisation – in much the same way as peasants were regarded as inherently incapable of 'rational' behaviour – see Wood, *The Baba and the Comrade*. For the impact of the revolution in rural Russia see Beatrice Farnsworth, 'Village Women Experience the Revolution', in Abbott Gleason, Peter Kenez and Richard Stites (eds), *Bolshevik Culture: Experiment and Order in the Russian Revolution*, Indiana University Press, 1985, 238–60. For the archetypal Bolshevik virtues, see the discussion in Barbara Clements, *Bolshevik Women*, Cambridge University Press, 1997, esp. 61–2.

10

Italian Women During the Great War*

Simonetta Ortaggi

(Translated by Guido M. R. Franzinetti)

1. History and memory

Our memory of Italian women's experience of the Great War has been influenced by Fascism in a number of ways. In the first place, Fascism liquidated the most energetic and militant Italian women who had opposed the war both in the countryside and the cities. Secondly, Fascism absorbed and undermined the drive towards emancipation which was inherent in movements such as the women's Red Cross.[1] In addition, Fascism marked not only a serious step backwards for women and for the consciousness which had emerged during the war years, but more generally it purged the political and ideological debate, previously dominated by the great events of socialism and of the Russian revolution. The Great War was thenceforth remembered in an instrumental fashion, as a way of demonising the socialist and popular movements, accusing them of having betrayed the country because of their firm and obstinate pacifism. Mourning, which affected women, workingclass women in particular, so strongly, was expressed in only one dimension – the pompous celebratory rhetoric of state monuments.

---

* Simonetta Ortaggi died suddenly on 24 October 1999. This text had been completed, with the exception of the title and some bibliographic references. Her husband Paolo Cammarosano has edited the Italian text and takes responsibility for any inaccuracies remaining.

This was the starting-point for Italian historiography between the end of the 1950s and the beginning of the 1970s. During these years, a body of work was produced by respected scholars, who carried out wide-ranging research in the archives and who confronted the political issues which were the immediate heritage of the traumatic divisions which had taken place during the Great War and of the rise of Fascism.

The extremely rich sources offered by the reports from the security services have revealed the importance of women's presence in popular protest against the war. This was a presence which the Italian *prefetti** described from an irredeemably male chauvinist point of view, by attributing the initiative to external male figures: the Young Socialists, soldiers returning home on leave, clergymen, or all of these figures together with others. With a fine touch of irony Paul Corner has remembered the list, 'brief but decidedly ecumenical', which was provided by a *prefetto* in Northern Italy, stressing that on one point local functionaries were in complete agreement: the fact that these movements were of a revolutionary nature.[2]

The first scholar to have explored these vast archival sources was Renzo De Felice, who at the beginning of the 1960s was interested in reconstructing popular and Socialist attitudes towards the war. In an article of 1963, which became famous, he focused his attention on the pacifist propaganda of the Socialist Party, and reached the conclusion that the effects of this propaganda were not to be overestimated. On the one hand, he pointed out that 'popular unrest, especially when created by women' was 'of a generally spontaneous nature, affected only indirectly by Catholic and especially Socialist propaganda'. On the other hand, he pointed out that 'until the end of 1916 and at the beginning of 1917 the Socialists' propagandising efforts were unable to have any real effect on the masses'. The author added that 'Socialist propaganda began to achieve indeed a measure of success *(especially amongst women)* at the beginning of 1917' [author's italics]. De Felice added as an appendix to the article detailed extracts from contemporary documents, summarising the reports in which (for the period December 1916 to January 1917) practically all the *prefetti* of the various provinces had described anti-war movements, led by women from the countryside, demanding the return of their husbands from the front, and most frequently of all protesting against the supplementary benefit which the state paid to the poorest wives of soldiers.[3]

The incidental and basically contradictory nature of De Felice's remarks regarding women are symptomatic of a lack of interest in

* Translator's note: There is no equivalent in British administrative language for the term *prefetto/prefetti*. It is derived from the French *prefet*, and by and large follows French administrative practice. In Italy since unification (1861) the *prefetto* has been the direct representative of central government in every province, and is an employee of the Minister of the Interior. His function is to coordinate state activities, to monitor (and if need be, control) local government, and last, but not least, to ensure the maintenance of public order.

women as true agents of this unrest, reflecting his own political agenda. This means that two statements which appear largely contradictory nevertheless have an identical general meaning: the fact that the protest against the war was carried out by women – and peasant women, at that – was a feature which reduced the political relevance of the protest itself in the overall context of his study. This approach was echoed by many, and for more than a decade it influenced research carried out by historians with a variety political viewpoints, including women.[4]

Piero Melograni, in his *Storia politica della Grande Guerra* (1969), also strove to correct the view (which was affected by the long shadow of the Turin insurrection of August 1917) that 'the proletariat of the big industrial centres was at the vanguard of the anti-war protest'. For this reason he emphasised reports of the *prefetti*, from which it would appear that 'protests emerged and spread especially in small municipalities, in the countryside, and were carried out mainly by women'.[5]

Compared to De Felice, Melograni proved more attentive to the role of women. He stressed the specificity of women's experience, which led them to be 'instinctively' pacifist. The 'hostility of women to the war in a certain sense belonged to the natural order of things', because of the instinctive refusal of wives and mothers to separate themselves from their husbands and sons. He reminded readers that while the middle classes in wartime had complained of loose morals resulting from the 'easy money' made through work connected with the military effort, in fact the war led women to emancipate themselves through work which was a harsh and unavoidable necessity, and which by no means gave them wealth. It increased their suffering and exhaustion, and at the same time deprived the family of attention precisely 'in a period in which the running of households became more complex because of the difficulty in obtaining supplies, and in which educating children became more difficult because of the absence of husbands'.[6]

The moral and patriotic inspiration which had initially guided Piero Melograni's studies on the Great War, together with his anti-Socialist sentiments which emerged on various occasions (for example in the antithesis between on the one hand the peasants who were infantrymen and on the other the workers and middleclass people who were shirkers [*imboscati*, literally 'in the woods']) constituted a challenge which was taken up in the work of Giovanna Procacci. Through wide-ranging archival research, and with the combination of intelligence and sensitivity which characterises Procacci's work, discussion of the role of women's anti-war initiatives acquired more relevance and depth. These were placed in the context of a general picture which stressed the deep-rooted hostility of the Italian state to the lower classes and the common people, a hostility which actually increased during the war.[7]

The 1980s witnessed a widening of the debate, which started with two equally provocative studies by Santo Peli and Anna Bravo. The starting-point of Peli's reflections was a radical critique of the 'public order vision of the Great war' which had been expressed by De Felice in 1963 and by Natalia Di Stefano in 1967, and which he described in the following terms:

> We know that, in examining the problem of 'public order' through the reports made by the security services, one has the impression that (especially in the provinces) the crowds typically emerge around groups of women who, in particular on the day when soldiers' pay arrived, gathered on the main village square to protest and, in many cases, even cry out 'Down with the War!'

On the contrary, Peli proposed to 'stress how the picture – that is, of workers getting on with their work in the factories, while women were involved in a bit of understandable but sterile protest – was arbitrary and tendentious'.[8]

In remembering the vast and important protest movements which emerged in a whole series of industrial areas throughout 1917 and 1918 (and which were led by women), Peli stressed the role of women workers in breaking the balance of power at factory level. He did not see this role as essentially subordinate (i.e. as 'a sort of commission given by skilled workers to the sector of the labour forces which was less vulnerable to repression'). He instead saw a need to explain this role by 'coming to terms with the *specifically female* exasperation' which derived from working conditions in the factory and 'from the repetitive, piece-work, underpaid labour on the one hand, and on the other from the vast price increases and from the consequent increase in domestic work'.[9]

A more radical challenge was launched in 1980 by the original approach of an oral historian, Anna Bravo. In her article, 'Donne contadine e prima guerra mondiale', Bravo proposed an approach based on oral sources rather than written, and concerning the world of the peasants rather than the workingclass struggles which Santo Peli had studied. Through the oral testimonies of a group of peasant women born at the turn of the century, Bravo proposed to study the 'modalities through which these women began to express a more radical change in their attitudes and in their vision of the world', 'the modalities according to which the war intervenes' in the mental structures of women, characterised by the contradiction between 'the importance and the complexity of the family and working role' and the 'extreme limitation of formal rights for women', 'between their self-image and the acceptance of the weakness of their social status'. Bravo saw this approach as a challenge on the one hand to studies on the Great War and the world of peasants (which in her view had been mainly centred on the 'peasant soldier'), and on the other to studies on women and the war, which until then had been confined to 'women's workingclass struggles and to urban reality'.[10]

These two kinds of studies presented a dichotomous view of reality, which focused first on one aspect or war, and then on another: the various studies did not communicate between each other, but proceeded as closed units, isolating peasant women and women workers, the country

and the city, Catholics and Socialists, working conditions and psychological and emotional conditions, although every unit represented a
piece of reality.

The 1980s witnessed the entry into the field of studies on the Great War
many women historians who addressed both class and gender issues.
The topic of class was addressed through research into a variety of
aspects of social and working conditions. Gender issues – despite Anna
Bravo's efforts to encourage studies in qualitative history, on oral testimonies and on feminine sensitivity as an intensely contradictory experience – have definitely played a much smaller role, mostly because of the
lack of documentary material illustrating subjective attitudes.[11]

An exception to this general picture is offered by the book *Donne
socialiste nel Biellese* (1984), written by an independent scholar, Luigi
Moranino. This book contains references to precious and rare written
sources. These are articles published during the war in a column which
a Socialist newspaper, *Corriere Biellese*, reserved for women. These articles are not the product of memory, i.e., an *ex post facto* reconstruction,
nor even of historiography, but are women's history as produced by the
women themselves: they speak in the first person, as events unfold, without the benefit of hindsight.[12] The preface is written by Gianni Perona, a
historian of great sensitivity, and a highly sophisticated critic, who poses
two fundamental theoretical questions. The first concerns the relationship between a mobilisation which was strictly connected to the war
(and therefore connected to the emotional and existential sphere) and its
subsequent implications in terms of a more general emancipation. The
second concerns the gap between 'the extremely long time scale of
changes in women's conditions and the extremely short time scale of
political action'. These are crucial issues, which will be discussed at the
end of this paper.[13]

2. Women and the Great War

In Italy, where the process of women's emancipation was much less
advanced than in other European countries, the Great War activated
women's moral and intellectual energies as never before. It forced them
to take a stand on a political issue, on a topic which had hitherto been a
masculine preserve. The 'abstract' problem of the lack of the political or
administrative vote could never have achieved such a result.

This point applied both to proletarian and middleclass women, albeit
with a crucial difference. Many middleclass women took the opportunity
to come out of the strictly domestic and family context not to oppose the
war (an attitude which would have clashed with their entire social and
family upbringing) but rather to devote themselves enthusiastically to
charities working to alleviate the suffering caused by war. This was also a
way through which women could emerge from a pre-occupation with

family, and develop a more altruistic role in the wider world. An excellent example of this can be found in Ursula Hirschmann's memoirs, when referring to her mother-in-law, Clara Pontecorvo. Clara's husband, who was connected to the business world and the cultural circles of Milan, had taken part, as a moderate Liberal, in the 'enthusiastic drive which brought Italy into the war'. Clara herself, who 'because of her nature put a bit less Liberalism and a bit more asceticism in what she did ... at the end of the day was engulfed by the patriotic wave to a much greater extent than her husband (who remained a worldly man) ever was'.[14]

In this context, an understanding existed between the middleclass women involved in care and assistance, and the women Socialist intellectuals who were in favour of the war effort, while a sharp opposition developed between these same Socialist intellectuals and those working-class women who refused to support the war as part of the defence of the Motherland. When asked if she would be pleased to live under German occupation, one of the latter answered, on behalf of workingclass women in Milan: 'we would oppose a foreign occupation, in the name of that same sense of rebellion against injustice and oppression which leads us to fight against Italian bosses.' She then added, as if to tone down the divergence in opinion: 'at the end of the day we think the same as they do, it's just that being closer to the people as we are born of the people we believe we understand better their feelings and that [desire for] absolute neutrality, which seems absurd, but which in reality is not at all.'[15]

The popularist women's opposition to the war was a movement which included peasant and workingclass women, young and married, of Northern, Central and Southern Italy. It undoubtedly had its roots in the emotional and existential context* which saw these women concerned for the lives of their husbands, brothers and fathers, but which did not necessarily imply a full mobilisation against the war. On the contrary, as Anna Kuliscioff aptly remarks in her book *Monopolio dell'uomo*, women's selflessness in the family context had always run the risk of being interpreted as selfishness in a wider social context.[16] This kind of 'selfishness' did not occur during the war, when women were moved by social inequalities, as well as by the strength of their affections, to invent thousands of kinds of protest.

3. Women's War

The links between women who were at home and men at the front were strengthened during these years, as is shown by the incredible number of letters and postcards sent in both directions.

Writing to loved ones at the front became a duty, which in the family and social division of labour was allocated to the younger[17] and less pro-

---

* Translator's note: 'existential' in this context is not the strictly philosophical term, but is used by the writer to mean personal problems in a wider sense.

ductive family members or, in rural centres where illiteracy was still wide-spread, to the village figure who personified education and culture – the village teacher. In the area around Biella (north-eastern Piedmont) reading out loud letters addressed to soldiers represented – for the young people who were joining the Socialist movement – an important time for discussion and for organisational activities.[18] In the countryside letters were read aloud, commented upon, and passed from one individual to another. Soldiers writing home asked for help, made suggestions and gave advice, or expressed approval. Peasants gave detailed instructions to their wives on the bureaucratic procedures to be followed to obtain leave in time for harvests. And the wives promptly carried out these instructions, hoping to get their men away from the front. In the province of Rome alone, the number of requests for leave in 1917 was 20,000 (of which 2,000 were accepted).[19] This took time away from the thousands of duties which kept them busy all day, both in the city and in the country. Everyday life was so deeply permeated and conditioned by war that women, who took over in its entirety the burden of the battle for survival, could rightly say: 'Oh yes, we also fought the war, staying at home. Men were at war, and women staying at home had to fight *an even greater war*, a measured bit of black bread, no sugar, no oil.'[20]

This last statement comes from a peasant woman in the area around Cuneo (south-west Piedmont). This is no coincidence, as life in the countryside could be much harder than in the urban centres, especially for those with no land. In families which owned or rented land, women could take over (with the assistance of the elderly and children) all the duties formerly carried out by men, but at least they managed to survive. However, landless peasant women, alone and 'mostly with large families',[21] either took on hard, often seasonal, work as farm labourers, for very low wages, or were forced to steal to survive (usually from the fields) or were driven to take over uncultivated land. Women went to the fields a few at a time, often at night, and marked with a stick 'their' territory, or they began to plough the land with spades and hoes, running away when the police came, and returning later. The uncultivated pieces of land were small, so these women still had to work as labourers on other people's land.

4. The Benefits War

Material difficulties caused deprivation, and thus protest, which usually took the form of a peasant *jacquerie* (against requisitions of wheat, the lack of flour, rise in the price of staple goods), but the rebellious state of women in the countryside was also closely connected with the general war situation, and this was often focused on a public occasion, namely the payment of war benefits.

The state provided assistance to the most needy families in the form of a benefit (*sussidio*), which in theory was supposed to compensate for the missing wages of the absent breadwinner. It amounted to very little, just as the wages women could earn were very small. In 1915 it was 60 centimes for the wife, and 30 for children under the age of twelve, at a time when bread in Milan cost 56 centimes per kilo, and a seamstress working on military clothing earned 82 centimes for a twelve-hour day.[22] In July 1917 the benefit was increased to 70–75 centimes for the wife, but in the mean time the cost of living had increased much more.[23]

On the day benefits were paid (usually a Monday) about a hundred women from the surrounding districts and houses gathered at each village square and then converged on the Town Hall. The benefit, which was declining in real terms, was often paid late and on an irregular basis. Collection of benefit itself represented a burden which peasant women, busy with labouring, could not always take on. Fairly naturally these meetings became an occasion for organising protest.

In effect women rapidly switched from a protest against the paucity of the benefit to a refusal to collect it, seeing it as a symbol in itself of war and its atrocities. To collect it implied a sort of tacit acquiescence to the massacre. It created feelings of guilt and of complicity. In any case, as long as benefits were being paid, the war went on.

Between December 1916 and January 1917 all the provinces of Italy witnessed peasant protests against the benefit, and demands from women that their husbands should be sent back home. In many areas female farm labourers refused to work, claiming that the wages were inadequate, or that they needed to go to the Town Hall to collect their benefit.

These movements were simply a gigantic action group directed at supporting the peace openings which were then appearing on the international scene. In Italy, on 6 December 1916, the Chamber of Deputies (the lower House) discussed a motion tabled by the Socialist Party. The motion asked the house to explore the chances for an equitable peace through an international conference. On 12 December the entire world (combatant and non-combatant) was caught off balance by the diplomatic initiative launched by Germany (together with Austria, Bulgaria and Turkey) which called for peace.[24]

The fact that all these peasant movements in Italy were directed at the sole objective of bringing about peace was perfectly clear to the Italian officials responsible for public order. The women's protests which had wreaked havoc in the province of Piacenza in December 1916, the *prefetto* wrote, were 'made with the specious pretext of wanting their relatives to come home and to obtain an increase in the benefit', whilst in fact 'they were directed at supporting the motion for peace which has been tabled at the Chamber of Deputies by the Socialist parliamentary group'.[25] One should take note of the fact that, as in Italy the cities and the countryside were traditionally strongly connected, and as the Socialist Party was widely present and rooted in the countryside, those peasant women had a whole range of antennae attuned to the world of politics, thanks to their connections with the

Young Socialists, or with the village teachers who wrote their letters to husbands at the front.

Most other *prefetti* agreed with their colleague in Piacenza. This interpretation was validated by subsequent protest movements in the spring: from the Polesine to Tuscany to Latium, rural districts witnessed demonstrations by peasant women who on this occasion were protesting against the increase of the benefit, which was seen as a sign that the war was going to go on.[26] Encouragement to follow this course of action came from the soldiers themselves, trapped in a war machine which cruelly crushed any attempt to resist. 'The government is tricking us, it sends us benefit and now, by signing, we condemn our men to another two years of war': this is what the peasant women of the Polesine said, and in saying this they were repeating 'what all the soldiers on leave say'.[27]

Women's protest movements carried on through the summer, lasting well into autumn. They affected not only the countryside but also cities and the big industrial centres. Significantly, they also coincided with the bloody but futile offensives at the front in June and September. At the beginning of September 1917 one soldier wrote, appealing to women to oppose the war in all possible ways, and start by refusing benefit: 'You cannot stay as you are without doing anything while soldiers are all being massacred'. So the women of his village, who in the previous month had demonstrated against the lack of flour, came out again into the streets: 'Down with the war, we want our husbands back, otherwise we will make a revolution'.[28]

In the summer of 1917 the 'benefits war' was joined by other, more incisive forms of protest. To end the war – and on this point the popular masses were unanimous – it was necessary to deprive the army of wheat, arms and men. In the irrigated areas of the Po Valley women farm labourers refused to work on the harvest: they wanted the wheat to rot in the fields so that – with the army lacking all means of subsistence – the war would come to an end. In some cases they had the support of their male fellow workers; the harvesters declared that they had given in to threats, or 'so as not to have anything to do with women'. The women explained why it was necessary to deprive the army of wheat; sometimes they issued threats, and sometimes they argued their case, recalling the sons they had lost in the war.[29]

The prevention of arms production in an attempt to end the slaughter was the other crucial aspect of the action programme. To interrupt production, women in the countryside gathered in crowds at railway stations to discourage the departure of young women who were going to work in armaments factories in urban centres, and also organised hundreds of trips to these factories. 'They are Furies': this was the expression used by Filippo Turati with reference to one of these incursions by women in Milan.[30] He described precisely what peasant women from a district of the Polesine did. Three hundred of them left from Polesella and travelled to Guarda Veneta to bring about the suspension of work by women workers at a depot for material destined for the front. They threw into the river Po 1,200 wooden hurdles, 1,500 stakes and another 1,500 pieces of wood which were destined to strengthen trenches.[31] One may note that in these actions peasant women generally had the support of female and male workers, who often came from the same villages and who in any case came close to them in their common hatred of the war.

From an instinctive feeling of solidarity, and a profound, deeply felt opposition to the war, boys, girls and women also offered sympathy and help to deserters. According to police reports, women were the first to hold back their husbands from returning to the front when they were home on leave, in order to deprive the war of the raw material on which it fed.

There are many different sources which demonstrate the widespread nature of protection offered by women to deserting soldiers. These testify to the audacity and courage of those who took such actions, which could even lead to them directly confronting the forces of law and order, especially when very young women, who were either friends or relatives of the soldiers, were involved. There are numerous references to different locations which attribute to women the initiative in holding back the men and encouraging them to desert. In Genzano (in the province of Rome) those who turned up for service 'were convinced not to by their fellow soldiers and by women'. In Agrigento [Sicily] soldiers failed to return from leave 'also because they [were] encouraged by the women, who had come to the conclusion that with a growing number of deserters the war would come to an end'.[32]

One might even suspect some male chauvinist malice in these reports, were it not for the fact that (in an intervention which sounds out of tune with the chorus against the war) one can read in *Difesa delle Lavoratrici* [Defence of Women Workers – a newspaper] of a woman exhorting women *not* to make their men desert, saying: 'if my husband were to become a deserter, it would weigh on my conscience.'[33]

A confirmation of the unanimous view of women's actions held by the *prefetti* may be found in oral testimonies of women who, when young, had helped the deserters in the countryside around Cuneo [south-western Piedmont]. At many years' distance, these women were able to remember accurately the individuals – even their nicknames – who were hiding in that area. Anna Bravo has pointed out that this is an incontrovertible sign of approval and emotional involvement. These women, who until then had been living in tight family groups, insulated from the enthusiasm of class solidarity and the lure of politics, had admired those 'courageous' young men, who were capable of challenging authority to the point of meeting to play football, exposing themselves to retaliation from the forces of order.[34] For example, Palma Gasparoni belonged to a workingclass family from Venetia living near Schio (close to Verona). Her recollection of two cousins who had deserted was positively tinged. She later followed the path of anti-Fascism. 'Already at that time' – she remembers – 'in my family the cousins were … not yet anti-Fascists [since Fascism had not yet emerged] but Socialists. Two of my cousins had deserted in the First World War. They hid in the mountains.'[35]

When, in the first months of 1918, during the repression which followed the Italian defeat at Caporetto, civilian and military authorities began demanding better results in the fight against deserters, young women who protected brothers, relatives or friends responded with great energy against attempts to capture the men. 'Rotten government spies f*** o**'; 'Screws, that's what you are … paid just to make the war continue and to kill our poor boys.'[36] In these words we can feel in all its depth the radicalisation of social conflict which the war had engendered.

We have already seen women advocated the return of their husbands, threatening revolution otherwise. Between these two extremes of private and public activity the dynamics of women's emancipation evolved during the war years. Women and girls, including children, all felt a tremendous responsibility for putting an end to the slaughter, not least because of the requests for help which were coming back from the front. They felt the profound iniquity of social divisions which the war had made intolerable – for what was now being distributed, according to one's income, was life or death. This enabled 'daddy's boys' (figli di papà) to avoid military service, and to be 'shirkers', flouting their privilege openly to the irritation of local authorities. It offended the popular masses' sense of justice, and particularly the feelings of mothers, wives and daughters.

5. War Work

Having been transformed into breadwinners the women agricultural labourers ended up organising themselves in leghe (agricultural labourers' leagues), fighting for a wage which was not simply a supplement to men's wages. Alongside the struggle against the war, women had to fight to survive themselves. Necessity led large parts of the population to abandon rural areas and the South, seeking work in other parts of Italy. During the war, the industrial centres expanded enormously: mere rural settlements became townships, with all the rationing problems which this involved. Cities such as Turin and Milan had to cope with the influx of thousands of people, who were mainly from the provinces or the region. The industrial belt around Milan increased rapidly. The population was migrating towards the only field in which work was available: military production. The migrants were overwhelmingly adult women who had suddenly become breadwinners when husbands were called up, or twelve to thirteen-year-old girls who had become the only form of support for mothers with young families, or girls who migrated with groups of friends, and who settled down in the outskirts of big industrial centres such as Milan.[37]

An enormous number of women were employed by the military simply sewing coats and blankets. It was quite another matter to actually produce weapons, weapons which killed: in this case there was an inevitable clash between the women's working role and the pacifism which was so deeply rooted in them. But it was in fact in the field of armaments production that many women and youngsters were employed, partly due to changes in technology and the process of stan-dardisation in the factory. A government memo dated 23 August 1916 ordered a tenfold increase in numbers of women and children employed in the production of bullets and munitions, so that by 31 October they together amounted to 50 percent of the labour force, and by 31 December to 80 percent.[38] There were, however, technical limitations to the deploy-ment of women, and limits to their availability for work (as shown by the textile sector, where women had been employed for a long time).[39]

So, while adult women with small children, or elderly women, pre-ferred to work at home – working on boots and shoes, sewing military uniforms, mending used clothes – a vast number of other women and girls worked in military factories: in foundries, in the munitions industry as turners, in fuse factories, and in explosives. This was an army of women which, although much smaller than the 600,000 working in sewing and mending military clothing (and smaller than that which was mobilised in other European countries), was nevertheless remarkable for the speed at which it developed and the size it reached. The few women workers of the prewar era had become 200,000 by 1918, and they repre-sented the most important component of the urban working class, next to male workers who had not been called up (*operai borghesi*).

Teresa Noce remembers, of Turin: 'Almost all working women – women of the people, mothers, mothers or daughters of soldiers and of men who had been called up – had been forced to work in military pro-duction workshops.'[40] This was due to economic necessity. Teresa Noce (who had worked at Fiat Brevetti herself) described in her autobiograph-ical novel how eventually the heroine resigned herself to work in an armaments factory for that reason, and defended those young women who had made the same choice – the young women held responsible for young men's call-up by wives and relatives.

In fact the young women workers who worked in munitions produc-tion felt a moral unease which was added to the physical and material suffering caused by the work itself, just as did Noce's heroine in *Gioventù senza sole* (*Youth without Sun*). As usual, their wages were lower than men's; they could compensate for this only partly through piecework. Fil-ippo Turati described their working conditions in the following terms:

These ever-increasing legions of women (often mothers or young wives with small children to look after) ... went into improvised or barely equipped indus-trial plants, without setting up any washrooms, separate facilities, rooms for breast-feeding and creches, canteens, in other words, everything which would have been necessary. These women were taken on with wages ranging between 1.50 and 2.40 liras, which were often reduced further because of fines, for exhausting work and long hours, standing up all day, militarised and therefore treated harshly, chased by the police and then punished as if they were soldiers abandoning their place in the field if they should ever be absent from work for a couple of day because of exhaustion. If one thinks of these conditions, one can imagine what state of affairs had been reached.[41]

This picture was no exaggeration. The outbreak of war marked the suspension of the few timid protective laws passed in the previous decade. Until 1917 nothing was put in their place. This affected both working hours and more especially provision for the inspection of working conditions. Until the end of that year there was no regulatory agency in existence for the inspection of hygiene in the buildings, to monitor hours worked, or to check the dangers involved in the manufacturing process. Indeed, the working week was so long that by October 1916 women workers in Emilia were asking to be able to rest at least on Sunday afternoons.[42]

Women and children, no less than men, came under the military penal code introduced in April 1915 in 'auxiliary' factories, so that breaking a factory rule was considered a form of insubordination and unauthorised absence for a few hours or days was punished as if it were desertion. To remedy this situation, in November 1916 a special disciplinary system was introduced for youths over the age of sixteen, but not subject to call-up, transforming many punishments into fines – but still retained was the sentence of imprisonment from two months to a year for absenteeism by women workers, even if this absence had only amounted to twenty-four hours.

These measures were directed against brief absences, which were deemed to occur particularly amongst women workers. This was in general a senseless and unfounded suspicion, as a doctor who worked as a consultant for the *Comitato di Mobilitazione Industriale per la Liguria* pointed out in August 1917, since most such cases of absence were due to accidents, i.e., verifiable, in which 'injury is manifest'.[43] Young women were in fact employed in many explosives factories, where the number of accidents at work was extremely high, with often fatal consequences for the women workers.

Married women with children, however, were often absent for a few hours or days. This was due to a variety of reasons, not least the fact that the working day was a minimum of twelve hours, work was frequently done at night, and was always performed at the intense pace caused by piecework. On top of this, women had the burdens of domestic and family life, which the war increased enormously. Buying food, for example, involved long queues at the shops, picking up benefits, picking up ration cards, and dealing with other bureaucratic matters which involved queuing at various offices. We should also bear in mind the chronic malnutrition of the masses, aggravated by shortages and rising costs of foodstuffs. It is no surprise that this state of affairs produced in women workers the condition which Professor Cosimo Rubino described as the 'indefinable pain derived from tiredness and which often leads to the sudden need to interrupt work.'[44]

In any case it was an incontrovertible fact (confirmed at national level in the summer of 1917) that those leaving factories 'after a few months of permanency' were chiefly women – 'married or married mothers'.[45] This was confirmed by some major companies, such as Pirelli in Milan, where the opposite had been the case prewar, as adult married women were the most stable component of the female labour force.[46] The reality of exploitation in Italy leaves little doubt about how impossible it was for a woman – who was no longer twenty years old, and with children to look after – to sustain the cumulative burden of household and factory work. This in my view leaves little room for discussion as to the usefulness of protective legislation or controls specifically directed at women's employment.

The domestic and family commitments which all women, whether married or not, had to carry out (for children, or for younger siblings in the case of girls) meant that the issue of rest days was vital for women. The women at the Ansaldo's bullet factory 'La Fiumara' wrote: 'We did not protest against working overtime or at night, despite the burden it represents for us as women; but we do believe it would be humane to allow a day off (on Sundays) or at least to allow those who feel the need for it to take that day off, because a woman working at a plant neglects the house, and herself, so she feels the need for the free day, for resting, for personal hygiene, and for cleaning the house.'[47]

A crowded trade union meeting had been held to protest against the Milanese employers' decision to impose work on Sundays (leaving a day off during the week). There had been a proposal for women to take the children to work with them. But the women workers adopted a less obvious but more radical solution by going on strike on the following two working Sundays in March 1917: those two days saw 17,405 case of unofficial leave of absence and entire workshops were paralysed.[48]

Once they started working in factories women rapidly joined trade unions. This process was accelerated by the war itself. Initially they tried to compensate for the inadequacy of their basic wages by increasing their piecework earnings, working long and intense hours. In so doing, they provoked a hostile reaction amongst male trade unionists, who had been trying for some time to slow down the pace of work.[49] The men expressed their displeasure 'in a vigorous and threatening way', because women were doing the same work as men for lower wages and no less industriously.[50] Men and trade unions then started taking an active interest in the problems of women workers not so much out of a desire to defend their own interests (as trade union leaders had advocated for some time) as out a feeling of solidarity, which united working people. They recognised the difficult situation in which many married women found themselves, trying to make up for the absence of husbands who had been called up.[51] Wage differentials between men and women remained significant, but some progress was made towards their reduction. For example, there was a strong egalitarian momentum expressed in the demand that the cost-of-living allowance (which by summer 1917 amounted to a large part of total earnings) should be equal for all (men, women and children). There was also a demand for the 25 percent pay increase for men working on hourly rates to be extended to women in the same category.[52] By the end of the war women had learnt from experience to demand a fixed daily wage sufficient for living (6 liras, in the case of the women workers from the Dora bullet factory in 1918), and for humane working hours: 'Of course – eight hours a day.'[53]

Nevertheless, women's experience of work in an armaments factory was very different from men's. For men this was a privileged position – not so much because of the wages (which were higher compared to other industries) but because it meant exemption from call-up. Women were compelled to deal every day with the increasing difficulties of ordinary life. In short, they experienced more intensely in a single existential dimension the specific problems of working conditions and the more general ones connected with the war.

One case well illustrates the interconnection between trade union demands and the anti-war mood which characterised the climate on the shop floor. On 2 August 1917 the *prefetto* of Leghorn reported that 'a woman worker at the Metallurgica was trying to convince the other women' to go on strike, so that there would have been no more bullets, 'and their respective husbands and relatives at the front would have been obliged to come back'. On 15 August a trade union meeting was announced. At this meeting there was going to be 'a discussion of the issue of the equality of sexes amongst workers, since at present a man earns 7 liras or more for every 700 slabs washed, while a woman earns 4 liras for every 800 slabs.'[54] The Workers' committee which signed the agreement with the *Società metallurgica* on 5 November included two women alongside seven men.[55]

The fact is that the war saw not only the old kind of conflicts (which of course did not disappear) but also new and more powerful forms of solidarity. Civilian workers exempted from military service worked next to women who had men at the front. They saw them exhausted at work, and also in long queues for food outside. This generated solidarity, and led to a greater understanding of women's protests and demands, and also encouraged a common sentiment against the war – which in turn often led to common political and trade union activity.

The revolt which exploded in the workingclass belt around Turin in August 1917 epitomises and exemplifies the combination of different elements which characterised social conflict in the great workingclass centres: the peasant *jacquerie,* with attacks on bread lorries and the ransacking of shops, urban guerrillas on the barricades, appeals to the troops to stop fighting, and the assignment of trade union representation to the *Commissioni interne.**

* Translator's note: this is similar to a works council.

The testimonies of the 'sisters' interviewed in the 1970s by Bianca Guidetti Serra have enabled us to rediscover this aspect of popular revolt. Women who were then girls, or even children, tell the same story: their arrival in Turin during the war, looking for work to help their mothers and younger siblings (at eleven or twelve years of age being the only source of income for families lacking male breadwinners), early experiences of trade union militancy in the traditional textile factories, and their first experience of gunfire on the barricades.[56]

Maria Barbero recalls: 'And then we girls would go to negotiate with those soldiers to ask them not to shoot ... and we did manage to keep them at a distance ... Because we would tell them – And what are you doing at home? We are workers struggling because our brothers are at war – I had three brothers fighting – and so we want them to come home and we don't want to suffer hunger and all these things.' She concluded: 'We did manage to get on more or less familiar terms with these soldiers.'[57]

Anna Fenoglio, who became the main source of income for her mother and younger brother when she was an eleven-year-old, remembered the hunger which had sparked the revolt: 'In front of the factory gates [where we were working] there was a co-op, and at 6 a.m. a lorry came with bread in baskets. One morning they could not stop us any longer ... we got onto the lorry, we grabbed the bread and we took it home to our hungry brothers.'[58]

In the trials held over the following months there were many female defendants, charged and sentenced for having ransacked shops or (as happened at the trial at the War Tribunal in Turin, 'in the case of Laida Celenghin') for 'having incited the soldiers not to shoot during the events of last August'.[59]

On that occasion, women's particular attitudes and their own psychological and sentimental reasons clearly prevailed over economic and trade union issues. The men – who generally had higher qualifications on the shop floor and who were often representatives of trade unions or of Socialist movements – had followed the momentum which women had created: 'despite everything we were pleased and proud to have fought with courage, even unsuccessfully, against the war, the government and the bosses. We at least had the feeling ... that we had done our duty ... to ... millions of mothers, sisters and wives who were living in the continuous and horrible expectation of receiving news of death [in their family]'.[60]

Maria Montagnana's testimony faithfully reproduces – at many years' distance – the sense of moral unease which was also experienced by men who worked in armaments factories (and who were exempted from military service) when they compared themselves to their less fortunate friends who had been called up, and their respective wives, mothers, daughters and sisters.

We repeatedly find women in this propulsive role. Maria Barbero remembers that at Fiat Lingotto [in Turin], when 'the war was almost over', she and her women friends at work ('all young, all young girls') had exhorted their male colleagues to go on strike, 'otherwise – they said – the war will not end and we will die of hunger and the others will die in the trenches. The men looked at us and came out with us. The Fiat guards looked at us but did not say anything'.[61]

There was one case of women's mobilisation which had few parallels in the rest of Italy, and is remarkable for its size and for the sophistication of its demands, and that was the movement in the Biella area [in north-eastern Piedmont], the birthplace of the Italian industrial revolution. This was another case of an emancipation process which, while not exclusively focused on the struggle against war, nevertheless derived its stimulus and impulse from the war. In those valleys the development of the textile industry had created, by the end of the nineteenth century, a workingclass population which consisted of girls and women who did not leave factory work on marriage: in this sense, economic emancipation had already been achieved. The war enabled these women to go a step further, and to move on to political organisation. From 1916 to 1918 almost one thousand women, most of them textile workers, created dozens of Socialist Party branches, held meetings, subscribed in their hundreds to political newspapers, wrote letters and articles for newspapers, and wrote their own column in the local Socialist newspaper, *Il Corriere Biellese*.

6. Gender and class dynamics

The war was a powerful force in polarising popular and middleclass worlds around respectively refusal or acceptance of the conflict. Women were a crucial component in the deep social division which emerged.

Women were bound to perceive class conflict in a much more intense and acute way, given their feelings about motherhood and women's traditional role. This represented for many women the starting point for a process of self-analysis and for discerning a specifically feminine point of view on the anti-war movement.

In the *Corriere Biellese* 'G.B.' wrote that '… women give life to men … and so she feels the sanctity of life much more than men do … How have we been able to renounce our natural instincts and to hand over our own flesh to the cannons? How can we explain such an unnatural thing?'[62]

A woman worker from the area around Biella explained how in Turin (where she was visiting a relative) she had met the countess from a nearby village, who told her of the deprivations which her son had endured, forced to sleep in barracks, and of her husband's trip to Rome to pull strings and get their son sent back home. When the countess asked her for news of her own husband and her three brothers, and was told that they had been on the front for sixteen months, she then exclaimed: 'How lucky they are to be already used to such deprivations. Do give them my best wishes when you write to them.'[63]

There is another episode which illustrates the depth of the abyss which separated workingclass and peasant women from middleclass women. In the climate of patriotic enthusiasm and witch-hunting which followed Caporetto,[64] a group of women of the *Lega patriottica tra le impiegate* (a women's white-collar organisation), animated by love of their country, had gone to propagandise in the industrial belt around Milan, which had been particularly affected by rapid industrialisation caused by the war. Here they were surrounded by the local inhabitants, and in particular by 'a group of women', one of whom responded: 'The Germans are welcome, I will keep the pot ready to give them *polenta*.'[65]

Workingclass and peasant women refused to sublimate their mourning on the altar of the Fatherland, seeing the war as an instrument of oppression by the ruling classes; they did not accept that mourning the dead should be a reason for forgetting their opposition to the war. Later, this division – a civil war – continued under Fascism, and in turn Fascism used the issue as justification for some of its vendettas against feminism.

A perfect example of this silent war was the official ceremony which was organised in March 1918 by the municipality of Limbiate. Through a commemorative ceremony for the men who had died at the front, the authorities strove to placate women, and to undermine their protests against the war, which were now radicalised and inspired by the example of revolutionary Russia. 'I appeal especially to the mothers, to the wives, to the daughters of those who have died in the war. Do let your tears fall freely. Your tears are sacred for us. But ... do lift your faces up with pride.'[66]

Appeals to women's patriotism had begun with the Libyan War (1911 to 1912), and had immediately been unmasked by proletarian women.[67] Pleas from politicians were strongly echoed by middleclass feminists. 'A mother' wrote in 1917: 'Women of Italy, serene and strong Italian women, you know, don't you? We must not cry. Our sons must be able to look at us in the eyes and to find us prepared; we must be worthy of them.'[68]

According to the myth of the 'virile' woman, which was put forward by Futurist Feminism, women who at the beginning of the war were 'in tears, weak as little girls when facing the drama of separation' were destined to become, thanks to the war, 'companions tempered by the grandiosity of time'.[69] This was a model which was unacceptable to the women of the people, who had opposed war with such audacity and courage. The evidence I have presented here should demonstrate this.

The impact of the war on these women also coincided with the renunciation by middleclass feminists of that crucial objective of emancipation – the right to vote. This happened at precisely the moment when the Socialist women's movement was attempting to acquire political rights and a more radical equality with men in the Socialist Party itself.[70] The women of Biella were those who put on the agenda (at a national, not just at a local level) the issue of parity with men. In political terms, this meant the right for women to have their own organisation, and the right to participate in joint party structures actively, not merely in a consultative capacity. In this regard, the movement was the most advanced expression of the transformation which had taken place amongst women during the war, and *because* of the war. With this experience before us, we may address the issues raised by Perona near the beginning of this chapter.

The first issue is that of the relationship between a mobilisation which was intimately connected to the anti-war movement (and therefore rooted in an emotional and existential context) and its effects in terms of women's emancipation. The conclusion must be that the capacity to mobilise and to take initiatives which women developed in their struggle against the war had a more general value and impact.

It is impossible to establish the relative impact of mobilisation in the countryside (which saw women developing peasant leagues and fighting for bread and against the war with such bravery) and the political and trade union organisation of the young Socialist women workers of the area around Biella. The latter reflected a level of consciousness and activity which derived from prewar developments, and the fact that they wrote down their thoughts and feelings allows us to examine their mind-set. We cannot do this with the rural women. They are remembered only through their dedications on tombstones for husbands who died in the war, now neglected and disappearing from country cemeteries.

The articles and the letters published in the women's column in the *Corriere Biellese* reflected a clear break with their traditional role within the family and with the lives lived by their mothers. Their feelings included pride at seizing a culture which had been denied to them when they left school early, feelings of liberation at breaking free from the restrictions imposed by the clergy, the sense of challenging older militants, who had turned a deaf ear to their requests for help, and the experience of affectionate sympathy and solidarity shown by the young men who helped them in their political activities. They reveal a reflectiveness which originated with the problem of war, but then led them to challenge orthodox views on specific aspects of women's condition.

The fact that this wartime emancipation was not merely a temporary or episodic experience is borne out by the fact that in most cases political participation did not end with the war, but continued in the difficult years of the immediate postwar period and (as the biographies collected by Bianca Guidetti Serra prove) during the years of Fascism and later Resistance. Many of the girls who had fought on the barricades in Turin in the days of August 1917 were active in the Workers' Councils, in the occupation of factories (at the Pirelli plants and at the spinning-mills in the Vittoriese area for example), and as Red Guards, involved in obtaining arms, which they would hide under their clothes. Those who had worked silently in the wartime years, oppressed by the immense apparatus of state repression, also took part in strikes and occupations. And the wave of emancipation now involved girls of the petty bourgeoisie, who were seriously affected by the exclusion of women from most kinds of state employment.

The change which resulted from such experiences could not be so radical as to sweep away overnight the subordination which had characterised relations between men and women in Italy, especially in the workingclass and peasant world. Political emancipation and general emancipation clearly do not neatly coincide. Even the young and brave Socialist women from the area around Biella could not escape the painful contradiction between immediate political change and the slowness of emancipation within the family and wider society. The latter required a profound change in men (who were used to having full and unquestioned authority) and in women (who had been used to suppressing their feelings during centuries of clerical oppression). How, for example, did the young Socialist women from the area around Biella think about love? Gianni Perona has noticed that their voices contain a 'reticence, inspired by profound modesty' when talking about love, together with absolute silence concerning their fathers. At the end of the war, in this area as elsewhere, women gave way to men who were coming back from the front, and who (because of the ordeal they had endured) felt they had a greater right to reclaim their past authority.

Conversely, the supposed liberalisation of sexual morals which took place everywhere, even Italy, as a result the exceptional wartime situation, did not constitute a clear indication of women's true emancipation. Greater 'freedom' in sexual relations was accompanied by a large increase in prostitution, both at the front and in urban centres.[71]

Even in Italy, however, relations between men and women, within the family or society, did not return to their previous state. Fascism came to power. On the one hand this meant the movement monopolised and amplified the myth of the heroic woman, working for the glory of the Fatherland (in anticipation of the next war), and awarded posts in government to middleclass and Socialist feminists who had accepted the rationale of the war, and who in the immediate postwar period had renounced the struggle for the vote.[72] On the other hand, Fascism took revenge on women who had not accepted the need to sublimate their mourning on the altar of the Fatherland. The Acerbo Bill, which was presented to parliament on 6 June 1923, proposed to give the right to vote to mothers and to war widows, 'but only to those who had maintained with an exemplary conduct the glorious cult of the heroes who died in the war'.[73]

But Fascism was unable to stop the process of women's emancipation which was inexorably connected to economic development and to the needs of the labour market. Barbara Curli[74] has recently published an important book, based on a wide range of archival and statistical sources. She has shown that the traditional view, according to which the end of the war marked the return home of all women who had found employment in different sectors, is simply a rhetorical myth. The reality was quite different: female employment grew consistently in the white-collar sectors after 1918, and did not decrease in the industrial sectors, as one might have expected. This is a very important demonstration of the fact that Fascist rhetoric, which exalted the role of the mother within the household while neglecting the wage-earning woman, has sometimes been taken all too easily for reality.

Notes

1. In 1926 the Women's Red Cross, whose activities had brought about important innovations for women, was absorbed into the assistance programme of women's *fasci*. Fascism developed an incessant propaganda campaign against the new generation of women, centred on women's duty to produce children and to sacrifice them for the Fatherland. The women of the Red Cross, who even under Fascism had reached the conclusion 'Never again war!', were forced into silence. On all these issues see Stefania Bartoloni, 'L'associazionismo femminile nella prima guera mondiale e la mobilitazione per l'assistenza civile e la propaganda', in A. Gigli Marchetti and N. Torcellan (eds), *Donna lombarda, 1860–1945*, Angeli, 1992, 65–91; S. Bartoloni (ed.), *Donne al fronte. Le infermiere volontarie nella Grande Guerra*, Jouvence, 1995.
2. Paul Corner, *Contadini e industrializzazione. Società rurale e impresa in Italia dal 1840 al 1940*, Laterza, 1993, 121.
3. Renzo De Felice, 'Ordine pubblico e orientamenti delle masse popolari italiane nella prima metà del 1917', *Rivista storica del socialismo*, 6 (20),1963, 467–504 (quotations taken from 471–472, italics added; the remark in brackets should be noted).
4. See Giovanni Gozzini, *Alle origini del comunismo italiano. Storia della Federazione giovanile socialista (1907–1921)*, Bari, Dedalo, 1979, 57 and note 33, 161–162; Natalia De Stefano, 'Moti popolari in Emilia-Romagna e in Toscana 1915–1917', *Rivista storica del socialismo*, 10 (32), 1967, 191–216.
5. Piero Melograni, *Storia politica della Grande Guerra, 1915–1918*, Laterza, 1969, 331.
6. Melograni, *Storia politica della Grande Guerra*, 336–337.
7. From Giovanna Procacci's vast output I would like to mention at least the following articles: 'Dalla rassegnazione alla rivolta: osservazioni sul comportamento popolare in Italia negli ani della prima guerra mondiale', *Ricerche storiche*, 19 (1), 1989, 45–112, and 'La protesta delle donne delle campagne in tempo di guerra', *Annali dell'Istituto 'Alcide Cervi'*, 13, 1991, 57–86.
8. Santo Peli, 'La nuova cl asse operaia', in Alessandro Camarda and S. Peli, *L'altro esercito. La classe operaia durante la prima guerra mondiale*, Feltrinelli, 1980, 91.
9. Peli, 'La nuova classe operaia' respectively 95 and 93.
10. Anna Bravo, 'Donne contadine e prima guerra mondiale', *Società e Storia*, 3 (10), 1980, 843–862. See also, by the same author, 'Italian Peasant Women and the First World War', in P. Thompson and N. Burcharat (eds), *Our Common History: The Transformation of Europe*, Pluto Press, 1982, 157–170, subsequently reprinted in C. Emsley, A. Marwick and W. Simpson (eds), *War, Peace and Social Change in Twentieth-Century Europe*, Open University Press, 1989, 102–115.
11. Together with the studies by Giovanna Procacci, Bruna Bianchi and Stefania Bartoloni mentioned in this paper, I would also like to mention Simonetta Soldani (especially ' La Grande guerra lontano dal fronte', in Giorgio Mori (ed.), *La Toscana (Storia d'Italia. Le regioni dall'Unità a oggi)*, Einaudi, 1986, 343–452), and those on women of the urban petty-bourgeois world by Alessandra Staderini, especially *Combattenti senza divisa. Roma nella Grande guerra*, Il Mulino, 1995.
12. Luigi Moranino, *Le donne socialiste nel Biellese (1900–1918)*, Vercelli, Istituto per la storia della Resistenza in provincia di Vercelli 'Cino Moscatelli', 1984. The scarcity of articles written by women in the Socialist press is mentioned. For example see *La Difesa delle lavoratrici. Giornale delle Donne socialiste* (henceforth abbreviated as *DL*), issue dated 6 August 1916.

13. Gianni Perona, Preface to Moranino, *Le donne socialiste*, i–xii.
14. Ursula Hirschmann, *Noi senzapatria*, Il Mulino, 1993, 144.
15. Maria Cerri, *DL*, 7 marzo 1915, 4.
16. Anna Kuliscioff, *Il monopolio dell'uomo*, 1st edition,1890, 2nd edition, 1894, Follonica, Zefiro,1995, 28.
17. This is mentioned, for example, in the interview with Albina Lusso, in a video edited by Paola Zanetti Casorati, deposited at the *Archivio nazionale cinematografico della Resistenza* in Turin.
18. Moranino, *Le donne socialiste*, 113 (with reference to the area of Cossato).
19. Melograni, *Storia politica della Grande Guerra*, 328–329.
20. Nuto Revelli, *L'anello forte. La donna: storie di vita contadina*, Einaudi, 1985, 23.
21. Procacci, 'La protesta delle donne', note 25.
22. *DL*, 7 March 1915, 2: the data are taken from an inquiry of 1914.
23. Bruna Bianchi, 'La protesta popolare nel Polesine durante la guerra', in Nicola Badaloni (ed.), *Gino Piva e il socialismo padano veneto. Atti del XX Convegno di Studi Storici*, Rovigo, 16–17 November 1996, Associazione Culturale Minelliana, 1998, 157–188, 158 n. 9.
24. Alberto Malatesta, *I socialisti italiani durante la guerra*, Mondadori, 1926, 124–125.
25. De Felice, 'Ordine pubblico', 486.
26. De Felice, 'Ordine pubblico', 483, 488, 491; Melograni, *Storia politica della grande guerra*, 330 and n. 144; Bianchi, 'La protesta popolare nel Polesine'.
27. Bianchi, 'La protesta popolare nel Polesine', 174 (telegram to the *prefetto* dated 16 May 1917).
28. Bianchi, 'La protesta popolare nel Polesine', 182–183 (Rovigo).
29. Bianchi, 'La protesta popolare nel Polesine', 175–177.
30. Filippo Turati, Anna Kuliscioff, *Carteggio*, Vol. 4, part 1, Einaudi, 1977, 501 (letter dated 3 May 1917).
31. Bianchi, 'La protesta popolare nel Polesine', 175.
32. Bruna Bianchi, *Crescere in tempo di guerra. Il lavoro e la protesta dei ragazzi in Italia. 1915–1918*, Libreria editrice Cafoscarina, 1995, 136, 138.
33. *DL*, 6 June 1915, 4.
34. Bravo, 'Donne contadine', 858.
35. Bianca Guidetti Serra, *Compagne. Testimonianze di partecipazione politica femminile*, 2 Volumes, Einaudi, 1977, Volume 1, 263.
36. Paola Peconi, Paolo Sorcinelli, 'Vittime e colpevoli nei processi della pretura e del tribunale di Pesaro (1910–1920)', in Paolo Sorcinelli (ed.), *Lavoro, criminalità, alienazione mentale. Ricerche sulle Marche tra Otto e Novecento*, Il lavoro editoriale, 1987, 51–81, especially 69.
37. Extremely interesting data may be found in Barbara Curli, *Italiane al lavoro, 1914–1920*, Marsilio, 1998, 129 (for the case of Pirelli).
38. Filippo Turati, *Discorsi parlamentari pubblicati per deliberazione della Camera dei Deputati*, Vol. 3, Camera dei Deputati, 1950, 1449.
39. Curli, *Italiane al lavoro*, 78.
40. Teresa Noce, *Gioventù senza sole*, Macchia 1950, 166.
41. Turati, *Discorsi parlamentari*, vol. 3, 15 December 1916, 1451–1452.
42. In August 1916 new regulations for the employment of women and children were passed, and in the spring-summer of 1917 the *Servizio di vigilanza igienico-sanitaria* (Hygiene and Health Inspectorate) was created, but these changes were not in fact carried out for a long time. See Bruna Bianchi, 'Salute e intervento pubblico nella industria di guerra', in Giovanna Procacci (ed.), *Stato e classe operaia in Italia durante la prima guerra mondiale*, Franco Angeli, 1983, 138–162, in particular 146–147 and 156. On working hours, see Maurizio Bettini, 'Orari di lavoro nell'industria italiana, 1907–1923', in Paolo Giovannini (ed.), *Di fronte alla Grande Guerra. Militari e civili tra coercizione e rivolta*, Il Lavoro Editoriale, 1997, 11–59.
43. See Bianchi, 'Salute e intervento pubblico', 158. Out of a 12–13 percent of total absences, 10 percent were due to illness. See also Camarda, in *L'altro esercito* (mentioned above, note 8), 155 note 11.

44. Bianchi, 'Salute e intervento pubblico', 158.
45. Circular sent by the newly created *Servizio di vigilanza igienico-sanitaria* to the regional committees, 16 June 1917, 156–157.
46. Curli, *Italiane al lavoro*, 145 (on Pirelli).
47. Letter dated 30 September 1916, reproduced in Bettini, 'Orari di lavoro', 22–23.
48. Rosalia Muci, 'Produrre armi, domandare pace: le operaie milanesi durante la prima guerra mondiale', *Storia in Lombardia*, 3, 1985, 59–60.
49. Muci, 'Produrre armi', 42 (note 22) and 48.
50. This is what happened, for example, at the Ansaldo shipyards of Sampierdarena, in the Bullets and Light Artillery Section, on 22 September 1916. See *Archivio Centrale dello Stato, Direzione generale della pubblica sicurezza, Divisione affari generali e riservati, Conflagrazione europea 1914–1918*, Cat. A5G (henceforth ACS, A5G), b. 49, Prefetto di Genova, 29 September 1916. ACS is Archivo Centrale di Stato, Roma.
51. This is the conclusion reached by a very detailed study on Milan: Muci, 'Produrre armi', especially 58.
52. See S. Ortaggi Cammarosano, *Il prezzo del lavoro. Torino e l'industria italiana nel primo '900*, Rosemberg & Sellier, 1988, 208–210. See also Curli, *Italiane al lavoro*, 88–89.
53. Ortaggi Cammarosano, *Il prezzo del lavoro*, 217.
54. ACS, A5G, b.50.
55. Ortaggi Cammarosano, *Il prezzo del lavoro*, 235.
56. Guidetti Serra, *Compagne*.
57. Guidetti Serra, *Compagne*, Vol. 1, 213.
58. Guidetti Serra, *Compagne*.
59. She was sentenced to six months in prison. See ACS, A5G, b.124, *Prefettura di Torino*, 22 January 1918.
60. Mario Montagnana, *Ricordi di un operaio torinese*, Edizioni Rinascita, 1949, Vol. 1, 78. (I have quoted some of Montagnana's testimonies in my article 'Testimonianze proletarie e socialiste sulla guerra' in D. Leoni and D. Zadra (eds.), *La grande guerra. Esperienza memoria immagini*, Il Mulino, 1986, 577–604, in particular 586–588.
61. Guidetti Serra, *Compagne*, Vol. 1, 213.
62. Moranino, *Le donne socialiste nel Biellese*, 153–155, (from *Corriere Biellese* dated 22 and 26 September 1916).
63. Moranino, *Le donne socialiste nel Biellese*,147–148 (*In piedi!*, Turin, 4 September 1916, signed Ada [Catella]).
64. On 24 October 1917 Austrian and German troops broke through the Italian lines above Caporetto in Venetia Giulia. The defeat turned into a rout and military collapse. (Translator's note.)
65. ACS, A5G, b.104, Prefettura di Milano, 15 April 1918.
66. Limbiate, marzo 1918, pamphlet in ACS.
67. See, for example, *DL*, 7 January 1912.
68. C. Del Soldato, *Tempo di guerra. Note di una mamma*, Firenze, Bemporad, 1918, 83 (quoted by Michela De Giorgio, 'Dalla "donna nuova" alla donna della "nuova" Italia', in Leoni and Zadra, *La grande guerra*, 307–329, 317.
69. Claudia Salaris, *Le futuriste*, Edizioni delle donne, 1982, respectively 297 and 295 .
70. See Tilde Momigliano in *DL*, 16 December 1917, 2: 'L'organizzazione femminile in seno al Partito'.
71. Emilio Franzina, 'Il tempo libero dalla guerra. Case del soldato e postriboli militari', in Leoni and Zadra, *La grande guerra*, 161–230.
72. Margherita Sarfatti, Regina Terruzzi and Giselda Brebbia were politically active with Mussolini in his Socialist phase, and joined the Fascist movement from its beginnings. See Victoria De Grazia, *How Fascism ruled Women: Italy, 1922–1945*, University of California Press, 1992, 31–32.
73. See Marina Addis Saba, 'La politica del regime fascista nei confronti delle donne', *Rivista Abruzzese di studi storici dal Fascismo alla Resistenza*, 4, 1983, 1.
74. Curli, *Italiane al lavoro, 1914–1920*.

Notes on Contributors

Keith Allen was formerly Director of the Wexner Learning Center at the United States Holocaust Memorial Museum, Washington. In 2003 he was a Research Fellow at the Woodrow Wilson Center for Scholars in Washington, DC. At present he teaches at the Corcoran College of Art and Design, Washington. His monograph, *Hungrige Metropole. Essen, Wohlfahrt und Kommerz in Berlin* (2002), considers the history of the midday meal in the German capital.

Gail Braybon is an independent historian, whose published work includes *Women Workers in the First World War* and, with Penny Summerfield, *Out of the Cage*. She has contributed to a number of books on aspects of women and the 1914–18 War, and has acted as Associate Editor for subjects in the category of 'Women in the Armed Services' for the *New Dictionary of National Biography*.

Peter Gatrell is Professor of History in the School of History and Classics at the University of Manchester. His most recent book is *A Whole Empire Walking: Refugees in Russia during World War 1* (1999), which was awarded the Wayne Vucinich Prize 2000 by the American Association for the Advancement of Slavic Studies. He is currently working on the aftermath of the war in the former Russian empire.

Susan Grayzel is associate professor of history at the University of Mississippi. Her first book, *Women's Identities at War: Gender, Motherhood, and Politics, in Britain and France during the First World War* was published in 1999. Most recently she has published *Women and the First World War* (2002).

Adrian Gregory is a lecturer at Pembroke College, Oxford. He has written widely on the War; his work includes *The Silence of Memory: Armistice Day 1919–1946* (1994), and, with Senia Paseta he is the editor of *Ireland and the Great War: 'A war to unite us all?'* (2002).

James McMillan is Richard Pares Professor of History at the University of Edinburgh. He is the author of *France and Women 1789–1914: Gender, Society and Politics* (2000) and of many other books and articles on nineteenth and twentieth-century France, including *Housewife or Harlot: The Place of Women in French Society 1870–1940* (1981), which was based on his Oxford D.Phil thesis 'The Effects of the First World War on the Social Condition of Women in France' (1976).

Catherine Moriarty is Senior Research Fellow in the Design History Research Centre, Faculty of Arts and Architecture, University of Brighton. Between 1989 and 1996 she was the first Research Co-ordinator of the National Inventory of War Memorials at the Imperial War Museum. She completed her doctorate on figurative sculpture and the commemoration of the First World War at the University of Sussex in 1995 and her most recent publication is *The Sculpture of Gilbert Ledward*, for the Henry Moore Institute (2003).

Simonetta Ortaggi was born in Rome, and studied at the University of Pisa. She was teaching Social History at the University of Trieste when she died in 1999. She had published studies on Gramsci, Trotsky, Lenin and the Third International. Her books include *Il prezzo del lavoro. Torino e l'industria italiana nel primo '900*, and *Liberta' e servitu'. Il mondo del lavoro dall'ancien règime alla fabbrica capitalistica*. She also edited *La formazione della classe operaia*.

Laurinda Stryker's doctoral thesis included research on shellshock and the war poets of the First World War. Her recent work is in the field of Holocaust studies and she is a member of the Pastora Goldner Holocaust Symposium. She has been a senior lecturer at the University of Brighton and an assistant professor at St. Cloud State University, Minnesota.

Deborah Thom is a lecturer and tutor in history at Robinson College, Cambridge. She has written a number of essays on women and work, and also on the history of psychology and children. Her most recent book is *Nice Girls and Rude Girls: women workers in World War I* (1998).

Index